THE NEW
CONSPIRACY READER

S- 20/2/22
F- 23/2/22

Also edited by Al Hidell and Joan d'Arc

The Conspiracy Reader
Paranoid Women Collect Their Thoughts

THE NEW
CONSPIRACY READER

Compiled by Al Hidell
and Joan d'Arc

Editors of *Paranoia* magazine

* * *

CITADEL PRESS
Kensington Publishing Corp.
www.kensingtonbooks.com

CITADEL PRESS books are published by

Kensington Publishing Corp.
850 Third Avenue
New York, NY 10022

Copyright © 2004 Paranoia Publishing, LLP

Previously published in *Paranoia*. For information write Paranoia Publishing, POB 1041, Providence, RI 02901; www.paranoiamagazine.com.

All Kensington titles, imprints, and distributed lines are available at special quantity discounts for bulk purchases for sales promotions, premiums, fund-raising, educational, or institutional use. Special book excerpts or customized printings can also be created to fit specific needs. For details, write or phone the office of the Kensington special sales manager. Kensington Publishing Corp., 850 Third Avenue, New York, NY 10022, attn: Special Sales Department; phone 1-800-221-2647.

First printing: May 2004
10 9 8 7 6 5 4 3 2 1

Printed in the United States of America

Library of Congress Control Number: 2003112312

ISBN 0-8065-2542-8

THIS BOOK is dedicated to those with the undying need to seek the truth, to look under stones, to lift curtains, to peel away and expose the layers of deception in which the history and political life of the human race is shrouded. We have been blessed to be in the midst of the most extraordinary and spirited of them.

ACKNOWLEDGMENTS

THIS BOOK would not be possible without the considerable assistance of many dedicated people, including the authors within, as well as our abiding proofreader and assistant, Devin LaRue, who was an enormous help during the long and arduous process of editing this book. Long may he live.

Contents

INTRODUCTION

Paranoia: The Conspiracy Reader emerged during the do-it-yourself 'zine craze of the early 1990s: before e-mail, before websites, and yes, even before *The X-Files*. Born in Newspeak bookstore in Providence, Rhode Island, in 1992, the first issue of *Paranoia* was the culmination of a group effort of The Providence Conspiracy League, a loose band of conspirators who had reported to Newspeak headquarters after seeing meeting posters on telephone poles. A red three-ring binder was established as the League's official information repository, emblazoned with a graphic of Lee Harvey Oswald on the cover. When several binders began to bulge at the seams, it was decided that something more should be done with the collection. The information needed to be liberated.

The first issue of *Paranoia* had a black-and-white tabloid-style layout, with feature stories starting on the cover and continuing inside. The first issue, which featured a cover story by Al Hidell about the assassination of Malcolm X, was copied at Kinko's. Our door-to-door attempts to get bookstores to sell the 'zine met with limited success, but the Kinko's sample was enough to convince several "indie" magazine distributors to help spread *Paranoia*. This in turn gave us the courage to dig into our pockets and finance a professionally printed second issue, printed on newsprint that has since yellowed with age.

Although it has since moved on to full-color covers and glossy paper stock, *Paranoia* really hasn't changed much. Since its inception, it has continued to lure its devoted following by presenting alternative views and marginalized theories of the inner workings behind sociopolitical events. Its refusal to accept the mainstream version of reality has made *Paranoia* one of the foremost conspiracy journals in America. More to the point, it's always been an entertaining and thought-provoking read. Or, as one early promotional flyer put it, *Paranoia* has served as "an anti-*Reader's Digest* for hip paranoids."

We'd like to take a moment to thank all those hip paranoids. *Paranoia*'s readers are both men and women, young and old. We don't know much more than that because, frankly, we don't think they're the types who'd allow for detailed market research.

Paranoia was a learning experience for us, its copublishers. Part of that learning curve had to do with the ups and downs of the 'zine publishing business. But the other part had to do with the fact that the cryptocracy's agenda over the years became increasingly undeniable. How could we have known that so many predictions of an impending New World Order would walk right off the pages of the magazine and into the real world?

Beginning with the Ruby Ridge FBI fiasco and the Waco travesty, to the Oklahoma City bombing and 9/11, *Paranoia* has—sadly for America—never lacked for content. Through it all, *Paranoia*'s contacts were out there taking notes, connecting the dots, reading between the lines, trying to prevent anything notable from slipping under the wire. Unbeknownst to its editors, during this awesome millennial time period *Paranoia* had become a time capsule, an ongoing project of a growing group of suspicious note-takers, most of whom had never met, aside from exchanging letters, e-mails, and telephone calls.

In its twelve-year history *Paranoia* has drawn from this talented pool of authors and visionaries in the conspiracy, occult, and paranormal genres. We'd like to thank all of our writers, regardless of whether they are represented in this volume.

Paranoia's pages contain a diverse collection of writings from the best minds in the business. The works in this book, the second *Paranoia* anthology, were carefully chosen from the bounty of articles that have appeared in *Paranoia* since 1999's *Conspiracy Reader*. We feel these articles are among the most provocative and entertaining of the lot. We have written new introductions for them, and have tried to note when articles became predictors of future events or trends.

We hope that you become absorbed in the pages of this book, as you bask in its visionary and paranoid rays. A protective tinfoil helmet is recommended, but not required.

* * *

HIDDEN
HISTORY

* * *

Moving Targets

The Real Strategies Behind the War on Terrorism

by Al Hidell

America's war on terrorism will have many victims, not the least of which may be our freedom. What are the real causes and implications of this new war? Learn how the CIA trained and financed Osama bin Laden and other radical Islamics during the Soviet Union's occupation of Afghanistan, and how America virtually created today's radicalized Islamic movement. Find out why the United States was "the main sponsor of the Taliban" prior to 9/11, until the Taliban threatened to wipe out Afghanistan's opium crop and the men behind Big Oil made it clear that they needed a stable, pro-American regime in Afghanistan in order to build a multi-million-dollar natural gas pipeline through the country. Decide for yourself if the war on terrorism is going to escalate into World War III—as a high-ranking American general has suggested—with China and Russia the wild cards in what could be the world's last hand.

AT THIS STAGE, it is likely that America's war on terrorism will have many victims—both foreign and domestic—not the least of which may be our freedom.[1] To better understand the reasons and aims of this New War, we will need to look beyond the bloodlust and comic book-level analyses offered by most of our pundits and politicians.

SMALLER RUBBLE

"Basically, we're going to bomb their rubble into smaller rubble." This is how an unnamed congressional staffer described the start of America's War on Terrorism, whose first military target is the impoverished and civil-war-torn country of Afghanistan. The official reason is that the country's radical Islamic rulers, known as the Taliban, have harbored and supported the presumed mastermind of the September 11 attacks, Osama bin Laden.

The apparent goals of the War on Terrorism are the death or extradition of Osama bin Laden, and the worldwide neutralization of radical Islamic regimes and networks. Yet the capture or assassination of bin Laden—who has followed Carlos the Jackal and Abu Nidal as the latest personification of world terrorism—would likely result in more terrorism, not less. Kill one Osama, it is said, and you create one hundred more. Furthermore, the military attacks against Afghanistan increase the chances of radical Islamic takeovers in countries that are supporting the U.S. strikes. In the case of Pakistan, you can add nukes to the scenario.

Moreover, the Taliban did not emerge in a vacuum. It was largely created and financed by Pakistan, Saudi Arabia, and the United Arab Emirates, countries that are now being sought by America as allies in the war on terrorism. In fact, the United States gave Afghanistan $124 million in aid in 2001, making it "the main sponsor of the Taliban," according to the May 22, 2001, issue of the *Los Angeles Times*. Indeed, the United States also trained and financed bin Laden himself and other radical Islamics when doing so served its interests.

This latter point deserves elaboration. Media commentators are now acknowledging that the United States made a "mistake" in the 1980s by supporting bin Laden and his fellow radical Islamics against the Soviet occupation of Afghanistan. This obscures the fact that the CIA flat-out created today's violent Islamic movement as a deliberate matter of policy. Furthermore, this policy amounted to much more than supplying the mujahedeen with some Stinger missiles, which is the popular conception of events. As reported in a laudatory 1992 *Washington Post* article ("Anatomy of a Victory: The CIA's Covert Afghan War"), the United States invested more than $2 billion and several thousand tons of weaponry and supplies in the project. The covert action involved everything from supplying copies of the Koran to constructing training camps—which we are now bombing—and teaching the future terrorists how to make bombs. All in all, this "mistake" was the single largest American covert action program since World War II.

If you think arming and supporting radical Muslims was just a tragic mistake of the past, think again. Osama bin Laden and an army of what the United States would otherwise label Islamic terrorists have been and are actively involved on the U.S.-backed side in the fighting in Bosnia, Kosovo and—most recently—Macedonia. In issue 27 of *Paranoia* ("Bankers and Generals: The Economic Interests Behind the Yugoslavian Conflict"), this writer quoted Ben Works, director of the Strategic Research Institute:

> There's no doubt that bin Laden's people have been in Kosovo helping to arm, equip, and train the [Kosovo Liberation Army] . . . The U.S. Administration's policy in Kosovo is to help bin Laden. It almost seems as if the Clinton Administration's policy is to guarantee more terrorism.

In addition, there are nations that the U.S. State Department has officially designated as "supporting terrorism"—Cuba, Iran, Libya, North Korea, and Syria—that have no known connection to Osama bin Laden. He does, however, maintain a residence in the London suburb of Wembly. In fact, on November 20, 1999, the London *Daily Telegraph* admitted:

> Britain is now an international center for Islamic militancy on a huge scale . . . and the capital is the home to a bewildering variety of radical Islamic fundamentalist movements, many of which make no secret of their commitment to violence and terrorism to achieve their goals.[2]

This is not meant to obscure the fact that the Taliban of Afghanistan is currently, and has recently been, bin Laden's main supporter and harborer; it is just to point out that the supposedly worldwide war on terrorism is at this point a highly selective affair.

Nevertheless, some argue that America has been forced to take action in response to the events of September 11. As we will see, America has other little-discussed reasons—that have nothing to do with 9/11—for wanting to control Afghanistan. Indeed, a former Pakistani diplomat told the BBC on September 18 that the U.S. was planning military action against the Taliban well before the hijack attacks. Niaz Naik, a former Pakistani Foreign Secretary, says he was told by senior American officials in mid-July that military action against Afghanistan would take place by mid-October. The larger objective, according to Naik, is to topple the Taliban regime and install a transitional government of moderate (i.e.,

U.S.-controlled) Afghans. The horrors of September 11, then, may have served as a convenient excuse to implement a preexisting Afghan war plan.

UNDER THE RUBBLE

So, why Afghanistan? Although not widely discussed, the country has more than "rubble" to offer its controllers. In 1999, Afghanistan produced 75 percent of the world's opium, from which heroin is derived. It should be noted that in February 2001, the fundamentalist Taliban destroyed the country's entire opium crop. While this unprecedented action was publicly applauded by the United States, it undoubtedly put the Taliban at the top of the enemies list of those elements within the United States and abroad that profit from the global drug trade.

Despite recent alarmist news stories about bin Laden and the Taliban "flooding the U.S. with heroin," pre-September 11 coverage of the Afghan opium situation provides a more objective view. A February 16, 2001, Associated Press story was headlined, "Taliban virtually wipes out opium production in Afghanistan." It stated:

> A 12-member team from the U.N. Drug Control Program spent two weeks searching most of the nation's largest opium-producing areas and found so few poppies that they do not expect any opium to come out of Afghanistan this year.

Of course, Taliban-controlled territory could begin to produce opium again. However, the earliest harvest date would be in May 2002. So British Prime Minister Tony Blair's recent vow to "bomb their poppy fields" neglects the fact that there are few if any poppy fields to bomb.

Regarding the addictive substances known as fossil fuels, the U.S. Department of Energy (DOE) estimates that Afghanistan has natural gas reserves of 4 to 5 trillion cubic feet, oil reserves of 95 million barrels, and significant coal reserves as well. Today, however, these riches remain unproven and untapped due to decades-long fighting and instability. The DOE says Afghanistan also has significance from an energy standpoint due to its geographical position as a potential transit route for oil and natural gas exports from Central Asia.

This potential would require multiple multi-billion-dollar oil and gas export pipelines through Afghanistan. One of the largest is a proposed 890-mile, $2 billion, 1.9 billion cubic-feet-per-day, natural gas pipeline project led by the American energy firm Unocal. However, in December 1998, Unocal announced that it was withdrawing from the consortium, saying low oil prices and turmoil in Afghanistan made the pipeline project uneconomical and too risky. Today, there is growing pressure to begin a trans-Afghanistan pipeline, in order to preempt plans for a pipeline out of Turkmenistan via Iran.

Significantly, Unocal has stated that their pipeline project will proceed once an internationally recognized government is in place in Afghanistan. John Maresca, vice president for international relations of the Unocal Corporation, stated in an important February 12, 1998, congressional hearing, "U.S. Interests in the Central Asian Republics"[3]: "From the outset, we have made it clear that construction of the pipeline we have proposed across Afghanistan could not begin until a recognized government is in place that has the confidence of governments, lenders, and our company."

At the same hearing, Robert W. Gee, the Clinton Administration's assistant secretary for policy and international affairs, Department of Energy, made no secret of the fact that "we have an interest in maximizing commercial opportunities for U.S. firms." Or, as Vakhtang Kolbaia, deputy chairman of the Georgian parliament, has observed regarding his own country, "Western countries understandably require security for their investments."

Afghanistan also has geopolitical significance because it borders three central Asian republics of the former Soviet Union: Uzbekistan, Turkmenistan, and Tajikistan. Uzbekistan and Turkmenistan are thought to have oil reserves; Turkmenistan also has the world's fourth-largest natural gas reserves; and Uzbekistan and Turkmenistan border the region's most extensive oil reserves, in Kazakhstan.

So the Taliban has become a major problem for both Big Energy and Dope, Inc., in ways that have nothing to do with terrorism.

BEYOND THE PIPELINES

Unocal's position on Afghanistan reflects the global energy cartel's broad desire to bring Western-dominated stability to the Caspian Sea region, as well as to the Balkans. This will make it easier for the cartel to get down to the business of exploiting the region's considerable natural resources, which the U.S. State Department has declared will be "crucial to the world energy balance over the next twenty five years."

In addition to an interest in energy and drug pipelines, there may be a broader U.S. geopolitical strategy at work, one directed at our old Cold War nemesis. The authors of "Why Washington Wants Afghanistan"[4] argue that Russia remains a significant threat and competitor to the United States. The authors consider U.S./NATO military actions in the former Yugoslavia (the Balkans region), and the current actions in Afghanistan, to be part of a larger plan:

> Central Asia is strategic not only for oil, as we are often told, but more important for position. Were Washington to take control of these republics, NATO would have military bases in the following key areas: the Balkans, Turkey; and [the central Asian] republics. This would constitute a noose around Russia's neck. Add to that Washington's effective domination of the former Soviet republics of Azerbaijan and Georgia, in the south, and the U.S. would be positioned to launch externally instigated "rebellions" all over Russia.

"If the U.S. can break up Russia and the other former Soviet republics into weak territories," they surmise, "Washington would have a free hand." The war on terrorism, these authors believe, is little more than a smokescreen. They believe that Washington, in fact, ordered Saudi Arabia and Pakistan to fund the Taliban "so the Taliban could do a job: consolidate control over Afghanistan and from there move to destabilize the former Soviet central Asian republics on its border."

They conclude that the tragedies of September 11 are being used by the Bush Administration "to create an international hysteria in order to drag NATO into the strategic occupation of Afghanistan and an intensified assault on the former Soviet Union." This, they warn, will move us closer to an all-out war with Russia.

For now, though, we know that Russian officials have charged that the Taliban aims to create "liberated zones" across Central Asia and Russia, and that they have linked their problems in Chechnya to the rise of Taliban fundamentalism (www.indiareacts.com). These facts, along with some very positive public diplomacy that took place in mid-October of 2001, suggest that a common enemy (the Taliban) has brought Russia and the United States closer together. Some commentators have gone so far as to suggest that we are witnessing a major strategic realignment. They say relations between the two countries are the strongest since World War II, when we fought another common enemy, Nazism.

Nevertheless, Bradford University professor Paul Rogers, in his book

Losing Control, has warned of "a near-endemic Russian perception that NATO expansion and U.S. commercial interests in the Caspian basin are part of a strategic encroachment into Russia's historic sphere of influence." The key question, then, is what will happen to U.S./Russian relations after the Taliban is defeated, and the war on terrorism moves beyond Afghanistan.

If one holds a darker view of Russia and its intentions, today's Afghanstan is like the Afghanstan of the 1980s with a twist. The country is again a Cold War-style battleground, but this time the United States wants the Afghan rebels (the anti-Taliban-, Russian-, Iranian-backed Northern Alliance) to lose. This would seem to conflict with the stated aims of the war on terrorism. So, if there is a U.S./Russia proxy war going on in Afghanistan, it will certainly be interesting to see what becomes of the Northern Alliance.

Already, soon after the start of military action, American officials have begun to promote the idea of a "broad coalition government" for Afghanistan, while downplaying the role of the Northern Alliance. In fact, Secretary of State Colin Powell had little to say while recently in Pakistan about the Northern Alliance, but offered a place in the new Afghanistan government for "moderate" Taliban leaders. Before we make too much of this, it should be noted that the Northern Alliance is made up of Afghan ethnic minorities, and the U.S. may have genuine concerns that the country's ethnic majority would never support a Northern Alliance–based government.

WHAT ABOUT CHINA?

A major regional player not considered in the above analysis is China, which has been using military force to keep order in its Xinjiang Province, where Muslim Uighur separatists have been fighting for independence. At this point, the massive, nuclear-armed Communist state is providing mixed signals, with modest words of support for the war on terrorism, and also some little-reported warnings against U.S. military action. China has said it opposes any unilateral military action in Afghanistan, and wants the United Nations to authorize any attacks. Also, it may be significant that Afghanistan's U.N.-recognized government-in-exile is located in Beijing, China (Reuters, September 12, 2001).

On October 4, 2001, the *Washington Times* reported that China had placed its military forces in the western part of the country on heightened alert and was moving troops to the border region near Afghanistan in anticipation of the U.S. military strikes. *The Frontier Post*, an English-language newspaper published in Peshawar, Pakistan, reported on October 1 that Chinese military forces had begun exercises near the Afghan border. Clearly, the intent is to suggest that China will enter the war on the side of the Taliban.

However, China would seem to have little motivation to support the Taliban. In fact, by coincidence two days after September 11, its fifteen-year struggle was rewarded when it was announced that China would be admitted into the World Trade Organization (WTO). China's recent successful campaign to host the Olympic Games is further evidence that the country wants to become part of the Western capitalist order, rather than destroy it. There is no doubt that there is already great economic interdependence between China and the United States, and that many U.S. businesses are committed to strong economic relations with China.

On the other hand, September 11 was also the day China signed a memorandum of understanding with the Taliban for greater economic and technical cooperation (*Washington Post*, September 13, 2001). Also, on October 18 the Associated Press made an unconfirmed report that bin Laden deputy Abu Baseer al-Masri was killed by a bomb in eastern Afghanistan, and that "two of his comrades, a Chinese Muslim and a Yemeni, were injured." It is quite a leap, though, to go from one Chinese Muslim to the "5,000 to 15,000" reported by the Israeli intelligence site www.debka.com. However, if these numbers are ever confirmed, the Chinese Muslims must have at least the tacit approval of Beijing. If China believes that the strategic realignment between Russia and the United States referred to above is taking place, it may well feel threatened enough to take these kinds of actions.

SUPPORT FROM THE OUTSIDE

It is strange that there has been relatively little domestic media attention given to the role of China in the war on terrorism, as well as that of Russia and India. These three countries, after all, are by far the largest and most powerful states in the Afghan region, and all are members of the nuclear club. Iran, too, has been a major player in Afghanistan, and the two nations share a long border.

So why have these countries been missing in much of the mainstream discourse about the War on Terrorism? Perhaps the U.S. government believes that these countries will become players in a larger war. In that case, our leaders would likely prefer that the American public stay in the dark about such complexities, lest public support for the war on terrorism erode. The more limited and straightforward goal of punishing those responsible for the September 11 attacks is a much easier sell.

Prior to September 11, such complexities were readily acknowledged. At the above referenced 1998 congressional hearing ("U.S. Interests in the Central Asian Republics"), Rep. Dana Rohrabacher of California observed, "At this point, you have got the Pakistanis and the Saudis on one side, and you have got the Iranians on one side. Every little faction has somebody who is supporting them from the outside." Likewise, Committee Chairman Rep. Doug Bereuter of Nebraska noted that "Japan, Turkey, Iran, Western Europe, and China are all pursuing economic development opportunities and challenging Russian dominance in the region. It is essential that U.S. policymakers understand the stakes involved in central Asia . . ."

Rep. Howard L. Berman of California defined the United States' major adversaries in the area as Iran and Russia, a sentiment that seemed to be shared by most of the Committee: "American interests in the region are simply to ensure its progressive political and economic development and to prevent it from being under the thumb of any outside power, be it Iran or Russia."

This concern was echoed by the Department of Energy's Robert W. Gee:

> REP. BERMAN: [You have said] our support for this pipeline derives from our belief that it is not in the commercial interests of companies operating in the Caspian States nor in the strategic interest of the host states to rely on a single major competitor for transit rights. Who are you talking about?
>
> MR. GEE: We are talking specifically about Russia and Iran, which would be potentially the two dominant players where most of the transit routes [would be] situated.

In case anyone missed the point, Assistant Secretary Gee then stated, "The U.S. government's position is that we support multiple pipelines with the exception of the southern pipeline that would transit Iran." However, he was more conciliatory regarding Russia:

> Our Caspian policy is not intended to bypass or to thwart Russia. . . . We support continued Russian participation in Caspian

production and transportation. We would also welcome their participation in the Eurasian corridor. U.S. companies are working in partnership with Russian firms in the Caspian, and there will be future opportunities to expand that commercial cooperation.

The United States government clearly viewed Iran as the greatest threat in the region. This, despite the testimony of hearing witness Frederick Starr, chairman of the Central Asia Institute at Johns Hopkins University. Starr noted that early Iranian efforts to "export" its radical Islamic revolution had completely failed:

> In the early years after the independence of the central Asian and Caspian states, Iran did indeed attempt quite vigorously to export its revolution and its ideology to the region. It pressed quite hard in some places, but without success. In fact, the uniformly secular regimes of central Asia and the Caspian firmly told them, "No. We're glad to trade with you, but keep your ideology at home."

Furthermore, Starr declared that "none of our friends in the region agree" with the U.S. position against economic engagement with Iran. He noted that French, Malaysian, and Russian firms were already investing in the construction of facilities in Iran, and that a pipeline was already being constructed across northern Iran from Turkmenistan. "The American [economic] quarantine of 1995–1996," he advised, "is not holding." Finally, Starr pointed out that Iran's historic election of a moderate and somewhat pro-Western leader, President Khatami, was making the U.S. policy of sanctions much harder to defend.

SHIFTING ALLIANCES

Of course, this Congressional hearing was conducted during the Clinton Administration, and we don't know how much things have changed under the Bush Administration. There has, though, been an obvious shift away from President Clinton's conciliatory and cooperative attitude toward China into a more adversarial relationship. Similarly, the Clinton Administration's strong tilt toward India at the expense of its bitter enemy Pakistan has been reversed by the Bush Administration's embrace of Pakistan as its leading ally in the war on terrorism.

However, despite continued conciliatory statements from President Khatami, it appears that the U.S. government's hard-line attitude toward Iran has remained unchanged. This is suggested by an October 18, 2001, report (www.worldtribune.com) that "the United States has rejected Iran's offer to aid the U.S.-led offensive against the ruling Taliban in Afghanistan." The report says that U.S. Secretary of State Colin Powell termed the offer by Iran—which has condemned the September 11 attacks, and which has long opposed the Taliban—as "not necessary." This, from an administration that has gone out of its way to court allies of all stripes and shades in its war on terrorism.

Of course, public rejections and a dearth of news stories may be masking behind-the-scenes cooperation between Washington and Iran, as well as with Russia and India. As early as June 26, 2001, an Indian public affairs web site (www.indiareacts.com) was reporting that "India and Iran will 'facilitate' the planned U.S.-Russia hostilities against the Taliban." (The American people, it seems, were the last to know about America's new war.) The article reports that Secretary of State Powell laid the groundwork for this cooperation in meetings with his Russian and Indian counterparts. No mention is made of any U.S.-Iranian meetings, although Iran is said to have participated in an unspecified "series of discussions" with Russia and India.

All in all, it seems that Russia, India, and Iran are supportive of the U.S. military action against the Taliban, while China is—as is often the case—a question mark. All four countries are dealing with Taliban-supported fundamentalist Muslim insurgencies to one degree or another. If the War on Terrorism extends beyond Afghanistan, however, their continued support is far from certain.

THE STRATEGIC TRIANGLE

Capitalism is about economic competition, and trade wars sometimes become shooting wars. Likewise, economic alliances often become military alliances. With this in mind, it may be instructive to consider recent developments involving China, Russia, India, and Iran, and see whether the seeds of a wider conflict are present.

The *New Federalist* newspaper (www.larouchepub.com) is one of the few nonspecialist publications to cover economic developments in the region. On June 25, 2001, it reported that Russia and China—along with Kazakhstan, Tajikistan, and Uzbekistan—had formed the Shanghai Cooperation Organization (SCO). Representing one-quarter of the world's population, the SCO is said to be based on a commitment to collaboration and cooperation in economic and security matters. Ironically, the SCO grew out of a 1999 agreement in which the countries vowed to work together to counter the threat of Islamic terrorism.

Regarding the Russia-China partnership, the *New Federalist* stated that relations between the two countries have been developing over the last three years; and that:

> The outline of the concept of the Strategic Triangle—Russia, China, India—[proposed] by Russia's former Prime Minister Yevgeni Primakov in 1998, has gradually been filled in, at least on the Russia-China leg of the triangle.

Furthermore, in July 2001, Russia and China signed a "Good Neighborly Friendship Cooperation Treaty," which promises extensive military and economic cooperation. The countries are also united in their opposition to implementation of President Bush's National Missile Defense System, which they think will encourage the U.S. to launch a nuclear first strike against them during a time of conflict.

In addition, on October 18, 2001 (www.worldtribune.com), it was reported that relations between India and Iran were advancing rapidly. Though not widely reported, for the first time, Iran and India have held strategic cooperation talks:

> India's Foreign Secretary Chokila Iyer and Iranian Deputy Foreign Minister for Asia and Pacific Mohsen Aminzadeh discussed security and defense issues. The two officials also discussed international disarmament and security cooperation and the situation in Afghanistan.

In addition, *Middle East Newsline* (www.menewsline.com) has related a *Washington Times* report that China is currently building an air defense network along Iran's border with Afghanistan, and that "China is said to have accelerated strategic and military projects in Iran over the last year," including "help for Iran's intermediate- and long-range missile systems."

As stated previously, The *Washington Times* appears to be promoting the idea of a major Chinese threat. Yet it is quite plausible that China is helping Iran, especially in light of the ongoing U.S. Iranian sanctions. India and Russia, too, are partnering with Iran on at least one major economic project, what *India Reacts* (www.indiareacts.com) has characterized as "a broad plan to supply oil and gas to south Asia and southeast Asian nations through India."

Furthermore, the London-based Arabic daily *Al Hayat* reported on

October 9, 2001, that Iran's Defense Secretary would be visiting Russia within a week to sign a weapons deal that will include "anti-aircraft defense systems and tanks." Russian Defense Minister Sergei Ivanov was reported as stressing that Russia is interested in developing the "military, economic, and scientific relations with its neighbor Iran." This relationship, according to an editorial in the March 5, 2001, *Guardian* (U.K.), includes Russia providing Iran with "nuclear know-how."

FLASHPOINT

So, is Iran the flashpoint that could bring the Russian strategic triangle of Russia, China, and India together against the United States? This frightening prospect is supported by an October 18, 2001, item on *Middle East Newsline*:

> Russian officials said Moscow would help Washington with the war on terrorism. But they said President Vladimir Putin would not allow the regime of Iraqi President Saddam Hussein or Iran to become a U.S. target in such a war. Both Iran and Iraq are on the U.S. State Department list of terrorist sponsors, [and] Moscow has indicated that this is where it would draw the line. Russia has emerged as an ally of both Baghdad and Teheran.

The article quotes Col. Sergei Goncharov, a leading Russian military analyst, as saying, "We can't allow the United States to wield its club the way it wants." He continues, "We are on good terms with Iran. We have tremendous economic investments in, and expectations of, Iraq. We can't afford to sever all these ties in one stroke. I foresee a major debate along these lines."

A debate, or a war? While Goncharov allowed for the possibility of limited air strikes against Iraq if there is proof that they are harboring terrorists, he made no such allowance regarding Iran. Regarding either country, the Russian colonel warned, "If they want to start carpet bombings, like in Yugoslavia, and then see what happens, it can't be allowed."

WORLD WAR III?

So, will the war on terrorism become World War III? *Al Hayat* reported on October 9, 2001, that U.S. tactical nuclear weapons are already in Afghanistan. Ranging in power from two to ten kilotons, they are said to be considered a "last resort" by American military planners. So, there is certainly the potential for a dangerous escalation of hostilities.

Fears of a geographically larger war were certainly not calmed by an October 21, 2001, Reuters report that Air Force Gen. Richard Myers, chairman of the Joint Chiefs of Staff, considered Afghanistan to be "only a 'small piece' of what he suggested might be the broadest campaign since World War II, possibly lasting more than a lifetime." Myers, America's top military commander after the President, added, "I think this is going to be a long, hard-fought conflict, and it will be global in scale."

Similarly, on October 3, www.newsmax.com quoted General Jack Singlaub, former chief of staff for U.S. forces in South Korea: "I think the war is going to broaden. I think that the president made it quite clear that this is a pure case of good vs. evil and those who want to live in peace must unite and eliminate those who want to kill one another." He added ominously, "We just have to recognize that it's going to develop into a larger war, and there [will be] lots of people and nations involved." ●

Notes

1. The September 17, 2001, *USA Today* warned, "Israelis and Europeans are used to seeing machine-gun-toting soldiers . . . stopping them at checkpoints. Soon, Americans may become accustomed to the sight also." Meanwhile, CNN has broadcast footage of National Guardsmen training at a mockup of a guard station with a road barrier and a sign that reads "Homeland Security Internal Checkpoint."
2. For a surprising and detailed argument to the *Daily Telegraph*'s article "Put Britain on the List of States Sponsoring Terrorism," see www.larouchepub.com.
3. commdocs.house.gov/committees/intlrel/hfa48119.000/hfa48119_0.htm.
4. Jared Israel, Rick Rozoff, and Nico Varkevisser, "Why Washington Wants Afghanistan," posted September 18, 2001, to www.emperors-clothes.com.

—Winter 2002

Richard Nixon and Conspiracy in the Kent State Shootings

by *Katie Klemenchich*

Katie Klemenchich refers to the Kent State student shootings of May 4, 1970, as an unresolved national trauma. Kent State is listed by The National Examiner *as #51 in its list of the top one hundred scandals of the twentieth century. The* U.S. Congressional Record *states that many facts of this event "strongly indicate the execution of a conspiracy." "The fingers on the trigger at Kent State point straight back to Nixon," Klemenchich writes. As she explains, "Unable to identify the enemies in his own mind, Nixon projected them onto others, including the innocent, idealistic minds snuffed out at Kent State, and the millions killed in Vietnam and Cambodia." Under the cloak of national security, she explains, hid "an insecure child, incoherent, unable to listen, retreating to a world of fantasy." Here is a rare look at Kent State and the enigma that was Richard Nixon.*

IN THE MIDST of the Vietnam conflict President Richard Nixon appeared on national television on April 30, 1970, to announce the expansion of the Vietnam War by an invasion into Cambodia. On May 4, 1970, the Ohio National Guard opened fire on unarmed students at Kent State University who were protesting the presence of the National Guard on their campus. The shootings left four dead and nine wounded. This tragedy, now officially known and referred to as "Kent State," is no more than a blip on the screen of our collective memory, an event so fleeting it no longer seems to matter. Yet the political and psychological agendas it exposed are still with us.

President Nixon was personally involved with the minutest details of the bombings in Vietnam and Cambodia. "Dick always planned things out. He didn't do things accidentally . . ." stated his brother Donald (Barber, *The Presidential Character*). As Stanley Kutler reports in *Abuse of Power*, in a "Secret-Eyes Only" Memorandum (Declassified E.O. 12958) personally typed by Nixon to J. Edgar Hoover, Nixon wrote, "thousands of Americans are determined to destroy our society." He wrote that because of "new threats" intelligence collection operations should be "reevaluated" with a view toward "accelerating the discreet and legitimate collection of vitally needed information." Nixon continued, "I wish to consider personally the issues involved and the options available."

It was probably this document Nixon referred to on May 23, 1973, when he said to Alexander Haig, "[Regarding the Huston Plan] The language in the first draft . . . which said that I told them, that they use any means necessary, including illegal means, to accomplish this goal. The President of the United States can never admit that."

There is a close relationship with the town house bombing March 6, 1970, in New York City, in which members of the Weather Underground died when a bomb they were making exploded and killed three members. This event, along with a wave of other bombings and violence by other groups, signified to the Nixon administration that the protest movement had crossed a crucial boundary and had gone over to violence.

THE HUSTON PLAN AND WATERGATE

A confidential White House memo dated March 25, 1970, from Bud Krogh to Tom Huston, included an attachment on the radical group known as the Weathermen or Weather Underground, and speaks of the secret service capability being factored into Tom Huston's "master plan." The administration was now fully justified in meeting fire with fire. A recently declassified "secret" White House memo addressed to Bud Krogh on internal security, dated March 20, 1970, specifies a new interagency working group, which came to be known as the Huston Plan, which included the FBI, CIA, the National Security Agency and Defense Intelligence Agency, in response to "the escalating threat to the internal security of the United States." The memo is from Tom Huston and says he will submit a "detailed game plan" with a deadline for a final report on May 1, 1970.

Another memo from Dwight Chapin to H. R. Haldeman, dated April 24, 1970, indicates that those attending the meeting of the final report were J. Edgar Hoover, head of the FBI, Tom Huston, H. R. Haldeman, John Ehrlichman, and Richard Helms, Director of the CIA.

The Huston Plan would include wiretapping, increased infiltration of left-wing groups, electronic surveillance, and use of informants. These recently declassified documents show that the Huston Plan may have been implemented in March 1970, before the Kent State shootings, rather than on June 5, 1970, as has been previously recorded in many Nixon biographies (Aitken, *Nixon: A Life*). When the Watergate scandal was unfolding in May 1973, Nixon and company tried to fall back on the Huston Plan as being necessary, along with the Watergate burglary, to combat domestic subversion. (Kutler, *Abuse of Power*) The Watergate hearings suppressed such critical evidence as the CIA background of J. Gordon Liddy, the Watergate burglar who proposed kidnapping campus radicals. (Alex Constantine, *Virtual Government*)

On May 16, 1973, while Nixon was discussing the Huston plan with White House attorney J. Fred Buzhardt, as a way of explaining the Watergate burglary, Alexander Haig reminds Nixon of the circumstances surrounding the reason for the Huston Plan. He says there were riots in the streets. Nixon is reminded of the time, "right after Cambodia." Buzhardt replies, "It was right after Cambodia and we just got Kent State." Buzhardt goes on to say that the break-in of Daniel Ellsberg's psychiatrist's office was justified by means of the Huston Plan. Buzhardt continues: "I think we ought to . . . give some thought to wrapping the psychiatrist office into this [Huston Plan] and justify it . . . We've got a major leak there, we got a threat to the national security. It's either wrap it up there, Mr. President, and hang it on this hat and the whole case, than to have to defend it separately. I think we may want to think about whether we just put this one under the umbrella." (Kutler)

The conversation of May 16, 1973, clarified the link, in Nixon's mind, between the May 1970, Kent State shootings and using the Huston Plan as a justification for Watergate. As Kutler reports in *Abuse of Power*, Alexander Haig says: "This was one helluva place to be along about May of 1970." Nixon replies: "This was simply an action plan [the Huston Plan] which was basically a contingency plan." Alexander Haig: "And we had a situation in which there were students killed at a school . . ." Nixon replies: "This will be the thing, they'll try to say this is grounds for impeaching the President." Nixon then recalls the invasion of

Cambodia along with May Day, Kent State, and the Huston Plan. "Cambodia was in [1970]. Yeah, May Day, I don't think the country is going to get excited about a damn plan that was drawn up by agencies to control the goddamn riots." On May 16, 1973, Nixon said to Haig and Buzhardt: "The President authorized a super-duper activity in 1970 . . . for the purpose of doing that which involves burglary, et cetera, and wiretapping . . ."

Speaking of Watergate and the resignations of Nixon's closest aides, a White House aide said that for Nixon, "the shortest distance between two points is over four corpses." (Hughes, *New York Times Magazine*, June 9, 1974) The comment was made in regard to the resignations of Nixon's closest aides in sacrifice for Nixon during the Watergate scandal, but it could have applied equally as well to the four dead at Kent State; they both served sacrificial purposes.

Richard Nixon learned the lessons of death in his family, where two young brothers died of tuberculosis. He learned this when the Kennedy brothers were killed. And he learned this at Kent State, where state-sanctioned abuse, and the sacrificial murders of four students, put an end to campus riots and drove other dissidents underground. The shootings, symbolic as well as literal, were meant to break the spirit of the anti-war movement, just as ritual abuse is used to break the spirit of the victim. In thirteen seconds of political terror heard around the globe, "a brutal scheme to end campus rebellion was enacted, and it worked," as Hal Dorland has noted in personal communiques. "We're really talking about domestic fascism with all this."

THE ROCKEFELLER "SIGNATURE"

At Kent State on May 4, 1970, the Ohio National Guard, stationed on high ground on a plateau on the campus of Kent State called "Blanket Hill"—19.8 feet above the intended targets—turned and fired on a group of unsuspecting protesters and passersby clustered in and around a parking lot below. They were given no warning. A single shot rang out, then a barrage of bullets. It was a massacre, no one was sure exactly what happened and no one was ever convicted for the killings. This is a familiar scenario; it is the Rockefeller "style" of putting down revolt, and keeping the masses under control.

As Rockefeller biographers Peter Collier and David Horowitz explain in *The Rockefellers: An American Dynasty*, at Ludlow, Colorado, striking miners of Colorado Fuel and Iron, owned by Junior Rockefeller, had set up a tent city. On April 20, 1914, National Guard troops, perched on a rim overlooking the camp, trained their Hotchkiss guns on the tattered tents and opened fire, supposedly in response to an unknown shot. In the end there were forty dead, including women and children. Just one month before this massacre, Junior Rockefeller had promised the Subcommittee of the House Committee on Mines and Mining in Washington that he was determined to keep the mining camps open in the face of poor working conditions and violent strikes, even if it meant death to all the employees. "It's a great principle," he stated.

On September 14, 1971, in response to the uprising of prisoners at Attica prison in upstate New York, without warning, a helicopter swooped down over the prison yard dropping a thick cloud of pepper gas. At that signal, snipers atop the prison battlegrounds let loose a hail of fire upon the prisoners trapped in the yard. In addition, an assault army of hundreds of state troopers and correction officers began a six-minute volley that ultimately left forty three dead and eighty wounded. It was the bloodiest one-day battle among Americans since the Civil War, except that in this case only one side was armed with fire-power.

According to Collier, Tom Morgan (Nelson Rockefeller's son-in-law) said, "Attica is the symbolic Rockefeller act. He delayed and hung back at each critical moment until all the 'liberal' options were exhausted and he was able to choose the reactionary solution, which was the one he had wanted all along." Rockefeller stated his feelings about the symbolic and political use of massacre in his remarks about Attica: "I think that we have to look at these things not only in terms of the immediate, but in terms of the larger implication of what we are doing in our society."

As at Attica, which resulted in the indictment of sixty one Attica inmates and no indictments against the assaulting army or prison officials, twenty five students at Kent State were indicted after the shootings of May 4, 1970. Eight guardsmen were later indicted and then exonerated in the shootings. A single, signal "mystery" shot that rang out at Ludlow, Attica, and Kent State was blamed on the miners, prisoners and students, respectively.

According to the U.S. National Archives, handwritten notes by H. R. Haldeman written May 5, 1970, the day after the shootings, says: "We have to get out the story of the sniper." The "story of the sniper" that Haldeman needed to "get out" to the public was that a student or radical had started shooting at the National Guard, triggering their barrage of thirteen seconds. No evidence was ever presented for this story. According to William Gordon, in *Four Dead in Ohio*, there is evidence that the FBI paid undercover informant, Terry Norman, who admitted firing his weapon and was seen standing over a prone student on the ground with his weapon raised. Another story by Don Fred, in the *Daily Kent Stater*, tells of a sheriff on campus who, responding to a sighting of a man with a rifle on the roof of Dunbar Hall, recalls meeting moments after the shooting an FBI agent after he retrieved two warm shells from the roof of Dunbar Hall. The agent confiscated the shells. The story of the sniper may be true, but the sniper could have been a government agent.

Like the massacres of striking miners at Ludlow, Colorado, in 1914, and of striking prisoners at Attica State prison in 1971, both of which involved Rockefellers (Junior and Nelson, respectively), the Kent State shootings bear the unmistakable Rockefeller stamp: a stated willingness to sacrifice lives by the officials, snipers stationed on higher ground over targets trapped below, a single, mystery shot, and a barrage of fire. A massacre ensues; the officials in charge and those who do the shooting are not punished.

The lesson taught to the striking miners at Ludlow was that their strike efforts were useless, at Attica that inmates cannot protest poor prison living conditions, and at Kent State the students' anti-war movement cannot stop the war, a war from which the Rockefeller family reaped large profits. The Rockefellers are and were the leading oil family in America, and owned much stock in Socony Mobil, which made over half its profits from investments in the Far East. In 1966, David Rockefeller opened the Saigon branch of the Chase Manhattan Bank. "Its business was often indistinguishable from foreign policy itself," write Collier and Horowitz.

Jim Garrison, JFK assassination prosecutor, wrote, "The oil-banking-military cabal in America creates dreadfully real structures to enforce its will." The various factions of power that control our society are capable of coalescing into a "central conspiracy" if the need arises, since so many of their interests overlap. The political objective for the Kent State killings was to stop the campus rioting in America, which threatened the war in Vietnam, which, in turn, threatened oil investments of the Rockefeller family.

The oil companies and big banks were unabashed in their desire to protect investments in the region. After an initial outburst of rioting on American college campuses in response to the Kent State shootings, the riots did indeed end. "The investigator of the Rockefellers will find that they have secretly had their hand in the politics of the United States during the twentieth century. The decisions and directions this nation has taken were the result of countless orders which the Rockefellers have given to their underlings," writes Illuminati expert, Fritz Springmeier. Hal Dorland sums up his view this way: "The Kent State shootings are what I'll call 'The David Rockefeller-Kent State-Anti-War Summary Executions.'"

CAPTAIN BRADY, NIXON, AND KENT STATE

"Indian hating," writes author Richard Drinnon in *Facing West*, "is the term that applies to the white hostility that for four centuries has exterminated 'savages' who stood in the path of Anglo-American expansion." In the case of the Kent State shootings, the expansion in question was the expansion of the Vietnam War into Cambodia.

Those who are perpetrated against at home sometimes grow up to be king-sized perpetrators; they come to identify with the all-powerful one who abused them, rather than with the helpless, pitiful child they once were. Nixon may have identified with the man his grandfather, Samuel Brady Nixon, was named after. Captain Samuel Brady, the famous Indian hunter/hater of Ohio, carried out a lifelong vendetta against Indians, and was known as an intelligent predatory animal. Men like Samuel Brady stalked America and were representative of the mindset of the founders of this country. Samuel Brady may even have been a friend of old George Nixon, Sr. (great grandfather of Richard Nixon) from the days of their military careers, according to Nixon biographer, Edwin Hoyt.

As Christian C. Cackler writes, in *Recollections of an Old Settler* (published in 1874), General George Washington appointed Samuel Brady in 1780 to be a spy and government-paid scout in the Western Reserve of the Ohio Territory, then the western border of America. Having been twice captured by Indians and sentenced to death, the Indians caught him in 1791 and made a big celebration in Sandusky, Ohio, where they planned to burn him at the stake. Brady made his dramatic escape by seizing an Indian baby, throwing it into the flames intended for himself, and fleeing naked in the confusion. Brady made his way a hundred miles from Sandusky to Kent, along the Cuyahoga River, finally jumping the chasm of the river at its narrowest point, at what is now known as Brady's Leap.

An estimated ten million Indians were massacred in the United States. George Washington, who received his military training in the French and Indian War (1754–63), centered in the upper Ohio Valley, participated in so many Indian massacres the Indians named him "baby killer" and "town destroyer." (Drinnon) In personal letters, Washington referred to Indians as "beasts of prey." President Andrew Jackson preserved the scalps of many native people he had personally murdered. According to Ward Churchill, in *Indians Are Us?*, Jackson supervised the mutilation of eight hundred Indian men, women and children at Horseshoe Bend in Alabama, slicing long strips of flesh to turn into bridle reins for horses. Such murder, mutilation, and celebration are signs of satanic cult rituals.

Nixon idolized President Abraham Lincoln, who ordered the largest execution of Indians of any president—the 1862 Santee Sioux uprising in Mankato, Minnesota—and under whose presidency many Indian massacres occurred. Colonel John M. Chivington, who killed at least 150 women and children, led a famous massacre in Cheyenne. He then led a triumphal parade through Denver, Colorado, displaying the scalps, heads and genitalia of their victims. During the Civil War, President Lincoln, as Nixon pointed out to H. R. Haldeman, "had the cannons in the streets in New York to shoot draft resisters."

The ritual-like public execution of young people at Kent State occurred in the heart of the Anglo-Saxon empire, the middle of the country, the point where all roads crossed for Nixon. It was a psychic dream come true; a logistical *coup d'etat* with two roads running in and out of the town of Kent to cordon and isolate the town. In the corridors of power and in America's delirium of violence, as in the Vietnam War and in the war against the Indians, this successful operation was measured in body counts.

Jewish Targets?

Another aspect of Richard Nixon's hatred shows up in the Kent State killings: the Jewish element. Jews represented only 2 percent of the student population at Kent State, yet three of the four killed were Jewish: Allison Krause, Jeffrey Miller and Sandra Scheuer, whose parents had fled the Jewish holocaust in Nazi Germany only to find another holocaust, or sacrifice, at Kent State. James Michener wrote: "A visitor is not long in Kent before someone informs him secretly, 'you've noticed, of course, that of the four students who were killed, three were Jewish . . . That was no accident.'" The students killed at Kent State were "the new Indians" or targets of hatred.

According to Stephen Ambrose, in *Nixon: Triumph of a Politician*, Nixon's paranoia and unbalanced mental state led him to select ever more specific targets. John Ehrlichman said, "Nixon would talk about Jewish traitors, and the Eastern Jewish Establishment—Jews at Harvard." As Woodward and Bernstein wrote in *The Final Days*, "The Jewish Cabal is out to get me," Nixon would lament to his close associates. The mathematical odds that 75 percent of those killed were Jewish is 1 in 32,189. "Nixon was raging against Jews, and then Jews were killed," said the late Richard Jaworski, high school teacher of Allison Krause, in a May 1994 personal interview.

How could Jews have been specifically targeted at Kent State? "Agent provocateurs posing as photographers were going back and forth between the students and the guard," says Richard Jaworski. It is documented that FBI informant Terry Norman, posing as a photographer, huddled with the guardsmen on the football practice field minutes before the shootings. It has been alleged that Norman enrolled as a student at Kent State and posed as a radical on campus the previous year. Jaworski points out that Norman was familiar with activist students and could have pointed out Jewish targets to the National Guard.

The family of Allison Krause received countless letters in the wake of their daughter's death. The Yale Archives, Kent State Collection, holds many of these hate letters directed against Jews, expressing the approval many Americans felt for shooting these students, and their collusion with Nixon's rage against Jews. A letter received by the parents of Allison Krause stated, "I join the many who regret that you had a daughter." Another read, "Juden, perhaps you realize now that there is no place in America for Zionist rabble-rousers." Another letter, signed only, "All American Parents," read, "Your daughter was raised to be sacrificed." The mother of Jeffrey Miller received obscene phone calls and hate mail smeared with feces.

NIXON'S DISINTEGRATION

Nixon wrote that the days after the shootings at Kent State were the darkest of his presidency. He felt utterly dejected; he had over-killed and it was irreversible. The deaths of these young people triggered in him the unresolved impact of deaths past, as well as his death wishes, which Nixon certainly had, according to Fawn Brodie in *Richard Nixon: The Shaping of His Character*. Handwriting expert Elaine Senko writes of Nixon from an examination of his handwritten letter, dated May 6, 1970: "He was rejecting painful or disagreeable memories from his past . . . his self-esteem was shattered, he felt responsible but he didn't want to feel that way. He holds onto his anger, he's not going to be up front with people. People and their criticism were getting to him." (Senko, personal interviews)

The elation Nixon thought he would feel from vanquishing his enemy was short-lived, for he had actually killed a part of himself. But first he needed to confirm the veracity of his belief system. Upon hearing of the shootings at Kent State, according to Nixon's own *Memoirs*, he asked his aide Haldeman, "Are they dead?"

Dr. Arnold Hutschnecker, Nixon's psychiatrist at the time, says Nixon suffered a "nervous breakdown." Roused from sleep at 4 A.M. on May 9, 1970, Nixon drifted to the Lincoln sitting room in the White House after logging fifty outgoing phone calls between 9:22 P.M. and 4:22 A.M. One was to the editor of *Reader's Digest*, to whom he would commission a book about Kent State, to be written by James Michener and serialized in *Reader's Digest*, that would whitewash the events and make them look like an accident. His conflicted state of being, self-described as agitated and uneasy, led to his strange foray to the Lincoln Memorial where demonstrators, spurred by the Kent State shootings, had gathered.

What drove Nixon there? "Guilt—nothing but guilt," his psychiatrist reported. Says handwriting expert Senko, "There is current guilt, and guilt from the past, he may have been involved in something similar in years past. He felt internally responsible for whatever happened [at Kent State]." Unable to sleep, Nixon went to the Lincoln Memorial, which was to him a temple to Lincoln where it seemed a divine presence dwelt. There he met young students like the ones who had died. He tried to "relate" to them by talking about travel and surfing, but they, like others, rejected his hollow overtures. First he told them he already knew what they were thinking and feeling. He described himself to them as an "SOB" and tried to justify his actions in Vietnam.

As Bruce Mazlich writes, in *In Search of Nixon*: "The vibrations in the air were scary," said nineteen-year-old Ronnie Kemper who met Nixon that day. "You had an impulse to reach out and touch him to see if he was real." A student newspaper reported, "He looked like he had a mask on. He was wearing pancake make-up. He looked scared and nervous like he was in a fog . . . his eyes were glassy." Nixon spoke to them about the great mystery of life, with words reminiscent of Masonic dogma, perhaps attempting to program his listeners as he himself had been programmed. "He was looking for shelter . . . he was regressing as a human being, needing help from a mother figure," says Elaine Senko.

According to Herbert Parmet, in *Richard Nixon and His America*, what Nixon really thought of the young people at the Lincoln Memorial is set out in his own words: "To try to lift them [the students] out of the miserable intellectual wasteland in which they now wander aimlessly around." H. R. Haldeman also wrote shortly thereafter, "regarding kids—get them out of their self-torturing, self-pitying attitude and see the world as it is." Those words are "Pure Nazism, I'm from Nazi Germany, I know," says Dr. Hutschnecker.

According to the *U.S. Congressional Record*, dated May 13, 1969, the traits Nixon manifested as a world leader were those of an ideological criminal: "He violates the law for a political purpose. He is driven by a vision—that his destructive action will bring about a better world. He is self-righteous."

RICHARD NIXON: WHITE REVOLUTIONARY

"His intensity could hurt others . . . he could be violent if put under pressure, he could be self-righteous," says handwriting expert Senko, of Nixon two days after the Kent State shootings. Self-righteousness is an extreme polarization, a belief that our motives are pure, but it soon leads to ruthlessness. "When righteousness comes, evil is not far behind," according to inner-child expert John Bradshaw. Richard Nixon was a "White Revolutionary"—"someone who will adopt radical or revolutionary measures to secure conservative ends." (Mazlich) Nixon could have been unconsciously describing himself when he wrote in his book, *In the Arena*, "We must remember that virtually every aggressor in history has claimed that his ultimate goal was peace, but peace on his terms."

What was Nixon's "secret plan for ending the war" in Vietnam—which remained unknown to Congress and the public? It was to use the punishing bombs of nuclear destruction on Vietnam that would have evaporated tens of thousands as they did in Hiroshima and Nagasaki, Japan, at the end of World War II. "Nixon went into a psychotic state from time to time, and that frightens me knowing he could have started a nuclear war. He was all set to strike when the demonstrations in Washington, DC, of October 15, 1969, and November 15, 1969, upset him so much he canceled his plans," says Hal Dorland.

Two of the slain students from Kent State had participated in those demonstrations, Allison Krause and Jeffrey Miller. Like Dorland, they experienced feelings of dissolution over the effectiveness of their efforts at protesting the war. As Dorland admits, "I was in on both those demonstrations and felt after that we were not achieving anything. Little did I know until much later!"

What does this infer about Nixon's state of mind? "I can say for certain that Nixon was psychotic at times . . . three of Nixon's psychiatrists were available around the clock for him." According to Dr. David Abrahamsen, in *Nixon vs. Nixon: An Emotional Tragedy*, Nixon was a psychopath, a person with a mental disorder marked by egocentric and antisocial activity. At the end of his presidency, when the Watergate scandal was closing in, he was "weeping, staggering, irrational . . . drinking heavily . . . enraged and raging." (James D. Barber) Like Hitler, he was suicidal. According to Hal Dorland, "there were a lot of people trying to get him to commit suicide . . . The political Nixon seemed to fluctuate between sadism and masochism," says Dorland.

The Richard Nixon revealed on the Watergate tapes was shockingly different from the one his colleagues had known. His entire speech pattern was different—the transcript filled with "grunts, unfinished sentences and meandering thoughts, which began almost nowhere and finished somewhere else," wrote Woodward and Bernstein. Arthur Burns, Nixon's chief domestic aide, had never heard some of the expressions before, like "candy-ass" and "the hang-out route," as Nixon had always spoken clearly, decisively and grammatically. He would be rational at meetings, then come back from meetings and not be rational. His alter-personalities may have helped him maintain a cover of control in front of others. Nixon almost went over the edge on national television during his goodbye speech to his White House staff. In a binge of free association, he rambled on about money, father, mother, brothers, death: the main themes of his life. Alone in the White House, he gave speeches to pictures on the wall.

UNDER WHOSE CONTROL?

Under layers of defensiveness, secrecy, passivity, and viciousness was an ideal stooge for superhuman forces of darkness to create chaos, disorder, and death. Nixon wrote in 1972, "Leadership itself is morally neutral; it can be used for good or ill." (Henry Morganthau, *Newsweek*, May 2, 1994) Nixon's spiritual advisor, Billy Graham, claimed that Nixon was under the influence of "sleeping pills and demons," stating, "I think there was definitely demon power involved . . . all through history drugs and demons have gone together." (Fawn Mackay Brodie) "He can be talked into things by others, he could be controlled by other people," says handwriting expert Senko. "He was programmed and made to be president," said John Mitchell in 1969. "He can be so easily led," says Dr. Hutschnecker, "Nixon told me, 'I'm guided by my party.'" *Richard* a film made in the late 1960s, also implies that the political handlers who drafted him into politics programmed Nixon.

Nixon was without proper boundaries between himself and others; he did not know what he really stood for. This is typical of adult children of dysfunctional families. Nixon's personality itself had no core, it was blank, wrote biographer David Abrahamsen. The heaviest bombing campaign in the history of warfare was carried out in Southeast Asia on villages of innocent women and children, perpetrated by a president who had surrendered his mind to the darkest of deeds and fears.

THE VORTEX OF KENT STATE

If Kent State sounded the death knell for violent student dissent on college campuses, it also sounded the death knell for the Nixon administration. According to H. R. Haldeman, Nixon's closest aide, May 1970 marked "a beginning of the downhill slide toward Watergate." (Jonathan Aitken, *Nixon: A Life*) First there was the scathing denunciation by the press and Congress for the Cambodian incursion and the Kent State shootings. The dirty tricks employed at Kent State were utilized again and again until he was finally caught.

The White House tapes of March 21, 1973, revealed Nixon discussing one million dollars in hush money to be paid to the Watergate burglars; reminiscent of the million-dollar bribe offered to the Krause family to drop their idea of a movie about Kent State. Watergate was the price Nixon paid for the bloodshed in Vietnam, Cambodia and Kent State. Ultimately he offered himself up as a sacrifice at Watergate—being the first president in US history to resign. As Nixon admitted to David Frost in *I Gave Them a Sword*, "I was one of the casualties, or maybe the last casualty, of Vietnam."

Nixon continued to monitor Kent State to the end of his life, seeking to find out what anyone knew about what really happened there, including having his friend, Ivan Boesky, pay for the Kent State statue created by Eric Segal at Princeton University. Elaine Senko's analysis of Nixon's handwritten letter to the Krause family reveals Nixon "was planning on being in a situation where he would be lying in the future, far into the future, as in a cover-up."

Kent State represented deaths of the young, viewed as property, who do not have a voice and are without power. The students represented a lower class of persons. The *U.S. Congressional Record* states, "Four human lives were not only inexcusably destroyed; they may very well have been deliberately taken by a number of men using their uniform, anonymity and subsequent lies to satisfy their personal animosity toward a 'class of persons' they had decided were long overdue for punishment."

The election of Richard Nixon as president is an example of the enormous denial that must be exercised when electing politicians. "We are Nixon; he is us," wrote Gore Vidal. Voters actually seek a leader of this kind who will act out for them the hostility that they feel and tell them what they want to hear. Abuse, incest, violation, and demoralization are part of the imperfect human family's legacy, which stretches back to our first parents and extends into the indefinite future. Repression, denial, and dissociation are the ways they are dealt with.

The fingers on the trigger at Kent State point straight back to Nixon. Unable to identify the enemies in his own mind, Nixon projected them onto others, including the innocent, idealistic minds snuffed out at Kent State, and the millions killed in Vietnam and Cambodia. Barber reports that Nixon once stated: "One day we'll get them, we'll get them on the ground where we want them. And we'll stick our heels in, step on them and twist . . . show no mercy." Under the cloak of national security hid an insecure child, incoherent, unable to listen, retreating to a world of fantasy, compartmentalizing his presidency as he had done his life. Nixon was a brilliant politician, but his personality may have been vacant and morally blank. Nixon died in 1994, but he will be back soon enough in some other form, because our world creates them, and our system continues to demand them.

The National Examiner (December 28, 1999) lists the Kent State shootings as number 51 in its list of the top 100 scandals of the twentieth century. The suppression of this unresolved national trauma creates a vortex of unresolved issues at the core of which lies not just four unpunished murders, but the unspoken hostility of elders towards the young—the belief that the young are not only expendable in war, they are no more than objects to be abused, molested or murdered at will. "Evil is a form of killing," according to Scott Peck in his bestselling book *People of the Lie*. "When I say that evil has to do with killing, I do not mean to restrict myself to corporeal murder. Evil is also that which kills spirit."

Did the deaths serve the intended purpose? The collective judgment of ex-activists, journalists, government officials, and historians determined that "the deaths at Kent State marked the end of the era of mass youth protest, the end of widely held aspirations for a rapid, substantive restructuring of society." (Susie Erenrich, Editor of *Vietnam Generation*) The "killing of spirit" was made evident in that the year 1970 marked not only the last season of protest for the Vietnam War, but also the beginning of the Postmodern period in art, this period ended the utopian optimism that survived two world wars, and began a period that marked no hope for the future (Marilyn Stockstad, *Art History*, Vol. 2, 1995). The killings at Kent State killed more than four innocents, it killed the spirit of an entire generation, which was its intended purpose.

The larger dysfunctional family that is our society continues to demand scapegoats and enforce silence. The *U.S. Congressional Record* states, "To deny the existence of an element in our society whose hatred for student protesters is such they not only approve of the killings, but genuinely wish more had been shot, is to deny reality. In this case, the victims are Americans, and the site of the massacre is an American campus. It is too much for the mind to contemplate, let alone accept." It also states, "The sudden turn upon the sound of a shot, the incredible precision of that turn, the number of guardsmen involved in that sudden turn . . . the deliberate aiming into the parking lot . . . the pointed disinterest in so many students close by . . . all of these facts strongly indicate the execution of a conspiracy."

George Shultz, Secretary of the Treasury under Nixon and a former marine, said the sound of gunfire at Kent State as replayed on television "was a salvo." A salvo, according to the Department of Defense, is "a method of fire in which a number of weapons are fired at the same target simultaneously." According to William Safire, White House advisor and speechwriter during the Nixon years, in *Before the Fall*, "The government, in an organized fashion, had executed some demonstrators on a command."

The young were slain abroad in Vietnam for reasons that still are unexplained, and they were slain at Kent State on their campus for reasons we are unable to face. Who was responsible for the conspiracy, and who supported it? "It's time we were told the truth," says Hal Dorland. The need for closure beckons in the "crime of the century," Kent State, to free ourselves from lies and second guesses. Says Dorland, "There was a huge outpouring of anger, and never total calm since." ●

References

Abrahamsen, David. *Nixon vs. Nixon: An Emotional Tragedy*. New York: Farrar, Straus and Giroux, 1977.

Aitken, Jonathan. *Nixon: A Life*. Washington, DC: Regner, 1993.

Ambrose, Stephen. *Nixon: The Triumph of a Politician*. New York: Simon & Schuster, 1988.

Barber, James. *The Presidential Character*. New York: Prentice Hall, 1972.

Bills, Scott L. "The Sixties, Kent State, and Historical Memory." In *Vietnam Generation*. Susie Erenrich, ed.

Brodie, Fawn. *Richard Nixon: The Shaping of His Character*. New York: W.W. Norton, 1981.

Cackler, Christian. *Recollections of an Old Settler*. Kent, OH: Roger Thurman, 1992, p. 39.

Chapin, Dwight. Memorandum for H. R. Haldeman, April 24, 1970. Declassified August 28, 1998.

Churchill, Ward. *Indians Are Us? Culture and Genocide in Native North America*. Monroe, ME: Common Courage Press, 1994.

Collier, Peter, and David Horowitz. *The Rockefellers: An American Dynasty*. New York: Holt, Rinehart & Winston, 1976, p. 115.

Constantine, Alex. *Virtual Government*. Venice, CA: Feral House, n.d., p. 257.

Dorland, Hal. Personal communications.

Drinnon, Richard. *Facing West: The Metaphysics of Indian-Hating & Empire Building*. Minneapolis: University of Minnesota Press, 1980.

Fred, Don. "Sheriff's Story of the May 4th Shootings," *Daily Kent Stater*, May 4, 1994.

Gordon, William. *Four Dead in Ohio*. Laguna Hills, CA: Northridge, 1990, Appendix.

Hoyt, Edwin. *The Nixons: An American Family*. New York: Random House, 1972.

Hughes, John Emmet. "A White House Taped," *New York Times Magazine*, June 9, 1974.

Huston, Tom Charles. Memorandum for Bud Krogh /Secret, March 20, 1970. Declassified August 28, 1998.

Krogh, Bud. Memorandum for Tom Huston/Confidential, March 25, 1970. Declassified November 9, 1995.

Kutler, Stanley I. *Abuse of Power*. New York: Free Press, 1997, p. 549.

Mazlich, Bruce. *In Search of Nixon*. New York: Basic Books, 1972.

Morganthau, Tom. "The Rise and Fall of Nixon," *Newsweek*, May 2, 1994.

Nixon, Richard. Draft Presidential Letter/Secret—Eyes Only. Declassified E.O. 12958, Sect. 3.6; August 28, 1996.

———. *The Memoirs of RN: Richard Nixon*. New York: Grosset & Dunlap, 1978.

Parmet, Herbert S. *Richard Nixon and His America*. Boston: Little, Brown, 1990.

Peck, M. Scott, Ph.D. *People of the Lie*. New York: Simon and Schuster, 1983.

Safire, William. *Before the Fall: An Inside View of the Pre-Watergate White House*. New York: Da Capo, 1988.

Senko, Elaine. Personal communication.

Thomas, Charles. *Kent Four*. Kent State Archives.

U.S. National Archives. Nixon Papers (notes April–June 1970).

White, Theodore H. *Breach of Faith: The Fall of Richard Nixon*. New York: Athenaeum, 1975, p. 130.

Yale Archives. Kent State Collection. "Letters to the Krause Family."

—Winter 2002

Bankers and Generals

The Economic Interests Behind the Yugoslavian Conflict

by *Al Hidell*

The United States and NATO bombed Kosovo and Serbia in 1999 and succeeded in removing President Slobodan Milosevic. Yet with the "ethnic cleansing" long over, our troops remain. Why? Al Hidell looks beyond the "humanitarian" rhetoric and discovers that control of the Balkans is, to a surprisingly large degree, about advancing our raw economic interests. Like Afghanistan, the region is a strategic point in the world's oil and drug trade routes. It is home also to significant coal, oil, natural gas, and gold reserves. Most incredibly, Hidell learns that in the battle for Kosovo, the United States, Iran, and Osama bin Laden were fighting on the same side.

WHILE THE MAINSTREAM American media have accepted the government's simplistic explanation for NATO's deadly attacks on Kosovo and Serbia, the region is more complex than President Clinton's "humanitarian" rhetoric. Ironically, both Bill Clinton and former banker Slobodan Milosevic seem intent on obscuring the region's true significance from their people.

Though they have not said so publicly, both men know the Balkan conflict is about more than the fate of the ethnic Albanians. It is about more than Serbia's desire to maintain its historic and cultural ties to Kosovo. Control of the Balkans is, to a surprisingly large degree, about raw economic interests.

According to the U.S. government, our military action in Yugoslavia has two main goals: to punish Serbian aggression, and to prevent further "ethnic cleansing," in particular to ease the plight of Kosovo's ethnic Albanians. In fact, President Clinton went out of his way to claim that this war was not being fought for territorial or economic advantage. With Orwellian logic, the government claimed the violence being committed against the Serbian people—which has actually resulted in an increased "cleansing" of most of Kosovo's ethnic Albanians—is a form of "humanitarian assistance."

With the notable exception of the Gulf conflict, this fits the pattern of justification for America's post-Cold War military excursions. In the official view, the bad old days of gunboat diplomacy and American imperialism are over. The U.S. military of the 1990s has become a kind of Red Cross with guns, serving the humanitarian and selfless impulses of America's benevolent rulers. In addition, because the United Nations (or in this case, NATO) is ostensibly calling the shots, America's military might is now held in check by the need to obtain an international consensus before it acts.

This last point is of particular concern to some conspiracy theorists, who fear the United States military has become little more than a servant to international elites. They believe the United States is increasingly surrendering its military and economic sovereignty (i.e., its ability to do what it wants) to supranational entities like the UN and NAFTA. In their view, the placement of U.S. troops in Kosovo as part of a multinational "peacekeeping" force—as will likely happen soon—would just be the latest example of this.

So, the official view holds that the U.S. military has become a rather benign source of "humanitarian assistance" and "peacekeeping," and even then only if it is allowed to do so by some degree of international consensus. A more extreme version of this viewpoint, held by some conspiracy theorists on the Right, depicts the United States as a puppet controlled by international bureaucrats who are out to destroy all notions of national sovereignty. Supporters of both views would point to U.S. actions in the Balkans as an example.

ANARCHY FROM THE U.K.

Another perspective is provided by statesman and former Democratic presidential candidate Lyndon LaRouche. Once again, we are presented a conspiracy theory that assumes that the United States is not the dominant actor on the world stage. In the April 12, 1999, issue of the *New*

Federalist, LaRouche warns that the war against the Serbs is, "like the ongoing war against Iraq, entirely a creation of the [British] Blair government, as 'Desert Storm' was adopted by [the Bush administration] at the behest of the former Thatcher government . . ."

Other articles in the same newspaper suggest that the U.K.'s motive in orchestrating the Balkan conflict is twofold. First, "to dismantle and loot the former Soviet-bloc states"; and second, to disrupt relations and prevent an alliance between the United States, Russia, and China. Presumably, it would take the combined strength of a U.S./Russian/Chinese alliance to thwart British geopolitical goals. In particular, the LaRouche publication claims that Britain was "pushed into its war rage" by the possibility that the United States was preparing to join Russia and China in an effort to completely reorganize the ailing world financial system. This reorganization would essentially put the economic welfare of the people ahead of the interests of the international bankers and currency speculators, whom LaRouche believes to be mainly British or British-controlled.

Summarizing the LaRouchian view of the Kosovo crisis, a recent *New Federalist* editorial declared:

> To understand this war, you have to recognize the reality of the terminal economic and financial crisis which is facing the world system. Without knowing that the British financial oligarchy is looking its own extinction in the face, it is impossible to comprehend the fact that this oligarchy would choose to launch wars in order to stop the consolidation of an alliance of sovereign nations, which would establish a new and just world monetary system.

Before dismissing LaRouche as simplistic due to his "blaming the British for everything," recall that for most of Clinton's two administrations, the president in fact cooled U.S. relations with Britain while strengthening our engagement with Russia and China. The U.S. also followed policies in Africa and the Middle East that, according to LaRouche, were antithetical to the British government's goals. Also, Clinton made peace in Northern Ireland a major policy objective, and even welcomed Sinn Fein leader Gerry Adams as an official visitor to the White House. Seemingly in response to Clinton's movement against British interests, the 1990s did see a major effort to "get" Clinton which in fact did originate almost entirely in the British media. [See "The Brits Bash Bubba," *Paranoia*, issue 9.]

The LaRouche organization's warnings of a "one world government"—which requires the ultimate destruction of political and economic national sovereignty—is actually similar to warnings that have been made for years on both the Right and the Left of the conspiracy theory spectrum. These warnings differ only in their identification of the ultimate orchestrator of the New World Order. For some, it is the international bureaucrats of the United Nations. For others, it is the international elites of such groups as the Trilateral Commission. For LaRouche, the strings are being pulled by the British Commonwealth.

The A-albionic conspiracy research group (www.a-albionic.com) takes the LaRouche viewpoint a step further. In their view, Britain is indeed a major force working for global domination. However, they believe there is another force battling Her Majesty behind-the-scenes: the Vatican. In the case of the Balkan conflict, it is interesting to note that the British are on the side of war, while the Vatican has repeatedly condemned the violence.

A more detailed system suggested by A-albionic pits a British/Masonic/Jewish axis against a Vatican/Jesuit/Islamic alliance. Elements of the current Yugoslavian crisis do fit into this conspiratorial scorecard. As stated above, the British are playing a major role in the war, while the Vatican is fighting against it. In addition, the Vatican has a natural connection to Eastern Europe's Orthodox Christians, including the Serbs. On the other hand, the fact that the Serbs are battling the mainly Muslim ethnic Albanians does not fit into the suggested constellation of forces.

THE U.S.: DOMINATED OR DOMINANT?

All these viewpoints ignore the simple truth that, since the collapse of the Soviet Union, America's military, economic, political, and cultural strength have made it the globe's only superpower. Indeed, a case could be made that the exercise of U.S. military power was constrained more during the Cold War by the Soviet military and nuclear threat than it is today. As a Pentagon analyst wrote in 1991, "Our status as the only superpower must be perpetuated by a military force sufficient to dissuade any nation or group of nations from defying the supremacy of the United States."

As noted by the Stratfor organization in its March 29, 1999, *Global Intelligence Update* (www.stratfor.com), "Since 1991, an extremely strange and even unnatural disequilibrium dominated the world. The United States presided over a global coalition and isolated any [rogue] state that would not participate."

However, Stratfor warns that the world is now in a "massive realignment designed to create an international system that can limit U.S. power." To an extent, this echoes LaRouche, with the major difference that LaRouche sees the emerging realignment as meant to counter British hegemony. In addition, while LaRouche sees Great Britain as the orchestrator of the conflicts in Yugoslavia and Iraq, Stratfor points the finger at Russia:

> By covertly supplying critical military supplies and providing public political support, Russia created a space in which both the Serbs and Iraqis could resist U.S. military pressure . . . The ideal for Russia [is] an ineffective, prolonged campaign in Iraq and an intensive one in Serbia. Neither can succeed, neither can end [and], both will together sap U.S. military strength while straining the American alliance.

The Stratfor publication goes on to declare that "the big story now is Russia's relation with China. In 1972, China and America ganged up on Russia in order to stop its tremendous momentum. Today, the players shift their partners but the game remains the same. Russia and China have a joint strategic interest in hemming in the United States."

Once again, there are surprising consistencies in the analyses provided by widely disparate sources concerning, for instance, increasing U.S. weakness, behind-the-scenes coordination of seemingly chaotic events, an emerging global realignment involving Russia and China, and efforts to recolonize and loot Eastern Europe. The differences emerge in their assessment of America's relative strength in the world, as well as in their assessment of which nation should most concern America.

Whether or not you believe a seemingly weakened Russia is still a threat to America, there is no doubt that the United Nations has become more powerful in this decade. In particular, the 1990s have seen a major increase in the strength and deployment of UN power, which is by definition a threat to the power of any individual nation. In a trend that signals an erosion of respect for national sovereignty, the UN has repeatedly deployed its military and inspectors within the borders of sovereign nations which the UN has decided are either too unstable (Somalia, Cambodia) or too much of a threat to regional stability (Iraq).

However, the only way we will know for sure that the UN has become a serious threat to American sovereignty is when it deploys its power in a way with which the U.S. strongly disagrees. So far, this hasn't happened.

Regarding the LaRouchian view of Great Britain as our true enemy, it is interesting that well before most Americans heard anything about Kosovo, on February 3, 1999, *The Times* of London was already declaring that NATO "is planning to deploy ground troops within a sovereign state, turning part of that state into a NATO protectorate." Also, *New Federalist* writer Umberto Pascali has noted in the April 19 edition that NATO special forces are dominated by Britain in terms of both leadership and personnel. Even the NATO bombing of the Chinese embassy in Yugoslavia, which took place during the preparation of this article, fits the LaRouchian picture. At the very least, LaRouche's focus on economic motives in the Balkans already puts him ahead of most of the mainstream media.

THE MEDIA FALL IN LINE

Whether following the orders of an international elite (the British Commonwealth) or its own desires, America's post-Cold War military actions have enjoyed an unprecedented degree of media support. Yes, they have sometimes been criticized by mainstream news pundits. However, these "objections" have tended to follow the naïve lament that "we cannot be the world's policeman," as if America is a neutral do-gooder with no interests to protect, or no territory it wishes to control. Our status as the most powerful nation on Earth has been thrust upon our reluctant shoulders by history, imply the pundits. Note that, unlike every other historic world power, we maintain our position by rendering "humanitarian assistance," rather than by aggressive military, political, and economic policies.

In the case of Kosovo, America's free press has been particularly docile. As Seth Ackerman of Fairness and Accuracy in Media (FAIR) charged in the May 16, 1999, issue of *In These Times*, "The first casualty of this war was dissent." He notes that every major U.S. newspaper editorialized in favor of the NATO campaign. In addition, on April 1, when the chief UN human rights monitor for Yugoslavia held a press conference to denounce the airstrikes as the "biggest mistake since Vietnam," not a single media outlet saw fit to report his criticism. However, his statement on the human rights situation in Kosovo—released at the same press conference, and more in line with U.S. propaganda needs—was widely reported.

FAIR's Ackerman goes on to note that the attacks have "elicited a great deal of bloodlust from the pundits," who once again rendered absurd any charges of a so-called "liberal media bias." For example, *New York Times* foreign affairs columnist Thomas Friedman virtually urged NATO to rack up more civilian deaths when he barked, "Twelve days of surgical bombing was never going to turn Serbia around. Let's see what twelve weeks of less than surgical bombing does. Give war a chance." This sentiment was echoed by *Washington Post* columnist Charles Krauthammer, who applauded the fact that NATO was "finally hitting targets . . . that may indeed kill the enemy and civilians nearby."

WHY KOSOVO?

To analyze U.S. and NATO motives in the Balkans, we need to look beyond the news media's shallow war-mongering and cheerleading. We should first examine the official motives and determine if they are an adequate explanation of events.

Are we there to punish Serb aggression? Perhaps, but there are simply too many governments in the world behaving as badly or worse than Serbia for this to be the major motive. Are we there to stop Serbia's "ethnic cleansing"? State violence against targeted ethnic groups is so widespread in the world that, again, Serb violence against Kosovo's ethnic Albanians—while certainly wrong—is not so unique as to merit special attention. For example, as Noam Chomsky has pointed out, the U.S.-supported country of Colombia has created over one million refugees, and the level of government-sponsored political killings there is about at the level of Kosovo. (As an aside, one of the world's most extreme and violent cases of "ethnic cleansing" was practiced by the United States against the Native American population, an irony lost on most news analysts and commentators.)

In addition, the western nations stood by and did nothing to halt the Rwandan genocide of 1994, in which literally hundreds of thousands of people of a certain ethnic affiliation were not just forced from their homes; they were brutally killed by machete-wielding gangs. The dead did receive a belated apology from the U.S. a few years later, one that made no mention of the possibility that the West's lack of interest may have had something to do with the fact that the victims were all black Africans.

Unlike Rwanda, the Balkans are very close geographically to western Europe, and instability there is naturally seen as more of an immediate threat. In addition, the ethnic Albanians have the PR advantage of looking more like "us" (i.e., western elites and news reporters). Both factors do explain to some degree why NATO has chosen to draw a "line in the dirt" in Kosovo. But is there more at stake in the region?

STRANGE BEDFELLOWS

Perhaps NATO has been inspired to act by the struggle of the Kosovo Liberation Army (KLA) to gain an independent Kosovo. The KLA, consisting mainly of Albanian Muslims and supported since 1992 by both the United States and Iran, may well become the Contras of the 1990s. Indeed, widespread KLA involvement in drug trafficking has been acknowledged even by its supporters. Meanwhile, opponents claim the KLA and the Albanian mafia are virtually one and the same.

In addition to Iran, the United States is joined in its support for the KLA by none other than America's Public Enemy No. 1, Osama bin Laden. Bin Laden's chief military commander, Ayman al-Zawahiri, is the brother of the KLA's head of elite forces, Muhammed el-Zawahiri. The connection does not end there. In fact, according to Ben Works, director of the Strategic Research Institute, "There's no doubt that bin Laden's people have been in Kosovo helping to arm, equip and train the KLA . . . The U.S. administration's policy in Kosovo is to help bin Laden. It almost seems as if the Clinton Administration's policy is to guarantee more terrorism."

Supporting the KLA, then, appears to be a politically awkward byproduct of the NATO intervention rather than a major reason for that intervention.

JOBS, JOBS, JOBS

In a rare bit of candor, Secretary of State James Baker admitted that the Gulf conflict was not about Iraqi aggression or saving Kuwait. No, he told a reporter at the time, it is about "jobs, jobs, jobs." In other words, it was in our domestic economic interest to punish Iraqi aggression and in so doing control the flow of oil from the region. Although it may seem unlikely at first glance, the crisis in the Balkans also concerns the politics of oil, as well as other critical natural resources. It is here, in the realm of naked economic self-interest, that the region's conflicts finally begin to make sense.

As a starting point, consider the Rambouillet Accord, the rejection of which by Slobodan Milosevic was the ostensible reason NATO began bombing. Ostensible, because as we have seen, NATO's decision to bomb and ultimately occupy Yugoslavia was made at least as early as February 3, 1999.

One little-known provision of the Accord demands, "The economy of Kosovo shall function in accordance with free market principles." So, not only would the Accord have imposed NATO military occupation, it also would have forced Kosovo to follow western "free market" economic policies. It is not too hard to understand why Milosevic rejected such a wholesale surrender of his government's political and economic policymaking authority.

This economic provision of the Accord was noted in an anonymous flyer ("Say No! Not NATO.") distributed on the streets of Washington, DC. The flyer succinctly places the conflict in a wider economic context:

> With NATO's growing military presence in Albania, Bosnia, Croatia, Greece, Hungary, and Macedonia, an occupation of Yugoslavia will only solidify NATO control in the Balkans and contain Russia. If the war against Yugoslavia succeeds, the goal of self-determination and economic sustainability for the other Balkan nations will only slip further away.

Likewise, Michael Colon of the Unlimited News Service dismisses NATO's "humanitarian" motives, calling the conflict in Yugoslavia simply "a new war for loot." In this, he shares Lyndon LaRouche's view that the conflict is at least partly about exploiting and looting the former Soviet bloc countries and the Balkan region.

No friend of Lyndon LaRouche, the Left's Noam Chomsky nevertheless sounds a similar theme. He asserts the West wants to turn eastern Europe into a "new, easily exploitable part of the Third World." He elaborates:

> There used to be a sort of colonial relationship between Western and Eastern Europe. In fact, the Russians' blocking of that relationship was one of the reasons for the Cold War. Now, it's being reestablished and there's a serious conflict over who's going to win the race for robbery and exploitation . . . There are a lot of resources to be taken, and lots of cheap labor. But first we have to impose the capitalist model on them.

Which brings us back to the Rambouillet Accord and its demand that the Kosovo economy follow "free market (read Capitalist) principles."

THE BANKERS AND THE GENERALS

Actually, the international financial community had its eyes on Yugoslavia long before Rambouillet. Beginning in the 1980s, economic "reforms" imposed by Yugoslavia's external creditors (i.e. International Monetary Fund [IMF]) resulted in "the impoverishment of both the Albanian and Serbian populations, contributing to the fueling of ethnic tensions," according to Spring 1996 *Covert Action Quarterly*. The area's much-lamented ethnic tensions, then, did not just materialize out of thin air. They are at least in part due to policies forced on Yugoslavia by the international bankers it is beholden to.

Covert Action Quarterly goes on to charge that "macro-economic reforms imposed by Belgrade's external creditors since the late 1980s have been carefully synchronized with NATO's military and intelligence operations." In other words, the generals have been dancing with the bankers in Yugoslavia for many years.

Commenting on the IMF's role in creating the Yugoslavian crisis, Professor Michael Chossudovsky of the University of Ottawa has written:

> By cutting the financial arteries between Belgrade and the [Yugoslavian] republics, the reforms fueled secessionist tendencies that fed on economic factors as well as ethnic divisions, and virtually ensured the de facto secession of the republics. The IMF-induced budgetary crisis created an economic fait accompli that paved the way for Croatia's and Slovenia's formal secession in June 1991.

OIL, OIL, OIL

Speaking of free markets, the *Sydney* (Australia) *Morning Herald* of April 28, 1999, reported the United States had no intention of following suit after the European Union banned oil sales to Yugoslavia. As the newspaper noted, "The disclosure that American firms have been selling oil to the dictator while American pilots have been risking their lives to bomb oil refineries and storage facilities is likely to undercut American efforts to moralize to the rest of the world." Indeed, two weeks into the conflict, Texaco shipped some 65,000 barrels of oil products from a British refinery to Yugoslavia. (Texaco has since stopped selling oil to Yugoslavia.)

In fact, though it has been overshadowed by events in the Middle East, the Balkans also have a history of "oil politics." For example, SUNY Associate Professor of Political Science Gregory P. Nowell has suggested that Italy's invasion of Albania earlier this century was "an oil-driven event." In addition, by 1928 western oil interests (in particular, British Petroleum) had come to dominate Italian and French markets, which had previously been purchasing large amounts of Soviet oil. This was achieved partly through British Petroleum's acquisition of oil concessions in Albania.

More recently, the *Moscow Times* noted on April 13, 1999, that the military conflict in Yugoslavia just happened to be hampering a project designed to provide Russian oil to the Mediterranean region. Such subtleties and parallels were not deemed worthy of significant coverage by America's free press, which continued to feed the public endless images of fleeing refugees and blown-up buildings.

BLACK GOLD

Michael Colon quotes a March 1996 issue of the German publication *Die Zeit* regarding what's really at stake in the Balkans: "The oilfields of Kazakhstan, the gas fields of Turkmenistan, [and] the enormous offshore reserves of black gold off Azerbaijan, make up a zone that can gain, over the next fifty years, an importance equal to that of the Persian Gulf today." Furthermore, Colon notes the world's most important gold mine is in Uzbekistan, and the largest deposit of silver is found in Tajikistan. There are even rumors of uranium in the area.

Colon goes on to note the interesting fact that "ferocious wars" always seem to "explode around the routes, real or projected, of [oil and gas] pipelines: Chechnya, Nagomy Karabakh, Georgia, and Kurdistan."

It should be pointed out that the Unlimited News Service for which Colon has written his article makes no secret of its pro-Communist/ Socialist bias. However, before you dismiss Colon's analysis, consider the following statement: "The Gulf War was a symbol of the American preoccupation [with] the security of oil and gas reserves. The frontiers of that preoccupation are advancing to the north and include the Caucasus, Siberia, and Kazakhstan." This farsighted analysis was uttered in 1992 not by some anti-Capitalist radical, but by former U.S. Senate Majority Leader and Republican presidential candidate Bob Dole.

Colon believes the Balkans are significant because "the oil transport routes must pass by there," in particular along the Danube river. Not coincidentally, "Belgrade [the capital of Yugoslavia] alone occupies a strategic position on the Danube." Furthermore, a proposed oil pipeline project—worth several billions of dollars—would pass through Bulgaria, Macedonia, Albania, and Kosovo. An area of such vital economic interest must be "protected," and "stability" must be imposed.

As Colon suggests, "To justify the installation of military bases [in the Balkan region], there is a need for a local conflict." This, he says, is the real reason why several western powers armed the Croatian nationalists in 1991, the Bosnian Muslims in 1993, and now the Kosovars of the KLA in 1998. "Those who call themselves firemen," he concludes, "need incendiaries."

In addition to oil, natural gas, gold, silver, and possibly uranium, the Balkan region also contains significant coal reserves. In fact, Kosovo itself has some seventeen billion tons of coal, according to the director of Kosovo's Stari Trg mining complex. Novak Bjelic has even gone so far as to state, "The war in Kosovo is about the mines, nothing else. This is Serbia's Kuwait—the heart of Kosovo."

Unless you are an avid reader of mining and metallurgical journals, however, you probably were not aware of these facts. The vast majority of U.S. media reports have portrayed Kosovo as an isolated and poor region with no natural resources of any consequence. As writer Sara Flounders pointed out in a recent article on the mines posted to an Internet newsgroup (alt.conspiracy), it is as if during the Gulf conflict the news media had repeatedly portrayed Kuwait and Iraq as little more than "barren deserts."

ANOTHER KIND OF PIPELINE

In a May 6, 1999, opinion piece for the *The Times* of London, analyst John Laughland also concerns himself with pipelines and their relation to the Kosovo conflict. However, Laughland speaks of a pipeline not of oil but of drugs, particularly heroin. Interestingly, he uses almost exactly the same language as Michael Colon, writing that "the 'ethnic' uprisings which convulse formerly communist states invariably occur at strategically important points on the Eurasian drug route." He defines this route as running "from the heroin fields of Afghanistan, through the former Soviet central Asian states, Turkish Kurdistan, and into the Balkans."

Laughland goes out of his way to deny the present conflict has anything to do with oil. "Just as previous wars were fought to control trade routes, whether for oil or other commodities, so this conflict is drug-fueled." Does this make the Kosovo conflict, in effect, little more than drive-by shooting on a global scale?

Certainly, the drug trade has been intertwined with military and covert operations around the world, particularly during the Vietnam war of the 1960s and the Contra's war against the Nicaraguan Sandinistas in the 1980s. And there is no doubt that drug profits have corrupted governments and rebel groups around the globe, including the Balkans. However, given the previously stated facts about the Balkan region's incredible natural resources, Laughland's rather weak argument that this is all just a drug "turf battle" smacks of disinformation. Also, the fact that this disinformation is originating out of London is no coincidence, if one believes the LaRouchian world view.

Know Your Enemy

Despite his region's wealth of natural resources, Slobodan Milosevic likely has noneconomic motives as well. However, because he is "the enemy," the mainstream media have no interest in examining his point of view with any measure of objectivity. It's much easier to parrot the official line that he is an evil madman/Hitler/tin-horn dictator (take your pick) who must be stopped at all costs.

The following scenario might help us to better understand his mindset. It is not a defense of Slobodan Milosevic's actions, but rather a mental exercise designed to demonstrate just how one-sided and incomplete the American media's seemingly intensive coverage of the Kosovo crisis has been.

Ask yourself what would be our president's response if America's agricultural heartland produced a group dedicated to achieving the region's independence from the United States. This group has been launching violent attacks on government buildings, and has assassinated a number of policemen and federal officials. Heavily involved in the drug trade, this group is known to be receiving support from Iran as well as Osama bin Laden's organization.

As the crisis intensifies, the president sends the FBI and federal troops into the region. NATO grows concerned, and tells the president that he must accept an armed occupation of the Midwest by foreign troops who will act as "peacekeepers." When the President refuses, the bombs begin to fall. •

—Fall 1999

The NFL: Professional Fantasy Football?

by Brian Tuohy

Have you ever watched a professional football game that was "too good to be true"? In 1969, the National Football League (NFL) merged with the American Football League (AFL), and a multi-million dollar business was born. From the Super Bowl of 1969 through the 2001 "storybook" victory of the appropriately patriotic New England Patriots, author Brian Tuohy uses quotes from the players themselves and other public sources to expose the NFL's hidden history. Tuohy wonders whether, in order to dramatize its "Cinderella stories" and "unabashed tragedies," and to get maximum output from its product, the NFL fixes, tweaks, or scripts its games. As Tuohy concludes, the ticket you purchase is for amusement purposes only. There is nothing on your ticket stating otherwise. If you take the game to be real (as some do pro wrestling) who is at fault?

> "Pro football provides the circus for the hordes."
> —CONGRESSMAN EMANUEL CELLER

IN 1969, the National Football League (NFL) was in the biggest developmental stage in its history. It was merging with its rival, the American Football League (AFL), and fans of the NFL weren't accepting the new competition. In both Super Bowl I and II, the NFL (represented by the Green Bay Packers) had proven its dominance over the younger, weaker

AFL. Now, with Super Bowl III looming, and the merger and the result-ant television contracts hanging in the balance, something had to be done.

This time, the AFL would be represented by the New York Jets, led by the highest-paid player of the time, quarterback Joe Namath. Repre-senting the NFL was one of its oldest franchises, the Baltimore Colts, who were made 18-point favorites by the bookmakers to win the game. Yet, just a few days prior to the game, Joe Namath brashly guaranteed the Jets would win. Namath was proven correct when the Jets beat the Colts 16–7 in one of the biggest upsets in NFL history. More than an upset, it was a turning point for the NFL. Not only did it give credibil-ity to the AFL teams in the fans' eyes, it further opened the NFL's doors to the TV networks, whose deep pockets finance football to this day.

The question remains, however, why was Namath so sure of victory? I would suggest Joe Namath is the "smoking gun" of the NFL, and that Super Bowl III was the first—but definitely not the last—time that the NFL fixed the outcome of one of its own games.

"Namath and his teammates' performance secured the two leagues, at the very least, $100,000,000 in future TV revenue. The game was almost too good to be true," commented former NFL player Bernie Parrish in 1971. "Considering other devices imposed by TV's needs to lift fan interest and raise the advertisers' prices, perhaps it was too good to be true."[1] Football great Bubba Smith, who played for the Colts in Super Bowl III, wrote in his autobiography that the game had been "set up" for the Jets in order to boost the AFL's credibility.[2] In a later *Playboy* interview, Smith elaborated, "That Super Bowl game, which we lost by nine points, was the critical year. The game just seemed odd to me. Everything was out of place. I tried to rationalize that our coach, Don Shula, got out-coached, but that wasn't the case. I don't know if any of my teammates were in on the fix."

FIXES AND TWEAKS

The NFL is a business, first and foremost. In 1996, *Financial World* magazine valued the worth of the average NFL franchise at $174 mil-lion. Consumers spent $3 billion dollars on NFL team-related merchan-dise. On average, more than 12 million viewers watch a regular telecasted game.[3] And it is television that feeds the most money to this ever-hungry beast.

Originally, each NFL team sold its broadcast rights individually. How-ever, in 1961, thanks in part to President John F. Kennedy, Congress passed the Sports Antitrust Broadcast Act, which paved the way for the NFL to market its games as a package. This first "package" was sold to CBS for $4.65 million. Three years later it was up to $14.1 million. By 1974, with the addition of *Monday Night Football*, it was a robust $57.6 million. A 1978 poll showed that 70 percent of the nation's sports fans followed football, compared to 54 percent pursuing baseball.[4] The prices escalated accordingly. By 1984, the networks were paying the NFL $434 million. In 1998, the last time the networks purchased the rights to the NFL's games, CBS paid $4 billion dollars for eight years, with ESPN shelling out $600 million and ABC adding an additional $550 million a year. That doesn't include more than $1 billion the Fox network paid just a few years earlier.

The only way these numbers can be recouped is through the ratings and the resulting advertising revenue. But how has football become America's number one spectator sport? Certainly, it offers drama, violence, and raw emotion for twelve hours every Sunday in the fall, and Cinderella stories, remarkable comebacks, and unabashed tragedies in every play, game, and season. However, to develop these stories and keep those ratings soaring higher, does the NFL fix, tweak, or script its games to get the maximum output from its product?

Over the years, there has been speculation about whether Super Bowls are "won," or whether they are "awarded." Some Super Bowls are awarded because of the stories they provide, others as rewards, but each for a reason: for instance, to Green Bay for bringing tradition back to the game; to Denver and John Elway in 1997 for their long-suffering seasons (perhaps at the League's insistence); to St. Louis and Tennessee in 1999 for their willingness to relocate for the League; to the relocated Baltimore Ravens in 2000 for their long-time owner, Art Modell, whose commitment to the NFL reaches back to the 1960s; and, most recently, in perhaps one of the most blatant examples of scripting an entire season, to the 2001 New England Patriots. In an immediately post–9/11 America, what more symbolic team could the NFL crown its champion than the Patriots, who were the biggest underdog in Super Bowl's thirty-six-year history?

PROFIT DRIVEN

Like any CEO, the NFL owners are profit driven. The fan is secondary in their scheme. Why else would they pull teams like the Baltimore Colts and the Cleveland Browns out of their respective cities when these teams constantly played to sell-out crowds? Both moves were made because the new cities (Indianapolis and Baltimore) offered the owners better stadium deals, and more cash in the owners' pockets. The media may label such moves "tragedies," yet according to author Jon Morgan in his book, *Glory for Sale: Fans, Dollars, and the New NFL*, "Television network executives said they didn't care where teams were based. The NFL had become a national broadcast product. It would garner high viewership wherever the games were played."[5]

Another huge source of revenue for the League comes from expansion teams. New teams are asked to pay an "initiation" fee of $150 million or more just to join the League. What, exactly, is this money for? Nothing. It is simply "profit divided up among the other rich kids that got there first."[6] Expansion is always on the NFL's mind. In fact, I believe it accounts for the success of the Carolina Panthers and the Jacksonville Jaguars in 1995. Both teams, in just their second year of existence, managed to reach their respective conference championship, just one win shy of the Super Bowl. Neither won, yet they were each hailed as success stories. This justified further expansion, with the addition of the new Cleveland Browns and Houston Texans.

"Football has become our national religion, and NFL owners are the druids. Men of business, men of state, men of war: All are inexorably drawn toward the people who own and control these teams."[7] The idea that this elite group of thirty two men sometimes reach down from their skybox and dabble in the happenings on the field is not a stretch of the imagination.

The NFL's Dirty Little Secret

According to Dan Moldea, in *Interference: How Organized Crime Influences Professional Football*, many early NFL owners were known to be gamblers. Moldea alleges that the following owners were known to have bet on football games, and some even bet on their own teams: One-time Dallas Cowboys owner Clint Murchison, Jr., Kansas City Chiefs owner Lamar Hunt (son of oilman H. L. Hunt Jr.), Cleveland Browns/Baltimore Ravens owner Art Modell, New Orleans Saints owner John Mecom, Jr., Chicago/St. Louis/Arizona Cardinals owner Charles Bidwell, and Philadelphia Eagles owner DeBenneville "Bert" Bell.

Moldea alleges that Carroll Rosenbloom, one-time owner of the Baltimore Colts, not only bet on his team, but also altered the outcome of a game because of it. Oddly enough, it was this very game that legitimized football for the television networks. It has been called the greatest game ever played: the 1958 NFL championship game. Rosenbloom's Colts were playing the New York Giants, who were 3½-to 5½-point underdogs. Moldea also alleges that Rosenbloom laid down $1 million on his boys to win.[8]

The Colts were losing until the last seven seconds, when Colts kicker, Steve Myhra, kicked a field goal to tie the game at 17–17 and send it into overtime. In overtime, the Colts marched eighty yards down the field to get to the Giants eight-yard line—easy field goal territory. But they never kicked. Instead, according to Moldea, Rosenbloom, knowing the game was won but his bet lost with a field goal, had his general manager force Coach Weeb Ewbank to go in for the touchdown. Final score: Colts 23, Giants 17, which covered the point spread, and Rosenbloom's money. (Sports gamblers generally bet not just on the victor, but on a particular "spread," or margin of victory.)

Players, too, have been tempted by the bookmaker. Several star players of the 1950s–1960s were known to have gambled, and some to have fixed games. Bookmaker/gambler Don Dawson has admitted that during those two decades, he had personally been involved in fixing no fewer than thirty two NFL games.[9] Washington Redskins quarterback Sammy Baugh, Pittsburgh/Detroit quarterback Bobby Layne, and Kansas City quarterback Len Dawson were alleged to have gambled (and perhaps shaved points), but were never charged or convicted of a crime. Green Bay Packers great Paul Horning and Detroit Lions star Alex Karras were not so fortunate.

On the January 16, 1963, edition of the NBC evening news program *The Huntley-Brinkley Report*, Detroit Lions star defensive tackle Alex Karras admitted that he had bet on football games in which he played. A national scandal erupted. It was quickly quelled on April 17, 1963, when NFL Commissioner Pete Rozelle suspended indefinitely Karras and Horning (who had also bet on games in which he played) and fined five other Detroit Lions players $2,000 each for betting on games in which they did not play. Rozelle also announced he had evidence that several other players around the League were gambling on the NFL, and these players had been "reprimanded, but not fined."[10]

THE NFL's FBI

As a result of the 1963 betting scandal, NFL Commissioner Rozelle created NFL Security. NFL Security (the League's FBI, if you will) has employed former intelligence officers, Justice Department officials, and ex-FBI officers throughout its years. It has branches in every city in which the NFL plays. Former director of NFL Security Warren Welsh has said, "These representatives [NFL Security officials] are on retainer to the League, and they specifically report to the League. In addition to their game-day coverage and their liaison with the local law-enforcement community, they would also do background investigations that we might have for game officials, an ownership group, impersonations, misrepresentations, whatever it might be, as opposed to just working for the local team."[11] They are on the watch for gambling, drugs, and whatever other troubles the players and coaches can get into. And these men are kept very, very busy.

In their extensively researched book, *Pros and Cons: The Criminals Who Play in the NFL*, Jeff Benedict and Don Yaeger chronicle just how rampant criminal activity is in the League. According to their 1998 research, one out of five (21 percent) of the players in the NFL have been charged with a serious crime. The crimes they detail go beyond the drinking and driving offenses we often hear reported. These crimes include rape, kidnapping, assault and battery, domestic violence, and homicide. Of course, there is a big difference between being charged and being convicted, but the fact that this many pro football players have such problems is alarming. Even worse, these players are allowed to continue to play in the NFL.

DRUG DEALINGS

Drugs are a way of life in the NFL. One of the first things discussed at the NFL rookie camp are drugs, but these talks tend to fall on deaf ears. Be they illegal, like marijuana or cocaine, or legal prescription drugs, like steroids and pain killers, drugs are very much in use in the NFL. Former NFL player Tim Green claims in his book, *The Dark Side of the Game*, "Moderate use of some drugs is just a necessary reality of big-time football."[12] He goes on to say, "One of the main reasons performance drugs [i.e. steroids] have played such a major part in the evolution of the modern football player is because the players themselves feel like they will never die. . . . They'll do whatever it takes to be the best they can be."[13]

Whether performance-enhancing or recreational, drugs are officially not allowed in the NFL. But this doesn't stop their use. The NFL's policy regarding drugs and drug testing has no effect because it is simply not enforced. Former Washington Redskin Dexter Manley was caught using drugs several times and finally was banned for life—twice. In his book, *You're Okay, It's Just a Bruise*, former Oakland Raider team doctor Rob Huizenga, M.D., tells of one player who tested positive for cocaine ten times with no action taken by the League.[14] He also recounts the story of an unnamed member of the Denver Broncos who was going to be suspended because of a second positive drug test. He never was, and was in the line-up the following week. According to Huizenga, "I knew then that something was wrong with the new drug penalty system. Either the fix was in at the commissioner's office or some major legal roadblock had been thrown up."[15]

MAINTAINING RANKS

"We have a basic rule in the NFL," says a former law-enforcement official who advises the NFL on security matters. "It is to keep it upbeat and keep it positive. But, above all, they want to keep everything quiet."[16] That's the way it is in the NFL today. Keep all potential problems within the League. The only press allowed is cleared by the League. According to the NFL's drug program, the League's "drug czar" has been banned from speaking with the press.[17]

In order to receive his pension, former League treasurer Austin H. Gunsel had to sign a contract with a gag clause reminiscent of those required of retiring CIA officers: "Neither shall Gunsel, without the prior consent of the Commissioner of this League, publish any newspaper or magazine article, book or publication, nor submit to any newspaper, radio, or television [an] interview or program which discusses, involves, or refers to the affairs or activities of the National Football League, its officers or employees, or to any of the member clubs thereof, or their owners, officers, employees or others holding any interest therein."[18]

Players, too, are not immune to this type of censorship. Both players and coaches are fined for making degrading remarks regarding poor officiating. They can even be fined for speaking about things not deemed to be in the NFL's best interest (like baseball's John Rocker). "The very nature of a football player, and one of the essential elements to ever get to the NFL, is to maintain ranks. . . . Football is a game that requires the discipline and unquestioning obedience of a soldier. Right or wrong, the fact is that all football players are programmed to march to a certain beat."[19] This is true both on and off the field. Players, throughout their playing career, are taught to toe the line. Break the rules, and you're cut. Even after players leave the game, it is rare to hear a bad word spoken about the NFL. Maybe this is because all ex-NFL players draw some sort of pension from the NFL and the player's union.

COINCIDENCE OR A FIX?

Anyone who has watched football has seen games or plays that seemed just too good to be true, games where the play on the field somehow matched or beat the pre-game hype. Could it be coincidence? Maybe. But I believe it to be more.

Take Super Bowl XXX, played in 1995 between the Pittsburgh Steelers and the Dallas Cowboys. The Steelers lost the game 27–17 because of two statistically-unusual plays—two Neil O'Donnell interceptions. Going into that game, O'Donnell had the lowest interception-per-pass-attempt ratio in NFL history. Yet, here he threw two passes that were seemingly gift wrapped for Cowboy Larry Brown (who was named Super Bowl MVP). In the following off-season, both O'Donnell and Brown signed multi-million dollar free-agent contracts with other teams, going on to careers of mediocrity.

Absent evidence of outright payoffs, a subtler mechanism exists for the NFL to potentially coerce its players into fixing games. Consider a player who gets into trouble, be it for steroids, drunken driving, etc. With 21 percent of NFL players finding themselves in some sort of legal trouble, there is plenty to choose from. When caught, would he perhaps be pulled aside and given certain options? Keep in mind that just one play, and just one player, can alter the outcome of a football game. Be it a field goal attempt, an interception, or a fumble, one player can change everything. Something as simple as a missed block, a botched snap, or biting on a pump fake, can be the difference between maintaining a drive or being forced to punt.

PLAYERS AS PATSIES

Certainly, not all games are fixed, and many NFL players engage in honest play for their entire careers. In fact, it may be that most players are unwitting patsies in the NFL conspiracy.

Coaches have a huge sway over what happens on the field and are directly responsible to the owner. It is the coach who decides who plays and how. Conceivably, a player who won't "play ball" might not see the ball at all during the game. This might explain an unusual benching in the 1999 AFC playoffs, when Buffalo Bills starting quarterback, Doug Flutie, was benched in favor of back-up Rob Johnson. Johnson hadn't started a single game during the entire year, but he was coach Wade Phillips' choice to play this critical game, while a healthy Flutie sat the game out. Buffalo went on to lose the game to the Tennessee Titans on the famous "home-run throwback" play (itself a disputed call). Could it be that Flutie was benched because he wouldn't lose the game for the League?

Coaches influence every play. What might seem like bad performance on a player's part may instead be an ill-advised play sent in from the sidelines. Take what happened in Super Bowl XXXII. Late in the fourth quarter, with Denver knocking on their goal line, Green Bay Packers head coach Mike Holmgren admittedly told his defense to lie down and allow Denver's Terrell Davis to score a touchdown. He defended his action, saying he wanted to leave enough time for his offense to come back and score. However they never did. Davis's touchdown won the Super Bowl for the Broncos.

Like the players they rule over, coaches also have "run-ins" with the law. As detailed in *Pros and Cons*, Minnesota Vikings head coach Dennis Green and assistant Richard Solomon were investigated by the team for charges of sexual harassment on more than one occasion in the 1990s.[20] To the frustration of their fans, the Vikings never seem to reach the Super Bowl despite a talented roster.

Then there are the referees—the only people on the field directly employed by the NFL. To a large degree, and despite claims to the contrary, they control what happens on the field. The penalties they call can alter a play, the score, and hence the outcome of a game.

NFL referees are actually only part-time employees of the NFL, even so they have to have a minimum of ten years of college experience and three years of monitoring by the League before even being considered to referee a game in the NFL. Each week, the NFL scrutinizes game tapes just to watch the officiating. They have to. Teams file weekly reports with the League on calls for which they want "further clarification." These reports never find their way into the media, however. "Conversations between the NFL officiating department and teams are confidential. We do not comment on them," NFL spokesman Michael Signora told ESPN.

Instant replay, a device television helped usher into the League, was supposed to clear up any controversies that may arise in a game. However, a referee is supposed to have "conclusive evidence" in order to reverse a call that has been challenged. "Conclusive" being the key word. What may seem conclusive to viewers at home is not always what's deemed conclusive to the referee calling the game. It's still a judgment call. And no matter how well instant replay supposedly works, it cannot—ever—overturn a penalty called by a referee.

TELEVISION'S INFLUENCE

With the wide variety of ways in which the game can be controlled, detecting a fix would be very difficult. The people who should be the public's eyes and ears, the sports reporters, are merely just another cog in the NFL's propaganda machine.

On a local level, the sports reporter is nothing but a cheerleader. He has to be. Should he begin to ask the "tough" questions, he will quickly find himself on the outside of the locker room looking in. Without the cooperation of the team, a local reporter will find it impossible to get close to the team, much less fill his column or broadcast.

On the national level, it is even worse. "All play-by-play TV and radio announcers are approved by not only the club management but by [the Commissioner] himself."[21] The list of current announcers/anchors of NFL broadcasts almost reads like a Pro-Bowl roster: Dan Marino, Deion Sanders, Boomer Esiason, Terry Bradshaw, Howie Long, Steve Young, Tom Jackson, Sterling Sharpe, Troy Aikman, Chris Collinsworth, etc. Even legendary commentators like Pat Summerall and John Madden have direct NFL experience. So whose interests are they more likely to represent, the fan or their former and current employer?

When a sticky situation arises within the League, or if the League has an issue it needs pushed (a need for new stadiums, higher ticket prices, etc.), it often relies on its phalanx of announcers to sway public opinion. As ex-NFL star, Bernie Parrish, put it, "The words we hear coming from our television sets don't seem to have the same meaning as they used to, whether they are coming from the White House or the NFL hucksters. The images we see are what the paid packagers want us to see. In the case of pro football, the packages are designed and decorated behind the closed doors of the Commissioner's office, and there is no consumer protection for the public."[22]

Television has changed the way football is played. It is because of TV that the two-minute warning exists (to allow for a commercial break when interest in the game has peaked). Former president of ABC Sports Roone Arledge (the man behind *Monday Night Football*), once said, "Most of what TV does wrong is done to generate more dollars for [NFL] owners. If we cram eighteen commercials into a football game it's because the owners and the Leagues are so damned greedy in what they ask for rights."[23]

In 1965, when CBS paid over $14 million for the rights to the NFL games, "they acted as if they had bought the sport, including the people who played it."[24] Perhaps they did. Former NFL player Tim Green wrote, "If you think that the players in an NFL game aren't only aware, but affected by the television cameras and microphones, you're wrong. Players often know when the cameras are on them, whether they can see the little red lights or not, and they play to them as if they were on a Hollywood movie set."[25]

So, is the NFL closer to what some feared the defunct XFL would become: A scripted soap opera much like professional wrestling? It could very well be. If it is, it is *not* necessarily illegal for them to be so. There is nothing printed on your ticket indicating that the game you see will be played by certain rules. There is no attempt at defrauding you, because the ticket you purchase is for amusement purposes only. And what they give you *is* a form of entertainment. If you take it to be real (as some do pro wrestling) who is at fault?

Just because it seems real doesn't mean it truly is. There is nothing anywhere that states the NFL and the networks couldn't script the season to get the maximum amount of fan appeal they desire. Does that mean every single game is fixed? No. But could they spot a potential story line in a team and play it for all it's worth? Certainly.

In 1971, former NFL star Bernie Parrish wrote, "With $139 million at stake for the owners, $84 million for the television networks, and up to $66 billion for organized crime's bookmaking syndicates, and with what I learned as a player, no one will ever convince me that numerous NFL games aren't fixed."[26] Now, thirty years later, with the dollar figures ten times what they were then, one would have to be naïve to believe that the NFL would leave everything—its name, its money, its very existence—up to chance. ●

Notes

1. Bernie Parrish, *They Call It a Game* (Dial Press, 1971), p. 128
2. Bubba Smith and Hal DeWindt, *Kill, Bubba, Kill!* (Wallaby, 1983), p. 130
3. Jon Morgan, *Glory for Sale: Fans, Dollars, and the New NFL* (Bancroft, 1997), p. 310
4. Ibid., p. 92
5. Ibid., p. 182
6. Parrish, p. xiv
7. Morgan, p. ii
8. Dan Moldea, *Interference: How Organized Crime Influences Professional Football* (Morrow, 1989), p. 91
9. Ibid., p. 28
10. Ibid., p. 126
11. Ibid., p. 35
12. Tim Green, *The Dark Side of the Game* (Warner, 1996), p. 59
13. Ibid., p. 76
14. Robert Huizenga, M.D., *You're Okay, It's Just a Bruise* (St. Martin's, 1994), p. 325
15. Ibid., p. 209
16. Moldea, p. 33
17. Huizenga, p. 325
18. Parrish, p. 219
19. Green, p. 49
20. Jeff Benedict and Don Yaeger, *Pros and Cons: The Criminals Who Play in the NFL* (Warner, 1998), p. 137
21. Parrish, p. 109
22. Ibid., pp. 130–131
23. Ibid., p. 126
24. Ibid., p. 122
25. Green, p. 136
26. Parrish, p. 183

—Spring 2002

I-Spies, Espionage, and 9/11

by Al Hidell

The American media have largely ignored one of the most explosive stories to emerge since 9/11: the breakup of a major Israeli espionage operation in the United States. The operation aimed to infiltrate several government agencies and may have been tracking al-Qaeda terrorists before the aircraft hijackings took place. Indeed, some sixty apparently suspicious Israeli Jews were quietly rounded up in the government's post-9/11 dragnet. Why were they rounded up? Has the U.S. media failed to "connect the dots" even more so than the U.S. intelligence establishment? Al Hidell investigates, and separates the rumors from the facts about Israel and 9/11.

MARIA, a New Jersey homemaker who does not want her last name to be used, saw something strange on the morning of 9/11, and it wasn't in Manhattan. Using binoculars to view the Twin Towers, her eye was caught by something happening in her apartment building's parking lot. She saw three young men—who appeared to be of Middle Eastern origin—kneeling on the roof of a white van, taking video or photos of themselves with the World Trade Center burning in the background. What struck Maria were the expressions on the men's faces. They appeared to be celebrating the attack. As she later told ABC News, "They were like happy, you know . . . They didn't look shocked to me. I thought it was very strange."

Things were about to get even stranger.

Later that afternoon, police—responding to an FBI bulletin based on Maria's description and plate number—pulled the van over, finding five young men inside. They were taken out of the van at gunpoint and arrested. One of the passengers had $4,700 in cash hidden in his sock, while another was carrying two foreign passports. On a day full of unbelievable events, the arresting officers may well have taken it in stride when the driver of the van told the officers their country of origin: "We are Israeli."

"DOCUMENTING THE EVENT"

After the men were taken to jail, the case was transferred from the FBI's Criminal Division to its Foreign Counterintelligence Section, which is responsible for espionage cases. One reason for the shift, sources told ABC News, was that the FBI believed the company to which the van license plate was traced, Urban Moving, may have been providing cover for an intelligence operation run by the Mossad, the Israeli military intelligence agency.

The FBI quickly obtained a warrant and "searched Urban Moving's offices for several hours, removing boxes of documents and a dozen computer hard drives," according to ABC News. However, the New York FBI agents ultimately ended their investigation, released the five suspects, and turned them over to the Israeli consul.

The Forward, New York's leading Jewish newspaper, reported that "top-ranking Israeli diplomats" had intervened with Attorney General John Ashcroft on behalf of the men. The article went on to acknowledge that "the nature of the investigation [had] changed after the names of two of the five Israelis showed up on a CIA–FBI database of foreign intelligence operatives." The men were eventually flown back to Israel, where an article in that nation's leading newspaper, *Ha'aretz*, criticized the FBI's treatment of the men, who were subjected to repeated interrogations and alleged beatings during their two-month detention.

Significantly, according to a report posted on www.americanfree press.net, one of the men appeared on an Israeli radio talk show and stated, "Our purpose was to document the event." If true, this statement is ominous in its implication: the Israeli government knew in advance that the 9/11 attacks were going to take place. Incredibly, the man's statement was confirmed—without comment—in a June 21, 2002, report on the ABC News website.[1] As for Urban Moving's owner, within days of being interviewed by the FBI—he answered all their questions, according to his attorney—he sold his home and returned to Israel.

The September 12, 2001, New Jersey-based *Bergen Record*, in an article since removed from its web site, went so far as to state the men in the white van were "carrying maps linking them to the blasts." The *Record*'s law enforcement source elaborated, "There are maps of the city in the car with certain places highlighted. It looks like they're hooked in with this. It looks like they knew what was going to happen when they were at Liberty State Park." However, this report has not been confirmed. In addition, it should be noted that Urban Moving's owner and his employees were never accused of or charged with any kind of involvement in 9/11.

CAUGHT IN THE DRAGNET

Many assume that the hundreds of people taken into custody (many not yet released) as part of the 9/11 investigation were all Arabs and/or Muslims. In actuality, the men in the white van were not an anomaly. They were among some sixty Israeli Jews quietly rounded up in the government's post—9/11 dragnet.[2] Most were present or former military or intelligence personnel—not unusual, since military service is mandatory for Israeli citizens. At least one was a "demolition/explosive ordnance specialist," according to John F. Sugg of the *Tampa Bay Weekly Planet* (April 22, 2002).

A November 23, 2001, *Washington Post* article by staff writer John Mintz noted that most of the Israelis were being held on immigration charges and were not suspected of any involvement in terrorism. However, in the language of international diplomacy, the phrase "immigration charges" is often a polite cover for more serious activities, such as spying. In addition, according to Mintz:

> In several cases, such as those in Cleveland and St. Louis, INS [Immigration and Naturalization Service] officials testified in court hearings that [the detained Israelis] were "of special interest to the government," a term that federal agents have used in many of the hundreds of cases involving mostly Muslim Arab men who have been detained around the country since the terrorist attacks.

An INS official who requested anonymity said the agency will not comment on the Israelis. He said the use of the term "special interest" means the case in question is "related to the investigation of September 11."

Fox News reporter Carl Cameron, who broke the "I-Spies" story to a national TV audience on December 12, 2001, also raised the possibility that some of the Israeli detainees may have been involved in 9/11.

Although he was careful to point out that there was "no indication" of direct involvement, he noted:

> Investigators suspect that the Israelis may have gathered intelligence about the attacks in advance, and not shared it. A highly placed investigator said there are "tie-ins." But when asked for details, he flatly refused to describe them, saying, "evidence linking these Israelis to 9/11 is classified. I cannot tell you about evidence that has been gathered. It's classified information."

LET ME SHOW YOU MY ETCHINGS

Carl Cameron's report also went beyond 9/11 to address the larger issue of Israeli spying in the United States:

> Numerous classified documents obtained by Fox News indicate that even prior to September 11, as many as 140 other Israelis had been detained or arrested in a secretive and sprawling investigation into suspected espionage by Israelis in the United States. . . . The first part of the investigation focused on Israelis who say they are art students from the University of Jerusalem and Bazala Academy.

According to Cameron and other sources, the Israeli "art students"—under the pretense of selling their creative wares—made repeated contacts with U.S. government personnel. Cameron detailed the scope of the operation, reporting that "they targeted and penetrated military bases [as well as] the DEA [Drug Enforcement Agency], FBI and dozens of government facilities, and even secret offices and unlisted private homes of law enforcement and intelligence personnel."

In fact, this writer even had a personal encounter with one of the Israeli "art students", although I do not work for any government entity. Several months ago, she entered my office and asked for my opinion on her portfolio. Oddly, she didn't try to sell me the artwork. She said she and her fellow students were simply seeking people's opinions as to which work they liked best. (I selected the most creative piece, a whimsical drawing of several elephants.) This visit occurred over a year before the I-Spy scandal broke, but even then I was suspicious as to why an Israeli art student would come all the way to America to seek my critique.

It gets stranger. According to Cameron, another part of the investigation, begun by U.S. officials in the mid–1990s, "resulted in the detention and arrests of dozens of Israelis at American mall kiosks, where they'd been selling toys called Puzzle Car and Zoom Copter." After the *New York Times* and *Washington Post* reported the Israeli detentions, "the carts began vanishing." Zoom Copter's web page quickly assured its customers, "We are aware of the situation caused by thousands of mall carts being closed at the last minute. This in no way reflects the quality of the toy or its salability."

A "High-Priority Target"

The Fox News story went on to cite a General Accounting Office report, which was based on a report by "a U.S. intelligence agency." The GAO report, which referred to Israel as "Country A," flatly stated that "Country A conducts the most aggressive espionage operations against the U.S. of any U.S. ally."

So why would Israel spy on the United States? Cameron quoted a Department of Defense intelligence report that noted, "Israel has a voracious appetite for information," and that "the Israelis are motivated by strong survival instincts which dictate every possible facet of their political and economical policies. It aggressively collects military and industrial technology, and the U.S. is a high-priority target."

Despite its newsworthiness, interested readers may have trouble finding Cameron's story. His four-part report was quickly yanked from the Fox News web site, replaced with the Orwellian message, "This story no longer exists."[3]

The Israeli embassy in Washington has denied all of the spying charges, with the rather comical assertion that "any suggestion that Israelis are spying in or on the U.S. is simply not true." On the other hand, *The Forward*, while denying Israeli spying on the United States, has at least acknowledged that Israeli spies are operating in the U.S., "spying on a common enemy, radical Islamic networks suspected of links to Middle East terrorism." Networks like al-Qaeda, perhaps?

If this is the case, which al-Qaeda operatives might they have been spying on? In his May 7, 2002, article for the online journal *Salon*, Christopher Ketcham reported:

[M]ore than one-third of the [Israeli art] students, who were spread out in forty two cities, lived in Florida, several in Hollywood and Fort Lauderdale, Florida—one-time home to at least ten of the nineteen September 11 hijackers.

In at least one case, the students lived just a stone's throw from homes and apartments where the September 11 terrorists resided. In Hollywood, several students lived at 4220 Sheridan Street, down the block from the 3389 Sheridan Street apartment where terrorist mastermind Mohammed Atta holed up with three other September 11 plotters.

PUTTING THE WOOMERS TO WEST

It would be untrue to say the mainstream media has not covered this story. Nevertheless there has been a troubling lack of coverage relative to its importance. Essentially, the Fox report was criticized by pro-Israeli lobbying groups, declared "completely baseless" by Israeli officials, and then was dutifully sent down the memory hole. The story literally disappeared.[4]

The reaction of Alex Safian, associate director of the Committee for Accuracy in Middle East Reporting, was typical of the backlash. Making the now familiar (and inaccurate) grouping of conspiracy theorists with the extreme Right, Safian lamented, "In the conspiracy media world and the hate groups, it's going to have lots of legs."

To its credit, the ABC news show *20/20* did air a report containing some of the above cited facts. However, Barbara Walters inexplicably concluded the report by reassuring America, as one Internet commentator has put it, "I hope we've put all these woomers to west."

Meanwhile, *USA Today* completely whitewashed the Urban Moving story. The September 28, 2001, issue of "The Nation's Newspaper" cited the story of the five detained Israelis as one of the "unsubstantiated rumors that implicate Israel" and on which "many in the Muslim world are endlessly chewing over and recycling."

The relative media silence hasn't gone unnoticed across the Atlantic. The highly respected British intelligence and military analysis service, Jane's Information Group, has remarked:

> It is rather strange that the U.S. media with one notable exception seem to be ignoring what may well prove to be the most explosive story since the 11 September attack, the alleged breakup of a major Israeli espionage operation in the United States which aimed to infiltrate both the Justice and Defense departments and which may also have been tracking al-Qaeda terrorists before the aircraft hijackings took place. (March 13, 2002)

HASIDIC MULES: THE DRUG CONNECTION

In his *Salon* article, Christopher Ketcham provided more details about the Israeli "art student" spy ring:

> Reports of the mysterious Israelis with an inexplicable interest in peddling art to G-men came in from more than forty U.S. cities . . . Agents of the DEA, BATF, Air Force, Secret Service, FBI, and U.S. Marshals Service documented some 130 separate incidents of "art student" encounters. Some of the Israelis were observed diagramming the inside of federal buildings. Some were found carrying photographs they had taken of federal agents. One was discovered with a computer printout in his luggage that referred to "DEA groups."

In fact, of all the listed agencies, Ketcham stated that "the majority of the 'art student' spying efforts targeted the U.S. Drug Enforcement Administration."

Now, it is certainly understandable that the Israelis would want to keep an eye on U.S.-based radical Islamic groups whom they believe have been involved in terrorist attacks against their citizens, but why would Israeli intelligence have such an interest in the DEA?

A key piece of evidence in the I-Spy allegations is a sixty-page document, a compilation of field reports by Drug Enforcement Administration agents and other U.S. law enforcement officials. Regarding the validity of the document, John F. Sugg of the *Tampa Bay Weekly Planet* (April 22, 2002) has reported:

> The author of the document is not identified. However, many DEA and other law enforcement agents are named. Three federal employees have confirmed the incidents described in the report. None disputed the authenticity of the report. One senior DEA official, when read paragraphs that mentioned him, said: "Absolutely, that's my report."

It should be noted that this DEA official added that he "didn't think the incidents were sufficient to prove an ongoing spy operation." On the other hand, according to Sugg, "the [Federal] Office of the National Counterintelligence Executive, in a March 2001 summary, reported on 'suspicious visitors to federal facilities' and noted the type of 'aggressive' activity recounted in the [DEA] document." Furthermore, as Sugg notes, "The specific incidents are richly chronicled, down to names, driver's license numbers, addresses and phone numbers of the Israelis."

In what may be its most significant passage, the DEA document links the I-spies to several ongoing drug investigations. The report states:

DEA Orlando has developed the first drug nexus to this group. Telephone numbers obtained from an Israeli art student encountered at the Orlando [district office] have been linked to several ongoing DEA MDMA [ecstasy] investigations in Florida, California, Texas, and New York.

The Israeli connection to MDMA trafficking was confirmed on July 25, 2002, when Ike Seamens, a correspondent for Florida NBC affiliate Channel 9, reported:

After a massive DEA investigation, Meir Ben David and Josef Levi will be the first Israelis sent to Fort Lauderdale to face a drug trial, said Thomas W. Raffanello, special agent in charge of the Drug Enforcement Administration's Miami office . . . The two Israelis were charged in October 2000 with conspiracy to import ecstasy and possession with intent to distribute ecstasy. . . . The Drug Enforcement Administration says the men are not only leading drug smugglers, they are also members of an Israeli organized crime syndicate. "This is really a significant event in the drug prosecutions in this district and nationwide," said former federal prosecutor Myles Malman. "It is the first time any Israeli has been extradited to the southern District of Florida for anything," Malman said.[5]

Seamens went on to reveal the rather astounding and rarely-reported fact that "Israelis control 75 percent of the American ecstasy market" and that "Israeli dealers have even supplied Sammy 'the Bull' Gravano, the former Mafia enforcer and ecstasy dealer." Furthermore, Seamens had some surprising news about some ecstasy ring drug couriers, commonly referred to as "mules" in the drug trade:

DEA officials say the Israeli drug rings have often used Hasidic Jews from Brooklyn to smuggle the drugs. Several Hasidim have been caught with the contraband and arrested by New York police, including seventy-two-year-old Machloof Ben-Chitritt, an Israeli-American who was used to smuggle 61,000 ecstasy tablets.

WRONG NUMBERS

So, if some of the I-Spies were working to foil DEA ecstasy investigations, how might they have done it? In the *Tampa Bay Weekly Planet* article referred to above, John F. Sugg reported that some time in the mid-to-late 1990s:

> American intelligence services were increasingly worried by the dominance of many highly sensitive areas of telecommunications by Israeli companies. Comverse Infosys (now called Verint) provides U.S. lawmen with computer equipment for wiretapping. Speculation is that "catch gates" in the system [allows the] listeners to be listened to. Software made by another Israeli outfit, Amdocs, [provides] extensive records of virtually all calls placed by the twenty-five largest U.S. telephone companies."

In particular, Amdocs generates billing data for virtually every call in America. As Fox News' Carl Cameron stated, "It is virtually impossible to make a call on normal phones without generating an Amdocs record of it." They also do credit checks. Both areas of expertise would, of course, be of great help to any intelligence agency. It should be noted, however, that neither the companies nor their employees have been accused or charged with involvement in 9/11.

According to Sugg, the relationship of Comverse Infosys and Amdocs to the detained I-Spies was detailed in the sixty-page DEA document referred to above. He wrote, "The DEA's intense interest in the case stems from its 1997 purchase of $25 million in interception equipment from Israeli companies," including, presumably, Comverse. Sugg then quoted a March 14, 2002, report by Intelligence Online, a French web-based service, that the DEA "was clearly worried that its own systems might have been compromised."

Interestingly, Carl Cameron's report referred to a 1997 local, state, and federal, ecstasy and cocaine investigation, "major" in scope and targeting "Israeli organized crime," that went awry. The problem?

> [A]ccording to classified law enforcement documents obtained by Fox News, the bad guys had the cops' beepers, cell phones, even home phones under surveillance. Some who did get caught admitted to having hundreds of numbers and using them to avoid arrest.

The surveillance, however, went beyond the communications of police detectives and other local law enforcement officers. The I-Spies were also monitoring FBI, Secret Service and, presumably, DEA communications. Amid growing concern in various federal government agencies, the super-secretive National Security Agency (NSA)—again, according to the Fox News report—issued a "Top Secret sensitive compartmentalized information report, TS/SCI, warning that records of calls in the United States were getting into foreign hands—in Israel, in particular."

Soon, as Cameron reported, federal investigators were focusing on two companies: Amdocs and Comverse Infosys. Regarding Comverse, Cameron revealed that "when investigators checked their own wiretapping system for leaks," they became concerned about "potential vulnerabilities in the computers that intercept, record, and store the wiretapped calls." Comverse was a major contractor in this area, according to the Fox report, which also declared that the company "works closely with the Israeli government, and under a special grant program, is reimbursed for up to 50 percent of its research and development costs by Israel's Ministry of Industry and Trade."

SUSPECTS ACTING DIFFERENTLY

So, the I-Spies—perhaps utilizing Comverse and Amdocs, and perhaps without the companies' knowledge—likely foiled at least one major drug investigation. Could the same be true of 9/11–related investigations? Possibly. As Cameron reported, "Fox News has learned that some American terrorist investigators fear certain suspects in the September 11 attacks may have managed to stay ahead of them, by knowing who and when investigators are calling on the telephone."

In particular, as Cameron related, "On a number of cases, suspects that they had sought to wiretap and survey immediately changed their telecommunications processes. They started acting much differently as soon as those supposedly secret wiretaps went into place."

Furthermore, Justin Raimondo (www.antiwar.com) has stated that there may be a "back door" in Comverse's software that "could have easily been opened by Israeli intelligence." It was possible, according to Raimondo, because "Comverse maintains a link to the wiretapping computers, on the grounds that it is necessary for system 'maintenance,'" something which Raimondo says was authorized by the 1994 Communications Assistance for Law Enforcement Act.[6]

Raimondo then raises a key point:

[It all] depends on the intended target of the wiretaps: was it the Israelis, or bin Laden's agents? If the former were acting differently after wiretaps were put in place, it means only that the Israelis were using their sources and methods to protect their own. If the latter, it means the Israelis were using their sources and methods to protect the bin Ladenites.

In a statement that could apply to many aspects of the I-Spies scandal, Raimondo confesses that this possibility is one that "no one—including me—wants to contemplate."

FACTS AND RUMORS

Poke around the Internet, and you'll find many allegations about Jews and 9/11. Following are the most common charges, along with what this writer believes to be the facts:

1. *4,000 Israelis didn't report to work at the World Trade Center on 9/11.* This allegation, which appears to have begun in the Jordanian newspaper *al-Watan*, is simply not true. It may have been based on an early and inaccurate statement issued by the Israeli Consulate that 4,000 Israeli citizens were missing in the New York attacks.

2. *Out of the thousands of 9/11 victims, only two Israeli citizens were killed.* This is, oddly enough, true, despite President Bush's assertion in his September 20, 2001, televised speech that Americans will never forget "the citizens of 80 other nations who died with our own: dozens of Pakistanis; more than 130 Israelis; more than 250 citizens of India. . ." Few of the 82 million Americans who watched Bush's speech noticed when the *New York Times* published a small retraction two days later: "There were, in fact, only three Israelis who had been confirmed as dead: two on the planes and another who had been visiting the towers on business." That number has since been reduced to two. Granted, President Bush doesn't appear to be a math whiz, but even he should know that two does not equal "more than 130." Whether deliberate or based on faulty information, his words served to further muddy the waters around Israel and 9/11. To return to the number two, it certainly does seem to be suspiciously low. That is, until you consider a recent breakdown of 9/11 victims by known foreign citizenship.[7] It appears that a grand total of one unfortunate Irish citizen died, as well as two Chinese

and sixteen Jamaicans. In other words, the Israeli total appears to have been the result of pure chance. (Or perhaps the two Israelis weren't home when world Jewry was making the phone calls from its secret control room, deep under the Swiss Alps.)

3. *A Jewish businessman closed on the purchase of a 99–year commercial lease on the World Trade Center just six weeks before the attacks of 9/11, and now stands to receive a large terrorism insurance settlement.* This is true. The man, Larry Silverstein, is currently involved in a major legal battle about whether the attacks on the Twin Towers constituted a single event or two separate events. A two-event ruling, according to an article seen on the *Wall Street Journal*'s RealEstateJournal.com website (homes.wsj.com), "would double the insurance payment on the destroyed property to about $7 billion." Although this may seem suspicious, one must remember that terrorism insurance on high-profile buildings was quite common even before 9/11. Furthermore, the lease purchase, which cost Silverstein's group $3.2 billion, was initiated in 1999, well before 9/11. The notion that Silverstein gained knowledge of the 2001 attacks some two years before they occurred, and then allowed 3,000 people to be killed for his personal financial gain, simply has no factual basis.

4. *An Israeli company pulled out of its World Trade Center lease shortly before the attacks.* This is true. Zim American Israeli Shipping Co., Inc., whose parent company is nearly half owned by the State of Israel, broke its lease when it vacated its North Tower offices shortly before September 11. Christopher Bollyn (americanfreepress.net) reported that "Zim's WTC office space had been leased until the end of the year, and the company lost $50,000 when it suddenly pulled out in the beginning of September." However, there is no evidence that Zim or its employees had any prior knowledge of 9/11, and the company says the pre-planned move was just a tragic coincidence.

5. *Just one day before the 9/11 attacks, the Army School of Advanced Military Studies (SAMS) predicted that the Mossad would stage a terrorist attack and blame it on Israel's enemies.* This is false, although it has a basis in fact. According to a September 10, 2001, *Washington Times* report, the Army SAMS did produce a report that stated that the Mossad was a "[w]ildcard. Ruthless and cunning. Has capability to target U.S. forces and make it look like a Palestinian/ Arab act." It was a speculation, not a prediction, and it per-

tained to hypothetical peacekeeping operations in the Middle East by the U.S. military.

Nevertheless, such a scenario does have a confirmed—albeit little-known—precedent. Could history be repeating itself? In 1954, Israeli agents working in Egypt planted bombs in several buildings, including an American diplomatic facility, and left "evidence" behind meant to implicate Arabs. After one of the bombs detonated prematurely, Egyptian authorities captured and identified one of the bombers, which in turn led to the roundup of an Israeli spy ring.

Israel responded to the scandal with claims that there was no spy ring, and that it was all a hoax perpetrated by anti-Semites. As the trial progressed, it soon became clear that Israel had indeed been behind the bombings. Eventually, Israeli's Defense Minister Pinhas Lavon was brought down by the scandal. Lavon, though, was most certainly a scapegoat, sacrificed to protect the real figures behind the bombing plan, which had been code-named "Operation Susannah." In the spy trade, it's called a "False Flag" operation.

6. *Secretary of State Colin Powell was scheduled to give a historic speech calling for the creation of a Palestinian State on September 11. The speech was never given.* This appears to be true. However, the 9/11 attacks didn't prevent the president himself from making a similar speech months later. Furthermore, orchestrating the horrific use of passenger aircraft as flying bombs to kill thousands of Americans would not appear to be a particularly logical way to influence U.S. mideast policy. The Israelis have much more effective financial and political methods to use in this regard.

The attacks did give Israel the opportunity to reframe its conflict with the Palestinians as part of the war on terrorism, and likely gained the country some empathy on the part of the American people. This appears to be what former Israeli Prime Minister Benjamin Netanyahu had in mind just hours after the 9/11 attacks, when he declared, "It's very good," when asked to characterize the attacks in terms of U.S./Israeli relations. Realizing that his words might appear insensitive to the tragedy, he then backpedaled, "Well, not very good, but it will generate immediate sympathy."

WEAPONS OF MASS DECEPTION

The sources for this article were not drawn from anti-Israeli Arab media, anonymous web postings, or al-Qaeda pamphlets. This writer has relied on mainstream U.S. and Jewish news sources whenever possible. This is an important point because articles that are critical of Israel or the actions of Jews are sometimes dismissed out-of-hand as being anti-Semitic.

Ironically, there are others who would dismiss this article precisely because it is based on mainstream sources. A conspiracy magazine, after all, should be an alternative to mainstream news sources. How can a magazine that is based on the idea of questioning mainstream reality turn around and say certain mainstream sources are credible? Is it inconsistent to trust the mainstream only when it supports a conspiratorial viewpoint, and to dismiss it when it rejects or suppresses such viewpoints? Not if this results from a good-faith effort to evaluate the particular material on its merits, which this writer has tried to do.

On the other hand, it would be naive to think that all "scandals" are exposed due to the muckraking and diligence of independent-minded reporters, mainstream or otherwise. While such efforts definitely exist and are to be applauded, the fact is that many scandals are exposed as the result of deliberate leaks of information by those in power. Scandals don't explode; they are allowed to emerge. This doesn't mean that the "revelations" that come out are false. In fact, they are true much of the time. Indeed, a governmental or intelligence organization will often volunteer some of the truth while still managing to withhold key and damaging facts. It is "damage control" or, in spy jargon, a "limited hangout".

So, evaluating the validity of scandal-related reports is only part of the equation. One must also consider the people or entities that are hurt by the revelations, and those who benefit. Is the scandal part of an inter-elite power struggle? In the case of the I-Spies scandal, could the leaks have been a "payback" of some kind? If so, there are at least two possibilities:

1. *The I-Spy leaks were payback for Israel keeping America in the dark about 9/11.* In other words, the leaks were meant to punish Israel for not sharing all the intelligence it had gained from its surveillance and possible infiltration of American and foreign al-Qaeda cells.

2. *The I-Spy leaks were payback for Israel's spying on the United States, i.e. the "art students" operation.* This is the most straightforward explanation. If this is the case, the leaks may have come from FBI and/or DEA agents whose investigations of Israeli targets may have been shut down or compromised, in particular, pre–9/11 DEA ecstasy investigations.

CRAZY LIKE A FOX

Finally, one must also consider whether a revealed scandal is meant to divert attention from a more damaging one, or intended to "muddy the waters" where legitimate investigators are treading. In this case, the real scandal may well be Israeli foreknowledge—or even connections to—the tragic events of 9/11. In other words, it may be a "limited hangout" on the part of the Israeli government.

In this vein, we might take a closer look at Fox News, the media outlet generally credited with breaking the I-Spy scandal. Fox News is owned by Rupert Murdoch's News Corporation. Murdoch is one of the world's most powerful media moguls. Most significantly, he has invested heavily in Israel and appears to be one of its strongest supporters. For example, he cochaired a 2001 America-Israel Friendship League black tie dinner, at which Ariel Sharon was the guest of honor (see "Corporate America stands by Israel," *Jerusalem Post*, June 27, 2001). In addition, at a recent twenty-fifth-anniversary dinner for the Jewish Community Relations Council held in New York City, New York Governor George Pataki stated with approval, "There is no newspaper in the U.S. more supportive of Israel than [Murdoch's] *New York Post*." In fact, the event was held, in part, to honor Murdoch. In his speech, according to the pro-Israeli magazine *15 Minutes* (www.15minutesmagazine.com), Murdoch bragged about the time he took a group of editors from New York and London for a weekend at Ariel Sharon's ranch, where the Israeli Prime Minister took Murdoch and his people "on a bird's-eye tour of Israel aboard a helicopter gunship."

Clearly, Rupert Murdoch is no enemy of Israel. This means that the Fox News report either flew in under Murdoch's radar, or was the product of a "limited hangout" operation by Israeli intelligence. This would imply a possible hidden "real" scandal: that the Mossad had advance knowledge of or involvement in the events of 9/11.

MORE THAN A THEORY

This disturbing conclusion, as we have seen, is supported by a significant amount of circumstantial evidence. Also, if the Israelis were able to devote so much effort to spying on the American government, isn't it likely that they would have devoted the same if not more resources to monitor and infiltrate anti-Israeli groups in America, groups like al-Qaeda? The proximity of at least one group of Israeli agents to Mohammad Atta's residence in Florida raises the possibility, as does the fact that an unusually high number of the I-Spies were concentrated in Florida—home to at least ten of the 9/11 hijackers at one time or another. We also have the disturbing revelation by one of the white van "movers" that he and his fellow Mossad agents were here "to document the event." Then there are the classified "tie-ins" between certain Israeli agents and 9/11 referred to in both the Fox News and *Washington Post* stories above.

This is not to take the CIA and the FBI off the hook regarding their own possible advance knowledge of the 9/11 attacks. For example, an article in the September 16, 2001, *Newsweek* reported that an FBI informant "who had been working closely with the FBI office in San Diego on terrorism cases related to Hamas" also had a "close relationship" with two of the 9/11 hijackers: he was their roommate from September to December 2000. Hamas, the radical Islamic group thought to be behind many Israeli suicide bombings, would of course have been of keen interest to the Mossad as well.[8]

GRUNT WORK AND BLACK OPS

On the other hand, despite their rather bizarre methods—using agents posing as art students and shopping mall kiosk operators—the Israeli spy rings were not particularly unusual. The fact is, friendly nations routinely spy on each other. And the I-Spies do not appear to have damaged national security nearly as much, for example, as the Israeli-controlled Pollard Navy spy ring of the 1980s. In fact, it is possible that the I-Spy efforts were merely the spying equivalent of grunt work, gathering basic information about American officials and agencies.

However, such low-level spying is often the first step toward more serious operations, such as infiltration and espionage. And, of course, the targeting of the DEA raises the specter of Mossad involvement in the lucrative drug trade—a potential source of funding for black ops, a fact our own CIA learned long ago.

Indeed, there is something of a symbiotic relationship between Israeli spooks and their American counterparts. As commentator Stephen J. Sniegoski (www.thornwalker.com/ditch/) has observed, "The U.S. government allows, even encourages, Israel to conduct covert operations here and elsewhere because Israeli agencies can perform certain tasks deemed helpful to American interests more effectively than U.S. agencies can." He continues:

Israel enjoys much more leeway to engage in dirty work than the United States does. It was for that reason that the Reagan administration relied on Israel to undertake certain covert activities in Central America. Those activities were little noticed by the media's dominant establishment liberals, who likely would have screamed to high heaven had those same activities been undertaken by U.S. operatives.

The intelligence information channel may not be a two-way street, however. Former Mossad agent Victor Ostrovsky has claimed that, while the CIA shares information with the Mossad, the favor is rarely returned. In fact, he has written that the Mossad has a policy of never giving secret intelligence information out—even if the lives of Americans are in danger.

As an example, Ostrovsky cited the devastating 1983 terrorist attack on U.S. military barracks in Lebanon, which killed 241 marines. According to Ostrovsky, the Mossad had foreknowledge of the terrorist attack, but did not warn America.[9]

A MEXICAN 9/11 OPERATION?

Other clues relating to the possible involvement of Mossad agents in 9/11 have managed to escape the memory hole. The following little-noticed news reports, if true, add much to the circumstantial evidence. At the least, they demand further investigation. Indeed, these reports also raise the question of whether it is the U.S. media which has failed to "connect the dots," even more so than the U.S. intelligence establishment. The first story, from the October 12, 2001, issue of the respected Mexican daily *Crónica de Hoy*[10] opened with a quite astonishing statement:

> The [Mexican] Attorney General is investigating and interrogating two Israelis (one, already a naturalized Mexican citizen) who were detained in the House of Representatives Wednesday with two 9 mm pistols, nine grenades, explosives, three detonators and 58 bullets, to determine if they belong to any group connected with terrorists or subversive groups.

The article went on:

> Both subjects were detained in the installations of the legislative palace of San Lazaro when a group of sugar industry workers that had met with the Speaker of the House, Beatriz Paredes, left to

discuss their issues in the lobby and the two arrested persons arrived and began photographing them.

Then, the following bizarre scene ensued:

This activity and the form in which they took the pictures (aiming their cameras below the belts of the workers) generated tension among the sugar workers, who proceeded to demand [the men's] identification. . . . The Israelis identified themselves as press photographers, but they were not believed and the workers overcame them and then discovered that they were armed with pistols and other high caliber arms.

The next day, again according to the *Crónica de Hoy*, spokeswoman Hila Engelhart of the Israeli Embassy in Mexico issued a statement that acknowledged the previous day's report. In a phone call to a reporter, she stated that her staff was "waiting to find out what happened," and expressed the hope that "in the case of the arrested Israelis, we hope the situation will be resolved quickly." On October 15, 2002, Mexican media reported that the situation had indeed been resolved. The two men had been released—after "intense pressure" from the Israeli embassy—with the official explanation that they had legal permits to carry their weapons.

Our second "dot" comes courtesy of a FoxNews.com report of May 13, 2002, again by the intrepid Carl Cameron. It seems that "a Budget truck was pulled over in Oak Harbor, Washington, near the Whidbey Island Naval Air Station" shortly after midnight on May 7, 2002. The truck was soon "found to have traces of TNT on the gearshift and traces of RDX plastic explosive on the steering wheel. . ." In a revelation that had a somewhat familiar ring, Cameron reported that the driver indicated that he and his passenger were "delivering furniture from California," and that both passengers "were Israeli nationals." Both men were taken into custody for immigration violations, and an investigation was said to be ongoing. There does not appear to have been a follow-up report. ●

Notes

1. At the time of writing, this report is located at abcnews.go.com/sections /2020/DailyNews/2020_whitevan_020621.html.
2. This total comes from the *Washington Post*. Other sources have reported numbers ranging from 100–160, but it is not clear whether those numbers include the many pre-9/11 detentions as well.

3. The ostensible reason was that Cameron used unnamed sources. As any news hound will tell you, this is a characteristic shared by many news reports. At this writing, a transcript of Cameron's Fox News report is still available at www. firefox.1accesshost.com/cameron.html.

4. The pro-Israeli inclination of the U.S. media is obvious, despite the occasional mild criticism of particular Israeli actions. A recent comment by CNN's Aaron Brown on Israel's killing of Palestinian civilians in an attempt to kill a Palestinian leader was typical. The newsman admitted, "We don't believe the Israeli government would risk killing a couple of hundred people in order to maybe—maybe—get one guy." Apparently, the fact that he had just described U.S. actions in Afghanistan, the "one guy" being Osama bin Laden, escaped his keen intellect.

5. Reached for comment, Ben David's Miami attorney Ruben Oliva gave Seamens a rather ambiguous answer when asked if his client is a major organized crime figure. His response was, "I don't believe so."

6. In fact, in a letter dated October 18, 2001, to Attorney General John Ashcroft and FBI Director Robert Mueller, fifteen federal and state law enforcement officers complained that "law enforcement's current electronic surveillance capabilities are less effective today than they were at the time CALEA was enacted." That was about as far as they could go, since even raising the issue of I-spying is, in the words of unnamed law enforcement officers who spoke to Fox's Carl Cameron "career suicide."

7. See www.september11victims.com.

8. There is in fact a precedent for a government infiltrator's involvement in a domestic terror attack, though it involves the American rather than the Israeli government. The FBI has admitted that they had an informer in the radical Islamic group that carried out the 1993 bombing of the Twin Towers. The informer was to have helped the plotters build the bomb and supply fake explosive powder. According to the informer, Emad Salem, the plan was called off by an FBI supervisor. As an October 28, 2003, *New York Times* article concluded, secret tapes that Salem made of his contacts with the FBI "portray the authorities as being in a far better position than previously known to foil the February 26th bombing of New York City's tallest towers."

9. See *By Way of Deception: A Devastating Insider's Portrait of the Mossad* (Toronto: Stoddart, 1990).

10. "Mexico Will Investigate if Israelis Were Terrorists," *Crónica de Hoy*, October 12, 2001, available at www.narconews.com.

—Winter 2003

UFOs and Supernatural Phenomena

* * *

People Are Strange

Unusual UFO Cults Examined

by Scott Corrales

Small armed groups defying the government are nothing new; one just has to look at Israel's mighty Masada fortress to be reminded of this. The 1990s had their share of armed resistance, most notably the Ruby Ridge and Waco incidents. In these cases, the common denominator was mistrust of the federal government and the desire to defend to the death a particular set of beliefs. As Scott Corrales suggests, had the following case been made widely known, a UFO factor might have been added into the mix.

IN MID-JUNE 1997, the UFOR (UFO Research) mailing list posted an item that remains shrouded in mystery. The list's owner, Francisco Lopez, did his level best to glean further information on the subject even many months later, when I pressed him for assistance in writing the kernel of what would years later become this article. But it was no use. In the age of the Internet, that hall of mirrors in which people can appear and disappear with impunity by changing e-mail accounts and assuming different names (and even identities), the source was well out of reach. The posted item may indeed prove someday to have been a compelling hoax, but there are certain details about it that have a ring of truth about them.

The narration begins *in medias res*, in the best tradition of classic epics: "I want to get the whole of the information first, and then release it, rather than just parts," begins its author. "Also, I need to edit out certain portions. Certain information does not need to be released to the public. In some cases the less they know, the better; it allowed us to work with fewer interruptions." He or she then adds, with chilling effect: "You should never be in the company of one with whom you would not wish to die."

This ominous opening would have soared to new heights were it not for the fact that the names and places mentioned in the message were redacted with a series of asterisks. The author, a man or woman with a military or law enforcement background, had participated in the raid of a compound which involved live arms fire in which "all brass was accounted for." The compound, a privately owned skiing or hunting lodge, was then gutted and made to look abandoned by the government forces involved.

"As little evidence as possible was left," states the cryptic author after indicating that a nameless group had been disbanded. "Only Terran humans were found, no XTs [extraterrestrials] or Greys."

This assertion might well relegate the unknown writer to the lunatic fringe, since belief in and or concern for the alleged alien Greys has waned in recent years. The message goes on to talk of how the "cult" in question had cooperated with a number of individuals over an unspecified number of years in the acquisition of "breeder semen from sperm banks" and from unsuspecting human males drawn into certain situations, only to be drugged and subjected to the removal of such a fluid with a syringe. It was then "flash-frozen by use of a portable D-flask of liquid nitrogen, to be stored at a central location," according to the author.

A spec script for *The X Files* or a description of a real event? The author continues:

> They used a group of "renegade" (omitted) as aides and "technical support," with a high priestess working closely with the upper echelons of the (omitted). It appears that, despite the usual (omitted) beliefs, this priestess and her companions were heretics, if such a term can be applied to (omitted) at all.

The cult mentioned in this mind-bending message appeared to be quite deft with the use of weapons, and a veritable arsenal of high-power rifles, shotguns and combat weapons, including "an HK-91 sniper rifle . . . a Steyr AUG Selective Fire Conversion, and a US Army M60, with about 7,000 rounds of .30 caliber ammunition . . . over fifty hand grenades, including explosive, flash, incendiary and smoke . . . 180 kilos of Czech plastique explosive and over a hundred military squibbs (detonators)," are mentioned in the text. It is a supreme irony that this arsenal of death should prove comfortingly familiar within such a high-strangeness context.

The allegations continue: the cult members were in contact with a human group claiming to act on behalf of the "Greys" and capable of projecting images of the entities from opaque, vitreous cubes. Although the author professes being unable to examine this information for him/herself, the putative alien messages appear to have been linked with clandestine UFO landings. "Techniques have been used to confirm that at least one incident took place during May 1995, but nothing further could be determined."

Many UFOR subscribers read this message and many, upon reading this article, may question the wisdom of reprinting more unconfirmed UFO-related speculation. One guesses the entire operation may have been a huge "psy-ops" exercise involving live fire, good guys, and "bad guys," with the entire alien scenario thrown in for good measure or even as a "sickener" factor for the trainees.

"HE DIED LIKE A SPACE COMMANDER"

The alien action-adventure story posted to UFOR smacked more of science fiction than of Sigma Draconis until Argentinean researcher Andrea Perez Simondini—widely known in her country for her contributions to the study of UFO incidents, along with her mother Sylvia, as well as for being an active political figure—forwarded a real-life account of a situation which, at first blush, hauntingly echoed the one scenario posted to UFOR.

"The mystery of the Radar 1 group has finally been solved," noted Andrea in her letter. A contactee cult known as Ashtar had apparently spawned a disturbed group of paramilitary types, led by one Guillermo Romeu, who assumed the name 'Radar 1.'"

The offshoot organization appeared to have been much more successful than its parent in gaining a following and making itself known. Romeu and his acolytes had access to the best technology and were not afraid to employ it. From their headquarters at 269 Wernicke in the village of Boulougne, Buenos Aires province, "Radar 1" (publicly known as Iglesia Manantial, the Wellspring Church) broadcast its own brand of ufolatry over the FM airwaves. Their station boasted a recording studio with three consoles and mixing board for special effects, eight computers (whose hard drives had been erased prior to the raid by Argentinean authorities on January 12, 1998, and Romeu's death by self-inflicted gunshot) and the same ominous arsenal as the improbable cult mentioned on the UFOR list: one surface-to-air missile, bullets of various calibers, gas masks, incendiary bombs, tear gas, Israeli-made Desert Eagle .50 caliber anti-aircraft handguns (*sic*) of the kind used during the Gulf War, an approach radar, chemical sample analysis equipment and radiation, electromagnetic, electrostatic, and heat detectors, etc. All of this gear was stored in a Bronco 4 x 4, which they would use for alleged field research.

Simondini's letter explained that all of this lethal and nonlethal hardware had been paid for partly by the 400- to 4000-peso contributions of the cult's membership and its affiliates. "We strongly believe," she wrote, "that the sect is a facade and there exists a cover-up concerning the weaponry."

Just who was this Guillermo Romeu? An electrician and occasional private pilot, he had joined a contactee study group directed by former UFO researcher Pedro Romaniuk before being expelled a year and a half later. It was during this time that the new cult was spawned, preaching messages received from the ubiquitous space brother known as Commander Ashtar Sheran concerning the "extraterrestrial evacuation plan." In a clever move, the cult leader insisted on the group being widely known as Iglesia Manantial in order to draw recruits from a large membership pool composed by Pentecostal worshippers from other churches.

Guillermo Romeu claimed that his extensive offensive capabilities, gathered since 1991, were devoted to a single purpose: defense against the alien Greys, whom he characterized as "extremely hostile and [who] are using us as a source of food." Two years later, his disciples were further cautioned that "an extraterrestrial race sent by the Antichrist prior to the Battle of Armageddon" would have to be held off by force of arms, thus prompting new arms purchases and further training. Radar 1's members were not averse to parading around in full battle array, showing off their weapons and alarming the general public. They boastfully termed themselves "Grey Hunters."

As in all cults, the price of dissent was high. Romeu was as authoritarian a leader as any, and those among his "Grey Hunters" who showed signs of wanting to part company with the group were threatened and harassed. Those who left lived in constant fear of being assassinated.

Romeu's wife called it quits in 1997, taking Cristin, the couple's seven-year-old son, with her. The cult leader successfully gained the court's permission to attend Cristin's eighth birthday. To everyone's horror, Romeu pulled a pistol from his jacket, stood straight, and placed a bullet through his right temple. "My father died like a space commander," said Romeu's grief-stricken son.

Cecilia Diaz, the late Romeu's mistress, told the press the cult would continue its activities from the location of San Isidro and would "have more weapons." Argentina's Secretary of Worship, Angel Centeno, ruled the cult's right to exist could not be challenged, as it was lawfully registered with his ministry. The Argentinean Foundation for the Study of Cults (FAPES) subsequently reported that Romeu's right hand man, Brian Bach, had assumed the reins of the cult, and urged the country's legislature to appoint a commission to study cults along the lines adopted by many European countries.

SPACE BROTHER BLUES

If we can bring ourselves to play the role of devil's advocate yet again, can we lend any credence to the UFOR story as representing a mop-up operation against a saucer cult in the U.S., much in the same way that Argentina's government moved against Iglesia Manantial? That country's authorities made it clear the cult was not being prosecuted for its beliefs but for its stockpile of weapons—the same argument wielded against the Branch Davidians at Waco.

There was clearly nothing in common between the cults except for the fact that the belief in UFOs and aliens was reason for their existence—the latter cult armed itself to the teeth against them, while the former served up man in a platter to these forces. It can be noted that both episodes serve as bookends to the Heaven's Gate and the Solar Temple suicides. The late 1990s were certainly not kind to saucer cults.

But Guillermo Romeu's violence is reminiscent, to a certain degree, of the activities of Brazilian contactee/terrorist Dino Kraspedon, the *nom de guerre* of Aladino Felix, who underwent an alleged contact experience in 1952 which was true to the contactee fashion of the time—nocturnal encounters in the wilderness with saucers and their humanoid occupants, disquisitions on "man's place in the universe" and life on other worlds. Kraspedon's nonhuman "handlers" apparently endowed him with psychic powers, giving him insight into future human events.

Kraspedon dropped from sight until 1968, when he was arrested under suspicion of terrorism (not at all unlikely, since Brazil at the time was seething with political unrest, best exemplified by the activities of Carlos Marighella, the "father of urban terrorism"). In his *UFO Encyclopedia*, saucer historian Jerome Clark notes that Kraspedon was sentenced in 1971 and was to be remanded into the mental health system, after which he vanishes from the record.

Was Aladino Felix truly contacted by aliens and steered wrong into a life of crime? He apparently recanted his alien contact experiences publicly, which should put an end to the story. Nonetheless, the connection between alleged "alien contact" which translates into violence cannot be overlooked.

PIROPHOS, UMMO'S LITTLE BROTHER

Thirty-two years after it first erupted on the scene, Spain's UMMO hoax still commands attention whenever it is mentioned. While not strictly a cult, given its lack of a leader and clear-cut objectives believers in the planet UMMO and the benevolent "Ummites" certainly carried on in cultish fashion. "Its very name ought to have given it away," says the hoax's creator, Jose Luis Jordan Pena, referring to the fact that UMMO shared the same sound when pronounced as the Spanish word for "smoke" (fumo).

Galician journalist Bieito Pazos managed to secure a lengthy interview with this fascinating character, gleaning details about the blond-haired space people from the star Wolf 424 and more importantly, a true cult which was formed in the wake of the UMMO experiment: a gathering of very intelligent men and women known as Pirophos.

The interest expressed in Kirlian photography by certain members of Spain's Sociedad de Parapsicologia prompted Jordan Pena to realize that people, regardless of their educational or economic background, are fascinated by any phenomenon from which light is issued in a strange way. This led him to create the fictitious deity "Pirophos" and gather some twenty-odd persons in a grimy room in Madrid. One of Jordan Pena's co-conspirators, known only as "C," read out a letter (a tool that had worked well for UMMO) to the congregation, from "our beloved charismatic leader Phoros," living somewhere in the United States. As the lights went out, the parties in attendance were startled to see a bluish light issuing from C's mouth—proof positive that the great god Pirophos had chosen the speaker as the "regional Phoselek" for all of Spain.

The hoaxer told his interviewer that the bluish light was "a basic yet uncommon triboluminescent phenomenon which requires the use of habitual and easily digestible substances."

But that wasn't the only surprise the master hoaxer held in store for his well-heeled disciples. On a table covered by a purple cloth stood a large glass container which contained a scintillating light which bathed the faces of all present in an eerie glow. Many of the economists, doctors, and engineers present dropped to their knees in the presence of the great god Pirophos—who was in fact an amalgam of bioluminescent bacteria in a nutrient agar culture. Later on, explained Jordan Pena, "Pirophos" would be created based on a compound of phosphorus diluted in kerosene or toluene.

The Pirophoreans (to give them a name) were entreated to follow a basic "moral code" crafted by the hoaxer himself: a commitment to study physics and biology, kindness toward spouses and children and, above all, to maintain their religion in strict confidence. The cultists were also told that their faith's supreme leader was a man named George Lipton from Albany, New York (Jordon Pena had successfully placed one Theodore K. Polk from Export, Pennsylvania, among the dramatis personae of the UMMO saga) who lived in complete seclusion due to having achieved the rank of "Phoros"—as high as could be achieved in the Pirophorean cult. Lipton owed his secrecy to the fact that his body now shone with a brilliant blue light.

"This was the ultimate reward," Jordon Pena stated, "to become the god Pirophos himself—immortal before dying and immune from all diseases. My eschatology was simple enough: The world would end in the year 4,634 due to the explosion of a supernova some 220-light years from Earth. At that time, all the adepts who reached the rank of Phoros would be forever joined to that universal light known as Pirophos."

In the early 1990s the master hoaxer decided to bring his cult to an end, in much the same way he had exposed UMMO. The cult's members accepted the fact that they had been duped, with a mixture of astonishment and amusement. "Only two," Jordan Pena told Pazos, "insist upon remaining faithful to that mysterious light." Jordan Pena's tone throughout the interview with Pazos is that of a mischievous schoolboy recalling youthful escapades. A highly educated man, the creator of the UMMO and Pirophos does not suffer fools lightly, and both of his fictitious communities seem to serve the purpose of holding human gullibility up to the harsh light of public scrutiny.

CONCLUSION

As we make the leap into the twenty-first century, many aspects of ufology can be safely deemed as no longer relevant. While there is a certain degree of hubris involved in the making of such a pronouncement, few will disagree that things like the "angel hair," which represented a major feature of the field's early days, retains any currency. The same applies to the "critters" or "zeroids," which troubled the sleep of many a researcher in the 1960s: Either the phenomenon ceased to occur, or it still occurs but researchers have gone off to pursue more fruitful endeavors, like abduction research or Roswell.

While it is undeniably tempting to consign contacteeism to the graveyard of lost pursuits, the "kind space brothers" and their adepts enjoyed a resurgence in the latter years of the decade. The reasons for this range from disillusionment with formal ufology (which is seen as having failed to "explain" the UFO riddle) to a desire to merge spirituality and the ufological avocation into a single current. Some might find humor in the realization that the very same arguments put forth by scientists regarding the public's dalliance with UFOs are similar to the ones used within ufology to explain the desertions within the field toward the "garden path" of contacteeism.

But 1990s- and early 2000s-style contactee groups seem to differ markedly from their mid-century counterparts, showing a more volatile and violent face to the world. ●

—Spring 2002

Giordano Bruno: 16th-Century Ufologist?

by Joan d'Arc

Dominican priest Giordano Bruno was burned at the stake in the year 1600 for his many heretical ideas. In this talk delivered at a meeting of the Rhode Island Mutual UFO Network (MUFON), Joan d'Arc puts the life of this iconoclastic thinker into historical perspective, along with the ideas of Nicolaus Copernicus and Galileo Galilei. She writes that Bruno identified the matter in the Earth with the matter of planets and stars, observing that "such living beings inhabit them as inhabit the Earth." Most importantly, she brings Bruno's espousal of the idea of universal consciousness, and his surety of life on other planets, into the arena of current Ufology.

FILIPPO BRUNO was born in Nola, Italy, in 1548. When he was thirteen years old, he entered school at the monastery of Saint Domenico. Taking the name Giordano, he became a Dominican priest in 1565, but was forced to run away eleven years later due to his shockingly inappropriate ideas. Author of countless obscure writings, originally written in Italian or Latin, the Theosophists claim Giordano Bruno as their own mystic and martyr. The Rosicrucians credit Bruno with the revival of their Egyptian-based religion. In Bruno are seen the first hints of Freemasonry in England, with its Egyptian mysteries, its overt philanthropy—its "good works." Bruno was a pioneer in the study of what is today called semantics, and he is a character referred to as "The Nolan" in James Joyce's complex tale, *Finnegans Wake*.

Modern environmentalists also credit Bruno as the forerunner of the

Gaian environmental movement. Gaia is the ancient name for the Earth, which is considered by "pagan" religions to be a living being with universal intelligence. Bruno was a pantheist, believing all of nature to be alive with divine spirit, intelligence, and consciousness. To Bruno, Nature is God, and God is Nature.

Bruno's works revived the basic heliocentrism of early Greek philosophers, which seems to have begun with Aristarchus of Samos in approximately 260 B.C. Even earlier, in 580 B.C., Pythagoras had taught that the Earth was a sphere. Ptolemy, too, had taught the Earth was a sphere, but was positioned at the center of Ptolemy's universe. Later, Aristotle's Earth-centered cosmology became the accepted doctrine for hundreds of years, in a tyranny of thought brutally enforced by the Catholic church.

According to the Catholic church, heliocentrism threatened the credibility of the holy scripture, which was believed to be the supreme authority in all matters, including science. The church allowed no "novel interpretations" of the Bible. The first sentence of the Earth-centered Genesis tale tells us that, "In the beginning, God created the Earth and the heavens." According to the Holy Book, He created the Earth first and placed the other bodies in the skies for the benefit of mankind.

BRUNO THE TIME TRAVELER

Bruno knitted into the fabric of his cosmic picture various systems of ancient knowledge. He merged into his system the pantheistic doctrines of the ancient Egyptians, Greeks, Hindus, and Persians, along with the essentially animistic physics of the twenty-first century. Some have even considered Bruno a time traveler, since his ideas touched those of the ancient past, as well as the distant future—the twenty-first century and beyond.

For instance, Bruno foretold the "many worlds" interpretation of quantum mechanics; the theory that the universe splits into many possible worlds as events unfold in time. He once reasoned as follows:

> I can imagine an infinite number of worlds like the Earth, with a Garden of Eden on each one. In all these Gardens of Eden, half the Adams and Eves will not eat the fruit of knowledge, but half will. But half of infinity is infinity, so an infinite number of worlds will fall from grace and there will be an infinite number of crucifixions. Therefore, either there is one unique Jesus who goes from one world to another, or there are an infinite number of Jesuses. Since

a single Jesus visiting an infinite number of Earths one at a time would take an infinite amount of time, there must be an infinite number of Jesuses. Therefore, God must create an infinite number of Christs.

Needless to say, this idea did not go over too big with church authorities when they got wind of it. Nonetheless, Bruno continued. In an extraordinary tide of information revelation, Bruno pulled past and future time together as though it were the folds of an infinite curtain. As one physics web site explains, "The physical world of things is embedded in the infinite, embedded in a space filled with all the other possible worlds. . . . We see a few of those other worlds in the probability waves of quantum mechanics." Bruno intuited the conditions of such a world as "the coincidence in the One of both the possible and the real."

As both quantum mechanics and Einstein's theory of Relativity suggest, we live in a "many worlds universe," where all the moments of the past, present, and future exist simultaneously as part of a single permanent existence. Oddly, Bruno the time traveler had this to say about God and Time:

> The single thought, which is Thy Word, embraces all and each in itself, Thy single word cannot be manifold, opposite, changeable. . . . In the eternity in which Thou thinkest, coincides all the after another of time, with the now of eternity. There is, therefore, no past nor future where future and past coincide with the present. (McIntyre)

Bruno also prefigured the idea of the atom, and smaller still, a unit which was divisible by nothing else, a unit of thought, when he wrote: "an atom, beyond which we cannot in fact go, although to thought it may be still further divisible; so there is in every figure, in every kind of thing, a definite number of atoms." (McIntyre) Today, quantum physicists suggest that thought, the act of human attention, is the force that gives birth to possibilities in the world of matter. Scientist Harold McGowan proposed the "thoughtron" to be an atom tinier than any other and to be contained in all things. In his book *The Thoughtron Theory of Life and Matter*, McGowan proposed that the thoughtron, as the smallest elementary particle, would be the mental bridge between the thought world and formal reality. (McGowan)

Bruno looked toward mathematics and geometry for the true method of natural science, writing that "number is the natural and fruitful principle of the understanding's activity . . . number is the unfolding of understanding." (McIntyre) Yet, Bruno also could not "conceive of a philosophy of nature, of number, of geometry, of a diagram, without infusing divine meanings into these." His philosophy was never divorced from divinity. Although he refused dogmatic teachings and always pushed the envelope, he was truly a holy man.

A HISTORICAL PERSPECTIVE

In 1543, when Bruno was five years old, Nicolaus Copernicus published his mathematical treatise *De Revolutionibus*, which vindicated the Greek Pythagoras who, at around 580 BC, argued that the Earth was a sphere. Copernicus reestablished the ancient Greek heliocentrism of Aristarchus of Samos by proving mathematically that the Earth revolved around the Sun. Yet, Bruno accused Copernicus of not fully understanding the meaning of his discovery, of being "only a mathematician." Bruno's divine intuition of the infinity of worlds picked up where Copernicus left off.

Bruno rejected the limits of the Copernican system, which posited a finite universe limited by a fixed sphere of stars just beyond the solar system. He argued the sun was not actually the center of the universe, saying that if one were able to observe the sun from elsewhere in the universe, it would simply look like any other star. Bruno even speculated that other worlds could be inhabited.

In 1588, Galileo Galilei began to teach Copernican theory at the University of Pisa, and in 1609, he discovered the moons of Jupiter via a hand-made telescope, invented by a Dutchman. Through this observation, Copernican theory ceased to be "esoteric."

Galileo was brought to Rome and interrogated by the Inquisition in 1615. He was forced to declare the Copernican system as scientifically false, and he was ordered to promise to stop teaching it. Galileo ignored his promise, returned to Florence, and continued with his work, publishing his *Dialogues on Great World Systems* sixteen years later, in 1632. Called back to Rome by the Inquisition in 1633, he was again forced to recant heliocentrism under threat of torture, this time being put under house arrest until his death in 1642. Although Galileo invited the inquisitors to look through his telescope and see for themselves the moons of Jupiter which revolved around it, they refused to do so. Heliocentrism was officially condemned in 1664, when Pope Alexander VII banned all books that affirmed any motion of the Earth.

Yet, almost a hundred years before, Giordano Bruno spoke to audiences in France and Germany, and taught heliocentrism at Oxford, England. Bruno and Galileo have much in common. Both were Italians, both espoused heliocentrism in the 1580s (although Bruno was teaching it a few years earlier) and both were an annoyance to the Inquisition authorities. However, Galileo does not mention Bruno because it was dangerous even to speak of such a heretic. Bruno was neither a mathematician nor an astronomer, but a member of the Dominican clergy who had the audacity to extend his theories to the fringes of thought.

In 1584, at the age of thirty-six, Bruno addressed a group in London, claiming that space is filled with an infinite number of solar systems, and that each has a central sun around which planets revolve. He taught that the planets shine by reflected light, but that stars are self-luminous bodies. He even spoke of sunspots, which he had learned about from Nicolas de Cusa, and the forward motion of our own solar system in space. In Bruno's philosophy, nothing stands still—everything is in motion, from the smallest atom to the largest star system.

Remarkably, Bruno was espousing these beliefs at a time when the flat, motionless Earth was believed the sole creation of a personal God and Father, who certainly had no other children anywhere else. The Father gave to His children the gift of the Earth, with its Garden of Eden, around which He placed for their sole pleasure the sun, the moon and stars. These points of light were far from being thought of by Europeans as universes of their own—solar systems perhaps inhabited by other intelligent beings like ourselves. Bruno's universe was infinite and included an indefinite number of worlds, each consisting of a sun and several planets. In Bruno's philosophy, the Earth was a small and insignificant body in an infinite universe. From this point of view, nothing was special about this "special creation."

This radical view was a heretical idea; yet Bruno shouted it, sometimes sitting near the door of the meeting hall so he could run from the crowd if he had to. Bruno made a public appearance in Paris in May 1586, in the library of the Abbey of Saint Victor. Bruno sat his assistant, Jean Hennequin, in the "great chair," while Bruno himself sat in a little chair near the door to the garden. Bruno apparently took this precaution in case he needed to leave hastily. (As it turned out, he did.) Bruno's assistant provided the following introduction to the lecture:

We have been imprisoned in a dark dungeon, whence only distantly could we see the far off stars. But now we are released. We know that there is one heaven, a vast ethereal region in which move those flaming bodies which announce to us the glory and majesty of God. This moves us to contemplate the infinite cause of the infinite effect; we see that the divinity is not far distant, but is within us, for its centre is everywhere, as close to dwellers in other worlds as it is to us. Hence we should follow not foolish authorities but the regulated sense and the illuminated intellect. (Yates)

When Bruno's speech was over, he called for anyone in the audience to defend Aristotle. When no one did, he left and was followed by several students. The students grabbed him and demanded he retract his insults to Aristotle. Bruno escaped on the condition that he would do so the next day—but he left town and never returned.

Bruno spoke of both the diversity of life and the sameness of life, referring to them as aspects of one substance: "the coincidence of contraries." He noted, "That there are more worlds than one is due to the presence everywhere throughout space of the same principle of life, which everywhere has the same effect." (McIntyre)

Bruno's dialogues were said by many of his peers to be "worthy of Plato." In his dialogue, *The Ash Wednesday Supper*, Bruno praised Copernican theory, yet went far beyond Copernicus himself in his intuition of the infinity of the universe. He identified the matter in the Earth with the matter of the planets and stars, and wrote of the possibility that "such living beings inhabit them as inhabit the Earth." Bruno wrote that the Earth and stars themselves are "living organisms," and observed, "there are not seven planets or wandering stars only, but innumerable such, for every world, whether of the sun-type or of the earth-type, is in motion, its motion proceeding from the spirit within it." (McIntyre)

In his 1584 work, *Cause, Principle, and Unity*, Bruno wrote of "the spirituality of all causation; the eternity of matter; its divinity as the potentiality of all life; its realization in the universe as a 'formed' thing; the infinite whole and the innumerable parts, as different aspects of the same . . . diversity and difference as aspects of one and the same substance." (McIntyre) He goes on to state:

This entire globe, this star, not being subject to death—dissolution and annihilation being impossible anywhere in Nature—from time to time renews itself by changing and altering all its parts. There is no absolute up or down, as Aristotle taught; no absolute position in space; but the position of a body is relative to that of other bodies.

Everywhere there is incessant relative change in position throughout the universe, and the observer is always at the center of things.

As he rightly argued, the sun was not the center of the universe, and
wasn't even the only sun, but was simply the center of one *part* of the
universe. In 1584, Bruno wrote *The Infinite Universe and Its Worlds*,
which "contained a masterly array of reasons, physical and metaphysical,
for the belief that the universe is infinite, and is full of innumerable
worlds of living creatures." (McIntyre) Bruno went on to write: "Innumerable suns exist; innumerable earths revolve around these suns. . . .
Living beings inhabit these worlds."

The theme of Bruno's *Spaccio de la Bestia Trionfante*, also written in
1584, is "the glorification of the magical religion of the Egyptians."
Bruno believed their worship was really the worship of "God in
things. . . . for diverse living things represent divine spirits and powers,
which, beyond the absolute being which they have, obtain a being com-
municated to all things according to their capacity and measure. Whence
God as a whole is in all things."

BRUNO THE UFOLOGIST?

Taken as a whole, Bruno's various sentiments sound uncannily similar
to a remark attributed to Harvard psychiatrist/ufologist John Mack,
quoted in the August 2001 issue of *New* Age magazine:

We are spiritual beings connected with other life forms and the
cosmos in a profound way, and the cosmos itself contains a numi-
nous intelligence. It's not just dead matter and energy. . . . Mack
has also stated: With the help of the abduction phenomenon we
will have discovered a new picture of the universe in which psyche
and world manifest and evolve together according to principles
we have not yet fathomed.

Mack has referred to the alien abduction phenomenon as "a kind of spiritual outreach program from the cosmos for the spiritually impaired."

Mack suggests: "We need to transcend the separateness that discon-
nects us from nature. If we could transcend this division, we might then
explore, enjoy, and travel ecstatically, lovingly, materially and nonmateri-
ally, among the unique particularities of our own being, our own natures
within the cosmos, experiencing at the same time an essential unity and
sacredness of creation." (www.peer-mack.org)

We might consider that this division—the removal of God from Nature as a power working from some lofty plain above Nature—is perhaps the cause of our spiritual impairment. Perhaps we can look to the many blasphemies of Giordano Bruno to reunite our lost souls with the sacredness of all creation.

Bruno's sentiments also reverberate in the words of UFO-tracker Steven M. Greer, who, in his book *Extraterrestrial Contact*, suggests that our "concepts of God, creation, life and religious meaning will evolve in the direction of accommodating the existence of intelligent life elsewhere in the universe, and this will cause an increasing 'universalization' of God."

We must realize that this *universalization* of God is just what turned the attention of the Roman Inquisition toward Giordano Bruno's heretical ideas nearly four centuries ago. Greer looks to a future where we will see God as "an infinite Creator whose glory is not confined to the Earth." This is an idea whose time has still not yet come, four hundred years after the first Universalist loudly proclaimed that there might be intelligent life in other worlds similar to our own.

Greer's universalism is evident when he writes, "Regardless of planet, star system, or galaxy of origin, and no matter how diverse, ETs are intelligent, conscious, sentient beings. We are, essentially, one. On this basis, we may speak of one people inhabiting one universe." Greer explains, "The simple thread of conscious intelligence which runs through all peoples elegantly weaves our unity. This unity is not subject to the trials of diversity, for it is pure, immutable and fundamental to the existence of intelligent life itself." Or, in Giordano Bruno's words, "diversity and difference are aspects of one and the same substance . . . the same principle of life." That substance or principle is Universal Consciousness, the First Cause, or God. The problem is that we are so used to thinking of God as an old guy with a beard that we cannot fathom this idea of universal consciousness.

The development of this attitude of "universality based in consciousness," Greer argues, is necessary for peace and unity to develop among peoples of the Earth, and to assure peaceful interactions between earth humans and other intelligent life in the universe. The endless diversity which our astounding universe may hold must be met with what Greer calls "the calmness of universal consciousness." Now, in the twenty-first century, we stand poised to take that same message one step further and over the great divide. If Greer is right, we are ready to meet our cousins, the once imaginary cousins of Giordano Bruno.

Whether we like it or not, the good old Earth is heading toward a paradigm shift. Pantheism has come of age. Gaia has spoken her mind. She has seen enough bloodshed, toxic destruction, and the reckless waste of resources that should have been bountiful enough for all her children. Strangely, the message from Mother Earth, as ufologist John Mack tells us, is coming in from a mysterious source—so-called Ets—distant cousins we never knew we had. It's hard to shake the feeling that there is an undeniable power behind this paradigm shift that may emanate from beyond Earth, and it's coming whether we like it or not.

We must realize that this *universality* is still a radical idea, almost as radical an idea as it was in Bruno's time. Greer's universality shines through when he states, "We must look to our inner reality to find our oneness with other intelligent life in the universe . . . for there is one universe inhabited by one people, and we are they." (*Extraterrestrial Contact*, 19)

The last time I spoke before MUFON, I quoted the Vatican official, Monsignor Corrado Balducci. As Balducci stated in an interview with Zecharia Sitchin:

> That life may exist on other planets is certainly possible . . . The Bible does not rule out that possibility. On the basis of scripture and on the basis of our knowledge of God's omnipotence, His wisdom being limitless, we must affirm that life on other planets is possible . . . credible and even probable.

It's interesting to see that a Vatican spokesman has publicly made such a radical statement. We must wonder how and why this has come about. Novel interpretations of the Bible, once considered punishable by torture on the rack, are now coming at us from all directions, including the Vatican. The Vatican has come close to apologizing for Galileo's hardships, but not Bruno's. It is unlikely that the Vatican will be quoting from Giordano Bruno's books anytime soon.

Scientific discoveries have always caused trouble for dogmatic Church teachings. In Bruno's time, astronomy was a threat to the teachings of the church. Two hundred years later, geology challenged the holy book's credibility, and it was maintained by Christians that Satan, the father of all lies, must have placed prehuman fossils in the earth to deceive mankind. A hundred years ago, evolutionary biology threatened the Genesis account of special creation. Now, many fundamentalist Christians believe that UFOs in the skies are piloted by Satan's "fallen angels."

We should not fail to appreciate that the belief in life on other planets was once dangerously heretical, a belief that present day ufologists assume as a bottom line. Not that Harvard University didn't try to excommunicate John Mack, the heretic. They certainly tried. But baby steps are still steps. We may even think of Giordano Bruno, therefore, as the first speculative ufologist.

REINCARNATION

Another idea Bruno wrote about continues to be frowned upon by the western world and mainstream religions: the concept of the reincarnation of the soul through various life cycles. Bruno brought back from ages past the Pythagorian and Platonic doctrines of the laws of karma and of reincarnation: that every act brings its appropriate reward or punishment in another life, and that each individual determines for itself by its actions its transition into another body. In his *Spaccio de la Bestia Trionfante*, Bruno described the condition of a soul who had misused its opportunities on Earth, saying that such a soul would be "relegated back to another body, and should not expect to be entrusted with the administration of a better dwelling if it had conducted itself badly in the conduct of a previous one." (Great Theosophists)

Although it seems a fate worse even than the Christian version of Hell—that we should continually need to repeat various incarnations until we get it right—the idea was heretical because, in essence, Bruno was charging that there was no Hell! Bruno's belief was that there was a spark of the divine in human beings and that we are in charge of our own fate. Bruno's ideas were nothing short of pantheistic: that "the Infinite has nothing which is external to Itself," that all living matter contains a spark of the divine.

THE ART OF MEMORY

Toward the end of Bruno's life, he was hired by an Italian named Mocenigo to teach him certain skills of mnemonics (memory), an art for which Bruno was well known, having written several books on the subject, including *The Art of Memory*, *The Shadows of Ideas*, and *Incantations of Circe*. Bruno had earlier fled Italy so that he could be as far away from the Inquisition authorities as possible, publishing his books while in England, France, and Germany. But he missed his homeland, and when he was invited back to Italy by Mocenigo, he walked directly into his trap. As one scholar writes, "People like Giordano Bruno are immunized from a sense of danger by their sense of mission, and a state of euphoria bordering on insanity." (Yates)

Bruno's *Art of Memory* is described as a "magical psychology." His complex magical memory system consisted of "wheels" on which groups of letters, symbols, and images corresponded to the physical contents of the terrestrial world, representing the whole sum of human knowledge accumulated through the centuries. It is presumed by scholars who have studied these diagrams that the person who committed this system to memory "rose above time and reflected the whole universe of nature and of man in his mind."

Bruno's memory wheel was a "Hermetic secret," since it was the "gnostic reflection of the universe in the mind." Bruno believed that when, in the mind, one conformed symbols and images to celestial forms, which corresponded to the figures of the zodiac, and when one held these images all at once in the mind, one would move from "the confused polarity of things to the underlying unity." In essence, one would become "like God."

Mocenigo got the idea that Bruno could teach him something more, something along the lines of sorcery. When Bruno denied knowing anything about such things, Mocenigo became angry about the money he had paid Bruno, and turned him in to the Venetian tribunal.

Mocenigo accused Bruno before the tribunal of teaching the existence of a boundless universe filled with a countless number of solar systems. He accused Bruno of saying the Earth was not the center of the universe, but rather a planet which revolved around the Sun. Bruno was also accused of "teaching the doctrine of Reincarnation; of denying the actual transubstantiation of bread into the flesh of Christ; of refusing to accept the three persons of the Trinity; and of rejecting the virgin birth of Christ." (Great Theosophists)

Bruno seems to have explained himself to the state authorities of Venice, who detained him for many months and were not at first keen on turning him over to the Inquisition body in Rome. Bruno's argument seems to be that his ideas were based on philosophical discourse and, therefore, should be protected. He argued that he was at all times speaking as a philosopher and not as a priest. Eventually, the counsel at Venice, wishing to keep peace with the Church, turned Bruno over to them. Thus began Bruno's seven-year prison ordeal at the hands of the Roman Inquisition.

The exact charges that were brought against Bruno by the Catholic authorities are unknown, since it is claimed that the records have been lost. Nor is it known why he was kept so long in their prison; it was the usual circumstance to house and harass a heretic for no longer than a year, most of the time discarding the poor victim's remains after just a few horrific months. But for some unknown reason, Giordano Bruno was tortured and interrogated for seven long years. Was it for his animistic belief that the spirit world pervaded all of nature? Was it for his insistence on a reform of Catholicism to the "natural religion" of the Egyptians? Was it for his belief in the heretical concept of reincarnation? Was it for his unshakable belief in the divinity of the human spirit? Was it for their belief that he was a magician? A Catholic web site called New Advent, which describes Bruno's system of thought as "an incoherent materialistic pantheism," makes the following claim:

> Bruno was not condemned for his defense of the Copernican system of astronomy, nor for his doctrine of the plurality of inhabited worlds, but for his theological errors, among which were the following: that Christ was not God but merely an unusually skillful magician, that the Holy Ghost is the soul of the world, that the Devil will be saved.

Is the claim that the Holy Ghost is the "soul of the world" connected to the age-old Christian sin of pantheism? According to what belief system is this system incoherent?

In the end, Bruno refused to retract his beliefs. On February 17, 1600, he was burned at the stake in the center of Rome, with a nail driven through his tongue—the customary treatment of all unrepentant heretics so they could not continue to insult the sensitive ears of the Inquisition.

Giordano Bruno stood for "the dignity of man"; of "liberty, tolerance, the right to stand up in any country and say what he thought, disregarding all ideological barriers." (Yates) Bruno dared to imagine many potential brave new worlds—like the one in which we are free to look out at the stars and wonder out loud if there is any life upon them, where I can stand *here* and say what I have said this evening, and not have to stand over there, near the door, ready to make a run for it. ●

References

"Great Theosophists: Giordano Bruno" (www.wisdomworld.org/setting/bruno.html).

Greer, Steven, M.D. *Extraterrestrial Contact: The Evidence and Implications.* Crossing Point Publications, 1999.

MacGowan, Harold. *The Thoughtron Theory of Life and Matter.* New York: Exposition, 1973.

McIntyre, J. Lewis. *Giordano Bruno: Mystic Martyr.* Kessinger, Montana, 1903. www.hiddenmysteries.com.

New Advent. www.newadvent.org/cathen/03016a.htm.

Yates, Frances. *Giordano Bruno and the Hermetic Tradition.* University of Chicago, 1964; see also www.pagesz.net/~stevek/intellect/bruno.html.

—Fall 2001

The Reptoid Invasion

by Alexandra Bruce

Just in time for the Chinese astrological Year of the Dragon, reptilian aliens invaded the conspiracy literature. From the "Dulce Wars" to David Icke, the reptoids have seized our collective imagination. Indeed, human beings do possess a "reptilian brain," and all human beings share some DNA structures with reptilians, but does this back up the idea that our planet is ruled by a race of shapeshifting reptilian overlords from another dimension? In trying to work out how to discuss such interdimensional issues as reptoids, Alexandra Bruce looks at both sides of this peculiar UFO-related phenomenon in her brief overview of the "reptilian mythos."

IN THE REALM of conspiracy, nothing since Fox News aired the "alien autopsy" footage has stirred up the amount of contention as the phenomenon of David Icke's book *The Biggest Secret* and the launching of his inflammatory website in April 1999. With a shrillness that is unparalleled, David Icke claims that the world's most prominent geopolitical players, and the governments and multinational industries that they operate, are all fronts for interdimensional reptilian puppetmasters. These controlling reptilians are described as semi-physical inhabitants of "fourth density," a plane of reality that is at a higher vibratory rate than the material three-dimensional world.

The reptilians' domination-oriented consciousness is said to resonate and express itself in the physical realm of our third-density reality. How? Via the institutions, ideologies and the DNA of the reptilian hybrid custodial caste that comprises the world's royal and elite bloodlines. To document his case, Icke has meticulously and convincingly traced the steps of these elites and their establishments over the millennia.

Despite the audacity and weirdness of his claims, the sheer mass of historical data Icke has accumulated to substantiate them is impressive. Whatever credibility this feat has earned him, however, is completely ruined by his ongoing, fervent, and surrealistic denunciations of public figures. For example, Icke claims that Queen Elizabeth and the Queen Mum are, in reality, "shapeshifting reptoids," intent on the satanic ritualistic eating of babies and the drinking of freshly-sacrificed human blood. [*Washington Post* writer Peter Carlson chose this sentence as his all-time favorite pull quote in an article entitled "Finally Making Headlines: The Pull Quote," July 30, 2002, page C4. —*Ed.*]

While it is amusing to picture these comically lurid tableaux, and it is fun to pretend for a moment that such stories are true (two thumbs up for entertainment value!), he has baited himself for derision with such ridiculous, wildly defamatory remarks. Icke's sensational slant has discredited the genuine value of some of his information. A disservice to serious scholarship has been done to the subject matter by himself and others.

Icke's most cherished refrain, "shapeshifting reptilian," is also his most misleading. All human beings share some DNA structures with reptilians; in fact, all biological life on Earth shares much of the same genetic codes. It is said that humans share up to 80 percent of our genetics with spiders! Furthermore, human beings possess a "reptilian brain," located at the very core of the human noodle. Indeed, the "intelligent" gray matter of the outer neocortex appears to be grafted abruptly on top of this reptilian core.

Icke has written an excellent article about the characteristics of this inner reptilian brain and the functions and attributes of the reptilian level of consciousness that exists within all humans (posted on his website www.davidicke.com). It is not surprising to learn that these human reptilian brain characteristics of territoriality, domination, and addiction are what typify the qualities of our supposed fourth-density reptoid overlords, something Icke duly points out. The existence of the reptilian brain and the limbic system within every human being is the first clue that the reptoid phenomenon is more complex and multifaceted than Icke's overly-literal shapeshifting accusations would indicate.

Dragons appear extensively in worldwide mythology. If only one could ask England's patron saint, George, so enshrined for slaying dragons: "Exactly what animal were you killing?" Was the dragon symbolic, literal, or both? In addition to the DNA codes humans share with reptilians and our reptilian brain stem, there is also an archetypal reptilian resonance, which echoes from the mists of time and legend, perhaps the legacy of the dinosaurs. This does not make any person a "shapeshifting reptilian," per se. A human being may have a resonance with reptilian energy or even direct resonance with evil extraterrestrial fourth-density reptilians. A psychic adept may be able to perceive such reptilian energetics overlaying the field of a human being, or to perceive other-dimensional reptilian aspects of that person's soul—but that is still not the same thing as a human person being a "shapeshifting reptilian"!

While there are numerous strange accounts of the fourth-density reptoids' ability to project holograms that make them appear as physical humans for limited amounts of time, it is highly doubtful that this is what is occurring with the Queen Mum. Even by most far-out eyewitness testimonies, no reptoid could sustain the ruse of appearing human for twenty-four hours a day, seven days a week. It is far more likely that the Queen Mum is a human host for a nonphysical reptilian entity, though I am not aware of evidence of that. Icke's miscommunication comes from his overly literal 3-D reading of fourth-density phenomena. This is done either out of a genuine, if misguided, sense of urgency on his part, or it is his conspiracy huckster's sales pitch.

The fourth density has been variously described as the astral plane, dream-time or the imaginal realm, among other terms. It is an order of reality that interacts with the physical plane. There is an archetypal or mythic quality to it, as opposed to the familiar "hardness" of 3-D reality. This does not minimize the "reality" of fourth density or its denizens. Dreams, ideas, and beliefs are quite literally what shape and inform the material world. Without the immaterial phenomena of dreams, ideas, and beliefs, no bridges would be built, no wars would be fought, nothing would be bought.

Theoretical physicists are currently working out the "long-division" that would mathematically explicate the hyperdimensions that interpenetrate the physical world. However, the more right-brained members of our species and countless native cultures have forever recognized these other realms.

The point I'm making is, there is some truth to what David Icke is espousing, even to some of his more ludicrous allegations. I think the way he chooses to discuss the information is misleading and self-defeating, or maybe I'm not getting the joke. Perhaps the tenor of his shrieking outrageousness, actually, is to provoke rebuttals and to spark lively commentary—even if much of it is derogatory. In that case, he is a master of the maxim that there is no such thing as bad publicity. He has certainly succeeded in getting people to talk about him *and* the reptilians.

To be fair, Icke's avocation is not an easy one to follow. Fourth-density phenomena do not translate neatly into third-density language, and proving their "truth" is a challenge, at best. I know, because I am also wrestling with the process of how to articulate interdimensional issues such as reptoids, while attempting to avoid the snickering wrath that has been visited upon Icke and others. I am completing a book that involves Phil Schneider, who lectured around the US about his seventeen-year stint as a government geologist in secret underground bases. Schneider was found strangled to death in his apartment within two years of going public. His more remarkable claims related to his personal involvement with back-engineered alien technologies and his physical skirmishes with tall, reptilian "big-nosed Greys."

Regardless of anyone's opinion of Schneider's credibility, the fact is that the legal investigation of his death was grossly mishandled. The evidence overwhelmingly indicates that he was murdered and that the murder was covered up. In my book's early stages, my editor and publisher, Peter Moon, advised me to remove all references to "reptilians" or "big-nosed Greys." He thought these just served to discredit Schneider in the eyes of the average reader, and to minimize the facts of Schneider's murder and its cover-up.

I understood Peter's point, but to avoid discussing these issues would be to miss a crucial element of Schneider's message—and of his untimely death. It would be like pretending there wasn't a slaughtered rhinoceros on your living room floor. Plus, there would not be much left to write about other than ascertaining that a series of local law enforcement personnel had suspiciously botched their jobs. If I could not mention Schneider's harrowing tales of hand-to-hand combat with aliens, there wasn't that much left for me to say about him. These claims are what got him on the lecture circuit to begin with, and are likely related to what got him killed. I was deeply aware, however, that to take some of Schneider's claims seriously would have the effect of transferring to me a certain lack of credibility.

The main argument used to dismiss certain claims of Phil Schneider, Preston Nichols, Stewart Swerdlow, or any percipient of the extraordinary, is to say that these claimants are insane, therefore, nothing they offer is valid. This is a unilateral and lazy way to avoid dealing with the unsettling implications of their information. That the hegemony would label such folks as "insane" is the pot calling the kettle black, in my opinion. The predominating orthodox scientific ideology about human existence, of which Darwinism and the "many worlds" interpretation of quantum mechanics are prime examples, is that "reality" is some kind of an arbitrary accident that replicates itself and echoes ad infinitum, for no good reason at all. This is sanctioned insanity and it is the state religion of America!

Don't get me wrong. I happen to agree with aspects of the many worlds interpretation. Yes, the gods must be crazy! What I love best about this postulate is that it actually validates the reality of the Queen Mum's being a cannibalistic practitioner of satanism! It validates every crazy thing ever asserted by Phil Schneider, David Icke, and every alien abductee and Montauk Project survivor, because on a quantum level, every possibility is true. For example, the many worlds interpretation of quantum mechanics would allow for the existence of parallel timelines where the Earth's dinosaurs never became extinct and, instead, continued to evolve. Could this explain the reptilian realities that are reported to be impinging on our own?

There is a certain condition, whereby some realities are more "true" than others. This has yet to be factored into the many worlds interpretation theory, as far as I am aware. The "truth" or pervasiveness of any given reality corresponds to the amount of conscious energy associated with it. The importance and power of mass conscious energy cannot be overlooked. This is the factor that makes advertising, public relations, "positioning," "perception," and mind control so important to people who wish to make huge profits. The more conscious energy is entrained into a concept, the more "real" or "true" it appears. It's simple: Thought and belief generate reality.

In any case, Icke is by no means an innovator in the field of reptiliana. My own first encounter with "reptoids" was in 1991, in a far-out channeled newsletter called "Revelations of Awareness." The vivid descriptions of planetoids hauling millions of invading reptoids Earthward at the "speed of gravity" (eighteen times faster than the speed of light, we were informed) completely gripped my imagination. This same mythos made headlines in 1997, with the advent of Comet Hale-Bopp and in the liturgy that resulted in the mass suicide of the Heaven's Gate cultists.

Yet there is a basic incongruity within the reptoid mythos, as promoted by the cosmic awareness, Icke and others, which short-circuits logic. Why are these flotillas of space rocks bearing giant, man-eating lizards "coming to get us," when it is also said that the "Lizzies" were always here, genetically-engineering the human race from day one? It is also said that the reptilians have been constantly tweaking human history toward their nefarious ends, using time travel tricks. How is it they supposedly have full mastery of our time and reality—yet they are schlepping their way toward us en masse, still yet to "arrive"? Perhaps, as suggested by Stewart Swerdlow, author of *Montauk: The Alien Connection*, the awakening of human beings to their presence has made them seem, in an archetypal sense, to be "arriving" to the growing body of those who perceive them.

Channeled by Paul Shockley, *The Cosmic Awareness* was the early-1990s forerunner to David Icke's website (www.davidicke.com) as a reptoid information clearing house. The awkwardly-phrased statements of the *Awareness* betrayed zero emotional affect, an interesting counterpoint to the banshee stylings of Icke, and other upstart conspiracy rant-meisters of late. This is true, despite the fact that many of the *Awareness'* readings were far more outlandish than Icke's claims, though they were free from his obsession with satanism.

Awareness would "indicate" that many of the political leaders of our world had been "switched" with cloned "robotoids" piloted by inter-dimensional reptilians. Again, fun weird stuff to contemplate, seeing as it was much more interesting (and actually seemed to make more sense) than *ABC World News Tonight*, et al., especially during that bogus, state-sponsored weapons infomercial that passed for coverage of the Gulf War!

Spurred on by the reptoid specter raised by *Cosmic Awareness*, I bought two books by the self-described ex-government cryptographer and Sumerian scholar, R.A. Boulay, *Flying Serpents and Dragons* and *Dragon Power* (www.thebooktree.com). He adds his own insights to the Sitchin information, saying the Anunnaki gods of Sumer were a custodial crossbreed of reptoids and primate hominids. According to Boulay, the Anunnaki were a "royal" half-caste engineered to lord over the slave caste created to mine gold and do menial tasks for the aliens. (It would be interesting to find out who that guy really is and his motives for writing his books. I do not think Boulay is his real name.)

Boulay's story dovetails quite nicely with the Merovingian myth about the origins of their bloodline, as outlined in the cult classic *Holy Blood, Holy Grail*, by Baigent, Lincoln and Leigh. As the ancient Merovingian legend goes, the queen was pregnant by the king and went for a swim in the ocean, whereupon she was raped by a "Quinotaur." The resulting hybrid offspring, Merovee, became the founder of the Merovingian bloodline, into which all the royal houses of Europe have since striven to marry, as detailed *ad nauseum* by Baigent-Lincoln-Leigh as well as by Laurence Gardner in *Bloodline of the Holy Grail*. The present generations of their offspring are the same folks implicated by Icke as the fearsome reptoid half-breeds who are selling out the rest of humanity to the "microchipped" New World Order.

The Quinotaur figure is somewhat reminiscent of the Oannes character of Sumerian lore, which emerged from the sea to teach agriculture, literacy, and architecture to the primitive locals, an amphibian figure similar to the west African Dogon tribe's "fishmen" from the stars, and reminiscent of the European children's fairy tale of the Frog Prince and the abiding obsession of the Chinese with dragons. "Japanese legends of serpent/dragon and human marriages, seductions, and liaisons abound," says William Michael Mott, in another excellent, extensively researched article posted on David Icke's website.

If you look at the legends of the origins of some Scottish clan names, you'll see a similar story. For example, the name MacLaclan is said to derive from "Lakeland," the underwater kingdom of Atlantis. The daughter of the king of Lakeland, who was described as a "dark," large, nonhuman sea creature, was said to have married an ancient warlord and, thus, founded the new dynasty. The name MacVeigh along with its cognates, such as MacFie, MacPhee and Duffy, also stem from this legend. This underwater princess bride would seem to bear a significant resemblance to "Nessie," the Loch Ness Monster. These are the clans' own legendary accounts.

Given my deeply-embedded fascination with these related subjects, I was not surprised to discover that, according to Icke, I myself come from a bigtime "shapeshifting reptilian" bloodline. Furthermore, there are numerous references to my celebrated clan mate, Robert the Bruce, as being the founder of modern Freemasonry. The Masons are the subject of endless calumny, implicated in nonstop satanic wrongdoing by Icke and other conspiratologists.

The good news is that I don't eat babies. Not human ones. I love organic baby salad greens, even if a bag sells for the weekly wage of the person who picked them. It's not my fault that the CIA's ongoing destabilization of the "developing world" has resulted in this state of affairs.

If anything, I am doing the opposite of selling out humanity to a microchip-implanted existence! (Perhaps I am of the brontosaurus line?)

The upshot of my investigation into all of this human-reptilian weirdness is that I have trained myself not to believe or to judge anything anymore, including the "common sense" we take for granted. I do my best to "hang out" with information, while endeavoring to discern its ideology and its agenda. I believe that the contemplation of all this bizarre reptilian information is worthwhile, in the sense that it can aid 3-D-bound consciousness in a better understanding of multidimensionality. If nothing else, it is excellent entertainment. ●

UFOs and Aliens in the Caribbean

What Is the U.S. Navy Hiding in Vieques, Puerto Rico?

by Jorge Martin

The actions of the Puerto Rican citizens of Vieques to make the U.S. Navy leave their island are truly heroic. As Jorge Martin explains, military practices in Vieques are unique in that it is the only place in the world where live ammunition is used in an inhabited area. What could possibly explain the U.S. Navy's presence in Vieques? According to the inhabitants of the island, the reason may be related to eyewitness reports of unidentified flying objects and non-human entities.

VIEQUES, under Puerto Rico's territorial jurisdiction in the Caribbean, has had two-thirds of its land occupied by the U.S. Navy, both in the west and in the east, ever since that military agency seized 26,000 of the 33,000 acres making up part of the island's territory, leaving the 9,500 inhabitants of Vieques in a small strip of land in the middle.

The Navy performs alleged military practices in Vieques, both aquatic and terrestrial, including bombings with live ammunition, which destroy the flora, fauna, and marine environment. These military maneuvers release toxic chemicals, metals, and fatal amounts of radiation, which are deposited into the air, soil, and water. In fact, Vieques is the only place in the world where military bombing exercises using live ammunition are performed in an inhabited area.

As a result, the population of Vieques has one of the highest cancer rates in all of Puerto Rico; more than double the incidence in the rest of Puerto Rico. It has been verified that the Navy has used in its practices in Vieques ammunitions containing depleted uranium, without informing the island's population or governmental authorities.

After the death of Vieques civilian David Sanes on April 19, 1999, which allegedly resulted from a bomb mistakenly released by a U.S. Navy combat jet, Vieques residents and representatives of various political groups, including the U.S. Congress, as well as environmental and religious groups, decided to establish protest camps in order to practice peaceful resistance and civil disobedience. Standing on the land used by the Navy as a firing range, and acting as human shields, these groups courageously prevented the U.S. Navy and other countries from bombing the island for a year. On May 4, 2000, federal authorities arrested and evicted these disobedients: priests, nuns, ministers, elderly people, women, politicians, and even U.S. congressmen. This event was broadcast live by local and international media.

VIEQUES: AN EXPERIMENTAL SITE?

Up until now, the U.S. Navy has stubbornly repeated as its reason for staying in Vieques that "Vieques is irreplaceable." Such reasoning, judged by experts and public opinion, brings about suspicion that something is being hidden from the people. Based on information obtained from confidential sources, as well as from a U.S. Navy web site, Puerto Rican journalist Jorge Seijo established that, contrary to official statements, Vieques is not used for military practices or exercises. Its real use consists of serving as an experimental field where newly developed armaments designed by the military-industrial complex of the United States are tested.

According to Seijo, David Sanes did not die due to a bombing mistake during Navy "practices." Rather, Seijo believes, the story of Sanes's accidental death was a fabricated incident intended to divert attention from the testing of a recently developed mortal weapon whose use is prohibited in populated areas like Vieques. It was later discovered that on the day Sanes died, and until April 23, 2000, both the U.S. Navy and the Raytheon Corporation were testing a weapon known as Phalanx Block AB-1, an automatic computerized armament that fires depleted uranium bullets, a weapon expressly prohibited by the U.S. Nuclear Regulatory Commission.

Seijo argues that the Navy created an "accident" to attract the attention of the Defense Department to the area where Sanes's body was found, in order to divert attention from the fact that several people had been killed, and even more wounded, by depleted uranium bullets in another area. According to Seijo, the Phalanx Block AB-1 fires 2,000 depleted uranium bullets in one minute. All of this proves that the island of Vieques is really a testing area, an illegal experimental site, and that in this situation its inhabitants are no more than mere laboratory guinea pigs.

It is precisely in such areas controlled by the U.S. Navy that other important events related to the presence of unidentified flying objects and non-human entities have been seen.

UFO Absorbs Water from the Ocean

During my recent investigations in the island of Vieques, a resident, Angel Encarnación, reported the following story:

> One night fishing out at sea, to the south of the shooting range, in the east of Vieques, we saw in the distance a really big and shining light. Getting closer we saw that it was suspended in the air. It was a huge object, a round flying saucer with lots of lights turning on and off intermittently all around the object. They were yellow, green, and red lights.
>
> On the bottom, in the middle of the saucer, it had only one really big green light, focused at the ocean's surface. It wasn't more than a hundred feet above the ocean. But that thing wasn't from this world. What shocked us most was seeing that the object was absorbing seawater from the ocean. You could actually see the water rising and entering the object through where the green light was coming from. It was a really big column of water going up. You could not see any fish or anything else . . . just the water going up. And all without a single sound.
>
> As we got closer to the saucer it stayed still for a while and then it immediately left, flew away very fast in the direction of El Yunque [a forested area in the east of Puerto Rico where there has been a lot of UFO activity] or Ceiba [where U.S. Navy Roosevelt Roads Naval Station is located] on the island of Puerto Rico. It was gone in seconds. We looked at each other and said, "We have seen something extraordinary that has never been seen before. Let's not say anything on land, because they won't believe us." I told only my family about what happened.

On another occasion, also fishing at night, the witness and his partners again saw a shining green light rising from the bottom of the ocean. They thought it could be a U.S. Navy submarine that was surfacing, but just at the time in which the "light" was due to surface, the green light disappeared and everything was again dark. Immediately they heard the sound of water falling to the ocean near them. Whatever emerged, it rose and took to the skies in the darkness of night and disappeared in total silence, while a subtle humid sprinkling fell over the group of fishermen. Encarnación continued:

> Besides that, we have seen shining objects coming out from the lagoons, after which they leave at high speed, and get lost in the sky. They are shining lights, orbs, or balls of light of a blue-white color. Of course, they could be something from the Navy, since they have lots of things of which we don't know yet. But what we saw in the ocean, was similar to what some people call a flying saucer. I have no doubts about it. And I don't think it is from the Navy, because nobody on Earth can manufacture, I believe, something like that, an artifact like the one we saw, because that object disappeared in the sky in seconds, in the direction of El Yunque.

ALIENS AND BALLS OF LIGHT

In another interview, several youngsters in Vieques who are members of the local "Cadets de la Marina" group (a Sea Cadets organization of the U.S. Navy), informed me about a series of enigmatic encounters they had experienced in some of the lagoons located in the eastern part of Vieques, specifically in lands near the shooting range of the Navy, in the area of Camp García.

On various occasions, according to the cadets, during drills and exercises in the area of El Tapon lagoon, they encountered some "very strange little dark men, gray or blackish in color, who are very fast, and ran speedily from one place to the other, sometimes in a zig-zag motion and at other times in jumps. They would stand suddenly in front of us, so that we could see them, and then they would leave, running really fast." The cadets reported that the little men "were three or four feet high, and were skinny, with long arms . . . and their heads were kind of big and egg-shaped." Due to the darkness of the night and the speed of the movements of the strange figures, the cadets reported that they couldn't see details, such as eyes, mouth, or nostrils.

The cadets added that on occasion the little dark men would jump into the lagoon, disappearing underwater. They also observed "various shining blue-white spheres varying in size from four to eight inches in diameter, that enter the water of the lagoons in the area." Due to the strange nature of these incidents, the young men decided not to perform any more exercise drills at night in these areas. At the end of the interview, one of their instructors corroborated what the young cadets reported, assuring me he had personally witnessed such encounters in the area.

FINAL COMMENTS

Encarnación, who gave me the initial information about the huge UFO that absorbed seawater from the ocean south of Vieques, also recounted the following:

> This type of thing has been going on here in Vieques for a long time now, but people were restrained to talk about it because of fear. But the weirdest thing is that all of this is more common in restricted areas controlled by the Navy. They must know something, or they're doing something with those people, those that are behind those objects [the UFO occupants] or they're together . . . and maybe that's the reason for the Navy's stubborn attitude of not wanting to let go of Vieques and letting us live in peace. They must be hiding something very important.

Everything we have found during our investigation in Vieques outlines an amazing scenario with important implications for Puerto Rico and the rest of the world, and indicates that the U.S. Navy, besides illegally using the island of Puerto Rico and Vieques as an illegal testing and experimental site, is also somehow related to the strange events going on there, events that make us wonder if that military agency is currently participating in an alien contact scenario using the territory of Puerto Rico.

I must emphasize that the Vieques issue, though it has a political angle due to Puerto Rico's ambiguous political relations with the U.S., is mainly one in which basic human rights are involved, such as the right to live in peace and health, and ultimately, the right to life itself. How can the U.S. argue that they had to attack Yugoslavia in order to protect the lives, well being and human rights of the residents of Kosovo, when that same nation submits the 9,500 inhabitants of Vieques, who are U.S. citizens, to the situation described in this article? It is unthinkable that such a situation can occur. ●

—*Winter 2001*

Excerpted with permission from *Evidencia OVNI*, issue 23. For more information about Vieques, visit the Vieques Libre web site at www.micronetix.net/virus/links.htm.

Chupacabras: A Study in Darkness

by Scott Corrales

From the first reports that emerged from Puerto Rico in 1995, the blood-sucking creature known as the Chupacabras ("Goatsucker") has grown into a worldwide phenomenon. Derided as a "phantasm of the Hispanic mind," the creature has been linked to everything from government genetic experiments, UFO activity, and NASA—whose scientists allegedly have taken several Chupacabras eggs from the Chilean military. A well-known expert in the Chupacabras phenomenon, author Scott Corrales looks at the evidence and the theories, while placing the creature in the context of Hispanic culture and the ancient global fascination with blood sacrifice and rituals.

NO ONE KNEW the darkness as well as the desert shamans responsible for supplying the sacrifices. They would stand in the cold desert night, the skies above filled with stars, waiting at a distance for the gods to appear. Generation after generation, they had learned the ritual and carried it out. Sometimes a dog, sometimes a young llama; the animal would be sacrificed and left out in the desert for the gods.

At sunrise, when it was no longer a sacrilege to approach the patches of desert where the gods had made their presence felt, the shamans would check to see if their offering had been accepted. It always was: the carcass would be completely drained of blood, with the tell-tale puncture mark visible somewhere on the body—neck, hindquarters, stomach—indicating that the gods' thirst had been satiated. It was now time for the priests and the tribe to share the meal with the gods by eating the sacrifice's flesh, whose remains would ultimately be buried under a cairn as reminder of the bond between mortals and their deities.

Anthropologist Juan Schobinger has written that the northern coast of Chile faces one of the richest seas in the world and one of the world's most barren deserts. This characteristic has granted a special archaeological value to the region's organic and ceramic deposits, causing experts to marvel at the preservation of so many fragile and perishable cultural elements, such as basketry, textiles, and food remains.[1]

It has been further possible to reconstruct the rituals of the inhabitants of the Atacama Desert from chronicles kept by the conquering Spaniards, or from oral traditions that still survive to this day. Dr. Virgilio Sanchez-Ocejo has noted that the museum of the city of Calama boasts an exhibit of one of the desert cairns, called *apachecta*, and the remains of a desiccated dog employed in a sacrifice. This is perhaps the only tangible link of a trade between gods and men that has gone on since the dawn of history.[2]

CHUPACABRAS IN THE SOUTHERN CONE

Derided by the intelligentsia as "phantasm of the Hispanic mind," the bloodsucking creature popularly known as the Chupacabras (or the Goatsucker) first emerged in 1995 in Puerto Rico, where its exploits in the municipality of Canóvanas became a matter of legend. But there was no reason why the Caribbean should have a monopoly over such an entity. In rapid succession, the Chupacabras and its kin spread throughout the southern United States (southern Florida, Texas, Arizona and California) in 1996, and began attacking both livestock and humans in Mexico during the same time period. By 1997, reports were coming in from northern Spain, and in 1998 Brazil bore the brunt of its depredations.

A world emerging from the threat of Y2K barely gave notice to the news stories indicating that northern Chile was in the midst of a strange wave of animal deaths. On April 20, 2000, Chile's prestigious *El Mercurio* newspaper told its readers that a multi-agency meeting had been convened to look into the bizarre sheep and goat deaths occurring in the northern province of El Loa. The task force's goals were simple: determine what had caused 135 animals to die under mysterious circumstances and put down the perpetrators, which officialdom had identified beforehand as dogs, dismissing all the talk among the locals that the dreaded Chupacabras might be to blame.

Lucas Burchard, chief of environmental hygiene and food control in Calama, posited the theory that dogs developed a taste for blood by biting each other during fights. Therefore, it followed that packs of blood-addicted canids would go on cattle-killing sprees after discovering that it was easier to drink their prey's blood than to eat its flesh. Another agency, the Cattle Farming Service (SAG, by its Spanish acronym), informed locals that it would install baited traps to capture the predators and remove them, while the country's national police force, the Carabineros, promised to use its infrared gear to conduct nocturnal patrols.[3]

Yet even as these agencies took a proactive stance regarding the mutilations, reports continued streaming in from all over El Loa province to the provincial seat at Calama. Dozens of dogs, hogs, and chickens were added to the list of mutilated animals, as reports of an outlandish predator were brought before the authorities. Jose Ismael Pino, a farm laborer from the village of Huepil, told the state police and the media that a creature he called "The Bird" had been responsible for the deaths of four sheep and a cow in the area.

On April 29, Pino had gone out for a bucket of water at around 10 P.M. under a moonlit sky when a shadow caught his attention. At first he thought it was a bull belonging to the ranch where he worked but, he claims, "that's when I saw it. It hardly moved. It just stood there, looking at me. It stood about 1.5 meters, like a big monkey, with long, clawed arms and enormous fangs protruding from its mouth, as well as a pair of wings." The farmhand ran back to the house for his hounds, sending them after the monstrous intruder. One of the hounds "returned with a bloodstained neck."[4]

Local schoolteacher Carlos Villalobos did not hesitate to remark upon the strangeness of the attacks: "I think it's linked in some fashion to an unknown life-form, probably alien in origin, but the problem is that the authorities do not wish to acknowledge it, and this course of action may probably be justified, since a collective panic situation may be unleashed."[5]

There were clear signs that the attacks were increasing in strangeness. On May 3, professor Liliana Romero was enjoying a good night's sleep in her apartment in the town of Concepción when she was wakened by the howling of five stray puppies she had adopted and kept in the building's courtyard as company for Black, her large mastiff. Fearing that a burglar might be at work, Romero looked through the window and was startled by what she saw. The mastiff was huddled in fear against the wall as the puppies continued to whine. "I could see the back of what appeared to be an immense man, standing some two meters tall. Its shoulder blades were split, as though it had wings," she would later tell reporters.[6]

The following day, Professor Romero gave the matter no further thought until her children informed her that they had found a dead dog near where the strange sighting took place. Her husband agreed to take a look at the carcass, which had "two deep holes in its jugular [vein], about as wide as a Bic pen, separated by five centimeters. What impressed me most was that [the carcass] was completely bloodless and light as a feather. The dog was incredibly woolly and, in fact, I had to move its fur to see the wounds."[7]

Within hours, three Carabineros reported to the Romeros' home to collect the mutilated dog, remarking on the similarity between the attacks on the canine and other animals found at other locations. The state policemen asked the Romeros for trash bags in which to carry their grisly find and then curtly ordered them to keep quiet about the event. The dog was brought to the precinct and left in an office near the local prefecture, where many local functionaries were able to get a good look at the carcass. Some of them confirmed Romero's remarks about the puncture marks and the dead animal's near weightless condition.

On May 8, Jorge Torrejón, writing for the *Estrella del Loa* newspaper, reported that three young men traveling aboard a refrigerator van had a close encounter with a similar creature. Mauricio Correa, an experienced tractor-trailer driver, was trying to park his rig not far from the María Elena salt mines, assisted by Oscar Robles and a hitchhiker named Ricardo.

After parking the truck at 5 A.M., he turned off the engine and the lights and became aware that the vehicle's cab was tilting toward the right, where Oscar was sitting. The vehicle's lights inexplicably began turning themselves on and off. To their horror they noticed that a "very ugly animal, very hairy and black, having a long oval head, fangs, and slanted, goggling yellow eyes" was staring at them through the side window. The apparition had pointed ears and "whiskers similar to those of a boar. It was something awful that was stuck to the glass for several seconds."

Recovering from the shock, the driver managed to start the truck. Oscar, his copilot, checked his wristwatch to ascertain the time for the report, but discovered that his digital timepiece had stopped. The drivers did not stop until they reached the vicinity of Victoria, where they waited for daybreak before getting out of the vehicle at a truck stop. They resumed their journey to the town of Pozo Almonte, presenting their report at the local Carabineros headquarters at 7 A.M. The only evidence of their experience was the prints apparently left by the creature on the back and side of the trailer cab.

Ghastly encounters aside, the number of mutilated animals was increasing almost exponentially, prompting Judge Flora Sepúlveda of the Third Criminal Court to open an inquest into the strange deaths. On May 10, the judge ordered the University of Concepción's Department of Pathology to conduct an analysis to determine the causes of the deaths, even if it meant exhuming the remains of all animals slain to date.

The phenomenon itself was clearly unimpressed by all of officialdom's fussing and flapping—twenty four hens were exsanguinated in the commune of Lebu on May 14, and thirty more on the following night in the vicinity of Concepción. These numbers would pale in significance when compared to the five hundred hens slain on July 3, on a single farmstead.[8]

CONSPIRACY IN THE WASTELAND

It is conceivable that the Chilean animal mutilations may have been completely overlooked outside the country had it not been for a development which catapulted them to worldwide prominence. On May 15, 2000, the newspaper *Crónica* told its startled readership that Pablo Aguilera, a talk show personality with Radio Pudhauel, had received a series of telephone messages from Calama and other points in northern Chile indicating that a family of strange animals, "possible Chupacabrases," as the paper put it, had been captured by the Chilean armed forces near the Radomiro Tomic copper mine. The male, female, and cub were allegedly handed over to FBI agents who arrived in Calama from the U.S Embassy in Santiago de Chile.[9]

The newspaper story made no mention of the creatures' taxonomy, nor whether the family had been taken dead or alive. "Police sources told Crónica that the capture of the specimens was real and that everything had transpired as originally told. Pure paranoia?" asked the unsigned journalist.

Chilean researcher Jaime Ferrer notes that the military stood fast by its "neither confirm nor deny" stance, but sources were able to determine that the three creatures were provisionally held in the stockade of the fifteenth infantry regiment based in Calama, but that an Army lieutenant was forced to kill the male specimen "because it was causing them too much trouble."[10] In addition, a retired air traffic supervisor named Patricio Borlone claimed that all flights arriving or departing Santiago's international airport had been put on hold while a cargo plane loaded two cargo containers with the NASA seal, allegedly containing the rare specimens in question. Borlone provided the flight numbers and departure times to substantiate his theory.

Transmitted via the Internet to the remotest corners of the world, the belief that the U.S. and Chilean governments might possibly be in collusion regarding these improbable creatures prompted a firestorm of speculation. Was the Chilean Chupacabras an American genetic experiment run amok in the barren salt deserts of Chile, as some believed? Or, given the area's history of animal predation, were the creatures natural inhabitants of the deep caves and passages under the dusty desert towns, perhaps brought to the surface by the mining companies' copper production?

Even more disturbing were rumors that a security guard for the Soquimich conglomerate had been clawed in the back by one of these hairy beasts, and that a Chilean soldier had allegedly been killed by one of the Chupacabras creatures during the operation that took them captive. If the U.S. was somehow involved, as many believed, the superpower saw nothing wrong with paying the price for its covert operations in Chilean blood.

Almost a month later, on June 10, Chile's largest UFO research group, Ovnivision, spearheaded by researcher Cristián Riffo, announced that it would formally petition the Chilean Ministry of Defense to look into allegations of NASA involvement with the Chupacabras, and the deaths of hundreds of animals in the country. During the press conference, Riffo noted that the belief that NASA had lost control "of at least three genetic experiments in Chile" was becoming increasingly widespread, and that the specimens in question were the creatures responsible for the massacres. "Many persons agree that they have seen a kind of ape or mandrill with human features but with very large eyes," added Ovnivision's leader. "An animal having these characteristics was hunted down by the Chilean military in the vicinity of the Radomiro Tomic mine near Calama, an operation in which one soldier allegedly died."[11]

Riffo was not being overly dramatic in his statements to the media. Residents of Calama and its encircling towns and villages openly blamed NASA for the Chupacabras apparitions and attacks. "The gringos had at least three genetic experiments run away from them and they've only been able to capture two," was the belief expressed by architect Dagoberto Corante, a respected citizen of Calama. Corante informed Spain's

EFE news agency that one of the captured specimens was kept "all day at the regiment's barracks until the NASA experts arrived to take it away."[12]

CHUPACABRAS EGGS

Perhaps the most curious twist in the chronicles of the Chilean Chupacabras came when the *Antofagasta Diario la Estrella* newspaper featured a story on the discovery of "Chupacabras eggs," which suggested that the predator might be an oviparous mammal, which produces eggs that hatch outside the female's body. A caller to the aforementioned Pablo Aguilera radio show claimed that Chilean soldiers had returned to their base near Calama—after having encountered a strange creature during their nightly patrols—carrying several of these "eggs," which were obtained the same day that NASA personnel allegedly came to collect the creatures.[13]

The story involving the Chupacabras eggs came to a spectacular, if not downright explosive, end when Chilean Air Force bombers dropped an unspecified number of bombs between 8:30 and 9:45 A.M. on July 20, 2000, causing the ground to shake and creating a good deal of consternation, something that isn't easy to do in a region accustomed to underground mining detonations.

The military aircraft allegedly took out a "Chupacabras nest" located in an area filled with small hills and mounds located between the town of María Elena and the abandoned Pedro de Alvarado mining camp. According to copper miners, this area was an ideal location for the creatures to hide.[14] Researchers suggested that an unknown number of breeding pairs of this creature may have entered their reproductive phase, and the government had seen this as the most opportune time for getting rid of them.

The forces behind the conspiracy to destroy the creature and to silence any further stories coming out of Calama employed a variety of tactics, including an all-out effort to purchase the silence of individual witnesses. One of the most unusual events involved a promise made by unspecified "authorities" to the owners of an automobile destroyed by a hairy, simian entity with bat-like wings. In exchange for their absolute silence in this matter, they were promised a brand new vehicle of the same make and model.[15] However, the victims could not resist telling their story to a friend, who in turn told the entire world on the Pablo Aguilera's television show. As the show's host noted, it was unlikely that the unidentified agency would make good on its offer after that.

A NEW IMPROVED GOATSUCKER?

In my monograph *Chupacabras Rising: The Paranormal Predator Returns* (Arcturus Books) I discussed the physical differences between the creature commonly identified as the Chupacabras—having a small head, wraparound red eyes, kangaroo-like body, small arms, and spines running down its back—and the creatures witnessed during the Puerto Rican events of 1995–1996, those witnessed during the Mexican events of 1996–1997 (a huge bat-winged entity), those seen during the 1997 events in Spain (a mandrill-like entity and another with more canid characteristics), and the ones observed during the Chilean events in 2000.

Most of the Chilean reports agreed that the mystery predator had large, luminous, yellow eyes that mesmerized its prey, as also reported in some of the Puerto Rican cases. On July 14, 2000, two motorists were unwilling participants in a case which illustrates the strange properties of the creature's eyes. As they drove toward Calama on their way back from a civic organization meeting, the two anonymous women saw two bright yellow lights up ahead. Thinking it might be a driver heading toward them, the driver flashed her high beams.

As they got closer, they realized that the "thing" standing in the middle of the road wasn't a car: it resembled a very large, earless dog with long gray hair and a pair of immense, slanted yellow eyes. The women and the "thing" exchanged looks for several seconds, after which the car drove off. The "animal" followed their departure with its head—in a 180-degree turn. "I felt a terrible panic," the driver told journalists. "I wanted to get out of the car but [my companion] calmed me down. We saw the two yellow lights again, but this time they lit up the entire road before disappearing. I hit the accelerator and kept up speed until we reached Calama."

Researcher Liliana Núñez Orellana mentions a case in which a Calama witness was able to take a good look at the creature, describing it as very similar to a mandrill with black and gray fur, and two very long eyeteeth. The nose was described as similar to that of a pig or bat, and the creature had a hyperkinetic, nervous attitude as it darted around. The witness frankly admitted having nearly lost control of his bowels during this sighting. "It is known," writes Núñez, "that males and females of this species exist and that they appear to reproduce sexually." She points out a case involving a firefighter who noticed that the creature's genitalia were quite similar to that of humans.

Yet, as the old saying goes, the scariest monster is the one you can't see. This was certainly the case in the early morning hours of June 9, 2000, when residents of the town of Maria Elena felt a strange presence that they identified as "dense air" falling over the town. "It was as if something went past, pushing against the walls, but without making any noise," according to a nervous local.

THE PARANORMAL POSSIBILITY

Since the Chupacabras made itself known in 1995, three possible origins for its existence have been suggested. Believers in extraterrestrial life consider the Chupacabras either part of the cargo manifest of an itinerant UFO that got left behind, or an extra-terrestrial experiment whose ultimate purpose we cannot fathom. Others have managed to weave the Chupacabras into the vast quilt of conspiracy theory by identifying it as either a genetic experiment gone astray, or as a biological robot dropped off in the Third World by the New World Order's minions, for equally unfathomable reasons.

Clearly, the Chupacabras' penchant for that sticky vital fluid called blood appears not to have made much of an impact among either of these two factions. Thus, a third faction composed of believers in the paranormal origin of the creature has paid closer attention to the blood factor.

Civilizations around the globe since the beginning of recorded history have considered blood a sign of invulnerability and potency, a substance to be sacrificed to gods in exchange for divine favor. Understandably, we are repulsed by the hideous blood orgies of the Aztecs and Mayans, whose high priests' hair was "caked with human blood," according to chronicler Bernal Díaz del Castillo. The demand for blood sacrifice by the God of the Old Testament is no less bewildering. The immolation of animals or humans for propitiatory purposes, according to German scholar Wilhelm Ziehr, stems from the fact that deities do not accept gratitude expressed through prayer or the acceptance of commandments—only sacrifice. The greatest sacrifice that can be offered is, of course, human blood.[16]

In many traditions, deities both good and evil have craved blood, or have performed services for a human sorcerer in exchange for it. In *The Odyssey*, Ulysses summoned the grim shades of the dead with an outpouring of blood from freshly slaughtered black sheep, and held the howling revenants at bay with his sword so that only one of them, the specter of the dead seer Tiresias, could feast on the blood's energy and foretell the circumstances of his return to Ithaca. The ancients believed that the spirits of the dead, and other beings belonging to the spirit world, lusted after blood and could be appeased with nothing less.

A number of contemporary authors—Salvador Freixedo, John Keel, Anthony Roberts, among them—have done their best to explain the seemingly insatiable need for vital fluids. Freixedo, for one, has noted that the entities crave not the substance, but the vital energy associated with it. Therefore, the manner in which the blood is released from the body becomes supremely important. The unwilling donor's pain and shock amplify the release of this energy, which, observes Freixedo, appears to be a pleasurable experience for them, much like the consumption of spirituous liquids by a human.[17]

THE MARK OF THE BEAST

The preceding paragraph may smack of obscurantism and superstition to many, but the accounts from Calama, which claim that the night air is rent by the howling screams of dying dogs, suggest that this theory is perhaps closer to the truth than any dreams of alien intervention.

Jaime Ferrer, director of the Calama UFO Research Center, has not shied away from this possibility, particularly after a conversation he had with a ninety-one-year-old desert native from Peine. The elder told Ferrer that "his grandfather's grandfathers" were well aware that these predators existed and that they were, in fact, gods who came to leave messages. In the past, these messages were articulated as complete sentences, but now they were numerical in nature. When Ferrer pressed him for an explanation, the elder replied: "Seven lowered by one, thirteen lowered by seven, four raised by two." In other words, 666—the "mark of the beast."

The reader may share the researcher's disbelief at hearing this item of Biblical numerology from the lips of a desert nomad, but Ferrer's written account goes on to mention that these predatory entities were known as *achaches* ("demon-slaves") in the ancient Cunza dialect, which predates the current Aymara tongue by centuries. This term is still commonly used among the tribal dancers, whose performances feature these improbable beings.[18]

Since 1995, researchers have reached agreement on at least one thing: whatever is draining animals of blood cannot possibly be doing it for its own consumption. Certainly the anomalous bloodsucking entities whose trajectory we have followed are drinking many times their own weight in the vital fluids of different animals. Could we speculate that the decline of blood sacrifice in regions where it was once practiced has led to the appearance of an order of beings in charge of collecting it?

Who or what are these strange deities feared and worshipped by the ancient Atacamans? Their existence has been recorded in a number of cultures ranging from Mexico to Mesopotamia, where blood sacrifices have been carried out at various points in history. What would occur if the Atacamans neglected to perform the ritual? Did their deities send monstrous minions to collect the blood they needed? ●

Notes

1. Schobinger, Juan. *Prehistory of the Americas.* New York: M.E. Sharpe, 2000.

2. Correspondence with Dr. Virgilio Sanchez Ocejo, January 10, 2001.

3. *El Mercurio de Chile*, April 20, 2000.

4. *Crónica*, April 30, 2000.

5. Ibid.

6. *El Sur*, "Mysterious Nocturnal Apparition in Building Courtyard," May 5, 2000.

7. Ibid.

8. Correspondence with Liliana Núñez Orellana, July 7, 2000.

9. Núñez, Raul. "Chupacabras in Chile." *Inexplicata* (Summer 2000).

10. Correspondence with Jaime Ferrer, February 2, 2001.

11. "Chileans Believe Chupacabras to be a NASA Creation," EFE News Agency, July 29, 2000.

12. Ibid.

13. "Chupacabras Eggs Discovered," transcript by Patricio Borlone Rojas, July 14, 2000.

14. *La Estrella del Loa*, "Bombardment Takes Place in Chile's Second Region," July 31, 2000.

15. "New Vehicle Exchanged for Silence in Antofagasta," transcript by Patricio Borlone Rojas, June 9, 2000.

16. Corrales, Scott. "The Paranormal and Blood Magic," *Unsolved UFO Mysteries* (Summer 1995).

17. Freixedo, Salvador. *Defendámonos de los Dioses* (Quintá, 1985).

18. Correspondence with Jaime Ferrer, January 29, 2001.

—*Fall 2001*

* * *

PSYCHOLOGICAL WARFARE

* * *

Heaven's Gate, Columbine, the Unabomber, and Other Atrocities

by Robert Guffey

Continuing his article "Honey, Did You Leave Your Brain Back at Langley Again?" published in Volume I of The Conspiracy Reader, *Robert Guffey's mind control update links government mind control experiments with the UFO phenomenon. Appearing in* Paranoia *in Winter 2001 and covering the years 1997–2000, Guffey's perceptive expose picks up with the Heaven's Gate mass cult suicide in 1997. Guffey outlines this tragic event from the point of view that this cult group was prompted to join their Aryan space brothers by certain agent provocateurs in the bizarre underworld of "remote viewing." Guffey's expose then discusses a peculiar pattern of conditioning which took place in Columbine high school before the shootings of 1999; and then moves on to assert that Theodore Kaczynski was a volunteer in a psychological experiment at Harvard from 1958 to 1962.*

IN THE FALL 1997 issue of *Paranoia*, I wrote an article entitled "Honey, Did You Leave Your Brain Back At Langley Again?: A Brief History of Modern Mind Control Technology." Since its publication, a number of significant events have occurred that may very well be connected to the covert world of government mind control programs. Four of them deserve special attention here.

HEAVEN'S GATE

In Rancho Santa Fe, California, on March 26, 1997, thirty-nine members of the Heaven's Gate group were found dead from an apparent mass suicide. The bodies were discovered by an ex-member who "just happened" to bring his video camera along. These grisly images were later shown all over the nightly news, something rarely allowed by normal network standards. The bodies were lying in their beds, triangular purple shrouds over their faces, their bags packed beside them. Videotaped farewell messages indicated that they committed suicide in order to advance to a "higher plane of existence," where they would rendezvous with a spaceship trailing Comet Hale-Bopp. They'd first heard of this supposed spaceship during an interview with Professor Courtney Brown on the late night radio talk show *Coast to Coast AM with Art Bell*.

On February 23, 1997, *The Washington Post* published a concise article on Brown, in whose 1996 book *Cosmic Voyage*, he claimed to have acquired the ability to "remote view" events from afar and carry on telepathic communications with extra-terrestrials. He claimed to have acquired these abilities from none other than Major Ed Dames, proprietor of Psi-Tech, a remote viewing school and research center founded by a group of "former" intelligence officers. "Major Dames is schooled in military intelligence," writes researcher Alex Constantine, "and is the former commanding officer of the Army's 'Psychic Espionage Unit,' which operated under DIA and Army INSCOM charter." Constantine maintains that Dames has utilized psychic research merely as a convenient cover story for mind control experimentation. (Constantine, 1)

The *Washington Post* article strongly suggested that Brown forged a photograph depicting a "mysterious object" trailing Comet Hale-Bopp. When Brown appeared on Art Bell's radio show in November 1996, he claimed that this object was an alien spacecraft, contending that the photograph had been given to him by a "top ten university astronomer" who would reveal his identity during a major press conference in a week. Brown urged Bell not to make the photograph public until the secret astronomer decided to step forward. The astronomer never emerged and the photograph was proven to be a fake on January 15, 1997, when Bell released the photograph on the Internet. The photo was almost immediately recognized by University of Hawaii astronomer Oliver Hainut as an altered version of a photograph taken by his colleague, David Tholen. A listener later sent Whitley Strieber, a frequent guest on Bell's show, the resumé of a man named Courtney Brown, who worked for the Pentagon.

Marshall H. Applewhite, the leader of Heaven's Gate, appears in Jacques Vallee's 1979 book *Messengers of Deception*. This is the first book to link government mind-control experiments with the UFO phenomenon. During the course of his research, Vallee spoke to a retired, high-ranking intelligence officer known as "Major Murphy." Murphy informed Vallee that a shadowy cabal is manipulating UFO cults to spread "belief in higher races and in totalitarian systems that would eliminate democracy."

Applewhite's faithful companion, Bonnie Lu Nettles, had once been his nurse while he was treated for mental instability at a Texas hospital (right in the middle of George Bush country) in 1972. A few years later, the pair began appearing on various college campuses, urging young and old alike to abandon their "earthly vessels" in order to take their rightful place among the friendly blond Aryans from the stars. At this time they began calling themselves "Guinea" and "Pig." Endearing nicknames, indeed.

Not surprisingly, soon after the news of the mysterious deaths broke on national television, Dr. Louis Jolyon West appeared on ABC's *Nightline* to explain the unique mind set that would cause normal, law-abiding citizens to join a cult and commit suicide. West is a CIA psychiatrist who has the unusual talent of attaching himself to such stellar American icons as Jack Ruby, Patricia Hearst, David Koresh, Timothy McVeigh, and O.J. Simpson, or at least he did until his death on January 7, 1999. Appropriately enough, just before Valentine's Day, on February 11, 2000, another infamous CIA mind-control scientist, Dr. Martin Orne, died of cancer. (Valentine's Day also marked the death of two teenagers who might very well have been the victims of Orne's mind-control milieu. More on this later.)

It should be noted that some researchers, like Richard Hoagland, have speculated that the Heaven's Gate affair was a complex intelligence operation to discredit the UFO community. [For more insight into this, see the interview with Dan Smith following this article. —*Ed.*]

6-6-98

In the researcher's edition of *Operation Mind Control*, Walter Bowart reported that many adult and child survivors of mind-control experimentation had been programmed to "snap" on a specific date: "Some therapists report the date as a multiple of 666 x 3 = 1998, which, following occult numerology, would make the exact day June 6, 1998." (ch. 11, pg. 16) I first read those words in the spring of 1994. In the weeks and days counting down to that date, the world watched in horror as violence exploded on school campuses all across the United States and beyond. In the U.S. alone there were school shootings (as well as attempts at violence that were halted just in time) in Lancaster, California; Springfield, Oregon; Ft. Pierce, Florida; Ft. Lauderdale, Florida; Clearville, Pennsylvania; Pittsburgh, Pennsylvania; Pahrump, Nevada; and St. Charles, Missouri; not to mention devastating church burnings, such as the one in Champagne, Illinois, in which thirty-three people were killed. Even more bizarre was the first homicide—or at least the first we know about—in the Vatican (perpetrated by the head of the Pope's elite guard, Alois Estermann) in more than 150 years. I suspect that David Yallop, author of *In God's Name*, which exposed the conspiracy behind the assassination of Pope John Paul I, would beg to differ.

It seems as if this transitory outburst of violence in our nation's schools was not the main objective of the operation, but merely a prelude for worse horrors to come. . . .

COLUMBINE

The Columbine case of 1999 is an intriguing one, to say the least. On April 18, 1999, I was hanging out with a few skeptical friends. Whenever I speak they tend to roll their eyes. On this particular evening I said, "Hey, in a couple of days it's going to be Hitler's birthday. You just watch, there's gonna be a bunch of 'lone nut' shootings goin' off all over the place, at post offices and high schools and McDonald's fast food joints, you just watch." They rolled their eyes.

Yet, sure enough, on the morning of April 20, I woke up and switched on CNN to see a massacre occurring in Littleton, Colorado, at Columbine High School. One of my friends called me and said, "Are you involved? How'd you know about this?" I said, "I read *Operation Mind Control*!" and hung up. I then proceeded to take fastidious notes. Within seconds, the sheriff of Littleton was telling a reporter, "Why do these kids' parents let them have automatic weapons and bombs? We need more gun legislation." As Dave Emory has pointed out, "If they had driven a truck into the high school nobody would've demanded the banning of automobiles."

One of my earliest notes reads, "Three white males, black jackets, black hats, camo fatigues." Please pay attention to the number three. Every single reporter on the scene described three white males entering the school. I sat there for hours and watched as the students rushed off the campus. The second they were in arm's reach, reporters began sticking microphones in their tear-stricken faces, saying, "So how do you feel?" Every single one of the kids said they saw three white males, two of them in black trench coats firing automatic rifles while a third man in a white T-shirt tossed bombs left and right. Hours later, however, after the media got to them, the kids began changing their minds. One girl even said, "I thought I saw three of them, but the news said there was only two so I guess I was wrong." And they say the media has no effect on children.

By that evening, President Clinton took to the White House podium and said, "We have to teach our children that we can't solve our disagreements with violence" (as Clinton was bombing the hell out of Kosovo). The cover story was nailed down, and the media abruptly followed in lockstep. The very same reporters who had spent the entire day fretting about the three armed men in black were suddenly fed a new batch of cue cards and maintained that the third man was only a phantom, perhaps a figment of their collective imaginations. Eerie shades of the equally elusive "John Doe 2" of Oklahoma City bombing fame.

At one point, while the rampage was at its height, a policeman told a CNN reporter that the gunmen tried to flee but were forced back onto campus by gunfire emanating from an unknown source. The policeman made it clear that they had not fired on the gunmen. So who was boxing the shooters into the trap?

And a trap it surely was. Prevented from fleeing, they were forced to take refuge in the library where most of the thirteen victims were found. After the bloodbath had played itself out, the shooters ostensibly turned their guns on themselves. At least that's what the president told us, even though an autopsy hadn't yet been performed. Wouldn't it be more logical to assume that the missing third assailant was responsible for the death of his cohorts?

By the next morning we discovered that the dead shooters were Eric Harris (age eighteen) and Dylan Klebold (age seventeen). My initial suspicions about the Hitler tie-in was correct, of course; Harris and Klebold had purposely scheduled the attack to coincide with Hitler's birthday. We now know that Harris's father was a colonel in the Air Force, which was no surprise to me. According to mind-control survivor Cathy O'Brien, her most horrendous episodes of torture occurred on Air Force Bases, such as Tinker near Tulsa, Oklahoma (Bowart, chap. 9, p. 9). In Harris's room the police found a dream machine, a device invented by Brion Gysin that induces a hypnotic state via flickering, rotating lights. Harris was also an avid fan of computer video games.

According to Dr. David Grossman, author of *On Killing*, "with the advent of computers and high-speed personal computers, [the military was] able to vastly improve the basic brainwashing techniques that had already earlier been developed. And all of it came down to desensitizing people to the idea of killing."

In a lecture delivered not long after the shootings, researcher Jeffrey Steinberg expands on Grossman's findings:

> In the 1980s and 1990s, the military spent enormous amounts of money through DARPA, the Defense Advanced Research Programs office at the Pentagon, in the computer industry, to be able to develop training simulators to get people into a situation where without even firing a gun, but using one of the "point-and-shoot" computer guns, you can go through the experience of killing an object that looks human, thousands, hundreds of thousands of times, until it becomes almost second nature.

What happened, after a point, is that the very people who were hired by the military to develop these systems, went commercial. They linked up with Hollywood, they linked up with the computer industry, and they began developing the identical techniques that were used in the framework of the military to train killers, and for no other purpose. There was no other reason why tens of billions of dollars of research money went into these technologies, other than to create a desensitized human being, who kills on instinct, and therefore violates everything human (Steinberg, 5).

I don't believe that video games alone can cause anybody to kill, but when you combine them with the complex sensorium of behaviorist conditioning that was surely occurring at that school, you have a recipe for destruction. What conditioning am I talking about? There are a number of mysterious happenings surrounding this school and these two young men in particular. For example, Eric Harris' parents were pumping him full of a drug called Luvox, as reported in *The Washington Post* on April 29, 1999. Though technically an anti-depressant, it is not approved in the United States to treat depression. Luvox is known to "activate mania in susceptible patients," and is contraindicated in patients with a history of "provocative, intrusive, or aggressive behavior," which clearly applies to Harris.

Stranger still is the intersection between Dylan Klebold and the son of FBI agent Dwayne Fuselier, as reported on May 22, 1999, in the *Denver*

Rocky Mountain News. Fuselier happens to be the lead investigator in the Columbine shootings. His son helped Brooks Brown, a close friend of Klebold, produce a "1997 videotape that shows trench coat–clad students armed with weapons moving through the school's halls and then blowing up the school. Incredibly, FBI spokesman Gary Gomes claimed there was 'no conflict of interest.'" (Hidell, 24)

The high school itself has been a lightning rod for controversy and death. In 1996 it was the focal point for a major censorship case involving the Bernardo Bertolucci film *1900*, which is about the rise of fascism in Italy. The film was shown in a Logic/Debate class in an ostensible attempt to expose the horrors of fascism. The film certainly does that. In one scene, the head fascist, portrayed by Donald Sutherland, sodomizes a little boy while whirling him around in a circle and then bashing his brains against a wall. This crime is blamed on communists, à la the German Reichstag fire, and used as an excuse for a crackdown.

The teacher who showed the film, Alfred Wilder, was fired for daring to teach high school seniors the true evils of fascism. Apparently in this predominantly white, wealthy suburb this is an outright no-no. During the firestorm of controversy that followed, Bertolucci testified on behalf of Wilder. He said, in part: "The puritanical urge to divorce the sexual material in my film from its context is only a prelude to a similar desire to cut politics and history from the context in which they are embedded. How will future generations of children grapple with the present if they cannot be allowed to bear witness and debate the past?"

In early February 1997, Alfred Wilder was vindicated and allowed to return to his job when the Colorado Court of Appeals found his dismissal to be in violation of his First Amendment rights. Ironically, the video in which Eric Harris and his buddies rehearsed the massacre-to-be was not allowed to be shown on school grounds because of the controversy surrounding Bertolucci's *1900*. If the video had indeed been shown, perhaps somebody would have realized the serious threat it represented, which may have prevented the tragedy from occurring. Researcher Dave Emory has wondered "whether perhaps Nazi elements, inside and/or outside [the] government, may have deliberately targeted Columbine High School because of the earlier case in which an attempt to remove Al Wilder from the teaching staff . . . was unsuccessful." (Emory)

Jeffrey Steinberg has a more sinister interpretation. He believes the violent Bertolucci film was shown to the children as part of a long program of desensitization. There seems to be some evidence that such a program was indeed underway at Columbine, and may still be occurring. Much earlier than the Al Wilder case, Columbine found itself locked into yet another national controversy. In 1990, around the time of that other notorious video game called the Gulf War, Columbine was featured prominently in an episode of ABC's *20/20* due to a rather strange course that was considered mandatory for graduation. It was unique in the history of American high schools. Indeed, its only precedent was a fictional one and can be found in Aldous Huxley's 1932 novel about dystopia, *Brave New World*.

The name of the course was Death Education, in which children were subjected to "experiencing" death vicariously in a number of different forms. The instructors would use films, but would also send the students on field trips to the local morgue where they were given a complete tour, shown corpses, and forced to sit in on autopsies.

In chapter 11 of *Brave New World*, Dr. Gaffney explains "the Slough Crematorium" to Huxley's protagonist Bernard Marx: "Death conditioning begins at eighteen months. Every tot spends two mornings a week in a Hospital for the Dying. All the best toys are kept there, and they get chocolate cream on death days. They learn to take dying as a matter of course." Huxley, it should be noted, worked for the CIA on the MK-ULTRA program and initiated Timothy Leary into their ranks (Bowart interview).

In an article entitled, "The Creation of the 'Littleton' Culture," Steinberg reports that the school's argument was, "Well, death is part of everyone's experience, and therefore it's good for people to learn to come to grips with it," and goes on to state:

> In reality, looking at Dr. Grossman, and other people who've studied this phenomenon in the military, this is all part of this process of desensitization . . . issues that are fundamental philosophical and moral issues cease to exist, and everything is one succession of sensory experiences that all lead you to abandon that which is essentially human in yourself.

Unfortunately, the milieu of death that surrounds Columbine did not end with Eric Harris and Dylan Klebold. According to the August 18, 1999, edition of *The New York Times*: "On the first day the school was to reopen, parents patrolling the halls before the start of classes found four swastikas carved into the walls. They covered the symbols with duct tape until school officials could remove them permanently. A parent named Tammy Theus, the mother of one of the fifteen black students at the school, said, 'It's like they're laughing in our faces.'" Who's "they," I wonder? Harris and Klebold are dead, are they not?

Perhaps "they" are the very same individuals responsible for the threats reported on September 5, 1999, in the *San Jose Mercury News*: "Grappling with the aftermath of the April 20 massacre at Columbine High School in Littleton, Colorado, education officials say five other high schools in the same district have received letters threatening violence in the past month." If Harris and Klebold were the "lone nuts" the mainstream media and President Clinton claim they were, who continues to threaten Littleton?

The latest fatality connected to Columbine High occurred less than a month ago, as I write this on March 9, 2000. The following brief paragraph appeared on February 15 in the *Los Angeles Times*: "Two Columbine High School sweethearts were found dead early Valentine's Day at a restaurant near the Littleton, Colorado school, reopening the wounds of last year's rampage. Sophomores Stephanie Hart, 16, and Nicholas Kunselman, 15—who were reportedly dating—were found in a sandwich shop near the school where Eric Harris and Dylan Klebold killed thirteen people April 20. Police said the shootings were being investigated as a double homicide and cited robbery as a possible motive."

You might assume the Columbine connection to this double homicide was a mere coincidence if you weren't aware of the program of desensitization I've outlined in the previous pages. I suspect the fallout from this ongoing experiment will continue to plague Littleton for years to come.

Before the end I should take note of one last interesting detail—or perhaps it's just a coincidence. Early in 1997, I wrote a short story that was inspired by the life of Joseph Grimaldi, the man who turned clowning into a respected artform in Victorian England. Grimaldi learned his trade from his father, who was obsessed with death and abused his son both physically and psychologically. Charles Dickens ghosted Grimaldi's autobiography, which I read for research purposes. While digging through some files in search of a *Skeptical Inquirer* article debunking the concept of government mind-control programs, I accidentally came across pages 108–111 of the autobiography. I had forgotten why I photocopied the pages, and yet there they were. One of the pages fell on the cluttered carpet. As I bent over to pick it up I spotted the word

"Columbine." Since I was in the midst of writing this update, I was taken aback for a moment. Then I read the following sentences:

> The nominal pretext for the harlequinade on this December evening is, as usual, the pursuit of the lovers by Pantaloon and Clown, and the excitement of the chase lends Zest to the buffoonery. But although the sympathy of the audience is officially with the runaways, and although a happy ending for Harlequin and Columbine is inevitable, the hero of the game is really the rascally Clown. Every one is on the anarchist's side. There is no end to his antics, and no particular continuity but the succession of familiar English scenes, as he races through Georgian London leaving havoc and destruction in his wake.

I hope Columbine really does have a happy ending, but I suspect the death-obsessed Clown will have the last laugh.

THE UNABOMBER

On July 6, 1999, investigative journalist Alexander Cockburn published a major revelation on the Internet edition of the *Los Angeles Times*. Apparently, someone on high felt the information was far too dangerous to print in the street edition intended for the mere "sheeple," those sorry besotted simpletons who lack access to the Internet (i.e., most of the planet). To correct this oversight, relevant portions of the article follow:

> It turns out that Theodore Kaczynski, a.k.a. the Unabomber, was a volunteer in mind-control experiments sponsored by the CIA at Harvard in the late 1950s and early 1960s. Michael Mello, author of *The United States of America vs. Theodore John Kaczynski*, notes that at some point in his Harvard years—1958 to 1962—Kaczynski agreed to be the subject of "a psychological experiment." Mello identifies the chief researcher for these only as a lieutenant colonel in World War II, working for the CIA's predecessor organization, the Office of Strategic Services. In fact, the man experimenting on the young Kaczynski was Dr. Henry Murray, who died in 1988.
>
> Murray became preoccupied by psychoanalysis in the 1920s, drawn to it through a fascination with Herman Melville's Moby Dick, which he gave to Sigmund Freud, who duly made the excited diagnosis that the whale was a father figure. After spending the

1930s developing personality theory, Murray was recruited to the OSS at the start of the war, applying his theories to the selection of agents and also presumably to interrogation.

As chairman of the Department of Social Relations at Harvard, Murray zealously prosecuted the CIA's efforts to carry forward experiments in mind control conducted by Nazi doctors in the concentration camps. The overall program was under the control of the late Sidney Gottlieb, head of the CIA's technical services division. Just as Harvard students were fed doses of LSD, psilocybin and other potions, so too were prisoners and many unwitting guinea pigs.

Sometimes the results were disastrous. A dram of LSD fed by Gottlieb himself to an unwitting U.S. army officer, Frank Olson, plunged Olson into escalating psychotic episodes, which culminated in Olson's fatal descent from an upper window in the Statler-Hilton Hotel in New York. Gottlieb was the object of a lawsuit not only by Olson's children but also by the sister of another man, Stanley Milton Glickman, whose life had disintegrated into psychosis after being unwittingly given a dose of LSD by Gottlieb.

What did Murray give Kaczynski? Did the experiment's long-term effects help tilt him into the Unabomber's homicidal rampages? The CIA's mind experiment program was vast. How many other human time bombs were thus primed? How many of them have exploded?

For far more esoteric, though no less significant, information on the Unabomber I recommend Michael Hoffman's article "Invoking Catastrophe: The Unabom [*sic*, per FBI] Ritual and Alchemical Process" published in the 1995 updated edition of his fascinating book, *Secret Societies and Psychological Warfare*.

Considering the severity of the atrocities described in these pages, one might become cynical about the fate of democracy in this mind-controlled society. However, reasons for optimism persist in the words of consciousness researcher David E. Worcester:

> When Pavlov went to the Russian hierarchy to report on his last findings before his death, he warned them that when you condition people . . . you condition them to receive something in exchange for that conditioning, and if that is not given to them they cannot be conditioned again. He warned them, "You may develop the first cosmically aware people, people who have been taken to the point where they cannot be conditioned by mass media."

Ask yourselves: Are you receiving what you want in exchange for your perpetual obedience? Are you receiving anything at all? ●

References

Bowart, Walter. *Operation Mind Control*. Ft. Bragg: Flatland Editions, 1994.

———. Telephone interview, March 14, 2000.

Constantine, Alex. "Ed Dames & His Cover Stories for Mind Control Experimentation." In "The Constantine Report," 1996, later published in *Virtual Government*, Venice: Feral House, 1997.

Dickens, Charles. *Memoirs of Joseph Grimaldi*. New York: Stein and Day, 1968.

Emory, Dave. "Something's Happening." Pacifica Radio (KPFK, Los Angeles), May 20, 1999.

Hidell, Al. "Columbine Update," *Paranoia* 21 (1999): 24.

Hoffman, Michael A. *Secret Societies and Psychological Warfare*. 1995 edition (Independent History and Research, PO Box 849, Coeur d'Alene, Idaho 83816).

Huxley, Aldous. *Brave New World*. Leicester: F.A. Thorpe, 1983.

Steinberg, Jeffrey. "The Creation of the 'Littleton' Culture," *The New Federalist*, August 30, 1999.

Vallee, Jacques. *Messengers of Deception*. Berkeley: And/Or Press, 1979.

Worcester, David E. "Genesis of a Music," Pacifica Radio (KPFK, Los Angeles), July 24, 1993.

—Winter 2001

The Aviary and the Eschaton

An Interview with "Chicken Little"

by Joan d'Arc

This interview, which was conducted in Washington, DC, during the winter of 2000–2001, explains that the Aviary was a UFO group formed in the 1970s by individuals with national security clearance. These individuals came together to share information from their highly compartmentalized government assignments in order to arrive at a bigger picture of the UFO reality. This loose network of individuals gave themselves bird names to obscure their identities. This interview is with Dan Smith, a self-appointed member of the Aviary who is known as "Chicken Little." In this interview, Smith tells Joan d'Arc how the Aviary "managed to keep the UFO pot stirred for the two decades or more that it has been in business." In particular, Smith admits that the Aviary leaked the Hale-Bopp UFO "companion" story, which ultimately led to the Heaven's Gate group suicide pact. Whether the end result was intentional, Smith doesn't say. But it is enough that he admits it was an intelligence psy-ops campaign.

THE AVIARY is an "ad hoc" UFO working group which has served as an information channel between military/intelligence self-appointed keepers of the facts (so-called Majestic 12 or "MJ-12") and the civilian UFO community, discussed in detail by Richard Boylan in issue 23 of *Paranoia*. In that interview, Boylan explained that the Aviary, which was formed in the 1970s, was made up of individuals with national security clearance, who decided to share information in order to better understand the enigma of UFOs and ETs. Some of its members were pro-UFO disclosure and others were not.

One self-appointed "auxiliary" member of the Aviary who has never maintained such cover is Dan Smith. As a volunteer civilian member calling himself "Chicken Little," Smith has openly shared information "leaks" from the Aviary to the UFO community. In this remarkable interview, he tells how the Aviary disseminated disinformation to the UFO community in an ongoing psyops campaign for at least two decades. He explains how the Aviary has contributed to UFO rumors in the public at large, and he wonders whether he and other members of the Aviary have been used in a high-level attempt to penetrate MJ-12.

JOAN D'ARC: Dan, as a civilian UFO researcher and attaché to an intelligence-affiliated UFO working group called the Aviary, your "bird name" was Chicken Little. How did you come to be involved with this group?

DAN SMITH: I became acquainted with one of the members, "Tom" (not his real name). "Chicken Little" was just my own concoction. My father was involved with the military in WWII and was later in the government as an economist. He had no interest in UFOs, but was in contact with some influential people who, I discovered later, had unusual interests. After doing some graduate work in physics I turned to metaphysics. An extended psychic experience led me to contact MUFON, and through them I came in contact with Tom at the CIA in 1991. He was known as the "keeper of the weird."

JD: What was your main impetus for wanting to be an information dissemination specialist between the intelligence community and the UFO community, using the Aviary as a go-between?

DS: I had no prior intent in that direction. I was well into my study of eschatology before meeting Tom. I wanted to find out what take the CIA might have on eschatology and possibly provide some input. Discussing the Aviary and the UFO community was a good excuse for a continuing contact with an intelligence officer who had relevant responsibilities.

JD: How would you describe your position as a "networker" between this group and the UFO community?

DS: From the beginning I was very open about my government contact. I began to network with some folks in the UFO community who were interested in sharing information. Through Tom I was put in contact with some other members of the Aviary and this all became grist for the mill. There was a lot of comparing notes and checking of information on both sides. At one point some of my UFO colleagues persuaded the CIA/IG (Inspector General) to conduct an internal investigation of Tom relative to his unusual methods of collecting information.

JD: Can you elaborate on these "unusual methods" and their implications in the field of civilian Ufology?

DS: Well, there was the fact that he was involved in domestic collections. He was making provocative statements to me about the possible presence of ET's. He spoke freely of his involvement with other members of the Aviary. On several occasions we met at nightclubs. He had "indelicate" conversations with a female researcher. It was far from clear what was in the line of duty. He was interviewed by an IG officer. He reported answering all the questions directly, but told the officer that he could not answer any questions about ETs.

JD: Your excellent web site, called The Eschaton, describes your end-times beliefs as well as other fascinating matters. What is the background of your end-times beliefs?

DS: After leaving school I struggled with mind/matter dualism for several years before reluctantly adopting an idealist or immaterialist metaphysic. It took a couple more years for me to see that some form of eschatology is inevitable for a mind-based cosmology. It also became clear that such a cosmology was compatible with some of the original beliefs and heresies stemming from the prophetic tradition of monotheism.

JD: How would you succinctly describe what you feel is going to occur in this "end of the world as we know it" scenario?

DS: If history is to have any meaning, it must have a beginning, middle, and ending, as does any story. Linear time will come to an end. Life will go on in some form, but not this one. The rigidities of space and time will dissolve. The boundaries between our different states of consciousness will become more fluid. The so-called millennium will be our time for wrapping our mundane affairs and preparing for our transition to a less physical existence.

JD: Your Eschaton revelation comes to you via science as well as religion. How would you succinctly explain this to people who aren't familiar with "new" physics concepts (realizing that people can go to your web site for more information)?

DS: As physics has evolved, the world it describes is becoming increasingly more abstract, much more "thought-like" than "thing-like." What is not abstract are the ephemeral qualities with which our minds imbue those abstractions. As we awaken to the fact that reality is a projection of the cosmic mind of which we all partake, we will begin to exercise more control over the nature of that projection. This will be an extension of psychosomatics to the sensorium that is our world.

JD: Do you know anything about a group called the Advanced Theoretical Physics Working Group, which was formed to integrate theories in "new" physics and remote viewing as these came to describe the nature of reality? In your opinion, how has quantum physics changed the modern view of reality, and what was the UFO's role in this?

DS: I don't know any group of this name, but there are many folks doing this. I was once a "quantum dualist" (i.e., the mind influences matter through the agency of quantum phase correlations). But once you have postulated a robust realm of the mind, it becomes increasingly difficult to view the world of physics as other than an abstract construction of the mind. The quantum realm may be weird, but UFOs are a lot more weird. With UFOs we are no longer talking physics. This is metaphysics with a vengeance. This is dream-time, not space-time. The UFOs are pulling the rug right out from under what we used to think of as our "reality."

In the case of MJ-12, with the best brains in the world it was like the cartoon of the fire alarm box. Behind the glass panel is a Bible. "In case of emergency, break glass." Now we know how MJ-12 felt. Imagine how much worse they felt when they opened the Bible to John 16:12 as I did one eventful morning about twenty years ago. The folks of MJ-12 concluding that an advent of this sort was being prognosticated by the Visitors have probably been anticipating this moment of truth with some trepidation.

JD: How would you characterize the relationship between your Eschaton and the intelligence community? Are there parallel beliefs, motives, or a modus operandi?

DS: Along with the rest of the UFO community, I believe that we have been visited. I believe that this visitation was in preparation for a messianic event which is imminent. That event will inaugurate our millennium of preparation leading up to the Eschaton. The Aviary is the part of the intelligence community most closely and publicly associated with the MJ-12/Visitor complex. The messianic event itself, however, must be as spontaneous and independent of MJ-12 and the Visitors as is possible. Thus the intelligence community will have very little direct input in this matter. National and global security will be largely redefined under the millennial aeon.

JD: OK, can we clarify this a little? What do the Visitors and UFOs have to do with the "messianic event"? What is the relationship between the Visitor phenomenon and the second coming of the messiah?

DS: I am suggesting that the Visitors could be playing several roles that would be relevant to a messianic event. They would be an off-world advance team helping in the preparation. This would involve alerting the powers-that-be to the inevitable advent of the messiah, millennium and Eschaton. They would convince those powers that it would not be in their interest to interfere in the cosmic plan. The Visitors might then negotiate with these powers in selecting a mutually acceptable individual for the role of messiah. The Visitors might also be overseeing the abduction phenomenon in as much as it could be part of the preparation for the millennium.

JD: Am I missing something here? Isn't there already a messiah assigned to this role?

DS: This is a heterodox scenario. This is divine minimalism. Christians will be mightily disappointed, those who were expecting a figure in white robes to descend from the clouds. The idea is that we do not need theatrics this time around. This is a package deal. Whoever can convince the world of its immateriality and of the rationale for the millennium and Eschaton, that person will be the second coming. Anyone who aspires to being this paradigm shifter should expect to play that role. I feel no need to apologize for personally wanting to put an end to the hegemony of materialism.

JD: You suggest that this messianic event must be separate from the Visitor phenomenon, meaning perceptually independent?

DS: Let's back up a bit. I am saying that we humans constitute a very significant aspect of the cosmic mind. The first and second coming, in particular, are designed to awaken humanity to their central role in the cosmic plan. We don't need to be told this, only reminded, so easily do we forget. Our memory only needs to be jogged a very little bit. Minimalism is the word when it comes to divine intervention, in keeping with the "prime directive." The perception of coercion is the very worst thing that could happen. If it appears that the cosmic plan is being imposed upon us, we would naturally react negatively. In reality, this plan is of us, by us, and for us. The messianic event is critical.

It may appear that I have just contradicted myself. From the previous response one might imagine a smoke filled room underground in Area 51 where the Visitors and MJ-12 haggle over the identity of the messiah to be "imposed" on humanity. This hardly seems spontaneous. However, if these negotiations can be kept secret, then the intervention remains minimal. There can only ever be informed speculation as to what might have actually transpired. The "designated" individual would have to convince her fellow humans as to the reasonableness of the hypothetical selection process.

JD: In your estimation, is it going to be possible to keep these events separate?

DS: The best I can do here is to give you a "for instance." Let's suppose that I was the selected one. My unusual interactions with Tom, and some other events, might lead me to suspect this to be the case. It would then be up to me, however, to make this case to the public, where it could be accepted or rejected. Even if some others could be convinced of this possibility, there would be no implied coercion in their acceptance of the outcome. If I were right, however, others would eventually come around to seeing and agreeing with the reasonableness of the choice, even if this occurred posthumously.

JD: Let's get back to your role in the Aviary. As a civilian networker for the Aviary, what types of information did you learn that most blew your mind? And how did this information affect your end-times beliefs?

DS: There has been a gradual realization that "MJ-12" and the Visitors are no longer playing a proactive role, and may no longer even exist here. This is the scariest piece of information that I can impart. Tom has been responsible for closing down the phenomenology and psychic warfare programs. He is also active in planning for the scaling back of the Navy and Air Force. It is reasonable to infer that he has similar duties relative to MJ-12. That may mean that I am a significant part of an effort to transfer the residual MJ-12 responsibilities to the civilian sector. That is a sobering thought for myself and for any others who are inclined to participate.

JD: What do you mean by "the Visitors are no longer playing a proactive role, and may no longer even exist here"?

DS: The Visitors got their message across to those who needed to be informed. That was the point of their Earth mission. There may exist now a sequestered "star gate" that can be activated for special purposes.

JD: What do you foresee will be your "duties" with regard to a transfer of what you call "residual MJ-12" responsibilities to the civilian sector?

DS: This transfer will occur in the context of a second coming. I consider myself a candidate for that role. Tom has partially abetted that illusion on my part.

JD: Has this transfer been requested by the Visitors?

DS: Presumably, yes.

JD: It concerns me that Tom, CIA "keeper of the weird" with his "unusual methods," might be pulling your leg. Does this not concern you?

DS: If there were proof that this was not a joke, that proof might easily trigger a financial panic, for instance. One has to proceed with great caution and virtual deniability. It is fair to say that we are pushing that envelope.

JD: Can you elaborate on this statement specifically with regard to your perceived role as a candidate for the Messiah? As you stated earlier, "my unusual interactions with Tom, and some other events, might lead me to suspect this to be the case." In what way has Tom abetted this illusion?

DS: The ultimate answer to this question will depend on whether one is assessing credit or blame.

JD: Your second project, the Aquarium, is described on your web site as an informal association of individuals who share a common realization and goal, and who recognize that society is rapidly approaching a "critical junction." I presume that this junction is the Eschaton? Do you believe the Eschaton will occur during your own natural lifespan?

DS: I hope that the second coming may occur during my lifetime. According to premillennialism, we would then have our allotted millennium to prepare for the Eschaton.

JD: The Aquarium's goal is to minimize the confusion and disharmony that will occur during the unfolding of this "cosmic plan" and to "maximize" the benevolent aspects of these coming changes. You also specifically state that the Aquarium has no political affiliations and no adherence to any one belief system. Are there members who are presently in government intelligence positions?

DS: The Aquarium name derives from the Aviary. It is an informal designation for those people who believe that mere humans are now in position to fulfill God's plan of salvation for the world. There is no formal membership.

JD: How would interested parties go about joining this group? What types of concerns would these individuals share?

DS: There is nothing to join. It is just those of us who wish to get on with the cosmic plan.

JD: Dan, what exactly do you mean by "get on with" the cosmic plan? Are you saying that there is a group of people who want Armageddon ASAP? Will the Eschaton be precluded by an Armageddon-like scenario?

DS: Yes, please hold the Armageddon. We still have another thousand years of recognizable, linear history. If that ever gets too boring, then hurry, Lord. The gross nonlinearity of inter-dimensional space-time, dreamtime will take some getting used to, even for those who fancy themselves spiritual virtuosos.

JD: You also state regarding membership: "everyone who wants to participate and a few select individuals who don't want to participate but are deemed useful by Dan T. Smith." Can you elaborate on this statement? What type of individuals would be deemed useful?

DS: Did I say that? I guess I was thinking of cosmic co-optation. No one can escape God's love.

JD: Would alternative publications like *Paranoia* be deemed useful?

DS: Of course!

JD: I'd like to talk about the Heaven's Gate cult suicide, which occurred after the remote viewing of several UFOs reportedly trailing the Comet Hale-Bopp in 1996. You have addressed this event in your web site as it concerns the Aviary. In your essay "Pecking Away at Heaven's Gate," you write the following: "The Aviary is not responsible for the deaths of thirty-nine innocents. It just looks that way. The Aviary always just manages to be in the wrong place at the wrong time, minding someone else's business. And I should know. . . ." Can you elaborate on how the Aviary manages to stir up this kind of trouble?

DS: The Aviary has certainly managed to keep the UFO pot stirred for the two decades or more that it has been in business. Rick Doty has probably contributed more to the UFO–government conspiracy rumors than everyone else combined. He has done so while in the government employ, and maintaining high-level contacts in the intelligence community. Tom weighs in on this scale as a not-so-distant second. It might be that the Aviary was being used in this manner in a high-level attempt to penetrate MJ-12. If this were the case, it seems probable that they experienced success, with Tom being the most likely beneficiary.

JD: In your Heaven's Gate essay, you wrote: "There is a larger agenda and those thirty-nine got caught at the short end of that agenda. The Aviary knows something of that agenda, and it shakes a lot of trees trying to find out more, and some of the apples will hit the ground pretty hard." Can you elaborate on that agenda? Whose agenda is it that the Aviary is trying to shake down?

DS: The larger agenda is eschatology. We presume that this is God's agenda, but it doesn't hurt to kick the tires once in awhile, just to make sure.

JD: In your essay, you admit that "the remote viewing of the alleged Hale-Bopp companion UFO was pretty much an Aviary spin-off." Can you elaborate on this? What did the Aviary hope to achieve with this story?

DS: Remember that this [event] was part of the run-up to Y2K. If this were deliberate, it was like the setting of the fires in the Bandolier Forest near Los Alamos. You take your chances. It might still be considered a success, compared to what else might have happened.

JD: Was it trying in some way to measure the public's gullibility?

DS: Gullibility? Perhaps it was more like measuring how dry is the powder in the keg. Another way to kick those tires.

JD: In this essay, you admit that the alleged April UFO landing was definitely an Aviary story and you admit that you were the one who passed it on to the public where it "quickly took a life of its own." You also state that you knew this UFO landing story was likely to be disinformation, but you put it out to the UFO community anyway. Dan, what were you thinking?

DS: As I recall, I put this story to [UFO researcher] Richard Boylan, and I did not have to be a brain surgeon to know that Rich would run with it. If Rick Doty had invited me to be on the "landing" team I might have taken him up on it. I am willing to believe Rick's claim to have been in communication with William Colby and that his canoe "accident" before this anticipated "landing" had some impact on whatever did or did not transpire. The Aviary was stirring the pot well before Y2K. If something was going to blow up, it was better to have it happen sooner rather than later. The fact that only thirty-nine people lost their lives that April perhaps should make us feel fortunate. And who knows, we might have thwarted a real landing or a hoax landing that might have made matters much worse.

Let us note that in this same time frame I had established an independent contact with the Senate Select Committee on Intelligence as another verification of Tom's bona fides. I was told that I was part of something called "unconventional collections" and that I could rest assured that I was involved with some very competent people. This was from a senior staff member who happened to be Jesuit trained and knowledgeable of eschatology. It was Tom who facilitated my contact with the other members of the Aviary in which Rick was a central figure. This is not to say that Rick was competent, but only that there was a much larger context.

JD: You stated you weren't surprised to see the Hale-Bopp companion story gain "considerable currency" in the UFO arena. What was your impetus for doing that?

DS: I could have chosen to have had no contact with the Aviary or to have kept quiet about it. I chose to have contact and to not keep quiet about it. I was shining my light on the Aviary and perhaps on MJ-12. I still am. I don't think this story is over by a long shot.

JD: Looking back, what had you hoped would come of this "networking" enterprise? Have you any idea how Art Bell was used in this scenario?

DS: I believe that an eschatological preparation is the most rational explanation for the observed behavior of the Aviary, especially of Tom, and for the inferred behavior of MJ-12. How well that end is being served remains to be seen. Art Bell was certainly influenced by the

Aviary. I don't know that he was "used" any more than you or I are being "used" right now.

JD: You state in your essay that "the Heaven's Gate affair is the Bennewitz affair written large." This is a most interesting statement. For readers who aren't familiar, Paul Bennewitz was a UFO researcher who was fed false information by the CIA operatives, and was basically driven crazy. What are the important similarities between the Heaven's Gate/Hale-Bopp affair and the Bennewitz affair?

DS: Perhaps Paul was being used as a guinea pig for Dan. Perhaps Dan is being used as a guinea pig for the next guy. Maybe the next guy will be the second coming. I am volunteering with that in mind. Maybe Paul did not have the opportunity to consider all the options. No one ever does. The actual messiah will have to explain the holocaust. Explaining Heaven's Gate is hardly in that ball field.

JD: In your Heaven's Gate essay you state that if you had it to do over again, you would do it over again. You write: "When one sheep goes astray, I am very reluctant to leave the other ninety-nine in the lurch, or the ends do sometimes justify the means." This messiah analogy is disturbing. How long have you held this self-perception? Was it before or after you met Tom, CIA "keeper of the weird," that this perception began to unfold?

DS: When I met Tom I was already "entertaining" the folks on CompuServe with the possibility that I was the "spirit of truth", i.e., third member of the trinity. Later on, Tom said, "Everyone knows that I'm Catfish and you are Sunfish" (this being apropos of the Aquarium). I chose to read that as "Sonfish" and to take it as something other than a joke. I was not at all surprised when the folks on CompuServe decided that it was not funny and kicked me off. Who's to blame? Why blame? The world is but a stage.

JD: You also comment, "In the field of eschatology, one gets paid mainly to keep track of the ends." This statement is a little confusing. So then, in the field of eschatology, one gets paid? As I understand it, you are a civilian. Can you tell me, do you work for a civilian business enterprise or are you self-employed?

DS: I have some independent income. As a piper I am piping a certain tune. I may just be entertaining myself and a few of your readers. We could do worse than that.

JD: In your Heaven's Gate essay, you have also written that, "I believe that we are all in good hands, and if two of those hands turn out to be mine, please forgive me for not being quite as surprised as you." What exactly do you mean by this puzzling statement?

DS: I'm just saying that I don't think my state of mind is completely my fault or Tom's fault. We all march to different drummers, some of which may be cosmic. We all hope for the best and don't spend as much time preparing for the worst as pure reason might otherwise dictate.

JD: Steven Greer has written that the eschatological belief system has pervaded the civilian UFO community. He describes "very strange bedfellows: war mongers and militarists in cahoots with industrialists who share a bizarre eschatological bent." He has warned that some of these people want Armageddon ASAP. Can you comment on these statements?

DS: This sounds reasonable to me. And if you want my opinion, I am against any more Armageddon. We have had enough of that already, no?

JD: In your estimation, is there a large group of persons in the intelligence community who believe as you do? Also, can you give me an idea of how many people are part of your "loose knit" Aquarium group?

DS: I don't know anyone in the world who believes quite like I do. But, heck, let's do an experiment. Run this article and see what happens with Tom. In the meantime we can all be thankful that we are not Tom.

JD: And why is that? Is Tom in some hot water right now?

DS: Tom has said that his continuing association with me is the greatest deliberate risk that he has taken with his career. Whatever may be the internal struggles relative to MJ-12 and the Visitors, Tom is riding shotgun for the Aquarium. ●

—Winter 2001

This interview has been edited for space considerations. The full version can be found at www.paranoiamagazine.com.

Cruisin' with the Spooks

Aboard the Maiden Voyage of a Different Kind of Spy Ship

by *Kathy Kasten*

In this fascinating travelogue, sleuth-reporter Kathy Kasten goes aboard a SpyCruise and interviews Oleg Kalugin, retired major general of the Soviet KGB, and Gene Poteat, president of the Association of Former Intelligence Officers. Kasten obtains some interesting first-hand information regarding MK-ULTRA and black operations for those interested in the history of government mind-control experimentation. She also comes away with the feeling that most of the "professors" on the SpyCruise, who have spent their lives in government agencies, went along with the "party line" on certain subjects and showed loyalty only to each other.

THE AD IN THE *Los Angeles Times* Sunday Travel Section was very terse and very small. It read "SpyCruise™" and provided an 800 number. I called and spoke with Judy McCabe, passenger services manager of Dynamic Cruises. Judy easily convinced me that the SpyCruise was the cruise for me. After I gave her my credit card number to reserve a place on the cruise, she suggested that I visit SpyCruise's web site, www.cicentre.com/SpyCruise.htm.

The web site was well designed, providing background briefings on the people and places involved in the SpyCruise. If you visit the site, you will note, as I did, that SpyCruise is promoted by Counter Intelligence Centre (www.cicentre.com). And, yes, you will notice that this "company" is made up of retired counter-intelligence agents of various governments from around the world, plus a couple of authors on friendly terms with intelligence agencies. Although I was interested in hearing what these "spooks" had to say, it was when I saw a photo of the Regal Empress that I knew it was the ship for me (ahaseminars.com/cruise/ship.html). The Empress was neither too big nor too small.

Perhaps you are wondering what motivated me to decide to sign on to this cruise. Was I delusional enough to believe I could actually ask these spooks specific questions and get specific answers? I thought if I could conduct some private interviews out of the glare of the majority of people on the cruise, there was a chance I might be able to get some questions answered. Yeah, I know the CIC "literature" claimed that nobody associated with them would discuss anything that wasn't already public.

Well, there is "public" and there is public. Utilizing humans—American taxpaying citizens, no less—for field-testing various types of electronic technology could be considered public, especially to those people who are targeted. I had to take a chance, and I thought I could get responses under the caveat that one of the things they consulted on was "personal safety."

SUNDAY, MARCH 10, 2002

The four-hour "red-eye" flight and six-hour wait in Tampa International Airport for the transport to Port Manatee Bay (forty-five minutes south of the airport) to board the Regal Empress was grueling. I slept a little on the bus. I was surprised when the Escot bus pulled into the Port and parked near a Del Monte warehouse. As you may remember, Del Monte and the United Fruit Growers Association were possible CIA cutouts, alleged to have attempted to topple governments that actually represented the people of those countries. I thought to myself, this is an appropriate beginning for SpyCruise.

After showing my I.D. to a local khaki-clad authority person, I got off the bus and headed to the dock for a closer look at the Regal Empress. However, a newly installed ten-foot high chain-link fence separated me from that closer look. I noticed two of the SpyCruise speakers were already on the other side of the fence chatting with another authority figure, this one in black. Two kinds of uniforms implied two types of policing authority. Personally, I liked the guys in the khaki better. They seemed to be more approachable and comfortable dealing with the public in a friendly, "fun" way.

All passengers passed through the gate, provided passports or a driver's license, had luggage tagged and sniffed/searched, and presented credit cards to people behind a desk—to take care of any on-board expenses (mainly liquor bills, as everything else was provided in the cost). As everybody mounted the gangplank up to the opening in the side of the ship, groups of two or three were corralled and photographed. Moving on, I found myself at the opening and entering into a very beautiful reception area that had a plush, nautical-theme rug in navy blue, wood paneling, etched mirrors and large art posters on the walls, and prints of ships and harbors. A cabin person quickly moved my luggage to my cabin on the Sun Deck, down the hall from the Commodore and Mermaid Bars.

MONDAY MORNING, MARCH 11, 2002

On the first day of the cruise, David Majors, one of the two people in charge of the SpyCruise, started off a series of on-board lectures with "Spies on the High Seas: A Hundred Years of Espionage on the High Seas that Have Affected World Events." This was a history of the United States's entrance into the spy/counter-spy business. Majors presented information on an incident at the start of World War I called "Black Tom," in which espionage was involved in blowing up an ammunition storage depot in New York City harbor at a time when America had remained neutral. This was the incident that helped America decide it needed intelligence agencies. Majors focused on the fact that ocean liners played a large part in espionage, using as an example the stealing of the plans for the Norden Bombsight, and Herman Lang's role in that theft.

Oleg Kalugin, retired major general of the Soviet KGB, presented the afternoon lecture that day ("The KGB's Targeting of America"). The motto shown in Kalugin's first presentation was: "Justice is truth in action." The highlight of Kalugin's lecture was newspaper photos of himself when he ran for Supreme Soviet/Parliament of the USSR and won during Gorbechev's push for perestroika. One fact he revealed in his lecture was that he was the Russian contact who "handled" one of the more famous spies in recent American history, Johnny Walker—not the John Walker who fought with the Afghans, but the one who ran the Walker spy ring between 1965 and 1970.

MONDAY EVENING, MARCH 11, 2002

There were more pointed questions I wanted to ask Kalugin regarding experiments in mind control that were done at the Academy of Arts and

Science in Moscow during his service with the KGB. After dinner that night, in the very beautiful wood-paneled Regal Empress dining room, I went over to his table and asked to meet with him at a later time. We made arrangements to meet in the Mermaid Bar around 10:30 P.M.

I arrived in the bar at the appointed time. Kalugin arrived moments later surrounded by a couple of people whom he essentially dismissed. He pulled over one of the comfortable lounge chairs and sat with his knees touching my leg. I took this as a sign that he was willing to be open and to try to answer honestly any questions I might have. I started the interview by introducing myself. However, before I could ask him any questions, a woman moved into our little circle, claiming she had learned some Russian. Basically, she had butted into my question mid-sentence.

Kalugin and I looked at her, and he explained that we would be finished in a couple of minutes. She left and returned with David Majors. He stood up straight, looking at me down his nose, saying something like, "Everyone wants to ask Oleg questions." I responded, "We arranged to have this interview. It will only take a couple of minutes."

Initially, Majors went away, only to return with Bart Bechtel, the other person in charge of the cruise. I explained to Bechtel that I was interviewing Kalugin for a magazine article. Bechtel said something like, "You can ask your little questions so that we can all hear them." Now, Majors was standing, looking down from his position on my right side, and Bechtel on my left in essentially the same stance. Both Kalugin and I protested, but neither Majors nor Bechtel would back off. So, Kalugin suggested we meet for a breakfast interview. I agreed and got up and left.

Moments later I was out at the fore of the Sun Deck trying to cool down after having been "handled" and manipulated—a paying guest—by the two guys from CIC who were in charge of the cruise. These guys were professionals all the way. They went about their job very quietly, very deliberately, and were used to having their way. Immediately, I was made aware of the dark side of this cruise. It was apparent that if Majors and Betchel wanted the SpyCruise to be successful, they would need to lighten up with curious members of the public.

TUESDAY MORNING, MARCH 12, 2002

My alarm was buzzing, and I hit the button. My watch said 6:10 A.M. Plenty of time until the 9 A.M. interview. I shut my eyes. I immediately opened my eyes when I realized that 6:10 was, in fact, 9:10. I was already ten minutes late. The next couple of minutes were a blur; all I know is I emerged from my cabin dressed, teeth brushed and make-up on. Dashing to the Promenade Deck, I finally found La Trattoria (the twenty-four-hour restaurant), but no Kalugin.

I was moving as fast as I could, even though my legs felt like rubber with the ship rolling under me. At the aft of the ship, on a set of stairs going up to the gym level, I spotted Kalugin. Upon reaching him, while tightly gripping the railing, I muttered my apologies that included, I hope, words to the effect that I was jet-lagged. We found a table away from La Trattoria, where it was relatively quiet.

Feeling pressured by time, I launched into my questions. I started off by bringing up the U.S. Army's 1974 report on the experiments in mind control at the Moscow Academy of Arts and Science. Kalugin claimed he knew about attempts at creating propaganda to influence the public, but stated those programs were abandoned by 1991. Kalugin stated that the leading institute of those programs was the Wolff Laboratory, and that the military ran those programs. The KGB, where Kalugin served as first chief director, was tasked only with developing technology for, and actually collecting, information.

Kalugin stated that the reformist KGB chairman Vadim Bakatin had invited a scientist to present his claim that he could teach talented individuals to kill remotely using only their mind. Nothing came of this presentation. Kalugin stated he knew about something called Seismology Warfare, a totally new concept to me, and one I have never read about anywhere. The concept involved remotely setting off an explosion in the sea to create a wave of massive destructive force.

The other project Kalugin mentioned was one familiar to most westerners: nuclear winter, the total destruction of the human race by radiation fallout. I brought my questions back to the topic of mind control of individuals, and raised Smirkov's name. Smirkov's experiments emerged from the Russian scientific community because of a 1995 program on German television. This was the year Kalugin left the KGB. He claimed he did not know about Smirkov's experiments.

I brought up the bugging of the U.S. Embassy in Moscow. Kalugin shared with me the fact that the Soviets were very proud of that project. Kalugin stated that the U.S. had the walls prefabricated in Helsinki and shipped to Moscow. When the walls were transferred to a freight train in Poland to carry the building materials to Moscow, the walls were switched. The original walls were replaced with ones that had listening devices built into them.

We finished the interview on a personal note. I asked him if he was doing okay in America, if he could make a living in America. He said he was fine, and he could always fall back on his retirement stipend of $135 from the Russian government. I found Kalugin very personable, intelligent and, as I was to find out, more honest and forthcoming than any of the other CIC "professors."

TUESDAY EVENING, MARCH 12, 2002

I was looking forward to Keith Melton's lecture the following day, since I thought maybe he would cover the more esoteric, modern technology. As it turned out, during his lecture, titled "Espionage and Counter-Intelligence Technology," I discovered Melton collects and displays (as part of the CIA's Cold War Exhibit located at CIA Headquarters) cameras that can be hidden and camouflaged in hundreds of different ways; cameras and equipment used by the KGB, HVA (East German Intelligence Service), and the CIA. The prize of his collection is one of the original Enigma encryption devices. This was interesting stuff, but not what I had come to learn.

I found everybody, including the "professors," in the Mermaid Bar that night, and located Melton. After stating that I wanted to interview him about microwave targeting, I mentioned that I was interested in the subject of shielding from microwave radiation. Melton claimed that copper would work. I questioned whether copper would work with heterodyning signals. He started to move away from me with the statement that he didn't think the American government had implanted anybody.

I countered that implants were no longer necessary, and that remote biotelemetry had probably replaced whatever implants had been intended to do. At this point, Melton complained that the loud talking behind us was disrupting our conversation and he excused himself. I noted that I had not brought up anything about implants. He had!

WEDNESDAY, MARCH 13, 2002

Prior to one of the lectures, Majors had made a plea for people to turn in the comment sheet that had been provided the first night at sea. At this point, based on attempts to interview the CIC professors, I was trying to decide whether I knew more than the professors. That night, I cornered David Majors to tell him that I didn't want to hand over my comments without chatting with him. Later, I expressed how disappointed I was with the lectures. In particular, I had looked forward to Ken Crosby's lecture, "The FBI Special Intelligence Service during World War II," which described how he survived monitoring the Perons while living in Argentina. All Crosby did, in my opinion, was drop names. Majors suggested that I wait—the best was yet to come.

Gene Poteat's Wednesday afternoon lecture, "The Science and Technical Wizardry of Intelligence: America's Crown Jewels of Espionage," had come and gone with minimal disclosure by Poteat on the CIA's part in covert testing. Poteat (president of the Association of Former Intelligence Officers and ex-CIA agent who had worked in the Science and Technology Directorate, as a scientific intelligence officer) was the manager for the development and operation of special reconnaissance systems for the U-2, SR-71, and various other space and naval reconnaissance vehicles. He developed and implemented new intelligence methods to detect low observable (stealth) aircraft by foreign air defense radars.

It was a remarkable lecture because Poteat stated he was able to electronically create a "phantom blip" on radar. By turning a few dials, he could make the phantom radar blip do extraordinary things—go very fast, slow to a stop, move up or down, or disappear, simply by manipulating the dials. One story involved a military airbase that sent a jet fighter out to intercept "the blip." The pilot had the blip on his on-board screen, but had no visual, even though he should have been on top of the "craft." Even though he did not have a visual, he claimed he had the target in sight and fired a missile claiming to have "taken it out." (I later read in *Body of Secrets*, by James Bramford, that the jet was Cuban and involved ferret craft flights.) This information suggests that some of the so-called radar evidence for "UFOs" will need to be discounted, as they can be explained away by the CIA's experimental technology.

One of the last points Poteat made was that it was not true that the U.S. Government handed over information downloaded from Echelon, the U.S. government's electronic eavesdropping operation, gleaned from private telephone conversations of European companies, to American corporations.

THURSDAY, MARCH 14, 2002

During lunch in the Regal Dining Room with a man and his wife, whose company I enjoyed (they are not public figures and these were private conversations), this man volunteered that he had been an engineer for Grumman's experimental craft operations on Long Island. He stated that the EA6B had the capability of "disappearing" from radar after a certain switch was turned on. He was the contact person for the Center for UFO Studies (CUFOS) in Long Island because of a sighting he had had many years earlier, and because he wanted to bring a more scientific process to the investigation of UFOs. I was discovering that the passengers on this cruise were *really* interesting.

There is one event outside of the SpyCruise lectures that I must mention. Before I do, there are two pertinent points: the Regal Empress's crew is from forty-seven countries; and whoever would want to "track" passengers would have known by July 2001 that I would be aboard, in a closed environment for a week. The voyage was to take place from March 10 to 17, 2002. As David Majors had pointed out, intelligence agents have used ships for many years. I am not saying I would have been the only target, if somebody wanted to target people for monitoring, but the environment was ready-made for such a purpose. Following is the gist of the event.

While sleeping on Wednesday night/Thursday morning, I experienced what some people call an alternate reality "dream." This "dream" involved seeing an individual standing very close to my window looking in. I was able to see the face very clearly and was able to "maneuver" my sightline to have a full view of the intruder. He looked Middle Eastern, with black hair. He was good-looking and wore a utility uniform—like an engineer or someone who would be involved in making repairs to the ship. I took note of this "dream" only because it was so lucid.

I usually spent my time after lunch on the Sun Deck reading. On Thursday, after the lucid dream, two men in utility uniforms were "pretending" to repair an area above my cabin. I was in a chaise lounge on the Sun Deck almost directly outside my cabin, and noticed them only because they didn't seem to be doing anything real. I decided it was time to leave the Sun Deck and return to my cabin.

As I approached the entry door, a good-looking young man stepped onto the deck, stopped and looked at me with a wry smile. He looked to the left and the right, and with his head turned to the left he continued to smile. I said, "They went that way," thinking he was looking for the other utility personnel. Of course, he matched exactly the image of the individual I had seen in my "dream." He continued to stand there, and I had to go around him to get through the entry. He seemed confused.

I turned and looked through the glass in the door, and noticed he was still standing in the same spot. I entered my cabin and walked over to the wall unit under the window that held the television. As I placed my book and purse on the counter, a face stepped up to the window and peered in. The window was covered with a silver reflective coating, which meant if someone wanted to look into the window they would need to stand very close and stare very hard to see anything. I moved closer to the window, leaned over the top of the TV and peered back into an Asian face. Our eyes met and he backed off very quickly. I thought: "Is he one of ours? Or, one of theirs?" I have no idea why I had that thought.

Suddenly, I looked at the little red light on the TV and realized the TV was really "on" at all times. I looked around for any large piece of clothing I could grab to cover the entire screen and red light. After doing this, I noticed that the involuntary muscle spasms I had been experiencing every night since I boarded the *Regal Empress*, had stopped.

THURSDAY EVENING, MARCH 14, 2002

Ray Wannall's Thursday evening lecture was, "Operation SOLO: The Double Agent Who Penetrated the Heart of the Kremlin." Wannall had served for many years as assistant director of the Intelligence Division directly under Hoover. As was the case with all the lectures, it would require an entire article to cover this man's material. However, I would like to mention an interesting fact: Wannall received an award for his years of service in counter-intelligence work from the same Masonic lodge where Hoover had been a lifelong member.

Many researchers have mentioned how closely Masonic lodges are involved in certain aspects of government policy. To my mind, there isn't usually a clear link. However, the above citation meets my criteria: First, Hoover was the member of a Masonic lodge. Second, Wannall claimed all of the myths surrounding Hoover were created by the KGB in their active measures program. Third, much of the SOLO file contained information about the J. F. Kennedy assassination, stating that two KGB agents had fronted the conspiracy spin Wannall claimed. In addition, in the interests of national security, the FBI had felt a strong need to deny the Church Committee's request for the file on Martin Luther King, Jr. The FBI maintained that Communist agents within the core group that surrounded him were advising King, and turning over the file would have compromised the FBI's investigation.

Friday, March 15, 2002

Since we were docked for most of the day at Cozumel, there was time for only one lecture. Paul Moore and David Majors presented "The Wen Ho Lee Case: What Went Wrong?" This lecture was very detailed and I will need to do an article on this case alone. Moore and Majors did make an "on site" video for CIC. (Contact www.cicentre.com for information about ordering the video *Overview of Chinese Intelligence Targeting of America*.) I learned that the Chinese method of spying was very different from that of the rest of the world. As an aside, I would suggest reading *Seeds of Fire*, by Gordon Thomas, which I read on board the cruise. In some ways, reading this book helped me understand the world of spooks and their "mission," plus there was additional information about the Wen Ho Lee case in Thomas's book.

During the day, I spent hours walking up and down the beach of Cozumel looking for *cubanos*. There was an interesting tobacco shop on the road to the airport filled to the roof with Cuban cigars. However, if anybody thinks they can go to Cozumel and pick up cigars at a cheap price, think again. It is no longer the case.

Saturday Afternoon, March 16, 2002

"The Robert Hanssen Espionage Case: An Insider's View from Two of His FBI Colleagues" was also presented by Majors and Moore. These lectures would require in-depth articles to do them justice. Those readers who cannot wait for any article I might write should contact www.cicentre.com and enquire about ordering one of their videos which discuss this case.

Getting information about the Hanssen case is a little more complicated, since it involves a one-day briefing and a one-day tour of Hanssen sites in north Virginia. CIC produces many succinct videos containing much more information than was provided during the SpyCruise. When I wasn't at the lectures, I was in my room watching one of these well-documented and interesting cases. They are worth the time and money to own. Another lecture, presented that day by Hayden Peake ("A Review of the Best and Worst of Intelligence Literature") bears mentioning to this audience. Described as the two worst books on the subject were Gary Webb's *Dark Alliance* and Alexander Cockburn's *White Paper*.

I had read Gary Webb's original series of articles in the *San Jose Mercury News*, had attended his lecture, and bought and read his book. I could not fault his documentation, and Peake provided no proof that Webb's documentation was faulty. Basically, the "party line" was that Webb was "crazy." I heard similar statements provided by Peake from two other "spooks" on the cruise—one who was identified as such and the other who I felt probably was one because of his comments during various interactions. The nature of Webb's craziness was never stated, but among the spooks there was the nodding of heads in agreement whenever Webb's "crazy condition" was mentioned.

SATURDAY EVENING, MARCH 16, 2002

Part of the cruise was supposed to involve "dinner with the professors." However, the professors didn't seem to want to dine with the general public. So, on the last evening of the cruise, Bechtel surprised our dinner table when he brought Gene Poteat over to our table. Please remember that Poteat is president of the Association of Former Intelligence Officers. Researchers whose subject is "mind control" will remember that Julia McKinney was a member of this organization. McKinney had presented "Valerie Wolff" (a targeted individual who is claimed to have died recently of cancer) to a presidential commission.

Wolff claimed to be a target of electronic harassment and a childhood participant in mind control experiments. Therefore, I am quite sure Poteat knew exactly what I was talking about when I began the interview with the subject of research involving MK-ULTRA, and the possibility that the projects went "blacker" after the congressional hearings.

Poteat stopped eating and began moving his food around with his fork. I waited for an answer. Then, I pointedly asked him whether the CIA had continued to create and develop new technology. At that point, Poteat stopped all movement, placed his arms flat on the table and stared straight ahead. I followed suit.

"The CIA contracted out all projects," he said. It took me a moment to digest what he had said. I asked the same question again, and got the same answer.

Now I became totally immobile and blurted out, "Then, the CIA lost all control of the projects." Poteat agreed. There was tension in the air as real information was disclosed. One of our dinner companions broke the tension by noticing that Poteat was not eating, at which point, Poteat got up and excused himself, saying he needed to join his wife at another table.

Whenever I have shared the above information with fellow researchers, none have failed to pick up on the import of Poteat's admission. First of all, anybody who has tried to bring a legal suit against the CIA for harassment has failed, simply because no one can sue the United States government. However, knowing the names of the private companies who were contracting with the CIA to create, develop, and test electronic equipment used for harassment is another story. A private company can be sued.

We must start applying for discovery under the Freedom of Information Act to find out which companies contracted with the CIA. I know this seems a step away from being able to stop harassment by entities that are not held to the same level of accountability as the government, but it seems like a path on solid ground.

What is my impression of spooks? Like most professional groups of people, they are a very closed society. However, some of the people retired from government agencies seem to understand that they were public servants (David Majors and Bart Bechtel, in particular) and would like to share what they learned during their years of service with the public who footed the bills. Most of those people on SpyCruise, the "professors" who have spent their lives in government agencies, still feel a loyalty only to each other. The incredible thing is that they pretend to, or really believe, the party line on certain subjects, for example, that Gary Webb is crazy. I watched as anything that was not the party line was squashed through derisive comments.

SUNDAY, MARCH 17, 2002

Toward the end of the cruise, on Sunday morning, while I chatted with an interesting couple from New York City (the husband was a psychiatrist), Poteat came over to our table to remind me of Peake's comment about Gary Webb. I stated that I didn't agree with Peake's comment, whereupon Poteat reached over and patted me on the head saying that I was "all right." He felt the need to say it twice and pat me on the head twice.

Just before leaving our table, he claimed once again that I was all right and patted me this time on the shoulder. •

—Fall 2002

CULTS AND SECRET SOCIETIES

* * *

Conspiracy, a Matter of Generations
Conspiracy Theories in History

by Scott Corrales

Are conspiracy theories just a modern phenomenon? Scott Corrales explains that our ancestors had their own secret cabals to fear and mythologize. Corrales traces the fear of "invisible rulers" back through the historical record, noting, for example, that Roman emperors believed that the nascent religion of Christianity was a conspiracy to destroy the Roman Empire. Likewise, leaders of the church would eventually persecute secretive groups like the Knights Templar for being part of a conspiracy to destroy the church. The author provides a concise overview of the roots of conspiracy theory, introducing the reader to such little-known groups as the "Council of the 98" and "The Order of the Holy Sepulchre."

"CONSPIRACY THEORIST" is a label which our society slaps onto anyone who dares question the possibility that something underhanded might be taking place at the highest levels of the government, the military, the world's financial institutions and, of course, the world's religions. The belief in a global conspiracy, regardless of the amount of evidence accumulated in its favor, must be stifled in order to maintain a perception of a lawful and orderly society in which people can go to work, mow their lawns, and pay their taxes without question.

The current interest in conspiracies might lead many to believe that we are dealing with a phenomenon no older than some forty or fifty years, when in fact our distant ancestors dealt with secret cabals of their own.

FREIXEDO'S CONSPIRACY FLOWCHART

Before embarking upon a voyage in quest of the forces who pull the strings from behind the scenes, it would be wise to examine the forces we can actually see and experience in our everyday lives.

In his book *La Granja Humana* (The Human Farm), Spanish paranormalist Salvador Freixedo plays the role of conspiracy theorist when dealing with "the visible rulers of the world," prior to launching into a disquisition on the world's "invisible" rulers. Freixedo condenses the main points of belief in conspiracy into the following four categories:

Politicians. This category of visible ruler despises physical violence and weaponry, but loves being consulted, loved, or even feared. Freixedo suggests that many elected officials have psychopathic personalities and, feeling the lack of something within themselves, find a suitable replacement by being engulfed in crowds of people.

Military. This segment of the power structure varies in importance from country to country (ranging from countries lacking armies, such as Costa Rica and San Marino, to military dictatorships such as Iraq). Freixedo theorizes that the military was created to defend its country from external threats, but once such threats have vanished the military soon turns upon its own country in search of internal enemies. In some countries, it is accepted practice for a civilian government to turn over the reins of power to the military when financial, social and political ruin is imminent.

Banks. Freixedo gives us a taste of the "international bankers" conspiracy, which is still prevalent in our times. In his opinion, "money maniacs" have less actual power and contribute indirectly to the prevailing tribulations by a fevered urge to increase the amount of money available to them, whether it bankrupts their countries or not. He observes that many politicians have sought safe haven in the banking world to mend their shattered political careers.

Clergy. Nothing has caused more dissension than religions, observes Freixedo. The clergy maintains its power by gathering masses and conditioning them to follow a specific belief, while at the same time telling them that others not sharing this belief are "the enemy."

These four tiers of the power structure rule the visible world. As if their vast power weren't enough, we now turn to those other powers who also hold sway over our lives.

ON THE WAY TO THE FORUM

Although it is perhaps possible to go farther back into the historic record, the Roman Empire gives us our best example of the fear generated among average persons, and within certain reaches of the government, that conspiracies are afoot.

The historian Suetonius, in his *Lives of the Twelve Caesars*, gives us a surprising parallel to our contemporary belief that Hitler escaped the bunker to live in South America, that JFK is alive and well in Switzerland, and that Elvis never died: A belief pervasive around 70 A.D. was that the emperor Nero, who had allegedly committed suicide, had in fact escaped alive and was a guest of the Parthian monarchy. A clever impostor, indubitably milking the Parthians for all they had, probably led to this particular belief.

Roman emperors feared any kind of dissension within their far-flung empire, and this gave rise to the belief that the nascent religion of Christianity was a conspiracy to destroy the empire. Bloody persecutions over a period of three hundred years killed thousands of "subversives." Adherents of Judaism didn't escape persecution either, since there was the belief that Jewish scholars, under the protection of the Parthian king, were plotting the overthrow of Rome from a safe distance in retaliation for the destruction of Jerusalem.

Roman authorities were also fearful of individuals with unusual powers and intelligence, such as Apollonius of Tyana, who claimed to have visited a "city of the gods" in the Himalayas, after a long trek from Nineveh in modern Iraq. The story tells that the "gods" who controlled human activity lived in a world vastly different from our own, were served by automatons, and possessed artificial light generated by "luminous stones." Apollonius learned much in this place before returning to Rome, where he became a trusted advisor to emperors Vespasian and Titus. The latter of these monarchs is supposed to have said: "I conquered Jerusalem, but Apollonius of Tyana has conquered me!"

As Roman power waned, beliefs in hidden forces took a turn for the more magical and sorcerous. It was believed that the Huns—whose leader, Attila, exacted tribute from the weakened empire—were the off-spring of demons and the prostitutes in the rearguard of the Visigothic armies.

MEDIEVAL WOES

People of the Middle Ages, a period during which Europe was racked by turmoil and disease, were held in a mental straightjacket by the church, and were prone to invasions by barbarian people. They held many beliefs which could be considered conspiracies.

Charlemagne, the most enlightened and energetic monarch of this period, felt that his kingdom was beset by Sylphs—nonhuman creatures whose magical powers affected the weather and caused the loss of crops. Many reams of paper have been written about the Sylphs and their mythical land of Magonia by a number of authors who have linked them to the UFO phenomenon. Most readers of this publication will remember Jacques Vallée's account of St. Agobard rushing to the rescue of three peasants who were about to be lynched by a frightened mob after having been deposited on Earth by a "sky-ship" hailing from this eldritch realm. Belief in the Sylphs persisted well into recent times: a Parisian bookseller at the turn of the century claimed to be in contact with a particular Sylph who would find rare volumes for him.

Earlier medieval beliefs held that inanimate objects were also engaged in a little conspiracy of their own. According to Gregory of Tours, church bells could be seen flying off into the sky; he concluded that bells were flying off the belfries to go to Rome, "since the Pope was there." So much for early UFO reports.

The medieval world was a theocratic state ruled by the Papacy. Simplistic maps showed a flat world composed of three continents and centered in Jerusalem. In later centuries, rumor would have it that a great monarch lived beyond the lands of the marauding Saracens. This was Prester John, who lived in a realm of amazing wonders and was the most powerful Christian king in the world. If only he could be contacted, argued the chroniclers of the time, he could attack the infidel from the rearguard while brave European knights led charges against the forces of Islam. Belief in Prester John, Rex Armenia et Indiae (King of Armenia and India) had a protean quality; when it had been established that there was no such kingdom in Asia, it was quickly relocated in the popular imagination of the time to Africa, where it would endure well into the Renaissance.

THE KNIGHTS TEMPLAR

In the year 1118, barely two decades after the conquest of Jerusalem by the crusaders, a French knight named Hugh de Payens approached the patriarch of the Holy City with an idea: a military order that would live in strict accordance to a religious rule, much like the Benedictines or other monastic groups, but devoted to patrolling the dusty roads of Palestine and protecting the flow of pilgrims and trade. King Baldwin of Jerusalem, who was in desperate need of experienced men-at-arms, also welcomed this idea.

One of the greatest downfalls of the Crusades was that as soon as the liberation of the holy places had been achieved, the crusading European noblemen often wished to return to their own fiefdoms rather than settling in the newly acquired territories. To this end, the monarch allowed Hugh de Payens to base his fledgling order on the ruins of the Solomon's temple, which would give the warrior-monks their name: The Knights of the Temple, better known as the Knights Templar.

The service provided by the Templars apparently was worthwhile. By the year 1127, notable figures in European history, including Bernard of Clairvaux, Pope Honorius II, and the Count of Champagne, had thrown their full support behind the order. Land grants, money, and supplies were heaped upon the knights, who would put them all to the best possible use—supporting their endeavors in the Near East. The land grants, which were numerous, were carefully husbanded and made to yield their maximum. The Templars were quickly on their way to becoming the wealthiest and most formidable fighting force Europe had known since the days of the Roman legions.

Then the accusations began pouring in. Ecclesiastical authorities charged the Templars with heresy and blasphemy. Rumor had it that initiation into the order called for stamping and spitting upon the cross, proclaiming: "I renounce Jesus!" New adepts were said to be stripped naked and received kisses upon different parts of their bodies before being led to the presence of Baphomet. Other chronicles stated that the idol worshipped was a statue of a dog or a cat—perhaps the statue of the Egyptian goddess Bastet, which the Templars had acquired during the crusaders' incursions into that country. It was also claimed that the remains of another effigy, known as the Goat, were confiscated by the Inquisition.

In the opinion of author Rollo Ahmed, these tokens were meant to represent the pantheistic concept of the Absolute: "The animal head, usually that of a goat with a torch between the horns, represented the responsibility of matter and the expiation of sin in the body; the human hands of the figure, betokening the sanctity of labor, were pointed above and below to two crescents, the upper white and the lower black, corresponding to good and evil, mercy and justice."

A substantial number of books written in the past hundred years point to the "black legend" surrounding the Templars and their works—a legend centered mainly around a belief that there was a hidden, special group within the order that adhered to unchristian beliefs, such as satanism, homosexuality, child sacrifice, and other abominations. Less extreme versions declare that the "inner circle" was in charge of forgotten occult lore, and likely candidates were initiated into these "mysteries" when the time was right.

The Templars' seal, depicting two knights riding on the same war charger, which symbolized the order's vows of poverty and modesty, has been reinterpreted by researcher Juan G. Atienza as a visible manifestation of the Knights Templar's understanding of the Kabbala and kabbalistic instruction, which stated that "only two men united in meditation over the word of God can create a living being." Gnostic dualism, the understanding of the teachings of eastern philosophies, would play a crucial role in the order's development. In a way, the Inquisition had been correct in its assessment of the Templars as heretics: they had embraced Gnostic principles (probably through contact with the Islamic Ophites) and probably denied the divinity of Jesus, while holding him in high esteem as a prophet or avatar.

More importantly, did the Knights Templar find the Ark of the Covenant, then ship it to France for safekeeping once the crusader kingdoms in the Near East crumbled before the advance of the Mamelukes? Perhaps they could have saved Indiana Jones a trip to Egypt.

THE ARK OF THE COVENANT

A legend closely associated with the Templars has it that Yolande, wife of Baldwin of Jerusalem, was greatly intrigued by these stern-visaged knights whose headquarters were located over the ruins of Solomon's temple. Entering their building by stealth, the queen found her way to a crypt, where she watched in amazement as six knights stood in silent meditation around an object that could only have been the Ark.

The available evidence suggests that the Templars' choice of the ruins of Solomon's temple was far from random, and that excavations began almost immediately in an effort to find something in particular that had been concealed centuries before the inception of the order. Before dismissing this possibility, it is perhaps worth pointing out that the oft-mentioned "copper scroll," which forms part of the Dead Sea Scrolls, describes an assortment of treasures and religious items allegedly interred beneath Solomon's temple. Could the Templars have been aware of a similar source?

A little history becomes necessary at this point. When the Roman legions of Titus sacked Jerusalem in 70 A.D., they took with them all the treasures of the Temple, including the sacred menorah, a golden table, and other items. These treasures were transported to Carthage after the Vandals sacked Rome, and were later shipped to Constantinople when the Byzantine army of Belisarius put an end to the Vandal kingdom. The superstitious emperor Justinian, fearing that the captured "treasure of the Jews" would spell the ruin of Constantinople, had the treasures sent to Jerusalem in 555 A.D. At this point, the treasure trove vanishes from history, so it is safe to assume that this hoard remained in the city of David and was never taken by the marauding Arabs who conquered Palestine a century later.

It is bold to suggest that the Ark of the Covenant was part of this lost treasure, but the great secrecy surrounding the Templars at this point suggests that the magnitude of their findings inspired awe within the order itself. The enigmatic "find" was sent back to Europe, possibly to the vicinity of Rennes-le-Chateau, which was ringed with Templar fortifications and concealed in a chamber hidden beneath the hill, upon which stood Castle Hautpoul and the surrounding village.

Was this the mystery at the heart of the Templar riddle? Did the order possess knowledge that the Ark was lost somewhere in the catacombs of the ruined temple, over which the al-Aqsa mosque had been built? Initiation into this secret would surely be as awesome and terrible as even the Templars themselves hinted, and knowledge of the custody of this holy and perhaps nonhuman item would have constituted a powerful source of élan, aside from other "powers" that may have been derived from it. This legend is connected to a host of others which have been handed down to our time.

RENNES-LE-CHÂTEAU

According to Michael Baigent and Richard Leigh, authors of *Holy Blood, Holy Grail* and *The Messianic Legacy*, the Knights Templar constituted merely the physical arm of a larger order that remained secret, and which went by a number of other names, including the Priory of Sion. This line of speculation and serious research opens the door to one of the most perplexing mysteries of our time—the enigma of the small French town of Rennes-le-Château, the nexus for a series of interlocking mysteries which have never been solved even after intensive research by American and European researchers. One of these, Lionel Fanthorpe, expressed this sentiment when he stated that investigating Rennes was comparable to the peeling of an onion, except that the researcher is within the onion, working from a smaller layer to a larger one.

Fanthorpe states that the sleepy village has earned a reputation as a repository of arcane knowledge and mystical treasures, such as the emerald tablets of Hermes Trismegistus, alchemical treatises, the lost treasure of the Cathar sect (which was brutally annihilated in the mid-1200s during a papal crusade), and other rare and mystical periapts. History tells us that while the Templars did not occupy the castle at Rennes, they surrounded the area with other massive fortifications, and it can be logically concluded that Rennes was part of their holdings. Centuries later, Bernard Sauniere, the parish priest, made a discovery at Rennes which made him wealthy. Could he have found the resting place of the Ark of the Covenant? Was he richly rewarded by an unknown, interested party, perhaps even the Catholic Church? An unsubstantiated and uninvestigated rumor has it that the Ark's final resting place is in the Vatican.

Baigent and Leigh's suggestion of the existence of the "Priory of Sion," followed by brilliant detective work, proves that this secretive, politically active European association inherited the Templar legacy, perhaps even exact knowledge of the resting place of the lost Ark. In 1979, during an interview with Pierre Plantard de St. Clair, putative "grand master" of the Priory, the researchers were told that the treasures taken from Jerusalem would be returned to the Israeli government "when the time was right."

A CABAL OF SCIENTISTS?

Narciso Genovese, an Italian scientist living in Mexico, was interviewed in the 1970s by Professor Mario Rojas, who asked: Is our world run by a conspiracy of scientists?

According to Genovese, a council of ninety-eight scientists from many nations and branches of scientific knowledge—physics, chemistry, mathematics, astronomy, and electronics—have pursued research into hidden avenues of knowledge, under the supreme commandment to never reveal a single iota of this knowledge to any of the world's governments. The "Council of the 98," to give it a name, has a doctrine based on three main points:

- There is only one religion: the belief in a wise, omnipotent God.
- There is only one country: the planet Earth.
- There is a single purpose: to bring forth peace through science on our world and create an alliance between humans and the inhabitants of other worlds in the universe.

Genovese's startling "scientocracy" was allegedly established in 1938, shortly after the death of Guglielmo Marconi, who refused to turn over his notes and discoveries to Italian dictator Benito Mussolini. Inspired by this courageous act, the "Council of the 98" has pursued its secretive work in the hopes of establishing a one-world government aided by secret technological developments. Yet, perhaps this scientific conspiracy is much older than we think.

THE IMMORTAL ALCHEMISTS

The alchemists, those protoscientists whose quest for knowledge was coupled with a profound esoteric philosophy, have captured the imagination of writers for the past two centuries. Traditionally, we have been told that alchemists sought to transmute base elements such as lead into noble elements such as gold. Many authors contend that this goal merely served the alchemists to receive funding from greedy feudal lords hoping to replenish their cash-starved estates. Some chronicles even tell us that small amounts of lead were turned into gold just to keep impatient patrons happy, but that the real quest of the alchemists was immortality.

This has led many conspiracy theorists to suggest that perhaps some of the alchemists were successful in this endeavor, and that human history may perhaps be controlled by a hidden council of alchemists who appear to us at critical moments to change the course of human history.

While the idea is laughable at first blush, our history books certainly are filled with enough strange encounters between important personages and unknown characters to add considerable weight to the argument. The most prevalent of these enigmatic characters is the Count of

St. Germain, who has been described as everything from an angel or "ascended master" to a time traveler or even a vampire. The legend of St. Germain has him appearing in the mid-1700s in Vienna, and at subsequent moments in that century through Napoleonic times, never looking a day older.

During his last recorded appearance, the Count told an onlooker that he was leaving to prepare the way for an invention that we would come to know as the railroad. While many authors have dismissed St. Germain as merely another eighteenth-century adventurer (like Alessandro Cagliostro), many have been convinced that he was in fact an immortal alchemist. Other strange characters, like the "Red Man" who persistently appeared to Napoleon Bonaparte at moments in his life, could also be members of this bizarre "Order of Immortals."

The closest evidence we have in our times for this fascinating belief is yet another controversy—one surrounding the legendary alchemist Fulcanelli and his two twentieth-century disciples, Eugene Canseliet and Jean Julien Champagne.

Fulcanelli is the only alchemist whose books remain in print to the present day: *The Mystery of the Cathedrals* and *The Dwellings of the Philosophers*. The first was published in Paris in 1926; the second in 1930. In the preface to the work, Canseliet observes. "It is a thankless and onerous task for a student to write a preface for a book written by a master . . . it is thanks to him that the gothic cathedrals have yielded their mystery . . . All the truth, all philosophy and all religion rests upon this unique, sacred stone. Many, filled with presumption, feel qualified to imitate it, yet how few are the Chosen whose modesty, wisdom and skill enables them to do so!"

The two books were the rage of prewar French occultist circles, who believed that acquisition of the "Philosopher's Stone"—the Holy Grail of alchemy—was close at hand. Yet many occultists refused to believe that Fulcanelli ever existed, and Canseliet himself declared that Fulcanelli had "ceased to be," suggesting that the alchemist had not only uncovered the Philospher's Stone but had acquired immortality as a result.

Fulcanelli was allegedly seen in 1954, living in Milan. Others saw him in Spain, where he stayed near the Andalusian city of Seville. Gérard Heym, another alchemist, claims that Fulcanelli's physical appearance as an immortal was entirely androgynous, one of the side effects of having ingested the elixir of immortality.

THE BLACK ORDER

The belief in "hidden manipulators" of the reality surrounding us continues unabated, and new conspiracies join the ranks of older established ones every few years.

In 1982, a strange little book appeared in French bookstores entitled *The Book of Secret Companions: The Secret Teachings of General de Gaulle.* Authored by Martin Couderc, it revealed the existence of a secret society know as the "Order of the 45," which was reputedly established by the soldier and statesman de Gaulle. A sequel appeared some time later, dealing with revelations about the author's struggle in Canada against the group of hidden controllers now calling itself the Black Order. According to Couderc, the Black Order had relocated to remote Tierra del Fuego, on the southernmost tip of South America.

While it is tempting to dismiss these tracts as nonsense, Couderc bases his "forbidden" knowledge on a series of letters left behind by de Gaulle himself, which exhorted members of the "Order of the 45" to fight for the restoration of France's greatness. This effort is associated with the coming of power of a "great king" prophesied by Nostradamus. The Black Order seeks to create a one-world government (another conspiracy chestnut) by instating this "great king" by means involving ritual magic and hidden technology.

Other sects, secret societies, and lodges have emerged in recent times. Some of them are decidedly religious in nature and involve only the top leaders of certain countries. To wit, the little-known Order of the Holy Sepulchre, created during the Crusades but still active, is run by Italy's Prince Lanchelotti and Count Senni, who occupy, respectively, the posts of grand master and governor general of the order. The "knights" of the order are financiers, industrialists and political figures from all over western Europe, sworn to defend Catholicism throughout the world. It is believed that the Order of the Holy Sepulchre has some two thousand members worldwide.

THE SECRET CITY OF DAMANHUR

Some secret societies are not quite so public and will go to great lengths to protect their anonymity, as was the case with the nameless group of Italian esotericists who created the amazing subterranean community of Damanhur.

Bruno Tinti, district attorney of the northern Italian city of Ivrea, scoffed initially at reports of a lost and magical city in the Piedmont foothills. In a country racked by extremist terrorism, Tinti took no chances: he promptly dispatched a regiment of *carabinieri*, who would later confirm the city's existence. Not far from the town of Baldissero Canavavese, near Turin, a secret entrance leads to the thirty-meter depth where the occult community of Damanhur thrives.

Tucked away in a seemingly endless maze of temples, labyrinths, and meeting halls, decorated with Egyptian and esoteric symbols, Damanhur boasts inordinate wealth: the floors and walls of its chambers are covered in marble, gold, mosaics and mirrors worthy of the grandest European palaces.

Founded in 1975 by Oberto Airuldi, the activities which led to the creation of the subterranean city of Damanhur were financed by the 300 members of Damanhur's Council of Elders—captains of industry and commerce whose activities net them a combined annual income of over $8 million dollars. Damanhur is a fully independent state, with its own government, constitution and minted coinage. Although its inhabitants resented the intrusion of the police authorities, the residents of the subterranean city of Damanhur are reportedly secretly pleased that word of their hidden city has reached the outside world. •

—*Winter 2002*

Jesus the Globetrotter

The Myth of the Mysterious "Lost Years"

by Acharya S

The following article sheds light on the infamous "lost years" of Jesus, during which he is rumored to have studied, sired children, and spent his post-crucifixion years in such places as India, Britain, and Japan. Although supposedly authentic "scrolls," housed in monasteries in Tibet and presumably written just after the crucifixion, pronounce that Jesus lived and studied there as "Issa," Acharya tells us that nothing could have been written in the Tibetan language prior to the seventh century. Acharya declares these documents to be Buddhist propaganda which attempted to demonstrate that Jesus was a student of the Buddha. As she explains, the real reason for the gap in Jesus's biography is because he was not a "real person" but a pagan sun god turned into a Jewish messiah.

OVER THE CENTURIES, the claim has been made repeatedly that Jesus Christ walked the Earth and spent his early and post-crucifixion years in a variety of places, including Egypt, India, Great Britain, Japan, and America. Indeed, traditions maintain that Jesus, the great godman of the West, lived, learned, loved, and died in such places.

Popular modern literature also purports that Jesus sired children, who then became the ancestors of various royal families of Europe, an allegation extremely convenient and useful for European royal families. Unfortunately for the European claimants, however, India also has a tradition that Jesus went *there* and likewise fathered children. So too does Shingo, Japan, allege that Jesus ended up *there* after the crucifixion, having children with a Japanese wife. Other tales depict Jesus "walking the Americas" or bopping about Glastonbury, England, with his "uncle," Joseph of Arimathea. Not all of these tales can be true, obviously, unless Jesus is polymorphous and phantasmagoric, a perspective that represents that of the mythologist or mythicist. Regardless of these fables, or, rather, *because of them*, the most reasonable conclusion regarding Jesus the Globe-trotter is that he is a mythical character, not a historical person.

THE GROOVY GURU

According to legend, Jesus, the great Jewish sage, spent his "lost years" (from age 12 to 28 or 30) in India, where he lived after surviving the crucifixion. The Jesus-was-a-guru tale was popularized more than a century ago by the Russian traveler Nicholas Notovitch, who asserted that in 1887, while at the secluded Himis monastery in Tibet, he was shown a manuscript which discussed the "unknown life" of Jesus, or "Issa," as he was supposedly called in the East. This Issa text, translated for Notovitch from Tibetan by a monk, alleged that during his "lost years" Jesus was educated by yogis in India, Nepal and "the Himalaya Mountains."

Stating that he felt the manuscript to be "true and genuine," Notovich maintained that its contents were written "immediately after the resurrection," while the manuscript itself purportedly dated from the third century C.E. Notovitch related that the "two manuscripts" he was shown at Himis were "compiled from diverse copies written in the Tibetan tongue, translated from rolls belonging to the Lhasa library and brought from India, Nepal, and Maghada two hundred years after Christ." (Notovitch, 44)

Notovitch's story was challenged by a number of people, which served to popularize it further. Noted Sanskrit scholar Max Muller came down hard on Notovitch, concluding that the Russian had either never gone to Tibet in the first place and had concocted the Jesus story, or that he had been fooled by waggish Buddhist monks. Others subsequently journeyed to Himis/Hemis and witnessed repeated denial by the lamas that Notovitch had ever been there or that any such manuscript existed.

On the other hand, in 1922, Indian scholar and swami Abhenanda eventually gained the confidence of the lamas at Himis, who revealed the manuscript to him. Other visitors to Himis, such as mystic Nicholas Roerich, verified this story. Aspects of Notovitch's story checked out, and he apparently did indeed stay at Himis and was shown a manuscript relating to Issa.

Notovitch claimed that Indian merchants brought the account of "Jesus" to Himis, and that they had actually witnessed the crucifixion. Indeed, the text begins, "This is what is related on this subject by the merchants who come from Israel," reflecting not that Jesus lived in India but that the Jesus *tradition* was brought to India and Tibet. (Notovitch, 32) Notovitch's text also did not state that Jesus was specifically at Himis. In fact, the lama stated that the Issa scrolls "were brought from India to Nepal, and from Nepal to Tibet." Through later visitors the story eventually morphed into "Your Jesus was here," in person at Himis. The "one book" or "two manuscripts" became "three books," which were displayed for later visitors, implying there was more to the tale.

Although subsequent visitors were presented such texts, none but Nicholas Roerich's son, George, could read them. By his translation, Nicholas Roerich was evidently shown the same text as Notovitch. Thus, it appears that there was only one text and it did not state that Issa himself was ever at the monastery. Furthermore, the text is based on hearsay provided by passing merchants and does not at all represent an eyewitness account of Jesus in India and Tibet, although the impression is given that this and other texts do constitute such records.

Also, Notovitch asked if Issa was reputed to be a saint, and was informed that "the people ignore his very existence" and that the lamas who have studied the scrolls "alone know of him." These remarks are a far cry from Roerich's claim that the tale of Christ in India and other parts of Asia was to be found widespread. They also contradict the Tibetan text's assertion that Issa's "fame spread everywhere" and that Persia and surrounding countries "resounded with prophecies" of Issa, causing the Persian priesthood to be terrified of him. This latter element sounds like typical mythmaking, especially since there were similar prophecies of godmen for centuries, if not millennia, prior to Christ's purported advent, particularly in India.

Moreover, the "originals" of the scrolls housed at the Tibetan capital, Lhasa, were composed in Pali, while the Himis library contained one copy in Tibetan. Yet, the Tibetan alphabet was developed by the king who "reigned in the days of Mohammed"; hence, nothing could have been written in Tibetan prior to the seventh century. Although older texts were composed in Sanskrit or Pali, it is clear that the actual physical manuscript revealed to Notovitch could not have existed before the seventh century. In fact, it would appear that very few Tibetan texts are dated prior to the ninth century. In any event, the manuscript itself certainly did *not* date from the third century, although it could represent tradition transmitted over the centuries.

While Notovitch claimed the Issa story dated to shortly after "the Resurrection," in it there is no mention of the resurrection, and the tale ends with Issa's death. In this regard, the text depicts the Jews, whom it calls "Israelites," in a favorable light, and is "the only [manuscript] ever to charge the Romans ["pagans"] solely for Jesus's execution." Unlike others, this account does not have Jesus being resuscitated and then returning to India, to father children and live a long life.

Notovitch's modern editor, Frank Muccie, relates that the manuscript states, "Pilate is responsible for removing Jesus's body from the tomb," noting that this development somehow does not "mean the resurrection hope is invalid." He then says:

> By the third century A.D., there were no fewer than twenty-five different versions of Jesus's death and resurrection! Some have him not being put to death at all, some have him revived back to life, and some have Jesus living on to old age and dying in Egypt! (Notovitch, 6)

THE MANY TOMBS OF JESUS

Obviously, not all of these twenty-five or more accounts can be "true and genuine," which casts doubt on the authenticity of one and all. It is interesting that Notovitch spent six days in the Vale of Kashmir, in its summer capital, Srinagar, "city of the sun," where the purported tomb of Jesus, the wandering prophet Yuz Asaf, is shown to tourists. Yet, the Russian traveler apparently never heard of the tomb, known as the Roza Bal or Rauzabal shrine, as he does not mention it in his writings concerning the Tibetan text, where its inclusion certainly would have been judicious in demonstrating that Jesus lived in India! Perhaps, however, as a believing Christian, Notovitch ignored this tale, much as the devout do today and much as skeptics may do with other fables concerning Christ.

Possessing the priestly touch of sculpted footprints "with nail marks" over the grave, the Roza Bal shrine may seem convincing to the uninitiated, who are unaware of the world's well-developed priestcraft. This "artifact" is another in a long line of so-called relics, like the twenty-plus shrouds or the multiple foreskins of Christ. In reality, there were many "footprints of the gods" in ancient times—and a number of Indian gods are depicted with nail holes in their feet.

Also, Yuz Asaf is not equivalent to Jesus but to Joseph, which was often a title of a priest and not a name. In fact, Eastern scholars, such as Dr. S. Radhakrishnan, state that the name Joseph or Joasaph is "derived from Bodhisattva, the technical name for one destined to obtain the dignity of a Buddha." (Prajnanananda, 107) Thus, this tomb of a Bodhisattva could belong to any of thousands of such holy men. In like regard, the purported graves of Jesus and his brother in Japan are in reality those of a sixteenth century Christian missionary and his brother.

The legends regarding Jesus's tomb in Srinagar, and that of the Virgin Mary in Kashgar, are apparently of Islamic origin. Such a creation would serve a couple of purposes: that, as asserted in the Koran, Jesus was not the "son of God" but a mortal prophet, whose body was buried in Kashmir, and that some presumably Moslem people are his descendants.

BUDDHIST PROPAGANDA

Proponents of the Jesus-in-India theory hold up a number of texts and artifacts which they maintain "prove" Jesus's existence on Earth and his presence in India. When such texts and artifacts are closely examined, they serve as no evidence at all, except of priestcraft. With one or two possible exceptions originating a few centuries earlier, the eastern texts regarding Issa seem to be late writings, some dating from the fifteenth and eighteenth centuries, based on traditions, not eyewitness accounts. Some of the "documents" are obviously fictitious, and others are downright ridiculous, such as the Bhavishya Mahapurana. A number of these texts merely relate the basic gospel story with embellishments depending on what the storyteller is attempting to accomplish.

Although some of the writings appear to be of Hindu origin, Notovitch's story of Issa seems to represent Buddhist propaganda. It appears that Buddhists were trying to demonstrate that Jesus, the great wise man of the West, was influenced by Buddhism, even having been taught by Buddha, an eternal disincarnate entity. In this regard, the Notovitch text states, "Six years later, Issa, whom the Buddha had chosen to spread his holy word, could perfectly explain the sacred rolls." (Notovitch, 35) In this way, Buddha usurps Jesus, becoming the Jewish teacher's guru.

That the text has been used as propaganda to raise Buddha and Buddhism over Christ and Christianity is further validated by Notovitch's foreword, in which he relates that the lama told him, "The only error of the Christians is that after adopting the great doctrine of Buddha, they, at the very outset, completely separated themselves from him and created another Dalai Lama." This "Dalai Lama," the monk subsequently informed the Russian, is the Pope. Concerning Christ, the lama continued, "Buddha did, indeed, incarnate himself with his intelligence in the sacred person of Issa, who, without the aid of fire and sword, went forth to propagate our great and true religion through the entire world." (Notovitch, 20) Hence, eastern traditions regarding Jesus are designed to show that Jesus is Buddha and that Christianity is an offshoot of ancient Eastern wisdom.

Nevertheless, the Notovitch text itself may have been composed originally by proselytizing Christians who attempted to use the natives' belief in Buddha to increase Christ's stature. These missionaries may have been appealing to women to follow Issa, as the text puts great emphasis on women, whose status in India has been abysmally low. The text would also appeal to the Sudra or Pariah groups in India, since it has Issa preaching on their behalf. To this day, these groups are targeted by Christian missionaries in India.

Considering that many missionaries, travelers, and scholars have been keenly aware of the numerous and profound similarities between the Tibetan and Catholic religions, it would not be surprising if the Issa fable were created in order to show that the Tibetan religion is merely a foreign derivative of the "true universal religion," i.e., Catholicism. The resemblances between various Indian sects and Christianity likewise led to tales about the Christian missionaries Thomas, Bartholomew, and Pantaenus proselytizing in India. Like the Jesus-in-India myth, there are other explanations for such resemblances, which are addressed in detail in my book *Suns of God: Krishna, Buddha and Christ Unveiled*, the strongest one being that the Christian religion and savior were already in India long before the alleged advent of Jesus.

By calling Issa Jesus or Christ, modern writers have cemented in readers' minds that the correlation is absolute—an erroneous conclusion. In reality, the name "Issa," "Isa" or "Isha" is a title and simply means "lord," "god" or "master," often referring to the Indian god Lord Shiva: " 'Isha' or 'the Lord' is another name of Siva." (Prajnananda, 19) Furthermore, Professor Nunos de Santos says, "a god variously named Issa, Isha, Ichtos, Iesus, Ieshuah, Joshuah, Jesus, etc., is indisputably originally from India." He also states, "Ishvara (Ishwar) is widely worshipped in the Far East, being also called Isha (or Ishana) in India, Issara in Pali, Isuan in Thai, Jizu (or Jizai) in Japanese, and so on."

Isa is likewise another name for Chandra, the Indian moon god, as well as for Shiva's Egyptian counterpart, the soli-lunar god Osiris, also called Iswara in India:

Iswara, or Isa, and Isani, or Isisi, are . . . unquestionably the Osiris and Isis of Egypt. Iswara, Siva, or Hara (for these are his names among nearly a thousand more) united with Isi, represent the secondary causes, whatever they may be, of natural phenomena; and principally those of temporary destruction and regeneration. (Moor, 151)

Numerous ancient legends, recorded for example in the writings of Diodorus Siculus during the first century B.C.E., depict Osiris as traveling all over the East, as well as the rest of the world, during the millennia when he reigned as Egypt's favorite deity. Osiris, or Isa, it should be noted, was put to death and resurrected, among many other correspondences to the Christ myth. Osiris/Isa too had a number of tombs in various places, especially in Egypt but likely also in India. However, Osiris was not a real person but a fertility and sun god. Mythologists recognize that it was not an historical Osiris but his myth that made it to India and diverse places. As in the case of Osiris, the same phenomenon occurred regarding Jesus, who is, in the end, a remake of Osiris, among others.

The title "Isa" or "Issa" could apply to others, and is a common name even today. Indeed, some part of these Jesus-in-India tales may revolve around the famed Greek sage Apollonius of Tyana. Not a few persons over the centuries have noted the similarities between the lives of Apollonius and Christ, and even in ancient times Christians were accused of plagiarizing the Apollonius legend.

THE BODHISATTVAS

The Issa myth apparently represents a christianization of legends regarding Osiris, Shiva, Apollonius, and other gods and Bodhisattvas, by the Nestorians, an early Christian sect who lived in India and elsewhere, and may well have spread the fable to other Asian ports of call. Indeed, Nicholas Roerich surmised that the ancient Nestorian sect spread the tales in the East:

We heard several versions of this legend which has spread widely through Ladak, Sinkiang and Mongolia, but all versions agree on one point, that during His absence, Christ was in India and Asia. . . . Perhaps [this legend] is of Nestorian origin. (Prophet, 261)

Roerich also stated, "Whoever doubts too completely that such legends about the Christ life exist in Asia, probably does not realize what an immense influence the Nestorians have had in all parts of Asia and how many so-called apocryphal legends they spread in the most ancient times." (Roerich, 89) In addition, George Roerich even proposed that there was a "floating colony" of Nestorians in Ladakh itself "during the eighth to tenth centuries," which could well be when the Notovitch text was composed. Roerich, one of the main writers whose works have led to the Jesus-in-India theory, almost invariably and misleadingly substitutes "Jesus" or "Christ" for "Issa," when Issa could be a number of individuals, mythical and historical.

Roerich further declared, "The teachings of India were famed far and wide; let us even recall the description of the life of Appolonius [sic] of Tyana and his visits to Hindu sages." (Roerich, 119) Again, one likely scenario regarding the title "Issa" ("lord" or "master") is that, whatever part of his tale is "historical," it refers to the Greek sage Apollonius.

As is well known, Apollonius was not alone in his journeys to the East. Decades and centuries prior to the Christian era there was much travel between India and the West, including the famous journey by Pythagoras and the Alexandrian incursion. Another pertinent example: one of the sects of Mandeanism, a Christian baptist sect, was Maisan, a Mesopotamian city colonized by Indians. As Dr. Rudolph Otto relates:

> Indian caravans passed through Maisan and likewise Nabatea. Indian merchants, wherever they went, were importers and missionaries of Indian ideas. There need be no surprise therefore if direct Indian imports are found in the syncretistic medley of Mandean Gnosis. (Prajnanananda, 41)

Space does not permit us to recount the numerous authorities who are in agreement as to the westward spread of Indian and Buddhist concepts centuries before and into the Christian era. A number of them may be found in Prajnanananda's book, including a "Mr. Cust," who offered evidence that trade between Indian and Yemen "was established not later than 1000 B.C." Yemen is very close to Israel, and by the first century C.E. there were plenty of Indians in the Roman Empire.

Despite the popularity of the Jesus-in-India tale, the claim is not accepted by mainstream authorities, either Christian or secular. The tale's proponents assert that scholars reject Jesus in India because of Western imperialism's inability to accept that Christ could have been influenced by Buddhism. In the case of mythicists, the reason Jesus's visit to India is denied is because he is a pagan sun god remade into a Jewish "human" messiah. Thus, it is not a question of a historical Jesus being in India and the East, but of a variety of solar cults that worshipped a similar deity with similar rituals, doctrines and myths.

JESUS THE DRUID

Another nation in which the native sun god was usurped by the Jewish son of god was Britain, where ancient Druidism was likewise appropriated by later Christianity. While the Indian theory asserts the Jewish sage spent his entire early years there, the British tale of Jesus has him travelling in his youth to Glastonbury in order to learn from the Druids.

As the story goes, many of the tin miners in Britain at the time of Jesus's alleged advent were Jewish, which is sensible since British tin mining was highly valued by the Jews' Phoenician predecessors and cousins. One such miner was purportedly Jesus's "uncle," Joseph of Arimathea, who, along with Jesus, allegedly founded the first Christian church at Glastonbury. Certainly there were Jews in England at the time of Jesus's supposed existence, as they were diffused throughout much of the world. However, the fact that Glastonbury was a "great pagan sanctuary" in pre-Christian times makes this story suspicious as myth-making and propaganda.

Among other things, Glastonbury was purportedly the seat of the Holy Grail or sacred chalice, a pre-Christian concept, and has been equated with the mythical pagan paradise Avalon. Legend holds that St. Patrick died in Glastonbury around 472 C.E. However, since it is evident that "St. Patrick" is an ancient Irish god turned into a Christian saint, it would seem that the apocryphal Holy Grail story points to the approximate date that Christianity began to circulate in England, "killing" the pagan gods.

The Glastonbury legends further hold that King Arthur and Queen Guinevere were buried there, and that Arthur and the Knights of the Round Table were descended from Joseph of Arimathea. The Glastonbury tales appear to have been created in order to give King Arthur Jewish ancestry and a divine pedigree as a descendant of King David, bestowing upon the British kings the divine right to rule as true Israelites. Indeed, one of the Jesus-in-Britain proponents, devout Christian-British Israelite, E. Raymond Capt, writes about the presence of both Jesus and Paul in Britain, and discusses the "remarkable prediction of Britain's glorious inheritance." Thus, the legend serves to establish British supremacy, as Great Britain is destined to inherit the biblical promise of God's kingdom on Earth to the descendants of the "lost tribes," the true sheep of Israel.

Adding to this notion, it was asserted that Mary's mother, Ann, lived in Glastonbury, and that Mary herself was buried there. After Christ's death, the story goes, Joseph was accompanied by Mary, the risen Lazarus and his sisters, Mary Magdalene, and a number of other "saints." Unluckily for the Mary-in-Britain fable, other legends place her burial in Kashmir, as noted, and in Bethlehem, Ephesus, and Gethsemane. Naturally, logic would dictate that were Mary a real person, she would not be buried in more than one place. The reason why Mary appears all over is that she is the ubiquitous ancient Goddess turned into a Jewish maiden.

Concerning the British gods, Capt states that the druidic trinity was composed of three "Beli" (cf. the Semitic Baal, Bal or Bel). Interestingly, "Yesu" (also "Hesus") was the name of the Druid "coming Saviour of the future." (Capt, 9, 10) Capt then naively remarks, "Druidism thus anticipated Christianity and pointed to the coming Saviour under the very name by which Christ was called." In reality, Christianity copied and incorporated countless elements of numerous religions within the Roman Empire and beyond. Moreover, per the Catholic missionary Huc, who traversed India, Tibet, and other parts of Asia, "Yesu" was also a name of the expected avatar of the Hindu god Vishnu, of which Krishna was an avatar.

The druidic inhabitants of Glastonbury Lake Village were highly-skilled woodworkers and carpenters; hence, their god was a woodworker and carpenter named Yesu/Esus/Hesus, long prior to the Christian era. When one understands the brotherhood and its priestcraft, it is not surprising that Jews who purportedly lived in the very heart of druidism— the fabled Avalon itself—and who would know about the future Druid savior and other doctrines, would return from Palestine with tales that "the" Messiah by that very name had been born in Judea.

In addition, the first "church" at Glastonbury was supposedly "circular . . . with the twelve huts of the other disciples forming a circle around it." (Capt, 42) Many Pagan temples had a similar astrological blueprint, i.e., the circle of the Zodiac, and it is clear that Glastonbury's sanctuary was appropriated by the mythical Christ and fictive Twelve, as the original Druid church was likely founded in the name of their patron carpenter god, Yesu/Hesus, long prior to the alleged advent of the Jewish savior. Indeed, Christianity is but a Judaized rehash of paganism, with the astrotheological pagan gods turned into the Jewish son of god, his disciples and a slew of saints. Ergo the tales of Glastonbury and elsewhere.

The reason for all this apparent chicanery can be summed up by Capt's words: "There can be no doubt that the Glastonbury Abbey is the oldest, continuous Christian foundation in the world." As we have seen, and would continue to see in *The Christ Conspiracy, Suns of God* and other books, this claim of primacy is commonplace and has at its foundation not the historical truth but a powerful political and economic agenda. In actuality, scholars have repeatedly discredited traditions regarding Jesus and Joseph in Glastonbury as having been devised in the twelfth century by monks trying to entice pilgrims and their tourist money. (Capt, 107)

The Glastonbury myth was apparently created in order to establish the supremacy of the church at Glastonbury, as well as to explain why Jesus and his purported teachings were so similar to the gods and doctrines of the Druids. The Druids in turn supposedly received their instruction from Pythagoras, who himself had traveled to India. Since the druidic and Vedic priesthoods, language and culture are one at root, separating perhaps three millennia prior to the Christian era (Ellis), it does not surprise us that Jesus legends are found in both India and Britain. In fact, such a godman and doctrines already existed in Britain for centuries, if not millennia, prior to the Christian era. By having Jesus and/or Paul establish a church in what is "the center of the druidic faith in Britain," the Jewish/Israelite version of the tale thus usurped the native religion. Also, druidism was a thorn in the side of the Romans, who could not totally rule Britain so long as it existed; hence, it would benefit the eventual Roman Church to have their supposed founder personally consecrate Britain.

THE "LOST YEARS" ARE ASTRO-THEOLOGICAL

Over the centuries, Jesus's so-called "lost years" and post-crucifixion life have provided much fodder for the fertile human imagination, leading to speculation, legends, traditions, and myths that the great godman and sage lived and studied in a variety of places. Once the fable of Christ became popular, numerous towns, villages, cities, and nations wished to establish some sort of connection.

Instead of recognizing that such a significant omission as Jesus's "lost years" is an indication of the mythical nature of the tale, individuals using typical priestcraft have come up with countless extraordinary adventures of the historical Jesus. Unfortunately for believers, the gospel story itself and the Jesus-the-Globetrotter tales are smoke and mirrors. The reason for the gap in Jesus's biography is because he was not a "real person" but a pagan sun god turned into a Jewish messiah. In the mythos revolving around the sun god, there need be no accounting for "lost years," as the "age" of twelve represents the sun at high noon, while the "ages" of twenty-eight or thirty represents the days of the lunar or solar months, respectively.

When religions are investigated with a knowledge of mythology, the profound correspondences are clearly revealed. It becomes evident that it is not the case that this miracle-worker or that godman traveled to this place or that, but it is the legends, traditions, and myths concerning these gods, godmen, or gurus that have been spread far and wide by their proponents, priests, and propagandists. As was the case with the missionary and his brother in Japan, who were taken for the object of worship they were proselytizing, so has it developed in other parts of the world over the millennia concerning Jesus and other deities, such as the virgin-born, crucified Mexican god Quetzalcoatl, whose similar life and religion led to claims that Jesus was in America. The reason for the similarities, however, is because both Jesus and Quetzalcoatl are sun gods with the same attendant holidays and practices.

In the final analysis, it is not possible that Jesus could have lived years after the crucifixion, fathered children and died in several different places, as legends represent. One explanation for such discrepancies has been metaphysical, deeming Jesus to be multidimensional and capable of simultaneous incarnations in various locations. Such an explanation, of course, will not satisfy the skeptic, scientist, or mythologist. Because the basic story of Christ revolves around the sun, which was highly esteemed the world over beginning many millennia ago, the myth is likewise found around the globe. To the basic mythos and ritual were added various embellishments according to the place and era.

In the end, Jesus the Globetrotter is not a historical personage who magically appeared all over the world, appearing in two places at once and flying on the backs of birds. Jesus Christ is a mythical creature who is found globally only between the pages of a book. ●

References

Capt, E. Raymond. *The Traditions of Glastonbury*. Muskogee, OK: Artisan, 1983.

Ellis, Peter B. "Our Druid Cousins," www.hinduism-today.com/2000/2/2000-2-16.html.

Huc, M. L'Abbé, *Christianity in China, Tartary, and Thibet*, Vol. I. London, Longman & Co., 1857.

Moor, Edward, Simpson, ed. *The Hindu Pantheon*. India: Indological Book House, 1968.

Notovitch, Nicholas. *The Unknown Life of Jesus Christ*. Tree of Life Publications, Simi Valley, California: 1980.

Nunos de Santos, Arysio. "The Unknown Life of Jesus Christ—Comments," www.rickrichards.com/jc/JesusComment2.html.

Prajnanananda, Swami. *Christ the Saviour and the Christ Myth*. Calcutta: Ramakrishna Vedanta Math, 1984.

Prophet, Elizabeth Clare. *The Lost Years of Jesus*. Summit University Press, Corwin Springs, MT: 1984.

Roerich, Nicholas. *Altai-Himalaya*. Kempton, IL: Adventures Unlimited, 2001.

—Spring 2003

Unholy Alliance: Nazis and the Occult
Peter Levenda interviewed by Tracy Twyman

What draws occultists into the dark world of spying and espionage? Peter Levenda, author of Unholy Alliance: Nazis and the Occult, *talks to Tracy Twyman about the links between the political and the magical. Learn how occultism, esoteric beliefs and secret societies influenced many Nazi leaders, and how Nazi occultism survived World War II and continues to be a dangerous influence in the present day.*

TRACY TWYMAN: Your book is about how occultism, esoteric beliefs and secret societies inspired many of the leading figures in the Nazi party. You also detail how several people in the upper echelons of the Golden Dawn and the OTO were involved in espionage: Karl Germer and Theodor Reuss for German Intelligence, and Crowley for the British. And certainly we know that a number of occult societies throughout history, such as the Bavarian Illuminati, various Masonic sects, the Knights of Malta, and the Templars, have been involved in espionage and political revolution. What do you think draws occultists into the field of spying and revolutionary activities?

PETER LEVENDA: Secret knowledge. The illusion of secret power. The man or woman who walks among us, ordinary and unremarkable, who is in reality a Magister Templi or a colonel in the KGB. It's the same attraction that comic book heroes hold for preadolescents. On a deeper level, I think that many people—intelligent people—resent having to obey authority. Openly resisting authority is usually a cause for arrest and torture, if not execution, in many countries. Secretly resisting authority, however, has its charms. One stays alive, and one resists. One has one's cake and eats it.

In the case of spiritual authority, an intelligent person cannot stomach that a black-robed eunuch with a wine-red nose would have some kind of direct connection with God, unobtainable by ordinary folk. The intelligent person wants to talk to God directly, and not to have to take direction from a tired old priest or minister. That person, through the act of contacting higher powers or forces on his or her own, becomes a kind of anti-priest, and thus a cult is born.

Conspiracies are a fact of life. Add God or occult powers into the mix—of politics, espionage, coups d'état—and you have an irresistible mix for a certain type of person. We all feel there is a mystery at the heart of reality. The spy and the occultist live at the periphery of this elemental, Ur-mystery. It has to do with authority, king, and reality.

The very word "reality" comes from the same root as "royal": reality was whatever the king said it was. "Real estate" was the kingdom; outside the kingdom, there was no king and, hence, no reality. To challenge the king, one had to be from beyond the border of the kingdom: one had to be in communion with non-real forces; one had to represent the anti-king. Spies and occultists live among us, but have loyalties elsewhere. There is a certain attraction to that, and a certain danger.

TT: Are politics and magic inseparably linked? Have politicians and political movements always used subliminal occult messages and archetypes to manipulate public consciousness for or against the prevailing power structure? Are political struggles basically magic wars, with power structures kept intact by magical means?

PL: In other words, to paraphrase Clausewitz, is magic a continuation of politics by other means? It depends on your definition of magic. Is it, as Crowley would have it, the "science and art of causing change to occur in conformity with will"? Then, yes. But, under those guidelines, so is selling used cars. We need a sharper definition of what we mean by magic. It also depends on whether or not you subscribe to the conspiracy theory of the day, I suppose. If real power is in the hands of a few secret people who pull strings behind the scenes, then politics as we know it does not exist. The will of the people, the voting booth, the mudslinging; in the end they come to naught because the boys in the back room will decide who gets elected. But if you define political power as the ability to move and mold masses of people, then you have a chance at proving the thesis that political wars are magic wars.

The key to this thesis would be, in my point of view, propaganda.

Propaganda is the use and manipulation of symbols. Whoever does it best is the better magician, and will probably win the "war." But the symbols of the political arena, especially in the United States, are not as sublime as we find in the occult symbol system. The political symbols are taken from the environment, from the times—the zeitgeist, if you will. No one actually goes around waving the tattvic symbols or the tarot deck during a political campaign; the manipulation goes in different channels. I think political wars are analogous to magic wars, but I don't think they are necessarily one and the same. A magician does not need a crowd to effect his or her will. A magician operates, like our spies, secretly, and manipulates forces of nature (or supernature) rather than directly massaging the psyches of people.

We are also in danger of considering all subliminal messages as occult messages. There may be some justification in this, in that any subliminal message probably has its occult analogue, but when you compare a run-off election in Iowa with what Hitler was doing at Nuremberg, you are comparing apples and oranges. Hitler was upfront about what he was doing; the symbolism was deliberately occult, pagan, anti-Christian, anti-Semitic. In fact, he was openly using ritual. Most of our popular politicians today would be unable and unwilling to do this, since virtually any public use of ritual for political ends would be considered cryptofascist.

King Arthur had Merlin for that. It was a separate department in his government, if you see what I mean. I believe that the CIA—specifically the boys at MK-ULTRA—came close to becoming our very own, home-grown version of Merlin, but I don't think Harry Truman was a black magician himself.

TT: In *Unholy Alliance*, you suggest that the Friekorps assassination of Foreign Minister Walther Rathau in June 1922, on the eve of the summer solstice, was a human sacrifice to the sun god Wotan. Do you think that in a larger sense the elimination of six million Jews could be considered one giant pagan sacrifice?

PL: We can consider the Holocaust a kind of pagan sacrifice, but more importantly I think it was something far more sinister than that. You don't sacrifice what you despise; you sacrifice something of value. Rathau, although Jewish, was considered an exemplary human being even by his executioners, and thus a fitting sacrifice. After all, he was an important element of Germany's war machine during the First World

War and had a lot to offer post-War Germany. His was a true sacrifice. But, the Holocaust? In the Nazi view, the slaughter of the Jews, Gypsies, homosexuals, and communists was designed to purify the planet of diseased blood and diseased spirit. That is why it kept going until the very end, regardless of the cost and regardless of the fact that the resources being used to keep the camps running could have been better utilized defending Berlin. It was not so much a sacrifice as a purification of the soil. The Nazis believed that the Jews and their fellow travelers were actual representatives of an evil force on Earth and had to be destroyed, at any cost. If this race disappeared, the Nazis felt that they had done the planet and its surviving human members a favor and would be remembered forever for their contribution.

TT: You state that Hitler himself did not perform any magical rituals, but had others do so on his behalf. But what about the rumors to the contrary? In the notes to your book, you dismiss Trevor Ravenscroft's book, *Spear of Destiny*, and its "wild tales of Hitler attending séances with Dietrich Eckart." But what makes you so sure? Also, Fred Berger of *Propaganda* magazine once published an article claiming that Hitler had gone to see the opera *Parsival* in 1909 while on peyote, and had "fallen to a transcendental state in which he perceived that he was the reincarnation of the evil black magician Klingsor," the bad guy in Wagner's opera. Any comment as to the veracity of this claim?

PL: I dispute this because there is simply no evidence for it. I feel that Hitler was more or less as I portrayed him in my book: Not a joiner, not someone who could sit still for long, waiting for the table to tip or a ghost to materialize. Hitler makes more sense as an unconscious medium, one being used by other magicians, than as a practicing occultist himself. The stories of his taking peyote and attending séances are all without substantiation, so far. I tried to document everything thoroughly, based as much as possible on primary sources (the Captured German Records section at the National Archives; the Rehse Collection at the Library of Congress), so that I would be immune from charges that I was "channeling" the information. In fact, using the primary sources, I came up with far more craziness than I could fit into *Unholy Alliance*. Avon cut my appendices, for instance, which would have contained more reference material. They wanted to cut the bibliography and index, as well, but I fought it.

TT: Why do you think the Nazis spent so much effort persecuting pagans and occult orders? Was it part of an attempt to placate the Catholic Church, or were they just eliminating competition? Were they afraid of the magical powers of these other occult orders?

PL: They were eliminating competition. Also, remember that the occult groups were a potential fifth column inside Germany. They had their own means of communication and contacts all over Europe. They had roots going back many years in many countries. They were indeed a threat. I believe that the United States has felt the same way.

TT: Why do you think the swastika specifically was chosen as the Nazi insignia? I know that their ideology was heavily influenced by theosophy, and the swastika was one of Blavatsky's favorite symbols. But what exactly was its significance to the Nazis? It gives one the impression of aggression and power, and I know that Crowley, in his book *Gematria*, describes the swastika as containing seventeen squares, and in a later chapter says of the number seventeen, "Here is a magic disc for me to hurl, and to win heaven by violence."

PL: I cover this in *Unholy Alliance*. The swastika was a popular symbol in Germany before the Nazis appropriated it. In fact, it was used by troops during World War I as a kind of talisman. The Germans clearly felt it had racial connections, and was more representative of their people than the Christian cross. Remember, too, that the Nazis idolized Tibet and the cults of northern India. The so-called Aryan race would have had its origins there, and India, Nepal, Bhutan, and Tibet are replete with swastika motifs. I live in Asia, and the swastika is everywhere out here, on Buddhist, Taoist, and Hindu temples alike. It represents, specifically, "auspiciousness," but is also taken to symbolize a kind of polar energy in the universe. A spinning sun disk, but also a deeper, more mysterious analog since the sun does not spin in two directions but the swastika does.

TT: You write that Guido von List borrowed the Golden Dawn's system of degrees, based on the Tree of Life, for use in his own *völkish*, anti-Semitic pagan order, the Armanenschaft, and that he might have gotten the information from a Golden Dawn initiate named D.R. Felkein, or from OTO initiate Rudolf Steiner. You write "That List would have based his hierarchy on the patently Jewish Tree of Life and borrowed the concept from the Golden Dawn—by way of the OTO—would seem merely ironic to a lay person, but positively frightening to an occultist, for what it implies about the relationship between the anti-Semitic List organizations and the ostensibly apolitical Golden Dawn and OTO lodges." So what is that implication, exactly?

PL: The implication is that the Blavatskian notion of a racial hierarchy—root races and all that—would have found a sinister manifestation in a proto-Nazi occult movement; that the Golden Dawn and OTO themselves might have been fellow travelers; that a spiritual hierarchy might imply a racial one; and that a magical war might develop into genocide.

TT: From my understanding, the Nazi idea of the Overman entailed much more that just increased physical strength and intellectual prowess. It was a creature whose ajna faculties (psychic powers associated with the Third Eye) had been fully developed. It entailed a creature more in touch with his higher self, a creature more advanced spiritually. What do you think men like Sebetondorf, Liebenfels, List, and Eckart imagined when they talked about the Overman? Did they imagine the Aryan race evolving into something with an entirely different physical appearance?

PL: Yes, the Overman was not merely a "superman," as it has been often erroneously translated. It was the next level of human evolution. As Hitler himself said, anyone who thinks that National Socialism is merely a political party had better think again: The goal is to create the New Man. I believe he meant that literally. Otherwise, why the Holocaust? Why the Lebensborn organization? Why the documented racial purity of prospective SS members? Germany was a laboratory where Hitler would create his homonculus. To the Nazis, this meant a human being that was above compassion, above sentiment, passionate in his ideals and self-image, but without conscience in comparison to the rest of us. A sociopath, probably. Intelligent, strong, perfectly proportioned. And a remorseless killer. Not exactly ET.

TT: You've mentioned that many of these Nazi occultists believed in the theosophical concept of ascended masters and secret chiefs. I know that Blavatsky believed them to reside in the Himalayas, while the Thulists deposited them underground, in a subterranean vault accessible by a tunnel which opens up in the North Pole. But is it possible that some of these people believed that the ascended masters were extraterrestrials or transdimensional beings? I know that the Nazis were suspected of conducting experiments with flying saucers, time travel and multiple dimensions, so it made me wonder.

PL: I think that recent neo-Nazi authors are toying with this idea, most notably Miguel Serrano in Chile. Crowley and his followers certainly hold these views—see the works by Kenneth Grant, for instance. The Nazis themselves? Well, going through their canon is a bit tedious, but I am sure the resourceful researcher could uncover the odd reference to an extraterrestrial abode for their secret chiefs. At that time, space opera was not nearly the advanced art form it is today and flying saucers were not yet the vogue, although the foo fighters had already made an appearance, as did the mysterious flying ships of the turn of the century. I think the Nazis understood the masters to be a kind of god force, like Odin or Thor. Horbiger was coming close to an extraterrestrial theory as he developed his World Ice concept, but it had little to do with the secret chiefs. I have not found documentation to show that the Nazis had a developed theory about the nature of the chiefs, and I have found very little support for an extraterrestrial theory of any kind among the Nazis so far. I am aware of the idea that they were working on a saucer or some kind of space ship, but that does not imply that they held significant alien life theories beyond those of a purely speculative nature.

TT: Please explain the World Ice theory, if you would. It makes no sense to me.

PL: Makes no sense to me either. The idea is that the basic building blocks of the universe are ice crystals, and that temperature and humidity are the determining factors for the various stages of life and evolution. The Nazis perceived themselves as "ice men" and their eden was a frozen wasteland. They looked down on the tropical edens of biblical lore as being the abodes of subhumans, much as tropical countries are the domain of non-Aryans. The theory is convoluted and self-referential, and gave rise to scientists running all over the world, taking its temperature, so to speak.

PL: You tell of Nazi mind-control experiments involving psychedelic drugs and torture techniques. You quote Rudolf Hess at the Nuremberg Trials saying that he himself was a victim of such mind-control techniques, and how he believed that the prosecution witnesses at the trial had been hypnotized because of their "glassy and dreamy eyes." You seem to think that the Nazis had become rather adept at mind control, and that our own intelligence organizations copied them. Do you have any more to add? What aspects of mind control do you think the CIA and others have copied from the Nazis?

PL: I don't think that Hess was implying the Nazis had mind control, but that the Allies had it. The man who interviewed Hess for CIA Director Dulles was Dr. Ewen Cameron, who went on to run the official CIA mind-control operation in Montreal. The Nazis were experimenting with hallucinogens and narcotics during the war. Their documentation on this was seized by American intelligence and has never seen the light of day. That much is known. The idea that the CIA ran a vast mind-control experiment from the 1940s to the 1970s, which involved all sorts of people and organizations, forms the central thesis of my next book, so I don't want to ruin the surprise. Suffice it to say that when the Nazis were being imported by the hundreds to the US and other American countries after the war, it wasn't only an "outer" space program that was being contemplated.

TT: You write that Jörg Lanz von Liebenfels created the Order of New Templars as "a secret society bent on reviving the chivalric brotherhood of knights, but in an aggressively Teutonic—and anti-Semitic—format." Since the original Templar order had so much to do with Judaism— Jerusalem, holy relics like the Ark of the Covenant, Jewish mysticism, and of course the Jewish priest king known as Jesus Christ—how did he reconcile the concept of the Templars with his own anti-Semitic beliefs?

PL: We enlightened types realize that Christianity has its roots in Judaism. The Old Testament should be proof enough of that, right? But just try telling the wrong people that Christ was a Jew and see what happens. If occult scholarship on the Templars is correct, however, these knights were less Christian than would appear at first blush. The Templars, an order of Catholic knighthood, went on an expedition to the temple of Solomon, and found something there that probably challenged their belief structure and caused them to deny the crucifixion and, possibly, to deny the entire Judeo-Christian edifice they had sworn to uphold and defend.

Recall the Nazis were fond of the Cathars, whom they considered— via Otto Rahn, at any rate—to be the "true" Christians rather than the persecuting Catholics. Remember that generations of scholars have posited some sort of Cathar/Templar connection. Remember that the Templars became enemies of the church and were ruthlessly exterminated (as were the Cathars). When someone like Lanz von Liebenfels decides to resurrect the Templars, it is not as the pious Catholic monk/knights, but as heroic enemies of Catholicism and, by extension, Judaism as well.

The Grail was no longer a Christian symbol to Lanz, but something more ancient, more "pagan." The bloodline of Jesus? Not to Lanz, unless that bloodline was purely Teutonic. One can no longer speak of templarism without the implicit challenge to papal authority. To the church in the fourteenth century, templarism was synonymous with satanism, idol worship, and all sorts of heresy. There has been no attempt by the modern church to rehabilitate the reputation of the Templars. Von Liebenfels and other "new Templars," such as Crowley and Reuss, bore no love for Catholicism.

They used esoteric Judaica purely as a key to other mysteries, as a tool and not as an element of their "faith." Crowley may have been a kabbalist, for instance, but by no stretch of the imagination was he a worshipper of the Jewish god. No tallis, tefillim or yarmulka for that boy. Same for von Liebenfels. The Christ that Christians worship—according to the Nazis, both then and now—is a Jewish impersonator. That Christ was Jewish is a lie perpetrated by the Jews to maintain some degree of control over the gentiles.

So, the "new Templars" were able to identify with a Christian knightly order while simultaneously reviling Christianity, since the "revealed" Christianity was a hoax. They were at least half right. What we know of Christianity today is a hodgepodge of other myths, other religions, and some political agendas. Strip away Mithraism, Gnosticism and paganism from Christianity—especially Roman Catholicism—and what's left? A messianic cult of Essenes with a narrow focus on regaining Jerusalem in its lifetime? The end of the nineteenth century saw a flurry of books and articles attacking the church and demonstrating how it obtained all its non-Christian trappings over the centuries. Cults like the new Templar orders were created as repositories of the "true Faith," the secret knowledge behind the Masons and the Jews and the Christians, the pre-Jehovah, pre-Garden of Eden consciousness of the Aryan people. As the old saying goes, "the enemy of my enemy is my friend," and the Knights Templar were obviously the enemy of the church.

TT: One chapter in your book that particularly interested me was entitled "Lucifer's Quest for the Holy Grail." In it, you describe how a mystical Grail scholar named Otto Rahn was enlisted into the SS and hired by Himmler to a write a book proving that Lucifer was the God of the Aryan race, that Jehovah was Satan, and that Christ was a Teutonic sun god and Christianity the corrupted result of Jews trying to co-opt the German Messiah.

All this led to the conclusion that the Holy Grail was actually a Luciferian relic that the Jews had also tried to co-opt. Rahn was even given a deadline of October 31, 1936, to finish his book, *Lucifer's Servants*. But a few years later, in February 1939, Rahn resigned from the SS for reasons unknown, and died a mysterious death one month later while hiking in the mountains. You intimate that he may have been assassinated because of something he may have discovered during his Grail research, something he'd confessed to another Nazi occultist named Karl Wiligut, with whom he was good friends. Is it possible that he discovered evidence that the Grail was actually the bloodline of Christ, the Judaic bloodline of David? This would of course have been thoroughly unacceptable to Himmler, and would have devastated his whole cosmology if such facts had gotten out.

PL: I don't know why Rahn was killed, although I am reasonably certain he was, and that his death was not the accident it was made out to be. He may be only another one in a series of individuals involved with Montsegur and Rennes-le-Chateau who died violent deaths. Was he murdered by the Nazis, or were other elements at play here? He was Himmler's pet for a while, and a friend of Wiligut (who designed the death's-head ring worn by the SS). Wiligut was a total psycho, so it is hard for me to imagine a less likely friendship since Rahn seems somewhat sane in his writings, if going a bit overboard at times. There is no evidence that Himmler ordered an investigation into Rahn's death, so either it was ordered by Himmler himself or he was satisfied that it was an accident. Had Rahn been cut down by a cult defending the Cathar/Templar secret, it is possible that more would have been made of his death, and that there would be a paper trail to follow.

Yes, if Rahn had discovered the secret I described in *Holy Blood, Holy Grail*, then possibly Himmler would have ordered Rahn killed to keep the secret safe. Or, he would have had him killed for having the temerity to suggest it. But I think that Himmler would have been fascinated by this discovery and would have had Pierre Plantard and his relatives rounded up and brought to Wewelsburg for some heavy interrogation. The Rahn mystery is one that concerns me to this day, for none of the reports, stories, theories I have heard so far have seemed conclusive enough. Perhaps, as the French say, *cherchez la femme*.

TT: You write that S.L. MacGregor Mathers had "aristocratic pretensions and was desirous of restoring the House of Stuart." I recently received a letter to the editor claiming this as well. The man, whose name is Kevin Coogan and who is a successful writer in his own right, said also that Crowley and other members of the Golden Dawn supported the Stuarts, and referred me to page 121 of Crowley's *Confessions*. Could you comment on this and tell me what evidence there is to support this? Also, please explain why they might have been supporting this long-exiled royal family.

PL: This could be a long story. I think the best source for background on this would be *The Temple and the Lodge* by Baigent and Leigh. They cover the links pretty thoroughly between the Stuart dynasty, the Jacobite movement, and Freemasonry, including data on the Rosicrucian societies and the Royal Society connections. According to Baigent and Leigh, Scotland was an early destination for Templars fleeing the Church, and there are Templar graveyards and chapels there and a history of Templar activism supporting the armies fighting the English.

Remember that restoring the House of Stuart would have been a romantic concept to Mathers, Crowley, et al. And this ties in with their opposition to Victorian English values. Mathers went so far as to have photographs taken of himself in full highland drag, and signed many of his writings MacGregor. Crowley made himself Laird of Boleskine on the banks of Loch Ness, and Boleskine is now the "Mecca" for Thelemites, the place they face when they pray.

I could go on and on about Bonnie Prince Charlie, "Charlie over the water," and the underground societies that supported him with their codes and safe houses; all those elements necessary to attract the devotee of secret cults and hidden meanings. Look at the similarities between the Catholic Church battling the Templars, and then the British Empire versus the Templars: the Templars as romantic champion of the underdog, fighting the minions of the Death Star. More to the point, the Stuart connection gives the Templars a dimension on the British Isles apart from its Gaelic origins and fame. It makes them more universal, and moreover is credited with being the source of Freemasonry. To restore the Stuart dynasty would be, de facto, to restore Templarism.

Mathers was passionately involved in Stuart-type intrigues and half-baked political movements. Crowley adopted it as a fashion and probably believed in restoring the throne to the Stuarts, but I think he was not as politically involved as his mentor in this cause. Crowley came first for Crowley, and unless he could prove to himself that he was a Stuart, I don't think he would have thrown his not inconsiderable weight behind the movement for any period of time.

TT: What do you think about the idea, put forth in *Holy Blood, Holy Grail*, hypothesizing that the *Protocols of the Learned Elders of Zion* was originally a Masonic document, doctored by Sergei Nilus in order to foster anti-Semitism?

PL: It is possible that *Protocols* is a corruption of another document; but once we go down that path, how do we know what was original and what was Nilus? At one point, Nilus himself says that *Protocols* was stolen by a woman from an influential leader of Freemasonry. (That was only one of his many stories of the background and origin of the *Protocols*; most are mutually exclusive.) It was originally entitled "Minutes of the Meeting of the World Union of Freemasons and Elders of Zion," according to Norman Cohn in his definitive *Warrant for Genocide*, which is probably the best source for anyone interested in the history of the *Protocols*. I should also mention Cohn's point that "in the eighteenth century, the Freemasons were on the whole hostile to the Jews (and so, incidentally, were the Bavarian Illuminati)." The irony is that the Nazis (and the Russian anti-Semites responsible for the *Protocols*) assumed a Jewish-Masonic conspiracy. Both groups were considered secretive, clannish, self-supporting, and outside the mainstream of culture; ergo, they were united in a single conspiracy. Paranoia has its own internal logic, I guess.

TT: In your book, you hint about your own involvement with the occult. What can you tell me about that? Why are you mentioned in the "Special Thanks" section of the *Necronomicon*? And what's up with the *Necronomicon*, anyway? I always thought it was something that Lovecraft had made up, but the preface to the edition edited by L. K. Barnes states that it was brought to him by some guy named Simon in a briefcase containing "additional material on the *Necronomicon* which provided his *bona fides*." He also says that the briefcase contained "correspondence from various Balkan embassies." At first I took this with a grain of salt, but after seeing your name in the special thanks section I grew curious.

PL: My involvement was on the translation side. I've been around occult groups in New York since the late 1960s. I was a friend of Herman Slater of the old Warlock Shop in Brooklyn Heights before it moved to Manhattan and became Magickal Childe. I was around during the famous Witch Wars of the 1970s, when it seemed that everyone was casting spells on everyone else. I was there when Gardnerians and Welsh Trads and Alexandrians and Sicilian Trads sat down around a table in the back of Herman's shop to settle the war and make peace once and for all.

Herman had once interviewed neo-Nazis in New York in the 1960s, and we had a lot of interests in common. I never joined any of the groups—that wasn't my intention or inclination—but I was a familiar face around the campfire, so to speak.

My fascination has always been the degree to which religion and occultism influence mainstream politics. *Unholy Alliance* began as an academic study of this theme before it turned into a Nazi history. As for the *Necronomicon*, it was part of a stash of stolen books. The story is told in other places, and I have been asked this before—also on the Internet—so to summarize: In the 1970s, two Eastern Orthodox monks pulled off the biggest rare book heist in the history of the United States. It was an ongoing, widespread crime, the books being taken from libraries and private collections all over the country (and, it was said, Canada and Mexico). They were finally busted, and did federal time, but most of the books were never recovered.

The *Necronomicon* was part of this swag, as were a lot of occult books. It was in Greek, handwritten, but the problem was that much of the Greek was unintelligible. My modest contribution was recognizing that some of the Greek was an attempt to phoneticize Babylonian and Sumerian words. I am not one of the people arguing that this *Necronomicon* is "the" *Necronomicon*, or that Lovecraft was even aware that it existed. I think Lovecraft heard the name through one of his friends in the Golden Dawn, and used it creatively. If the Simon *Necronomicon* is a hoax, I think it would have been better done, and more closely followed the Cthulhu mythos. I kind of like the fact that William Burroughs was into it, and wrote Simon and L. K. Barnes a letter praising it as an important spiritual breakthrough.

TT: In *Unholy Alliance* you talk about how the Nazi occultists believed there was an "Aryan spirit" and a "Jewish spirit," passed along through the genes by way of racial memory. Is this not the same concept espoused in the *Necronomicon* when it talks about how we all have the blood of the Ancient Ones pumping through our veins, poisoning us? It says, "a man, being born, is of sadness, for he is of the Blood of the Ancient Ones, but has the Spirit of the Elder Gods breathed into him." Also, I believe Abdul Alhazred, if there was such a person, refers to the pentagram as "The Sign of the Aryan Race."

PL: Yes, this is similar to what we find in the *Necronomicon* but is also what we find, for instance, in ancient Sumerian religion. Man is formed from the blood of the slain gods, but has the spirit of the victorious gods blown into him. Hence, his naturally schizophrenic nature.

TT: In the final chapters to your book you explain how Nazi occultism is being spread throughout various youth countercultures, such as the skinheads. One of my readers, Kevin Coogan, recently sent me an article he'd written for *Hit List* magazine about a phenomenon popular throughout Europe known as "black metal," hardcore heavy metal called "black" ("an adjective used by Europeans for right-wing," he claims) because of the radical views espoused by the musicians. Many within this counterculture blend Nazism, anti-Semitism, fascism, Satanism, sado-masochism, and Odinist ancestor worship, supposedly as a means of shocking themselves or others out of a mundane, linear mindset. He traces this cultural anomaly back to Genesis P-Orridge, one of the forefathers of industrial music (Throbbing Gristle/Psychic TV) and a thelemic essayist with whom you're probably familiar. Genesis used a lot of these elements in their work as well, calling it "entertainment through pain." Any comments on the usefulness of such practices?

PL: I'm not sure it's necessary to shock oneself out of a linear mindset, although that would be the fast approach. Satanic ritual does that, properly performed. But what happens to the psyche thus shocked? Who is in control at that point? In the case of black metal, the musicians are ostensibly in control but often their sole contribution has been the "shock" factor. Where does the psyche "go" at that point? What does it learn from the experience? Growing up in the 1960s, we understood acid to be a similar shock factor that disrupted linear time and linear thinking, but our trips were guided. The acid was used as a tool for other purposes and not an end in itself. I think it is more useful that way. The same for black metal. I think the music should be part of a larger format—a ritual, if you will—to enable the effects to be more lasting, more profound. But where's the fun in that?

TT: Do you think that members of the OTO are involved in espionage today? If so, how prevalent do you think that is? Do you think that by joining the OTO a person is entering into a den of spies and government agents?

PL: No, not really. I have known a lot of OTO people in my time—from various countries—and for the most part they would make poor spies. There were some lodges operating in the former Yugoslavia, though, that might have become involved in the murder and mayhem taking place there now. I don't know, as I have lost touch with them. But I do believe that the OTO was involved in espionage for, perhaps, the first fifty years of its existence. I think, as it became "hippified" in the States, it lost some of its attraction for the intelligence agencies, but that does not mean that it would not be involved somehow in such activities in other parts of the world, or that individual OTO members would not be involved in such activities even in the US. I feel that US intelligence investigated—and possibly infiltrated—the OTO in the 1960s, as they did the Klan and the neo-Nazis, and that the full extent of the FBI and/or CIA "cult awareness" program has never been adequately revealed, or the right questions asked. •

—Spring 2001

* * *

Planet X

* * *

Planet X, NASA Cover-up

Does a Runaway Wrecking Ball Belong to the Solar System?

by Joan d'Arc

This article surveys more than a decade of extensive media coverage of a tenth Solar System planet. On June 17, 1982, a NASA press release officially recognized the existence of this "mystery object," now known as Planet X. News stories variously described the wayward body as three to four times the size of Earth, or as a gaseous planet larger than Jupiter. Other press releases described it as a brown dwarf star, and the Sun's "dark companion," indicating we live in a binary star system. Yet, NASA was cautious in its appraisal that the wayward object was not "incoming mail," on a potentially destructive path toward Earth. A 1998 British report indicated that "earth-shattering" information, such as the discovery of incoming comets or asteroids, has been ordered to go through NASA first. What does NASA know about Planet X?

ANCIENT SUMERIAN TEXTS indicate that the Earth ("Tiamat") was struck by a large planet, which moved it into its present orbit, and created the Moon and the asteroid belt. In his books *The Twelfth Planet* and *The Cosmic Code*, Zecharia Sitchin outlines this "celestial battle" as described in the Babylonian text called *Enuma Elish*. The Sumerians counted the Sun and the Moon as planets; the twelfth planet means the twelfth celestial body in the solar system.

The twelfth planet "Marduk" (the Sumerian "Nibiru"), as it came into the solar system on its clockwise elliptical course, struck Tiamat, which was moving in its ordained counterclockwise orbit. One of Marduk's satellites struck Tiamat first, followed by two more of Marduk's moons. Then Marduk itself, an enormous planetary body, struck Tiamat, smashing one half of the planet into pieces, which became the Earth's Moon and the "Great Band" (asteroid belt). The other half of the planet, which was struck by a smaller moon of Marduk, was moved into a new orbit, along with a chunk of material which became its moon. The new planet was then called "KI," meaning "cleaved one." The Earth's original moons were dispersed, many changing the direction of their orbits.

Sitchin has also written in *Divine Encounters*, that the planet where God the creator resides is referred to in the Bible as Olamin, the plural of olam. The meaning of "olam" in the ancient world was a measure of a very long time, specifically related to the span of time between the periodic disappearance and reappearance of the planet Marduk on its 3,600-year-long elliptical orbit. The domain of Olamin was described as a kingdom which encompasses many worlds. According to Robert Temple, in *The Sirius Mystery*, the Dogon tribe of Mali call this planet "the egg of the world," and they say it is the origin of all things. They say of this planet that it is "the center of all things and without its movement no other star could hold its course." They say it is made of a heavy metallic compound called "sagala." The Sumerians also wrote that this planetary "god," Nibiru, "remade our solar system and remakes the Earth on its near passages."

According to commentary posted on the web site http://xfacts.com, the twelfth planet's periodic appearance and disappearance from Earth's view confirms its permanence in solar orbit. In this way, it acts like many comets. The writers on this web site ask why our astronomers are not aware of the existence of this planet. Even an orbit half as long as that of the comet Kohoutek (7,500 years) would take the solar system's tenth planet about six times farther away from Earth than Pluto. At this distance, the planet would not be visible from Earth.

The ancient tale of Nibiru's Celestial Battle is actually scientifically sophisticated, and current advances in astronomy have recently corroborated certain aspects of the Sumerian cosmogony, among them the following:

- The March 16, 1999, announcement by NASA at the Thirtieth Lunar and Planetary Science Conference in Houston of the theory of the origin of Earth's Moon as a catastrophic collision with a "Mars-size planet."

- Hubble's recent discovery of (at last count) eighteen stars, and numerous Jupiter-size planets (last count nine) with highly-elliptical orbits and retrograde (clockwise) orbits. Such orbits are now understood to be the norm in nearby solar systems; with the exception of Venus and Uranus, the orbital direction in our solar system is prograde. Some comets and small asteroids orbit the Sun in retrograde orbits, but these are exceptions rather than the rule.

- The 1994 announcement by NASA of a one-mile-wide moon orbiting the thirty-three-mile wide asteroid Ida, which follows the expectation that if a planetary body in this solar system exploded (or collided), the debris will be gravitationally bound in orbits around a primary body.

- The discovery of water, atmosphere, and perhaps previous life on Mars, the Moon, and Europa.

- Speculations on a strange gravitational "pull" exerted on Uranus, Neptune, and Pluto, which indicates the possible existence of another body of significant size beyond their orbits.

PLANET X—MYTH OR FACT?

Mathematical irregularities in the orbits of the outer planets, in particular the strange wobbles and gravitational anomalies noted in the orbits of Uranus, Neptune, and Pluto, have prompted astronomers over the past hundred years to search for a large planetary body in the outer solar system. Based on mathematical evidence, astronomers have been so sure of the reality of this planet that they named it Planet X. The name stands for the tenth planet, as well as the mathematical symbol for an unknown quantity.

On June 17, 1982, a NASA press release from Ames Research Center officially recognized the possibility of "some kind of mystery object" beyond the outermost planets. Various press releases around this time confirmed that scientists were indeed looking for the infamous Planet X. *Astronomy* magazine published an article in December 1981 entitled "Search for the Tenth Planet," and another in October 1982 entitled "Searching for a Tenth Planet." *Newsweek* covered the story of Planet X on June 28, 1982, in the article "Does the Sun Have a Dark Companion?" which implied that we live in a binary star system and stated:

A "dark companion" could produce the unseen force that seems to tug at Uranus and Neptune, speeding them up at one point in their orbits and holding them back as they pass. The best bet is a dark star orbiting at least 50 billion miles beyond Pluto. It is most likely either a brown dwarf, or a neutron star. Others suggest it is a tenth planet . . . since a companion star would tug at the other planets, not just Uranus and Neptune.

The Washington Post covered the story of Planet X on December 31, 1983, in a front page piece called "Mystery Heavenly Body Discovered." This story reported that the Infrared Astronomical Satellite (IRAS) detected heat from an object about fifty billion miles away. Reporting on an interview with chief scientist Gerry Neugebauer from Jet Propulsion Laboratories, the story stated:

A heavenly body possibly as large as the giant planet Jupiter and possibly so close to Earth that it would be part of this solar system has been found in the direction of the constellation Orion by an orbiting telescope aboard the U.S. Infrared Astronomical Satellite. "All I can tell you is that we don't know what it is," said Neugebauer.

The *Post* article went on to explain that this mysterious object has never been seen by optical telescopes on Earth or in space, but its infrared heat signature was detected twice by IRAS as it scanned the northern sky between January and November of 1983. If it's a brown dwarf star, it glows in the infrared band, which eludes optical detection; its presence must be detected by other means. This explains why we are not able to see the object, even though it's massive.

The second infrared observation of the body noted that the body appeared not to have moved in six months. This suggested the object is not a comet, since a comet probably would have moved. According to this article, the infrared telescope aboard IRAS, which is able to detect very cold objects, calculated the body's temperature to be about 459°F below zero.

Astronomers suggested the object was a "giant gaseous planet, as large as Jupiter," and is so close that "it would be the nearest heavenly body to Earth beyond the outermost planet Pluto." This would make it part of the solar system. There was also speculation that the object "might be moving toward Earth." However, Neugebauer was careful to "douse that idea with as much cold water as I can." He pronounced with certainty that this object "is not incoming mail."

On September 10, 1984, *US News and World Report* published an article called "Planet X—Is it Really Out There?" stating that:

> Shrouded from the sun's light, mysteriously tugging at the orbits of Uranus and Neptune, is an unseen force that astronomers suspect may be Planet X—a tenth resident of the Earth's celestial neighborhood. Last year, the infrared astronomical satellite (IRAS), circling in a polar orbit 560 miles from the Earth, detected heat from an object about 50 billion miles away that is now the subject of intense speculation.

The report went on to say that scientists are hopeful that the space probes Pioneer 10 and 11 will locate the object, which they noted was possibly a "brown dwarf," a protostar which never got hot enough to become a star. Others astronomers, however, argue that the object is a "dark, gaseous mass that is slowly evolving into a planet." Neugebauer was quoted as stating: "If we can show that our solar system is still creating planets, we'll know that it's happening around other stars, too."

Contrary to this information, according to the ancient Sumerian texts, our solar system is not still creating planets, and this planet has been with us a very long time. It would appear that the media spin being put on Planet X is an attempt to avoid the potential panic of "incoming mail."

INTO THE FRIGID FRINGES

The media was quiet on the subject of Planet X for the next few years. Finally, in the *Astronomical Journal* of October 1988 R. Harrington supplied the details of continuing mathematical modeling of this planet. Harrington suggested the mysterious planet was three to four times the size of Earth, and its position was three times further from the Sun than Pluto. Mathematical modeling also suggested that Planet X had an extreme elliptical orbit of thirty degrees.

A NASA/ARC press release quoted in *Newsweek* on July 13, 1987, disclosed that "an eccentric tenth planet may—or may not—be orbiting the Sun," stating that NASA research scientist John Anderson "has a hunch Planet X is out there, though nowhere near the other nine." The report concluded, "if he is right, two of the most intriguing puzzles of space science might be solved: What caused mysterious irregularities in the orbits of Uranus and Neptune during the nineteenth century? And what killed off the dinosaurs 26 million [sic] years ago."

The reference to killing off the dinosaurs (actually closer to 45 million years ago) seems to indicate that something more is known about this planet than NASA is letting on. Is this a reference to the planet Nibiru of ancient infamy, the planet which, according to ancient sources, struck the Earth (Tiamat) in ancient times, and gave us a moon for a thank-you? Regardless of what NASA really knows, silence is golden, and, for the most part, mum was the word on the issue of Planet X throughout the 1990s. Instead, scientific journals began to debunk the issue of a tenth planet and news stories began to dwell on "runaway planets" and "rebel planets" discovered in other solar systems. The issue of the existence of Planet X became entirely muddled by the discoveries of eighteen nearby stars with Jupiter-class planets orbiting them (last count as of October 1999). (See the web site astron.berkeley.edu.) Now, locating any new developments regarding a tenth planet is akin to finding a needle in a haystack, since it's difficult to know which "new planet" they are talking about.

For instance, an October 23, 1996, AP article entitled "New Rebel Planet Found Outside the Solar System," disclosed the following:

A new planet that breaks all the rules about how and where planets form has been identified in orbit of a twin star about seventy light years from Earth in a constellation commonly known as the Northern Cross. The new planet has a roller coaster–like orbit that swoops down close to its central star and then swings far out into frigid fringes, following a strange egg-shaped orbit that is unlike that of any other known planet.

Thus, the issue of Planet X became lost in the information shuffle, with the Hubble space probe's discovery of many distant galaxies, stars, planets, and brown dwarfs. This situation affords NASA the opportunity to avoid the societal chaos that will surely ensue once everybody realizes that a sizable object somewhere out there may be destined to circle our own sun in the near future. (Some have opined 2003, but others, including Andy Lloyd and Zecharia Sitchin, say it will be in at least 2,000 years.) After all, who would bother to go to work, go to school, pay their bills, play the stock market, be a loyal taxpaying John or Jane Doe, if the end of civilization were near?

PLANET X—THE COVER-UP

Contrary to what happens in Hollywood movies, which depict the government coming clean about comets (in the film *Deep Impact*, authorities wait almost a year after official knowledge to announce an imminent collision to the public), wouldn't it make sense that such an announcement would not be made public, at least very far in advance? Tom van Flandern of the U.S. Naval Observatory, quoted in the 1982 *Newsweek* article ("Does the Sun Have a Dark Companion?"), admits that a tenth planet is possible, but argues that it would have to be so huge that it should have been observed by now. There is a possibility that more details regarding Planet X are known, but the public is not being informed. Is there a major cover-up of Planet X?

This possibility was discussed in an article in *CCNet Digest* on May 18, 1998, entitled "The Secrets of Asteroid Peril, British Media Smells a Rat." This report claimed that the *London Daily Mail* accused US astronomers of trying to cover up scientific data until NASA has had a chance to look at the information. The report indicated that information that might cause public hysteria, such as the discovery of incoming comets or asteroids, has been ordered to go through NASA first. The original *Daily Mail* report of May 15, 1998, entitled "Delayed Impact, or the Secrets of Asteroid Peril," stated the following:

> If a giant asteroid is hurtling in the general direction of our planet, we will be the last to know about it. For astronomers have decided that the news would be too earth-shattering for ordinary mortals to handle, and would likely cause widespread panic. In a week that sees the release of the film *Deep Impact*, a fictional account of just such a catastrophe, astronomers funded by the American space agency NASA have now agreed to keep asteroid and comet discoveries to themselves for forty-eight hours while more detailed calculations are made. The findings would then go to NASA, which would wait another twenty-four hours before going public.

A Los Angeles AP article reported on May 19, 1998, about this seventy-two-hour delay rule imposed by NASA on announcements to the public of asteroids or comets by private astronomers. The report indicated that these measures were undertaken to avoid the "doomsday alert" which occurred in March of 1998 with regard to an asteroid which was initially warned to be on a collision course with Earth in 2028, and which course was "soon found to be a mistake." These new procedures, the article stated, are "not an attempt to hide anything but to make sure the information is accurate." How can we be sure that, if the information is found to be accurate, NASA will not (a) find it to be a "mistake," or (b) withhold the message for a longer period of time?

X MARKS THE SPOT

In February 1999, J.B. Murray presented a paper to the Royal Astronomical Society entitled "Arguments for the Presence of a Distant Large Undiscovered Solar System Planet" (posted on www.blackwell-synergy. com). Murray's paper explored various explanations for what he called a "non-random clustering of long-period comets," which his research concluded are "aligned along a great circle inclined to both the ecliptic and the galactic planes." His paper examined the possibility that this non-random clustering was due to "orbital perturbations by an undiscovered object orbiting within the . . . distances of 30,000 to 50,000 AU from the Sun." Murray's mathematical modeling predicted that the object would have a retrograde (clockwise) orbit inclined at 120 degrees. Retrograde is the direction opposite that of the rotation of the Earth. In the solar system, all major planets orbit the Sun counterclockwise (prograde) as seen from the pole star (Polaris).

In an October 16, 1999, *Economist* article entitled "X Marks the Spot," Drs. John B. Murray and John Matese, after looking at the orbits of approximately 300 long-period comets, have separately concluded that too many of them are coming from the same regions of space. They suggest that the galaxy's "tidal wobble" is "being modulated by the gravity of something big within the Oort Cloud itself."

The new object must be very faint, these astronomers suggest, or it would have been spotted. They predicted the object to be three times the size of Jupiter. They also suggested that the object is not a "proper planet," because, take note: "its orbit appears to run in the opposite direction from those of the nine known planets." We can add this factoid to our "anomalous" discoveries list regarding the existence of Marduk/Nibiru. As the *Enuma Elish* tells us, the planet Marduk entered the solar system on its "clockwise, elliptical orbit," and struck the Earth, which was moving in its "ordained counterclockwise orbit." (Chalk up another one for Sitchin.)

According to the *Economist* article, the orbit of this object appears to be so unstable that it is unlikely it could have maintained this orbit for the 4.5 billion-year lifetime of the solar system. Therefore, these astronomers suggest, it is more likely that the object is an extra-solar body that was captured by our sun's gravity only "recently," in astronomical terms. (Otherwise, it would have wreaked havoc throughout the history of the solar system. Of course, we are presuming our neck of the galactic woods is serene because life here has been left in peace to "evolve" for so long that Planet X would have to be a relative newcomer to fit into this preconceived scenario.) These astronomers predict that we should be detecting Planet X soon, even if we have to wait for the next generation of infrared space telescopes.

It's interesting to note that many of the newly discovered extra-solar planets have extremely eccentric orbits. It is suggested in "New Discoveries, A Planetary Mystery" (posted on the web site astron.berkeley.edu) that circular orbits may not be the rule in nearby solar systems. Nine of the recently discovered extra-solar objects travel in unusually elliptical orbits, "several of them plunging in relatively close to their stars and then swinging far out again." Several of these planets may be three times as massive as Jupiter, and one is estimated at eleven times the mass of Jupiter.

These new discoveries are teaching us that our own solar system may be very unlike others. Even considering our catastrophic past, we may inhabit a relatively peaceful end of the cosmos. As Dr. Geoffrey Marcy explains, powerful gravitational forces exerted by huge planets or passing stars over smaller planets are capable of upsetting their orbits. Likewise, he explains, two or more huge planets orbiting in close proximity can generate a "gravitational slingshot" effect, which could fling one of the objects into an elongated orbit within the inner planetary system, while the other could at the same time fly off in the other direction, into interstellar space.

In another possible scenario, this brown dwarf star (which Andy Lloyd refers to as Sol B) could be part of a binary star system, locked in a gravitational embrace with our primary star, Sol A. Although discussion of this possibility is avoided in what little news is released on Planet X, the existence of this mysterious outer solar system traveler suggests that we could unknowingly be living in a binary star system. Aside from the danger to civilization the existence of such an object implies, what would be the implications of such a reality on our current scientific paradigm? If the solar system has two suns, Sol A and Sol B, what are the physical effects of Sol B on Sol A and the other planets? How does this affect the mathematics scientists use to describe the relationships between planets, the so-called "Music of the Spheres"? And last but not least, does the existence of a second sun supplant Darwinian gradualism in place of which science must admit catastrophism best describes reality: the cyclic catastrophic destruction of earthling life forms? Are there, then, many reasons to squelch this information? As Andy Lloyd explains in this volume, ancient peoples may very well have known about this second sun, Sol B, and encoded it into their esoteric writings and artwork.

As Dr. Marcy writes: "We are realizing that most of the Jupiter-like planets far from their stars tool around in elliptical orbits, not circular orbits, which are the rule in our solar system." Why our largest planets remain in circular orbits is, therefore, a mystery. Dr. Marcy goes on to say:

> Jupiter sized bodies plunging toward and away from their stars are likely to sweep aside smaller worlds, sending them crashing into their star or flying out of orbit into interstellar space. Current technology is incapable of detecting Earth-size planets around other stars, but they almost certainly could not exist near their star's warmth in a system so unsettled by large planets in wrecking orbits.

A huge planet in an elliptical orbit would probably scatter or destroy smaller planets as it crosses their paths time and again. As Dr. Marcy writes, "if our Jupiter were in an eccentric orbit, the Earth and Mars would likely be gravitationally scattered out of the solar system." Therefore, our very existence, he observes, is dependent upon both Jupiter and Earth being in mutually stable and circular orbits. Lucky for us, we have no big bullies, no freewheeling wrecking balls, in our solar system. Or do we?

EXPLODED PLANET CULT

Interestingly, astronomer Tom van Flandern wonders if Planet X has exploded! In his book *Dark Matter, Missing Planets and New Comets* van Flandern wonders if this planet was responsible for disrupting the moons of Neptune. In his 1995 paper entitled "Origins of Trans-Neptunian Asteroids," van Flandern notes that a new asteroid belt has been discovered beyond Neptune, suggesting that Planet X may have exploded. (On the other hand, why wouldn't this be the result of one of Planet X's fly-bys?)

In his book *The Phoenix Solution*, Alan Alford asks why, if Planet X has exploded, do the Mesopotamian texts imply that it was seen by the Sumerians during the third and fourth millennia B.C.? Alford makes the preposterous suggestion that the planet Nibiru was not actually seen, and is a "metaphysical" planet. He believes that the descent and ascent of the Egyptian gods was metaphysical, and that the Egyptian religion was "an exploded planet cult." The story of Osiris was based on this exploded planet; the deity Osiris had been mythologically "dismembered" and his body distributed among the other gods in the solar system. The resurrection of Osiris (continued in the Jesus myth) was based on his metaphysical journey to the stars, which restored the exploded planets to their primeval and pristine form; essentially a metaphysical trip back to "The First Time."

Alford charges that Sitchin has misinterpreted the gods as interplanetary astronauts, and that Planet X actually did not come into the vicinity of Earth, but was essentially a "play" or metaphysical replay of an even more ancient event. He also tries to establish a Darwinian evolutionary trajectory that implies human evolution was "quickened" by this explosion of planets. This is, in fact, an anti-Darwinian thesis, but more importantly, are we expected to believe that what IRAS spotted in 1983 was a metaphysical planet?

So this means that what NASA officials mistook as a heavenly body in the direction of the constellation Orion, a body that could be as large as Jupiter, and close enough to Earth to be part of this solar system, was just a mythological planet. And the mysterious heavenly orb, which mathematicians now predict may be three times the size of Jupiter, with a highly elliptical orbit, moving in the opposite direction from the other nine planets in the solar system, and with a retrograde orbit inclined at 120 degrees, is just the replay of an ancient event in the solar system. Lucky for us, that means we can all continue to pay our bills, go to work, go to school, play the stock market, and be a loyal taxpaying John or Jane Doe.

And we can all go back to sleep now. •

Planet X Updates

Blakemore, Paul. "Does the Sun Have a Doomsday Twin?" Telegraph.co.uk, October 18, 2002. www.telegraph.co.uk/connected/main.jhtml? = %2Fconnected %2F2002%2F10%2F18%2Fecfuniv116.xml

JPL NASA News Release. "Satellites Reveal Mystery of Large Change in Earth's Gravity Field." August 5, 2002. www.jpl.nasa.gov/releases/2002/release_2002_ 156.html

Onion, Amanda. "Red Planet Warming: Images Show Mars' Ice Caps Are Melting Fast." ABCNews.com, December 7, 2002. abcnews.go.com/sections/scitech/DailyNews/mars011207.html

Roach, John. "New Planet-Shaped Body Found in Our Solar System." National Geographic News, October 7, 2002. News.nationalgeographic.com/news/2002/10/1003_021007_quaoar.html

———. "Why Is Earth's Girth Bulging?" National Geographic News, August 7, 2002. news.nationalgeographic.com/news/2002/08/0807_020807_earthgirth.html

Royal Astronomical Society. "Puzzle of Cometary Orbits Hints at Large Undiscovered Object." October 7, 1999. www.xs4all.nl/~carlkop/planetx.html

Sepehr, Robert (producer). Planet X videos: *Unveiling the Mystery* and *Assessing the Science*. www.planetxvideo.com

Stenger, Richard. "If the End Is Near, Do You Want to Know?" CNN.com, February 28, 2003. www.cnn.com/2003/TECH/space/02/28/asteroid.alert/index.html

———. "North Magnetic Pole Could be Leaving Canada." CNN News, March 20, 2002. edition.cnn.com/2002/TECH/space/03/20/north.pole/index.html

———. "Pluto May Be Undergoing Global Warming." August 23, 2002. www.cnn.com/2002/TECH/space/08/19/pluto.warming

Tyrell Corp. Solar Storm Monitor. "Pioneer Spacecraft Slowing." 2002. www.geocities.com/solarstormmonitor/Pioneer.html

Whitehouse, David, "Neptune's Moon Is Getting Warmer." BBC News, June 25, 1998. news.bbc.co.uk/1/hi/sci/tech/120259.stm

—Spring 2000

Sol B: The Messianic Star?

by Andy Lloyd

In this fascinating article, British researcher Andy Lloyd provides a brief overview of current ideas surrounding the infamous Planet X, focusing on news reports that this enigmatic solar system wanderer is a brown dwarf star: Sol B. Lloyd provides an overview of ancient literature and artwork that suggests ancient peoples witnessed this wandering star, "alight with red flame and accompanied by seven moons, known to the Mesopotamians and Egyptians as the 'Winged Disc.'" He provides provocative evidence that Planet X may have been the Star of Bethlehem, or the Messianic Star. Lloyd concludes that the actual Nativity account is itself probably allegorical, and the emergence of Christianity may be connected to this anomalous celestial event.

THE POSSIBILITY that our solar system may have another, as yet undiscovered, planet has been the subject of serious debate by astronomers for decades.[1] Orbital perturbations by the outer planets point to a distant object's gravitational effect; yet, this so-called "Planet X" has eluded discovery despite advances in telescopes and space probes. Even the recent IRAS sky survey failed to pinpoint the culprit, leading many to drop the idea of a tenth planet.

The assumption has always been that this planet would be similar to the known planets, and located about six times as far away as Pluto. This distance is staggering, but it is nothing compared to the gravitational range of our star, Sol. Within its sphere of influence is thought to reside a truly enormous field of comets known as the Oort Cloud. It is entirely possible that a massive planetary body lurks undetected in this comet cloud around the Sun—so massive, in fact, that it could be considered a "failed star."

THE DARK STAR: SOL B

This possibility was forwarded by two independent astronomers, Drs. John B. Murray[2] and John Matese[3] in October 1999, based on evidence from long-period comet perturbations. The two researchers proposed different parameters for this proposed "planet," but the generalities were very similar.[4] This planet was several times the mass of Jupiter (the largest planet in our solar system), was orbiting in a slow circular procession around the Sun, and was affecting comets tens of thousands of astronomical units away (one astronomical unit, or AU, is the distance from the Sun to the Earth). This possibility was an exciting breakthrough that caught the imagination of the world's media, even though the "planet" had not even been detected directly. The astronomers pointed out that this object might be a brown dwarf, or failed star. They posited that although it had insufficient mass to become a star, it could be massive enough to emit low-frequency light and heat, thereby falling into a category of object that is neither star nor planet.

Recent astronomical discoveries have shown that young planets only five times the mass of Jupiter can emit light.[5] The unspoken implication of this finding is that our Sun might have a distant sister, a "dark star" in orbit around it. In a loose sense, then, it could be claimed that we are living in a binary system. This proposition has vast repercussions, not the least of which is the possibility that this dark star might have its own system of planets, lit and warmed by the brown dwarf itself.

Take Jupiter's moon Europa. Europa is warmed by the gravitational pull of the nearby gas giant to such a degree that an immense ocean lies under its frozen, billiard ball–like surface. Imagine the effect, then, if Jupiter were even larger, and emitting heat and red light. It is highly likely that Europa would have developed an atmosphere and would have become an ocean-covered terrestrial world. This is how a brown dwarf could maintain a series of inhabitable moons. Not only that, but the more harmful high-frequency radiation that bombards our planet from the Sun would be absent. One can imagine the potential for extraterrestrial life if a "light-emitting planet" were found in orbit around the Sun—a dark star I will refer to as Sol B.

NIBIRU

A couple of months before the story broke about the light emitting potential of young planets referenced above, I had proposed that a brown dwarf would be found in the Oort Cloud.[6] The basis for this hypothesis was that the ancient Sumerian description of the "twelfth planet" seemed more in keeping with our understanding of brown dwarfs than of presently known planets. This massive celestial entity, reintroduced to a skeptical world by the eminent scholar Zecharia Sitchin, was a fiery world which emitted flares and lightning, and roamed around "planet-busting."[7] These descriptions of the "Winged Disc," as Nibiru was known to the Mesopotamians and Egyptians, were in keeping with our present knowledge of light-emitting planets.

According to the ancient Mesopotamians, following its initial catastrophic entry into the planetary solar system, the wandering god Nibiru (also known as Marduk) was catapulted out after a collision with the watery planet Tiamat, whose main remnants became the Earth and its moon. The Mesopotamians stated in their astronomical and religious texts that this wandering "god" described an elliptical orbit around the Sun, which Sitchin likens to that of a comet.

Sitchin had always assumed this entity to be the habitable home world of the Anunnaki, an assumption dogged with practical difficulties. By definition, a habitable world would have to be warmed by an external heat source to maintain its atmosphere. At the distances from the Sun involved, an Earthlike planet's atmosphere would be so frigid that it would simply become a snowdrift-covered planet, as on Neptune's moon Triton. Internal heat sources resulting from massive gravity or radioactivity clearly would preclude life as we know it. Yet, according to the Sumerians, the Anunnaki are our god-like ancestors, and presumably they enjoy conditions on their own world that are similar to those on Earth.

Encouraged by the discoveries of Murray and Matese, I produced a research paper to show that Nibiru was a dark star, not a planet, and that the home world of the gods was one of its moons.[8] More shocks were to come. Upon reading Murray's paper, I realized that his "planet" moved in an orbit whose angle to the ecliptic (the plane of the other solar planets) was 30 degrees, a figure precisely the same as that indicated by Sitchin for Nibiru.[9] The ancient accounts of Nibiru's visible movement around the Sun indicated that it attained its perihelion (that is, its closest point to the Sun) in the area the Egyptians know as the Duat, between Sirius and Orion.[10] Murray's "planet" was located opposite the Duat, in a region of the sky north of Sagittarius. If Nibiru really is Murray's brown dwarf, then it is presently near aphelion, its most distant point from the Sun.

Many people interested in the twelfth planet believe that it last appeared around the time of the Exodus; thus, its return should be imminent. I think it is safe to assume that this is incorrect, as we would certainly have located it by now as it bears down on us from the void. Instead, the lack of direct astronomical evidence for Planet X indicates that it is at a great distance from the Sun, eliminating the argument for an appearance during the Exodus. This argument owes more to the discredited Velikovsky than to Sitchin, I suspect. Any tilt of the Earth's axis that occurred at the time of the Exodus would suggest that the older monuments, like the Pyramids, could no longer be in line with astronomical indicators; a condition that is clearly not met.

Sitchin's work indicates that Nibiru reached the perihelion point of its cometary orbit in 3760 B.C., the year when the Nippurian calendar began, as did the Jewish count of years.[11] Since Nibiru is supposed to orbit the Sun every 3,600 years (itself clearly an archetypal approximation), the last passage should have been in the two centuries preceding Christ, and the "planet" would now be at aphelion. Therefore, the only differences between Murray's data and Sitchin's hypothesis are its distance and orbital shape. Everything else fits, and this seems enough of a coincidence to pursue the possibility that we are looking at the same celestial body.

Furthermore, aspects of Matese's paper point to the possibility of an elliptical orbit and bizarre orbital changes known as occultation,[12] a review of which is beyond the scope of this paper (but will be tackled in my book in the near future). The recent discoveries about extra-solar planets, many of which exhibit wildly eccentric orbits, have shown us that we should not assume regularity based solely on the knowledge of our own planetary system.[13] This opens the door to multiple possibilities regarding Nibiru. It is no longer necessary to simply consider a regular, elliptical orbit. There may be other, more bizarre factors at play here.

THE MESSIANIC STAR

If Nibiru was supposed to have appeared in the skies in the centuries before Christ, why was its remarkable countenance not recorded? After all, a Jupiter-sized world, alight with red flame and accompanied by seven moons, must have been quite a sight at perihelion. This problem was not lost on researcher Alan Alford, who seemed to toy with the idea that this entity was the Star of Bethlehem.[14] The stumbling block was the 3,600-year orbit, which moved the window of opportunity to a period long before the lifetime of Christ, as agreed upon by biblical scholars. Also, it seems highly likely that the actual Nativity account itself is allegorical. It is possible that, even though the historical existence of Christ is open to question, the emergence of Christianity was the result of an anomalous celestial event. However, there is no objective evidence available in the astronomical records of the time.

An anomalous event recorded by Seneca in A.D. 25 might hold the key. In the "dark star" theory,[15] I have shown that perihelion occurs near Sirius, the brightest star in the sky, which is of blue-white appearance. In comparison, a Babylonian astrolabe carried a crystal-clear description of Nibiru's appearance to observers on Earth: "The red star, which when the stars of the night are finished, bisects the heavens and stands whence the south wind comes, this star is the god Nibiru-Marduk."[16]

While the Roman writer Seneca discussed fiery celestial phenomena, he described Sirius as being a "piercing red" star.[17] No satisfactory explanation has been found for this so-called "red Sirius" anomaly, an old astronomical chestnut that has done the rounds over the last few centuries.[18] Yet, one solution has never been considered: Seneca and others were not looking at Sirius at all! If this record points to Nibiru's appearance toward the end of Christ's life, a great many loose ends fall into place. The appearance of the messianic star near Sirius (which would appear pale in comparison) would explain the very emergence of Christianity; a religious cult originally built on ancient pagan mystery cults of dying-and-rising gods. The messianic star is the Egyptian god Horus, born of the goddess Isis (Sirius). It is also the phoenix, a fiery celestial entity reborn in the heavens after a great absence, associated with the meteoric bombardment of the Earth. Nibiru, after all, is likely to enter the planetary solar system shepherding a flock of attendant comets and asteroids, as well as its seven moons.

The Talisman of Orpheus, an amulet depicting the crucified Christ under an upturned crescent and semicircle of seven stars, indicates a very real link between the mystery cults and Nibiru and its moons, especially since the crucified figure is labeled Osiris-Dionysus.[19] The amulet is from the third century A.D. and its language is Greek. The inclusion of a planetary crescent and seven attendant "stars" has been ignored until now, but the imagery is consistent with the ancient description of the winged planet. After all, Jupiter's four largest moons are visible through binoculars. The seven moons of Nibiru, which are probably larger and lit by the dark star's red light, in addition to the Sun, would be visible to the naked eye at perihelion. This would explain the "wings" of the phoenix itself. Other pagan mysteries allude also to a young, dying celestial messiah as a "shepherd of white stars."[20]

The appearance of Nibiru would also explain the unexpected resurgence at the same time of the Persian mystery god Mithras in Rome, a sun god who sacrificed the zodiacal Taurus and dragged it off into a cave (the Primordial Deep). This cult seems to acknowledge Nibiru's disappearance into this constellation as it exits our planetary solar system. The sacrifice of bulls is an integral part of the rituals of many ancient religions. These cults have strong stellar links, with hidden esoteric messages, similar to the ancient Egyptian stellar religion of Osiris, Isis, and Horus.[21] Is it possible that ancient underground cults represented the secret knowledge of the winged disc in the hostile world of monotheistic Judaism and imperial Rome?

In setting out to discover the truth about the Sumerian account of Nibiru, it has gradually become apparent that the winged planet was an essential part of the fabric of many ancient religions and cults. Its reappearance during the life of Christ, the messianic event awaited since the time of Alexander the Great,[22] triggered a surge of new esoteric cults, including Christianity, which were devoted to attaining heavenly resurrection for their followers. Christ, like the many dying-and-rising pagan gods of the time, has stellar significance that owes more to the Babylonians and Egyptians than to orthodox Jews.

I think it likely that the "literal" existence of Jesus is built upon allegorical teachings about the messianic star's appearance in the heavens. The Nativity contains zodiacal imagery, and the crucifixion is based upon the Osiris myth, in turn pointing to an event in the constellation of Orion. The esoteric teachings of Christianity are spiritual teachings aimed at preparing initiates for life as a reborn god in the realm of the gods.

It is my contention that the Egyptian practice of mummification and the stellar significance of the pyramids at Giza[23] owe much to the awaited arrival of the Nibiruan system in the Duat. Mummification holds the *ka*, the spirit body, of the deceased to the Earth, while the Great Pyramid provides a time-activated device aimed at focusing the *ka* toward the reappearing system of Nibiru for its final astral journey. This may explain why the pyramid is empty, and why the star shafts point to Sirius and the belt of Orion; both significant markers on Nibiru's perihelion passage. I suspect that the *Egyptian Book of the Dead*[24] was meant to be an esoteric manual for departed souls to locate the gods' heavenly world in orbit around the Sun's dark sister, and for those souls to gain the opportunity of reincarnation as one of the Anunnaki, and thus to become immortal.

The cathedrals of the Roman Catholic Church are orientated towards significant stellar locations, and one wonders whether the tombs and graveyards in and around them are a more modern version of the Egyptian tombs around the Great Pyramid.[25] The souls of faithful Christians wait patiently in the "house of the Lord" until the second coming, when they too will rise to Heaven and will be resurrected into everlasting life. As Christians no longer believe in reincarnation, mummification has become redundant. The burial of remains is now considered sufficient to tie the soul to the church.

The claim that Christianity is a later adaptation of ancient Egyptian esoteric teachings is controversial, but it certainly makes much sense of the Book of Revelation. The celestial phoenix will be reborn once again, in about 1,800 years, giving the awaiting souls their next opportunity for resurrection and eternal life. However, the apocalyptic omens for our own planet, as the wandering planet-busting brown dwarf closes in, seem less optimistic. •

Notes

1. d'Arc, J. "Planet X: Is a Runaway Wrecking Ball Part of Our Solar System?" *Paranoia* 23 (or see www.paranoiamagazine.com).

2. Murray, J. "Arguments for the presence of a distant large undiscovered Solar system planet," *Monthly Notices of the Royal Astronomical Society* 309 (1999): 31–34.

3. Matese, J. "Cometary Evidence of a Massive Body in the Outer Oort Cloud," *Icarus* 141 (1999): 354–66.

4. "X Marks the Spot," *The Economist* (October 1999) (or see www.economist. com/editorial/freeforall/16/10/99/st7748.html).

5. "Mystery of free-floating 'planets.' " news.bbc.co.uk/hi/english/sci/tech/ newsid_957000/957518.stm 5/10/2000.

6. Lloyd, A. "Ancient to Modern," *UFO Magazine* (Sept.–Oct. 1999): 76.

7. Sitchin, Z. *The 12th Planet.* New York: Avon, 1976, chapter 7.

8. Lloyd, A. "The Dark Star Theory," www.darkstar1.co.uk.

9. Sitchin, Z. *Genesis Revisited.* New York: Avon, 1990, pp. 326–27.

10. Lloyd, "Theory."

11. Sitchin, Z. *The Lost Realms.* New York: Avon, 1990, p. 268.

12. Matese, "Evidence."

13. Marcy, G. and P. Butler. "Hunting Planets Beyond," *Astronomy, 28,* 3 (March 2000): 42–47.

14. Alford, A. *Gods of the New Millennium.* London: Hodder & Stoughton, 1996, p. 552.

15. Lloyd, "Theory."

16. Van Der Waerden. *Sciences Awakening II*. New York: Oxford Univ. Press, 1974, pp. 66–68.

17. Ceragioli, R. "The Debate Concerning 'Red' Sirius," *Journal of the History of Astronomy* 26 (1995): 187–226.

18. Whittet, D. "A Physical Interpretation of the 'Red Sirius' Anomaly," *Monthly Notices of the Royal Astronomical Society* 310 (1999): 355–59.

19. Freke, T. and P. Gandy, *The Jesus Mysteries: Was the Original Jesus a Pagan God?* London: Thorsons, 2000, pp. 15, 16, 114.

20. Ibid.

21. Gilbert, Adrian. *Magi*. UK: Bloomsbury, 1996.

22. Bauval, Robert, *Secret Chamber*. UK: Century, 1999, pp. 100–105.

23. ———, and Adrian Gilbert. *The Orion Mystery*. UK: Mandarin, 1994.

24. Wallis Budge, E.A. *The Egyptian Book of the Dead*. New York: Dover, 1967.

25. Heilbron, J. *The Sun in the Church: Cathedrals as Solar Observatories*. Cambridge, MA: Harvard, 1999.

—Spring 2001

The Chinese "Guest Star" of 1054 A.D. and Earth Catastrophism

A Preliminary Report

by William Patrick Bourne

An important paper published by Ho Peng-Yoke in 1970 indicates that in 1054 Chinese stargazers witnessed a bright object that was visible for 653 days, and visible during daylight for 23 days. There is some indication that the object was moving, but a comet has been ruled out. Over time, records of this awesome event were edited or destroyed for religious and political purposes. William Bourne suggests that this was not a supernova event, but was more likely the approach of a large planetoid in a highly elliptical orbit about the Sun.

THE CRAB NEBULA and its accompanying pulsar have long been assumed to be the result of a supernova explosion in 1054 A.D. What is not often discussed in the literature, though, is an important paper by Ho Peng-Yoke et.al. (1970), which minutely examines the original Chinese and Japanese evidence for this assertion. On the basis of the extant historical record, their conclusion is that there must be considerable doubt whether the object of 1054 A.D. and the Crab Nebula are connected at all.

Although the Crab Nebula may in fact be a supernova remnant, the evidence indicates that most supernovae throughout the past two millennia have not been seen by earthbound sky watchers or, at any rate, have not been recorded. Supernovae are relatively rare events, occurring in our galaxy perhaps once every 25 to 100 years (Fesen). Studies of ancient records from Europe, China, Japan, Korea, and the Arab world indicate that there have been fewer than ten such events witnessed over the last 2,000 years, out of a possible maximum number of eighty events. Some of these would be too far away, obscured by dust clouds in the galaxy, to have been observed.

One example, Cassiopeia A, is only a little farther away from us than the Crab and it was not observed at all when its star exploded some 300 years ago (Mitton). Presumably this is because it took place in a region of our galaxy that from our viewpoint is heavily obscured by dust. The viewing conditions today in the direction of the Crab are much better, but a thousand years ago the conditions could have been different. We must remember that every part of the galaxy is in constant motion.

It seems odd that there are no contemporary European or Arab observations of the 1054 A.D. event, whereas other supernovae were witnessed and recorded by those cultures. They accurately reported the position and other properties of another supernova that occurred in 1006 A.D., only forty-eight years earlier, as well as many other astronomical phenomena, such as Halley's comet. After great efforts, one possible example of an Arab observation has been found, though it is not very helpful (Brecher et.al.). Furthermore, Trimble's careful study of the expansion of the Crab Nebula showed convergence at about 1140 A.D., not 1054 A.D. (Mitton).

CHINESE STARGAZERS

According to the work of Ho Peng-Yoke et.al., the Chinese "guest star" of 1054 A.D. first appeared at a sky position perhaps several degrees away from the Crab Nebula. The Crab is northwest of the star Zeta Tau, whereas the Chinese stargazers placed the new object southeast of Zeta Tau. The object was very bright and was visible for a total of 653 days, during 23 of which it was visible in daylight! However, there is nothing in the recorded observations to indicate that the object was visible initially for 23 days in daylight, which is what one would expect of a supernova, which reaches its maximum brightness quickly, then fades. The records also seem to leave open the possibility that the object was moving, but a comet has been ruled out.

The Chinese and Japanese records that have come down to us are fragmentary and may represent an edited version of original observations. We are not used to this today, but a thousand years ago, when very few people anywhere in the world could read and write, central authorities kept very tight control over information and utilized it to reinforce their own positions of power. The Chinese emperors employed official stargazers to create accurate calendars and to observe the heavens for celestial events that might reflect upon the condition of the emperor and his government, according to their philosophy that the celestial abode echoed the condition of the world. If the news was bad, it was a problem for all concerned. Might it be a matter of interpretation, which could change with a little editing?

A recent study of the chemical composition of the Crab Nebula concludes that it is unlikely that the supernova could have burned brightly enough for 653 days to be visible from Earth (Sollerman et. al.). I suggest that the event of 1054 A.D. was far more than a supernova, but rather was the approach toward perihelion of a large planetoid in a highly elliptical orbit about the Sun; and that over time most of the records of this awesome event in cultures all over the world were edited or destroyed for religious and political purposes.

Jesuit scholar Franz Kugler suggested, based on his close study early in the 20th century, of Mesopotamian clay tablets that the ancient cultures of the Middle East had knowledge of a large celestial body orbiting in a great elliptical path like a comet (Kugler). Author Zecharia Sitchin asserts in *The 12th Planet* that Mesopotamian and biblical sources present strong evidence that the orbital period of this object is 3,600 years.

ARIZONA PICTOGRAPHS

William C. Miller found pictographs in northern Arizona that many scientists associate with the supernova of 1054 (Brandt et.al.). The pictographs seem to indicate a large planetary body about the size of our Moon. Two separate images show one circular object next to a crescent-shaped object. Current thinking on this suggests that the pictographs describe conjunction of the Moon and the first appearance of the supernova on July 5, 1054, which would have been visible to native Americans from that location. The crescent represents the Moon, which did have that shape on that date, and the circular object represents the supernova. However, the circular object is about 86 percent of the Moon's diameter in one pictograph and about 73 percent in the other.

Current thinking suggests that the great size of the circle emphasizes the great brightness of the supernova, but no supernova has ever come close to the 0.5 degree size of the full Moon. A very close and extremely bright supernova might appear about twice the size of Venus in the night sky, just a tiny fraction of the size of the full Moon.

I suggest that the pictographs may be composite artistic representations of the complete 653-day event; and that the artists were showing the conditions of the first appearance of the object on July 5, when it became visible to the naked eye (~magnitude 6), in a composite with a later period of the orbit as the object approached the Sun and passed some distance beyond the orbit of our Moon. Using the information in the pictographs literally, the apparent size of the guest star (GS) at closest approach to the Earth was about four fifths the size of our Moon.

If GS is about the same size as the Moon, its apparent angular diameter would indicate that it passed about 680,000 km from the Earth. By comparison, the Moon averages about 385,000 km from the Earth. Ho Peng-Yoke et.al. have suggested that one interpretation of the Chinese historical record implies that the object may have had an apparent angular size comparable with that of the Moon, which is supported by the Native American pictographs from half a world away.

As GS approached the Sun on a highly elliptical orbit, any type of ice on its surface would have begun to evaporate, increasing its brightness. The object would have become visible during daylight (~magnitude −4 or −5) as it approached the Earth, months after its first sighting in July 1054. The Chinese stargazers' records say that during its 23 days of daytime visibility the object's "color was reddish-white, with pointed rays in all four directions."

COMPUTER SIMULATIONS

When GS was first sighted with the naked eye (~magnitude 6), it was probably something like 4 AU from the Earth. This exact distance is difficult to calculate, as we can't be certain of the size of the object or the extent to which its brightness was increasing. During its departure from Earth proximity it would of course have been in a totally different region of the sky from where it was first sighted. The fragmentary Chinese records provide no real help here, merely leaving open the possibility that the object was moving. I have run some simple computer simulations to look at this more carefully. Some of the orbital elements that I used:

- Semimajor Axis: 120 AU
- Eccentricity: 0.9917
- Inclination: 170°
- Longitude of Ascending Node: 50°
- Argument of Perihelion: 90°

- Perihelion Distance: 0.996 AU
- Orbital Period: 1,314 years
- Date of Perihelion: May 1, 1055

Note that this is a retrograde orbit, i.e. it is moving in the opposite direction from the other planets. Using these values, GS was several degrees southeast of the star Zeta Tau on July 4, 1054. This is where the Chinese observations place it. As I run the simulation, GS approaches the Sun, reaches perihelion at about 1 AU, and swings away to the outer solar system to disappear again from view.

Using these orbital elements, it appears in the correct position in July, approaches the Sun and disappears from view in about 653 days. When it first appears it is about 4 AU from the Earth, and 653 days later it is again about 4 AU away, albeit in a different part of the sky. One slight wrinkle: my simulator program only allows a maximum orbital period of about 1,300 years, not 3,600 years, so these elements would need to be fine-tuned. But this is, nonetheless, strong evidence of proof-of-principle.

An object with an orbital period of 3,600 years has a semi-major axis of about 235 AU. If its perihelion is, say, 1 AU, then its aphelion would be about 469 AU (by comparison, the aphelion of Pluto is about 49 AU). If this is the case, then its current distance from the Sun is about 250 AU, still moving away and due to return to the inner solar system around the year 4655.

According to my rough calculations, it may still be barely visible to the big Keck telescope, which can reach magnitude 28. If the object can be spotted, parallax will easily give us its precise distance from the Sun and exact orbital parameters. In order to calculate its current position, highly accurate orbital simulations would be needed, taking into account gravitational perturbation by the Earth, Moon, and other planets.

EARTH CATASTROPHISM

If we count back from 1054 A.D., subtracting 3,600 years each time, we arrive at the following dates: 2546 B.C., 6146 B.C., 9746 B.C. The last date is very close to Plato's date for the destruction of Atlantis. This can be deduced from his dialogue *Timaeus*, in which he relates the speech of the Egyptian priest, in conversation with Solon, who says that the events regarding Atlantis occurred "nine thousand years ago." Since Solon died circa 559 B.C., this gives a calendar date of circa 9500 B.C.

Circa 9500 B.C. is about the time of the Pleistocene-Holocene boundary in the geological record. At this time, a mass extinction occurred in North and South America (Martin and Klein), although there is no iridium signature in the strata (such as there is at the Cretaceous-Tertiary boundary, indicating that the impact of an asteroid was at least partly responsible for the demise of the dinosaurs 65 million years ago). The Natufian village sites in the Levant also were abandoned or destroyed circa 9500 B.C. (Olszewski 1986).

Evidence is also accumulating for a global culture collapse around 2300 B.C. The Akkadian empire in Mesopotamia, the Old Kingdom in Egypt, the Early Bronze Age civilization in Israel, Anatolia and Greece, as well as the Indus Valley civilization in India, the Hilmand civilization in Afghanistan, and the Hongshan Culture in China, all fell into ruin at more or less the same time (Peiser). Current studies point to a radical climate change as a major factor (Dalfes et.al.). Fast climate change on this scale is highly anomalous, unless viewed in the context of catastrophic theory. This date falls very close to one of the proposed perihelion points for the large planetoid discussed in this report. Although I am not suggesting a close encounter, dust and debris carried in the wake of GS could have rained upon the Earth and significantly altered climate.

MULTIPLE CATASTROPHIC MECHANISMS

I suggest that the last close approach of this object by the Earth occurred around 9500 B.C., ending the Pleistocene and altering somewhat the surface of the Earth. After that event, GS settled into its current orbital period of some 3,600 years, after which the ancient civilizations began to observe it. The orbital period of GS fluctuates somewhat around this average. Such an object would have an unstable orbit. Planetary perturbations would change its period randomly on the order of 10 percent per revolution, even without a close approach.

This unstable object, like the long-period comets, would eventually be ejected from the solar system. Statistical studies of this process indicate that its maximum residence in the solar system would be about 6 million years (Yabushita). Interestingly, the last few million years constitute a period of accelerated mountain-building movement of the Earth's crust (Flint), exactly what would be expected due to occasional close approaches of such an object.

This object cannot explain the mass extinctions 65 million years ago.

Over long periods of geological time, we may be looking at multiple "catastrophic" mechanisms, including comet and asteroid bombardment. Also note that Sitchin's model also does not explain these extinctions. Whatever the object is, if it's in a highly elliptical orbit, it is unstable.

POSSIBLE SCENARIO OF GUEST STAR EVENT

Circa 9500 B.C., the Guest Star made a close pass by the Earth as it approached the Sun. The scenario I suggest would approximate the following events:

- Gravitational effects caused high tidal waves moving at thousands of miles per hour as GS swept past the Earth, moving in the opposite direction. In addition to the ocean tide, the body tide in the solid structure of the Earth is sufficient to lift up large portions of the crust and cause major shifts along tectonic boundaries. Some portions of the ocean tide achieve escape velocity, freezing as they hit space and going into orbit around the Earth and the Sun to return later as the strange periodic "ice falls" recorded in the literature of Charles Forte, who inspired the creation of *Fortean Times* magazine.

- Small living creatures trapped in these masses of ice survive in suspended animation for long periods of time, to be revived as the ice melts during reentry and appearing as the rains of frogs and fishes also seen in the Fortean literature. Recent scientific analysis on a large icefall in Spain revealed that the fragments contained earthly substances such as chalk and salt, and were generally inexplicable (*Fortean Times*). Usual explanations, such as cometary debris and meteorological or aircraft origins, were ruled out. Other portions of the escaping frozen mass are lost forever to the Sun, or eventually collide with other planets.

- Preliminary work by Brian Tonks at the University of Arizona (personal communication, 1992) indicates that about 40 percent of the ejected material would eventually return to Earth, and another 40 percent would collide with Venus. Less than 5 percent would strike Mars and Mercury, with the rest scattered about the outer planets. Radar evidence indicates that Mercury may have a north polar water ice cap (*Astronomy*). This is quite a surprise, because Mercury was considered too hot to hold any ice deposits. This water ice may in fact be from Earth, and sampling it could constitute one test of this hypothesis, as would tests of the possible deposits of water ice on the Moon.

- The killing mechanism of the mass extinction event of 9500 B.C. was a large tidal wave, which stretched from pole to pole and swept across the Earth in less than an hour, leaving no iridium signature. This model is supported by the fact that the extinction event was weight-dependent, i.e. the larger species tended to die out, the smaller species tended to survive (Martin and Klein). Small species tend to be burrowing creatures, and can more readily hide underground or in rock caves and cracks than larger species. Thus, they essentially had little bomb shelters in which to ride out the devastation. Large species would be out in the open and subject to the full impact of the event.

- The tidal waves probably did not cover every part of the Earth; some areas may have been affected more than others. The extinction event struck North and South America, but not much in Africa and Asia. It is fair to assume that the Earth's orbit, the length of the year and perhaps the length of the day, were changed somewhat by this event, but we have no way to determine that now. However, ingenious work studying historical eclipses has determined that the day length is growing longer by an average of 1.7 milliseconds per century in an oscillating pattern (Stephenson), something which cannot be explained by any known force. This oscillating pattern may be one remnant signature of the event at the end of the Pleistocene.

EARTH'S INTERNAL HEAT

Another important anomaly is the high temperature of the interior of the Earth. During the nineteenth century, British scientist Lord Kelvin calculated that the Earth should have lost all of its primordial heat of formation after a maximum span of 400 million years (Thomson). The Earth is supposed to be more than 4 billion years old. Why is the interior of the Earth still hot?

Geologists believe that radioactive elements such as uranium, thorium and potassium contribute to heating of the Earth. But it is generally accepted that these elements are concentrated only in the outer crust of the Earth (Press and Siever), and do not affect deep internal heating.

Measurement of the flux of alpha particles (produced by the radioactive decay of uranium and thorium) on the Earth's surface should agree with estimates based on the Earth's content of these elements and the observed heat flow. Yet, actual measurement of the alpha particle flux is much less than what is predicted (Keken et.al.). Where is Earth's internal heat coming from?

Catastrophism suggests that tidal forces in the solid structure of the Earth during close encounters are responsible for much of the continued heating of the planet. Indeed, those areas that are most geologically active, such as regions showing recent mountain-building, are precisely those areas radiating the most heat. This is not an argument for a "young" Earth (i.e. greater internal heat equals youth). Although there are indications in the scientific literature of some problems with radiometric dating techniques, I can accept that these techniques, used carefully, are giving us useful information on the age of the Earth. Radiometric dating techniques should not be affected by the heat of the Earth, and thus should be independent confirmation of the Earth's age.

This preliminary report does not attempt to address all issues, but constitutes a work in progress. Further work is required, especially in precise orbital simulation modeling. ●

References

"AstroNews," *Astronomy* (February 20, 1992).

Brandt, J.C., et al. "Possible Rock Art Records of the Crab Nebula Supernova in the Western United States." In *Archaeoastronomy in Pre-Columbian America* (Austin: Univ. Texas Press, 1975) pp. 45–58.

Brecher, K., et al. "A Near-Eastern Sighting of the Supernova Explosion of 1054." *Nature* 273 (1978): 728–30.

Dalfes, H.N., et al., eds. *Third Millennium B.C. Climate Change and Old World Collapse.* Berlin: Springer-Verlag, 1996.

Fesen, R.A. "Supernovae, General Properties." In *The Astronomy and Astrophysics Encyclopedia* (New York: Van Nostrand Reinhold, 1992) pp. 883–86.

Flint, R.F. *Glacial and Quaternary Geology.* New York: Wiley, 1971.

Ho Peng-Yoke et al. "The Chinese Guest Star of A.D. 1054 and the Crab Nebula." *Vistas in Astronomy* 13, (1970): 1–13.

Keken, P.E., et al. "A Dynamical Investigation of the Heat and Helium Imbalance." *Earth and Planetary Science Letters* 188 (2001): 421–34.

Kugler, F.X. *Sternkunde und Sterndienst in Babel.* Munster in Westfalen: Aschendorff, 1907–1924.

Martin, P.S. & Klein, R.G., eds. *Quaternary Extinctions.* Tucson: University of Arizona Press, 1989.

Mitton, S. *The Crab Nebula.* New York: Scribner, 1978.

Olszewski, D. *The North Syrian Late Epipaleolithic.* Oxford: B.A.R., 1986.

Peiser, B. "Comets and Disaster in the Bronze Age." *British Archaeology* 30 (December 6–7, 1997).

Press, F. & Siever, R. *Earth.* San Francisco: W.H. Freeman, 1982.

Sitchin, Z. *The Twelfth Planet.* New York: Stein and Day, 1976.

Sollerman, J., et al. "Why Did Supernova 1054 Shine at Late Times?" *Astronomy and Astrophysics* 366 (2001): 197–201.

Stephenson, F.R. *Historical Eclipses and Earth's Rotation.* Cambridge: Cambridge University Press, 1997.

Taylor, R.E. *Radiocarbon Dating: An Archaeological Perspective.* Orlando: Academic Press, 1987.

Thomson, W. "On the Secular Cooling of the Earth." *Transactions of the Royal Society of Edinburgh* XXIII (1864): 157–69.

"Weird Ice Chunks Fall on Spain." *Fortean Times* (April, 6, 2000).

Yabushita, S. "A Statistical Study of the Orbits of Long-Period Comets." *Monthly Notices of the Royal Astronomical Society* 187 (1979): 445–62.

—Spring 2003

Occult Symbolism of Nibiru, the Planet of the Cross(X)ing

by Andy Lloyd

This article by a well-known Planet X researcher explores the implications of the existence of a tenth solar system planet, which the ancient Sumerians called Nibiru, and its symbolism within various powerful esoteric movements. As Andy Lloyd postulates, even though scientific evidence and ancient mythological systems continue to strengthen the case for this "dark star" and its contingent of habitable moons, the media and the mainstream scientific community will continue to ignore it.

WE LIVE IN AN ever-changing world where scientific knowledge adapts to new, sometimes startling, discoveries. However, our ability as a society to adapt to these new revelations is often below par. We have short lifetimes, and the strength of conviction that the "facts" taught us in school are immutable is often overpowering. Sometimes this reflects a need to be fastened to a fundamental rock of truth—a religious doctrine perhaps, or a political philosophy. Yet, the world does not conform to these models or ideals—many of the truths we hold dear are as afloat on the sea of knowledge as we are.

Take, for example, what we think we know about the solar system. Having rid ourselves of the notion that the planets and the Sun circle the Earth, we have replaced this geocentric notion with another palliative. Because the planets circle the Sun in an amiable, orderly fashion, we take it as a truism that they have done so since the very beginning of the solar system. Inherent in this belief is the assumption that there cannot be another major body in the solar system interacting with the known planets in any kind of destabilising manner. Otherwise, the planets would be chaotically arranged, and the solar system would be a desperately dangerous place.

To confront this assumption with a few uncomfortable facts is a difficult task, even for astronomers. We quickly embark upon a journey into what, as far as most scientists are concerned, is purely speculative. With this in mind, I will ask the reader to grant me a little leeway within these pages as I consider a number of modern solar system discoveries and see where they take us. The ideas that I will promulgate will be speculative, but they explain a great deal and seem worthy of consideration.

GALACTIC WANDERERS

The solar system is an arena that extends well beyond the planet Pluto. The area of the Sun's influence may extend as far as the halfway point between this solar and the nearest star. It is likely, although not proven, that comets orbit the Sun at extraordinary distances, perhaps 100,000 times the distance between the Earth and the Sun. It should not surprise us, then, that other much larger bodies may be similarly in orbit within the Sun's sphere of influence. There may be many large planetary bodies out there, dark and distant, that await discovery. What if there are? Any number of sizeable planets could exist in the Oort Cloud, but it would make precious little difference to our understanding of our place in the cosmos. After all, such bodies would be frozen in the deep cold of interstellar space, existing as lifeless rocks gently circling a dim and remote star.[1]

But as the size of a planet increases, so does its ability to warm itself. We can start to talk about failed stars, or brown dwarfs. These entities are likely to have been formed in the coalescing matter of emerging multiple star systems, and to have been ejected as the "runts" of the litter during the gravitational struggles of the new stellar families.[2] Brown dwarfs, or dark stars, tend to be found wandering the interstellar void; yet they were created within the celestial nests of stellar incubators. Rarely discussed in scientific papers about brown dwarfs, however, is what might happen when one of these cosmic wanderers inadvertently finds itself passing through another star system. Given that it is statistically probable that regular stars have passed through the outer reaches of the solar system during the lifetime of the Sun, it seems more likely still that smaller bodies would similarly have encroached into Sol's domain. Astrophysicist Jack Hills of the Los Alamos National Laboratory has calculated that stars pass within 3000 Astronomical Units of the Sun every

100 million years or so. (An Astronomical Unit is equal to the Earth's average distance from the Sun.)[3]

Our knowledge of dark bodies wandering independently through interstellar space is just beginning. Clearly, these bodies are very difficult to pinpoint, but the Hubble Space Telescope has inadvertently discovered some planetary bodies doing just that. They were detected through a "micro-lensing" effect as they passed in front of background stars, and some of these remote bodies have been dubbed "sub-brown dwarfs."[4] We now know that there are dark planets, "light-emitting planets"[5] and failed stars floating freely in interstellar space, and that they could pass through our solar system on a random basis.

THE LATE, GREAT BOMBARDMENT

Our notion of a planetary system hugging the Sun and safely cocooned from the dangers of the galactic environment is a fallacy. Looking at the action of passing stars and planets, Hills ran computer simulations to predict the outcome of various scenarios.[6] His results were illuminating. It is evident that a planetary body ten times the size of Jupiter could pass directly through the planetary solar system without causing major disruption to the known planets. It is also the case that, upon interacting gravitationally with the Sun and major planets, the wanderer could be captured into a highly eccentric orbit around the Sun. But instead of disrupting the orbits of the known planets chaotically, their orbital distances from the Sun would be subject to change. Since the "binding energies" of the planets are linked, a major new planet going into orbit around the Sun would change these energy relationships.

Such an event would also trigger a short, but violent, period of cometary bombardment upon the planets.[7] This might explain the extinction events during the history of the Earth, as well as a remarkable event that occurred 3.9 billion years ago. Dubbed the "late great bombardment" by scientists, this time witnessed a sudden barrage of cosmic debris against the Earth and Moon. Many thousands of impacts occurred, some of them even greater than the impact believed to have wiped out the dinosaurs. These impacts created continent-sized craters and vaporised oceans.[8] This bombardment appears to have lasted about 100 million years, but occurred too late and too violently to be a result of random asteroid collisions after the birth of the solar system 4.5 billion years ago.

Scientists are struggling to explain this cataclysmic event in the solar system. An interaction with a wandering celestial body would fit the bill well. It would likely mean that such a body remains in orbit around the Sun, undiscovered. Were it not for the lack of evidence of such a planet's existence, this idea would most certainly be a prominent theory. Instead, mainstream astronomers and physicists have proposed the wildest and most speculative ideas about the induction of this monstrous cataclysm. However, their musings ignore an entire collection of further evidence about this wandering planet.

ANCIENT KNOWLEDGE

Many ancient religions and mythologies have involved the study of the stars and planets. The ancient cosmologies were understood in terms of the character and actions of deities, but they referred to heavenly bodies. For many of the ancients, there was no distinction to be made between deities and heavenly bodies, and there is much to learn about their understanding of the cosmos from their religious myths.

The Egyptians, for instance, almost certainly worshipped stellar deities prior to the later domination of the solar figurehead. Constellations, stars and planets represented gods and goddesses, and the Pharaohs expected their spirit bodies, or *ka*s, to rise to the stars after death. But where much of the ancient Egyptian material pertaining to such beliefs is symbolic in nature and subject to differing interpretation, the religions of the early Mesopotamians are far more explicit. In particular, the texts of the ancient Sumerians, our planet's earliest known civilization, describe cosmic events that leave us in no doubt about the origin of the late, great bombardment.

The Sumerians lived in what is now Iraq and produced a relatively advanced society seemingly overnight, replacing the more primitive neolithic cultures prevalent in the area 6,000 years ago. Their own origin is mysterious, but they made it quite clear that they derived their knowledge and expertise from a race of superhuman gods known as the Anunnaki. These extraterrestrial colonists on planet Earth created humans in their own image, put them to work in their mines and their gardens, and then looked on from above as mankind was almost entirely wiped out by a cataclysmic deluge. Following this catastrophe, the Anunnaki allowed humans to spread freely over the face of the Earth and, eventually, bequeathed them the knowledge necessary to advance to a state of civilization.

This version of the Sumerian account of prehistory was first described by the scholar Zecharia Sitchin in 1976.[9] It goes without saying that his conclusion about the physical reality of the Anunnaki is not shared by mainstream Sumerologists, who prefer to interpret these myths in terms of psychological constructs of the primitive mind. Yet the Sumerian texts are complex in form and explicit in their declaration that they apply to a physical reality, not to allegory. Sitchin has since written a series of books to back up his initial claims, and to provide further evidence that this origin of our species is based in reality. Other writers, taken with this new mode of thinking, have pursued parallel research; they include Alan Alford,[10] Lloyd Pye,[11] Neil Freer,[12] and Joan d'Arc.[13] Their school of thought has produced a wealth of scientific data and evidence to back up Sitchin's theory; yet the so-called "Twelfth planet theory" remains on the very fringes of scientific speculation.

NIBIRU: PLANET X?

One particular aspect of Sitchin's writings that has interested me is the nature of the home world of the Anunnaki. In their text called *Enuma Elish*, the Babylonians derived a cosmology and story of the genesis of the solar system from the Sumerians.[14] It is a remarkable account that recreates the solar system almost exactly as we now recognize it, but with a hidden extra planet. This is no normal planet, it seems, but is an enormous fiery realm with attendant moons, known as Nibiru. Prior to Sitchin's first book, the nature of Nibiru was being argued by scholars, and remained "Planet X," an "unknown factor."[15]

Sitchin determined this celestial body to be an undiscovered tenth planet orbiting the Sun. Its orbit is a highly elongated ellipse, and it remains hidden from view. Like a comet, it becomes visible only at its closest approach to the Sun, during its relatively short-lived perihelion. The origin of this body was interstellar space, having been captured by the Sun when it wandered through the solar system. The resultant changes to the solar system were catastrophic, and Sitchin indicated that this event, described in the *Enuma Elish*, occurred when the solar system was still young. The Earth was the battered result of multiple impacts, and had previously been a much larger planet whose oceans had been vaporised.

This description from a 4,500 year old creation myth sounds remarkably like the late, great bombardment. Nibiru's capture by the Sun into a highly elongated orbit also correlates well with the computer simulations conducted by Hills in 1985. We are now aware of planetary bodies greater in size than Jupiter that wander freely in interstellar space, many of which are dark stars known as brown dwarfs. This substantiates the claims of the ancient Babylonians that a wandering fiery planet could encroach upon the family of planets formed with the Sun. It also consolidates my claims that the ancient descriptions of Nibiru are consistent with a small brown dwarf.[16,17,18] But even though the scientific evidence continues to strengthen the case for the dark star and its contingent of habitable moons, the mainstream scientific community ignores it.

There isn't any particular reason why they should do so, at least from a purely objective point of view. After all, the far reaches of the solar system remain very much uncharted territory. When an astrophysics group from Harvard released details of an anomalous Kuiper Belt object known as 2000 CR105, one of the team members, Matthew Holman, indicated its bizarre orbit might be the result of a massive perturber in the comet clouds, beyond the planetary zone. He went on record as saying that a Mars-sized body might "easily" have evaded detection at a distance as close as 200 AU from the Earth.[19]

Nibiru is a substantially larger body, but it is also likely to reside a great deal further away than 200 AU. So not only could Nibiru still have evaded detection, but its presence beyond our current range of observation could explain the anomalous orbital behaviour of known objects. It would also explain the nonrandom pattern of comets entering the planetary zone, which led two groups of researchers to propose the existence of a brown dwarf in the outer Oort Cloud in 1999.[20,21]

Although the astronomical community continues to ignore the remarkable "coincidence" between the ancient knowledge of the solar system and continuing scientific discoveries, if Nibiru is out there it is simply a matter of time before it is located. Meanwhile, the symbolism of this hidden celestial entity becomes the focus. Any expectations or implications to draw from the existence of Nibiru can only be done through a rigorous study of its place within comparative religious thought and symbolism. It has become increasingly evident that Nibiru played a central role in many religions and cults through the ages, and its iconography is of the utmost significance.

PLANET OF THE CROSS(X)ING

The earliest symbol used to depict Nibiru, or the "Planet of the Crossing," was a Sumerian pictographic cross. (Strangely, if it's the same body, it is still being similarly depicted as Planet X.) Sitchin notes that this cuneiform symbol also meant "Anu" (the leader of the Anunnaki) and "divine." This symbol evolved in the Semitic languages to become the letter "tav," meaning "the sign."[22] Nibiru means "ferry" or "ford," and is applicable to a celestial phenomenon.[23] The symbolism used to depict the Planet of the Crossing became more complex and took the form of the winged disc. This important symbol was popular throughout early Mesopotamian cultures, and found its way into ancient Egypt, presumably as part of a general transfer of early Sumerian culture.[24]

The Mesopotamian winged disc symbol took the form of a feathered cross, and the central disc often had the image of the supreme deity within it. The Persians depicted Ahura Mazda in the symbol, while the Assyrians showed the god Assur.[25] The ancient Egyptians used the symbol to denote Horus Horakhti, synonymous with the Horus falcon. In the Egyptian texts references were made to Horus flying up to the Sun as a "great winged disc," emphasising that Horus the winged disc and the Solar disc were not synonymous in the ancient teachings.[26]

I consider it highly likely that the Christian image of a dying-and-rising godman depicted at the center of a cross owes much to this symbolic tradition, and denotes the messianic star as a celestial phenomenon. In this way, we can follow the evolution of symbolism from the Sumerians, through the ancient Egyptian culture and, via the Hellenistic Mystery schools, to the deification of Jesus the Nazarene. It may come as a shock to some, but the symbolism of a deity upon a cross is by no means unique to Christianity, and the earliest Mesopotamian examples were quite evidently of purely celestial significance.

NIBIRU'S APPEARANCE

Nibiru currently orbits the Sun in a similar way to a comet. But far from being an icy rock ejecting volatile gases as it is flung around the Sun at perihelion, Nibiru is a fiery world of immense proportions. The ejected gases from comets are blown back from the Sun by the solar wind, whether the comet is travelling towards the Sun or away from it.[27] This display constitutes the famous cometary tail, a visible phenomenon of significant size that dwarfs the cometary core from which the volatile gases are driven off.

The planets with their own magnetic fields have a similarly shaped but invisible field around them known as their magnetosphere. Jupiter's magnetosphere is very substantial indeed, and it seems likely that the magnetosphere of a brown dwarf would be greater still. In recent times, evidence has emerged showing that the auroras of Jupiter are subject to deflection by the solar wind around the magnetic field of the gas giant. Dr. John Clarke of the University of Michigan notes that Jupiter's magnetosphere is "so vast that if it shined at wavelengths visible to the eye, it would appear from Earth to be two to three times wider than the disc of the Sun, even though it is more than four times as far away."[28]

Brown dwarfs may not shine like stars, but they still manage to "glimmer darkly forever," as Bo Reipurth of the University of Colorado has described.[29] They are also known to emit small solar flares, and have unpredictable periods of intense activity.[30] Astronomers consider it probable that brown dwarfs in the vicinity of stars are likely to be more active than those floating free in interstellar space. Therefore, we can conclude that Nibiru would become more active in the vicinity of the Sun during perihelion, throwing out solar flares and auroras in abundance.

Indeed, this heightened level of stellar activity is described in Mesopotamian accounts of Nibiru as it approached the primordial planet Tiamat (Earth):

> In front of him he set the lightning,
> with a blazing flame he filled his body;
> He then made a net to enfold Tiamat therein . . .
> A fearsome halo his head was turbaned,
> He was wrapped with awesome terror as with a cloak.[31]

If Jupiter's aurora follows the magnetospheric field lines, then it seems equally likely that the coronal discharge of an excited brown dwarf will be similarly swept back from the Sun by the solar wind. Furthermore, the celestial halo effect will be of truly awesome proportions, making Nibiru's size appear much greater than the Sun to viewers on Earth. As Nibiru approaches the inner solar system, it will be seen to grow immense, fiery wings, swept back from the Sun.

This explains the descriptions of the falcon god Horus flying toward the Sun as the winged disc. Not only that, but it allows us to recognize within this celestial image the symbolism of the firebird so prevalent throughout the world's mythologies. Nibiru at perihelion becomes the cosmic phoenix, reborn from glimmering embers of its exiled solitude in the comet clouds. I imagine it to be a truly awesome sight, one that remains the focus of countless mythologies and religions through the ages, despite Nibiru's millennia-long periods of absence.

NIBIRU'S MOONS

According to the Sumerian texts, Nibiru entered the solar system with seven moons before engaging the primordial planet Tiamat in the celestial battle. Known in the creation myth as the "seven winds," the moons became an important focus of Nibiru's onslaught of Earth's primordial mother planet.[32] It is unclear how many moons Nibiru has, and how visible they are from Earth during its perihelion transit. Some depictions of the winged disc contain seven distinct discs in either the wings or the tail.[33,34] Other motifs contain the image of two discs attached to the central disc by curved lines, and looking like the feet of the celestial bird.[35] It may be that the number of moons is indeed seven, but that a variable number are visible from Earth, depending on their relative positions in their orbit around the brown dwarf. Perhaps two of the moons are sizeable bodies, similar in size to the terrestrial planets orbiting the Sun, while the rest constitute more elusive bodies.

The number seven is a holy number in many religions. There is a wealth of evidence about how ancient celestial symbols often involved seven stars or discs, often accompanied by a crescent.[36] These range from Sumerian cylinder seals to Judaic and Christian symbols. It is evident that not only has the Nibiruan cross survived into modern times as an archetypal symbol, but the depiction of the dark star's attendant moons remains a powerful icon.

The moons of Nibiru perform another important role involving the incubation of life. Warmed by gravitational interaction and the considerable heat output of the dark star, these moons are potentially far better environments for supporting life than even Jupiter's own moons, such as Europa.[37] These would be relatively dark worlds, perhaps lit by only dim red light, but the warmth of their environments would enable water to exist in liquid form, and I suspect the brown dwarf's radiation output would facilitate atmospheres, unlike the Galilean moons of Jupiter.

The question is whether the Sumerian claim that Nibiru itself is home to a god-like race of extraterrestrials, known as the Anunnaki, is plausible. Brown dwarfs themselves seem incapable of supporting life, but not so their moons. Conditions on the moons would make the establishment of intelligent life potentially viable, and there would be no constant bombardment of the kind of harmful solar radiation to which we are subject. This may facilitate longer life spans, reflecting the remarkable longevity claimed for the gods. This has to be a possibility, although it is also equally possible that the rare visible passage of Nibiru was sufficient in itself to engender several complex polytheistic mythologies.

Sitchin argues that our evolutionary development was subject to direct intervention, and he may well be correct. But the existence of Nibiru would not, in itself, necessarily indicate the presence of the Anunnaki. However, if a massive planet or failed star were found to be following a cometary orbit around the Sun, the chances of Sitchin being vindicated would be high. The future discovery of this body would change our entire perception of who we are and of our place in the cosmos.

WINGED DISK: THE EVOLVING SYMBOL

The bizarre orbit of Nibiru creates a unique characteristic for any deity associated with the "winged planet." Instead of being a cyclical visible phenomenon like the Sun, Moon and known planets, Nibiru's appearance is confined to a brief period of time every 3,600 to 3,800 years. Its appearance is sudden, and it quickly brightens to become a quite remarkable celestial event, before disappearing once again into the void. The fiery wings of Nibiru become the phoenix, reborn in the heavenly Duat.

The deity associated with this anomalous planet would be linked with dying-and-rising symbolism, a god of heavenly resurrection. This polytheistic deification may have evolved differently in monotheistic religion, taking the form of legends and myths regarding "the lost king." We can expect that the belief in the Nibiru archetype would have taken on a different guise during the purging of the pagan religions in the first millennium after Christ. According to writers of antiquity, the extensive spread of the pagan mysteries originated in Egypt, and were modeled on the mysteries of Osiris, Isis and Horus. The mysteries traditionally include Dionysus in Greece, Mithras in Persia (and Rome), Adonis in Syria, Attis in Thrace, and there has lately been an argument to include early Christianity.[38] The Osirian and Isian cults extend back to pre-Dynastic times, and there is a strong case for believing that early Egyptian civilization itself originated in Sumer.[39]

This presents us with an alternative and parallel expansion of Sumerian knowledge, as described by Sitchin. The Sumerian religion was taken up by the Assyrians and Chaldeans, and expanded into Persia in the guise of Ahura Mazda. It also has resonance in the Ugaritic god Baal in Canaan (depicted as part of a trinity with the Sun and Moon), and Hittite dragons and lost gods.[40]

Sitchin documents the importance of the winged disc in Egyptian culture and religious beliefs,[41] and goes on to propose the migration of the Anunnaki culture to South America and Meso-America.[42] The later claim seems less likely to me, although there was evidently contact between the ancient world and the New World in the past, possibly through the Phoenicians and Vikings. I think it more likely that the evolution of beliefs about the winged disc took a different course; it was retained in archaic Egyptian symbolism and became embodied in the pagan mysteries— and eventually early Christianity.

The problem with such an assertion is that the nature of these mystery schools is secretive and closed, based on rites of initiation. It is difficult to chart the evolution of a particular religious tenet through schools of thought that remain closed to non-initiates, but enough evidence now exists in the public domain to allow us a closer look at this private world. ●

Notes

1. Lloyd, A. "Sol B: The Messianic Star?" *Paranoia* (April 2001): 2–6.
2. Reipurth, B. "Brown dwarfs are stellar embryos evicted by siblings." CU Boulder press release, July 2, 2001.
3. Hills, J. *Astronomy Journal* 86 (1981): 1730.
4. spaceflightnow.com/news/n0106/27hubble/.
5. "Mystery of free-floating 'planets.'" news.bbc.co.uk/hi/english/sci/tech/ newsid_957000/957518.stm 5/10/2000.
6. Hills, J.G. "The Passage of a 'Nemesis'-like object through the Planetary System," *Astronomy Journal* 90 (1985): 1876–82.
7. Hills, *Astronomy Journal* 86.
8. Semeniuk, I. "Neptune Attacks!" *New Scientist* (April 7, 2001): 27–29.
9. Sitchin, Z. *The Twelfth Planet.* New York: Avon, 1976.
10. Alford, A. *Gods of the New Millennium.* London: Hodder & Stoughton, 1997.
11. Pye, L. *Everything You Know Is Wrong.* Adamu Press.
12. Freer, N. *Of Heaven and Earth.* www.thebooktree.com, 1996.
13. d'Arc, J. *Space Travelers and the Genesis of the Human Form.* www.thebooktree. com, 2000.
14. Sitchin, *Twelfth Planet.*
15. de Santillana, G. and H. von Dechend. *Hamlet's Mill.* App. 39, pp. 430–51, www.apollonius.net/trees.html.
16. Lloyd, "Sol B."
17. ———. "The Dark Star Theory." www.darkstar1.co.uk [February 2000].
18. ———. "Synopsis of the Dark Star Theory," *UFO Magazine* (August 2001): 50–55.

19. Beatty, J. Kelly. "Big-orbit Object Confounds Dynamicists." www.skypub.com/news/news.shtml#bigorbit [April 5, 2001].

20. Murray, J.B. *Monthly Notes of the Royal Astronomical Society* 309 (1999): 31–34.

21. Sitchin, *Twelfth Planet*.

22. Hills, *Astronomy Journal 86*.

23. Matese, J.J., P.G. Whitman and D.P. Whitmire, *Icarus* 141 (1999): 354–36; see also Professor Matese's homepage: www.ucs.louisiana.edu/~jjm9638.

24. Rohl, D. *Legend: The Genesis of Civilization*. London: Arrow, 1999.

25. Plunket, E. *Calendars and Constellations of the Ancient World*. London: Senate, 1997.

26. Geddes & Grosset. *Ancient Egypt: Myth and History*. Chicago: Gresham, 1997, pp. 145–47.

27. Sagan, C. and A. Druyan. *Comet*. London: Headline, 1985.

28. Webster, G. "Jupiter Particles' Escape Route Found," www.jpl.nasa.gov [May 31, 2001].

29. Hills, *Astronomy Journal* 86.

30. Leutwyler, K. "Bright X-rays, Dim Dwarfs," www.sciam.com/exhibit/2000/071700dwarf/ [January 17, 2000].

31. Sitchin, Z. *Genesis Revisited*. New York: Avon, 1990, pp. 324–28, 334.

32. ———, *Twelfth Planet*.

33. ———. *When Time Began*. New York: Avon, 1993, p. 143.

34. ———. *Twelfth Planet*, p. 240.

35. Willis, R. ed. *World Mythology: The Illustrated Guide*. Duncan Baird, 1996, pp. 64–67, 169.

36. Lloyd, A. "Winged Disk: The Dark Star Theory," www.darkstar1.co.uk.

37. Milstein, M. "Diving into Europa's Ocean." *Astronomy* (October 1997): 38–43.

38. Freke, T. and P. Gandy. *The Jesus Mysteries: The "Original Jesus" Was a Pagan God*. London: Thorsons, 1999.

39. Rohl, *Legend*.

40. Willis, *World Mythology*.

41. Sitchin, Z. *The Stairway to Heaven*. New York: Avon, 1980.

42. ———. *The Lost Realms*. New York: Avon, 1990.

—Winter 2003

Biological and Chemical Warfare

* * *

Blaming Gays, Blacks, and Chimps for AIDS

by *Alan Cantwell, Jr., M.D.*

In this well-documented article, Dr. Cantwell explains that the origin of the HIV virus can be traced back to the Special Virus Cancer Program (1964–1977). Conveniently overlooked are the epidemics of a simian AIDS-like virus which began to break out in primate centers in 1969, a decade before AIDS. Virus-infected animals were shipped to labs worldwide and some of these primates were let back out into the wild. In fact, most of the major researchers promoting the African primate origin of AIDS were connected with this primate cancer retrovirus experimentation. As Dr. Cantwell concludes, the theory of man-made AIDS is rational, based on an awareness of the species-jumping virus experiments of irresponsible scientists during the two decades before the epidemic.

SINCE THE BEGINNING of the AIDS epidemic there have been persistent rumors that the disease was man-made, and that HIV was deliberately "introduced" into the American gay and the African black populations as a germ warfare experiment. This so-called conspiracy theory was quickly squelched by virologists and molecular biologists, who blamed primates in the African bush and human sexuality for the introduction and spread of HIV.

In the fall of 1986, the Soviets shocked the world by claiming that HIV was secretly developed at Fort Detrick, the U.S. Army's biological warfare unit. Although the claim was dismissed as "infectious propaganda," Russian scientists had worked hand in hand with biological warfare scientists in the transfer of viruses and virus-infected tissue into various nonhuman primates (monkeys, apes, chimps) during the 1970s, before AIDS appeared. With improved international relationships, the Russian accusation vanished.

Although evidence supporting the theory has never been mentioned in the major U.S. media, the theory continues to be ridiculed. For example, in the *San Francisco Chronicle*, ("Quest for the Origin of AIDS," January 14, 2001), William Carlsen writes:

> In the early years of the AIDS epidemic, theories attempting to explain the origin of the disease ranged from the comic to the bizarre: A deadly germ escaped from a secret CIA laboratory; God sent the plague down to punish homosexuals and drug addicts; It came from outer space, riding on the tail of a comet.

AIDS certainly did not come from the hand of God or from outer space. However, there is ample evidence to suspect the hand of man in the outbreak of AIDS that first began in the late 1970s in New York City.

CREATING AIDS IN ANIMALS BEFORE THE EPIDEMIC

Lost in the history of AIDS is evidence pointing to HIV as a virus whose origin traces back to animal cancer retrovirus experimentation in the "pre-AIDS" years of the 1960s and 1970s. Evidence linking the introduction of HIV into gays and blacks via vaccine experiments and programs in the late 1970s has been totally ignored in favor of the politically correct theory which claims that HIV originated in chimpanzees in the African rain forest, and that HIV "jumped species" into the African population around 1930 or even earlier.

Conveniently overlooked is the series of outbreaks of AIDS-like epidemics that broke out in U.S. primate centers, beginning in 1969. A decade before AIDS, the first of five recorded epidemics of "simian AIDS" erupted in a colony of stump-tailed macaques housed in a primate lab at Davis, California. Most of the macaques died. Two types of primate immunodeficiency viruses were eventually discovered as the cause. A few silently infected monkeys transferred to the primate colony at Yerkes in Atlanta subsequently died of simian AIDS in the late 1980s. Veterinarians claim that the origin of the simian AIDS outbreak is unknown. However, one obvious possibility is the experimental transfer of viruses between various primate species, which is common practice in animal laboratories.

In 1974, veterinarians actually created an AIDS-like disease when newborn chimps were removed from their mothers and weaned exclusively on virus-infected milk from cows infected with "bovine C-type virus." Within a year the chimps died of leukemia and pneumocystis pneumonia (the "gay pneumonia" of AIDS). Both diseases had never been observed in chimps before this virus-transfer experiment.

Also downplayed is the laboratory creation of feline leukemia and "cat AIDS" by the transfer of HIV-like cat retroviruses in the mid-1970s. These experiments were conducted at Harvard by Myron (Max) Essex, later to become a famous AIDS researcher. All of this man-made creation of AIDS in laboratory animals directly preceded the "mysterious" 1979 introduction of HIV into gay men, one of the most hated minorities in America.

Nowadays, scientists hunt for "ancestor" viruses of HIV in chimps in the African wild and ignore all the immunosuppressive viruses that were created in virus laboratories shortly before AIDS. No consideration is given to any of these lab viruses as possible man-made ancestors of the many strains of HIV (and HIV-2) that jumped species to produce AIDS in humans.

GAY EXPERIMENTS PRECEDING AIDS (1978–1981)

Scientists also discount any connection between the official outbreak of AIDS in 1981 and the experimental hepatitis-B vaccine program (1978–1981) at the New York Blood Center in Manhattan, which used gays as guinea pigs shortly before the epidemic. Curiously, the exact origin of AIDS in the United States remains unstudied. Health authorities simply blame promiscuous gay men, but never adequately explain how a black heterosexual African disease could have transformed itself exclusively into a white young gay male disease in Manhattan.

Researchers claim HIV incubated in Africa for more than a half-century until AIDS broke out there in 1982. However, in the U.S. there was no incubation period for gay men. As soon as homosexuals signed up as guinea pigs for government-sponsored hepatitis-B vaccine experiments, they began to die with a strange virus of unknown origin. The hepatitis-B experiments began in Manhattan in the fall of 1978; the first few cases of AIDS (all young gays from Manhattan) were reported to the Centers for Disease Control (CDC) in 1979.

Scientists have also failed to explain how a new herpes virus was introduced exclusively into gays, along with HIV, in the late 1970s. This herpes virus is now believed to be the cause of Kaposi's sarcoma, the so-called "gay cancer" of AIDS. Before AIDS, Kaposi's sarcoma was never seen in healthy young men. Identified a decade after HIV, in 1994, Kaposi's is closely related to a primate cancer-causing herpes virus extensively studied and transferred in animal laboratories in the decade before AIDS.

Also downplayed to the public is a new microbe (*Mycoplasma penetrans*), also of unknown origin, that was introduced into homosexuals, along with HIV and the new herpes virus. Thus, not one but three new infectious agents were inexplicably transferred into the gay population at the start of the epidemic—HIV, the herpes KS virus, and *M. penetrans*.

In his 2000 book *Virus*, Luc Montagnier, the French virologist who co-discovered HIV, blames promiscuous American gay tourists for bringing this new mycoplasma to Africa, and for bringing back HIV. He provides no evidence for this homophobic theory. Nor does he mention the various mycoplasmas that were passed around in the 1970s in scientific labs, and the fact that these microbes were frequent contaminants in virus cultures and vaccines.

Why are all these simultaneous introductions of new infectious agents into gay men ignored by scientists? Surely a credible explanation would be important in determining the origin of HIV and AIDS. Why are scientists so opposed to the man-made theory? And why do they believe so passionately in the chimp theory? One explanation might be that scientists don't want the public to know what happened to the tens of thousands of imported primates who were held captive in laboratories throughout the world in the decade before AIDS.

THE FORGOTTEN SPECIAL VIRUS CANCER PROGRAM (1964–1977)

Rarely mentioned by AIDS scientists and media reporters is the fact that surgeons have been transplanting chimpanzee parts (and chimp viruses) into people for decades. When Keith Reemtsma died in June 2000, at age 74, he was hailed as a pioneer in cross-species organ transplants (now known as xenotransplantation). By 1964, he had already placed six chimpanzee kidneys into six patients. All his patients died, but eventually Reemtsma succeeded in many human-to-human organ transplants.

The largely forgotten Special Virus Cancer Program (SVCP) is much more likely to have spread primate (chimp and monkey) viruses to human beings. This research program was responsible for the development, production, seeding, and deployment of various animal cancer and immuno-suppressive AIDS-like viruses and retroviruses. These laboratory-created viruses were capable of inducing disease when transferred between animal species and also when transplanted into human cells and tissue.

The SVCP began in 1964 as a government-funded program of the National Cancer Institute (NCI) in Bethesda, Maryland. Originally designed to study leukemia, the program was soon enlarged to study all forms of cancer. The scope of the program was international and included scientists from Japan, Sweden, Italy, the Netherlands, Israel, and Africa. The mission of the SVCP was to collect various human and animal cancers from around the world and to grow large amounts of cancer-causing viruses. As a result, thousands of liters of dangerous man-made viruses were adapted to human cells and shipped around the world to various laboratories. The annual reports of the SVCP contain proof that species-jumping of animal viruses was a common occurrence in labs a decade before AIDS.

The SVCP gathered together the nation's top virologists, biochemists, immunologists, molecular biologists, and epidemiologists to determine the role of viruses and retroviruses in the production of human cancer. Many of the most prestigious medical institutions were involved in this program.

Connected with the SVCP were several Americans who would become the most famous AIDS scientists, such as Robert Gallo (the co-discoverer of HIV), Max Essex of "cat AIDS" fame, and Peter Duesberg, who claims HIV does not cause AIDS. Gallo and Essex were also the first to promote the widely accepted African green monkey theory of AIDS. This theory was proven erroneous as far back as 1988, but was heavily circulated among AIDS educators and the media until the theory was superseded by the chimp theory in the late 1990s.

BIOWARFARE AND PRIMATE RESEARCH

Also joining forces with the SVCP at the NCI were the military's biological warfare researchers. On October 18, 1971, President Nixon announced that the army's biowarfare laboratories at Fort Detrick, Maryland, would be converted to cancer research. As part of Nixon's so-called war on cancer, the military biowarfare unit was retitled the Frederick Cancer Research Center, and Litton Bionetics was named as the military's prime contractor for this project.

According to the SVPC's 1971 annual report, the primary task of the now jointly connected National Cancer Institute–Frederick Cancer Research Center was "the large-scale production of oncogenic (cancer-causing) and suspected oncogenic viruses to meet research needs on a continuing basis." Special attention was given to primate viruses (the alleged African source of HIV) and "the successful propagation of significant amounts of human candidate viruses." Candidate viruses were animal or human viruses that might cause human cancers.

For these cancer experiments, a steady supply of research animals (monkeys, chimpanzees, mice, and cats) was necessary; and multiple breeding colonies were established for the SVCP. Primates were shipped in from west Africa and Asia for experimentation; and virus-infected animals were shipped out to various labs worldwide.

By 1971, a total of 2,274 primates had been inoculated at Bionetics Research Laboratories, under contract to Fort Detrick. Over a thousand of these monkeys had already died or had been transferred to other primate centers. Some animals were eventually released back into the wild. By the early 1970s, experimenters had transferred cancer-causing viruses into several species of monkeys, and had also isolated a monkey virus (*Herpesvirus saimiri*) that would have a close genetic relationship to the new Kaposi's sarcoma herpes virus that produced the "gay cancer" of AIDS in 1979.

In order to induce primates and other research animals to acquire cancer, their immune systems were deliberately suppressed by drugs, radiation, or cancer-causing chemicals or substances. The thymus gland and/or the spleen were removed, and viruses were injected into newborn animals or into the womb of pregnant animals. Some animals were injected with malaria to keep them chronically sick and immunodepressed.

The U.S. is the world's leading consumer of primates, and 55,000 are used yearly in medical research. Primates (especially newborn and baby chimpanzees) are the most favored lab animals because they are similar biochemically and immunologically to human beings. Humans share 98.4 percent of their DNA with chimpanzees. Chimps were extensively used by SVCP because there would be no official testing of "candidate" lab viruses on humans.

In the decade before AIDS, Robert Gallo was a project officer of a primate study contracted by Bionetics which pumped cancerous human tissue, as well as a variety of chicken and monkey viruses, into newborn macaques (a small species of monkey that carries a close relative of the KS virus). Recorded in the 1971 SVCP report (NIH-71-2025), Gallo's project notes state:

Inasmuch as tests for the biological activity of candidate human viruses will not be tested in the human species, it is imperative that another system be developed for these determinations, and subsequently for the evaluation of vaccines or other measures of control. The close phylogenetic relationship of the lower primates to man justifies utilization of these animals for these purposes.

Researchers at Bionetics injected human and animal cancer material into various species of monkeys to determine the cancer effect. Newborn and irradiated monkeys were injected with blood ("using multiple sites and volumes as large as possible") taken from various forms of human leukemia. In other studies, tissue cultures infected with various animal viruses were inoculated into primates. How many "new" and "emerging" viruses were created and adapted to human tissue and to various primates is not known.

Some primates were released back into the wild carrying lab viruses with them. The possible spread of these lab viruses to other animals in the wild has been ignored by scientists searching for the origin of HIV and its close relatives in African animals.

Cats were also bred for leukemia and sarcoma cancer studies. Germ-free colonies of inbred mice were established. Mouse cancer viruses were manipulated to produce resistant and nonresistant strains. These adapted viruses would be employed in the 1980s in human gene replacement experiments. Such experiments utilized a weakened strain of the mouse leukemia virus to infect and "taxi-in" the missing genes to genetically-defective human beings.

THE BIRTH OF AIDS

By 1977, the SVCP came to an inglorious end. According to Gallo, "Scientifically, the problem was that no one could supply clear evidence of any kind of human tumor virus, not even a DNA virus, and most researchers refused to concede that viruses played any role in human cancers. Politically, the Virus Cancer Program was vulnerable because it attracted a great deal of money and attention and had failed to produce dramatic, visible results."

Despite all this, the SVCP was the birthplace of genetic engineering, molecular biology, and the human genome project. More than any other program, it built up the field of animal retrovirology, which led to the vital understanding of cancer and immunosuppressive retroviruses in humans. As activities at the SVCP were winding down, thousands of gay

262 / Biological and Chemical Warfare

men were signing up as guinea pigs in government-sponsored hepatitis-B vaccine experiments in New York, Los Angeles, and San Francisco. These same cities would soon become the three primary epicenters for the new "gay-related immune deficiency syndrome," later known as AIDS.

Two years after the termination of the SCVP, the introduction of HIV into gay men (along with a herpes virus and a mycoplasma) miraculously revived retroviral research and made Gallo the most famous scientist in the world.

Could virus-contaminated hepatitis vaccines lie at the root of AIDS? In the early 1970s, the hepatitis-B vaccine was developed in chimpanzees. To this day, some people are fearful about taking the hepatitis-B vaccine because of its original connection to gay men and AIDS. Was HIV—along with KS and a new mycoplasma—introduced into gays during vaccine trials on thousands of homosexuals in Manhattan beginning in 1978, and in west coast cities in 1980 and 1981?

As mentioned, the first gay AIDS cases erupted in Manhattan a few months after the gay experiment began at the New York Blood Center. When a blood test for HIV became available in the mid-1980s, the Center's stored gay blood specimens were reexamined. Most astonishing is the statistically significant fact that 20 percent of the gay men who volunteered for the hepatitis-B experiment in New York were discovered to be HIV-positive in 1980—a year before the AIDS epidemic became "official" in 1981. This signifies that Manhattan gays in 1980 had the highest incidence of HIV anywhere in the world, including Africa, the supposed birthplace of HIV and AIDS. Epidemic cases in Africa did not appear until 1982.

Although denied by the AIDS establishment, a few researchers are convinced that these vaccine experiments served as the vehicle through which HIV was introduced into the gay population. My own extensive research into the hepatitis-B experiments is presented in *AIDS and the Doctors of Death: An Inquiry into the Origin of the AIDS Epidemic* (1988), and in *Queer Blood: The Secret AIDS Genocide Plot* (1993). These books also debunk the preposterous "Patient Zero" story of 1987, which claimed that a promiscuous gay Canadian airline steward brought AIDS to America. The highly implausible story was sensationalized in the media and served to further obscure the origin of AIDS in America and blame gay promiscuity. Even Montagnier is doubtful that the U.S. epidemic could have developed from a single patient.

Never mentioned by proponents of the chimp theory is the fact that the New York Blood Center established a chimp virus laboratory in west Africa in 1974. One of the purposes of VILAB II, at the Liberian Institute for Biomedical Research in Robertsfield, Liberia, was to develop the hepatitis-B vaccine in chimps. A few years later this vaccine was inoculated into gays at the Center.

Chimps were captured from various parts of west Africa and brought to VILAB. Alfred Prince, head of virology at the New York Blood Center, has been the director of VILAB for the past twenty-five years. The lab prides itself by releasing "rehabilitated" chimps back into the wild.

Also closely allied with "pre-AIDS" development of a hepatitis-B vaccine is the little-publicized primate colony outside New York City called the Laboratory for Experimental Medicine and Surgery in Primates (LEMSIP). Until disbanded in 1997, LEMSIP supplied New York area scientists with primates and primate parts for transplantation and virus research. Founded in 1965, LEMSIP was affiliated with the New York University Medical Center, where the first cases of AIDS-associated Kaposi's sarcoma were discovered in 1979. Researchers at NYU Medical Center were also heavily involved in the development of the experimental hepatitis-B vaccine used in gays; and the Medical Center received government grants and contracts connected with biological warfare research beginning in 1969, according to Leonard Horowitz, author of *Emerging Viruses: AIDS and Ebola* (1996).

SCIENTIFIC DISINFORMATION: THE 1959 HIV-POSITIVE BLOOD TEST FROM AFRICA

By predating HIV back to the 1930s, the chimp theory effectively discredits the man-made theory of AIDS, which dates the introduction of HIV to the late 1970s. Only time will tell whether the chimp theory will hold up to further scientific scrutiny.

Conspiracy theorists believe that some wildly popular AIDS-origin stories reported in the press reek of scientific disinformation. One example is the "Patient Zero" story. Another is the media blitz surrounding the English sailor who supposedly contracted AIDS in 1959. This now-disproved story made worldwide headlines in 1990 and obviously served to contradict the underground conspiracy theory that AIDS (particularly among African-Americans) was man-made.

The New York Times on July 24, 1990, declared: "The case also refutes the widely publicized charges made by Soviet officials several years ago that AIDS arose from a virus that had escaped from a laboratory experiment that went awry or was a biological warfare agent. The human retrovirus group to which the AIDS virus belongs was unknown at the time. Nor did scientists then have the genetic engineering techniques needed to create a virus." Several years later, the case was discovered to be not a case of AIDS because the sailor's tissue remains were accidentally (or deliberately) contaminated with HIV.

In 1998, the media alerted the public to further evidence that AIDS started in Africa. The proof consisted of a frozen blood specimen, stored in 1959, discovered to be HIV-positive. Researchers claimed the tiny amount of serum contained fragments of HIV "closely related" to a virus found in three chimpanzees in the African wild, and in the frozen remains of a chimp named Marilyn discovered in a freezer at Fort Detrick.

The 1959 specimen was obtained from a Bantu man living in Kinshasa, the Congo. His name and health status were not recorded. Details of the history and testing of this specimen (later heralded as the "world's oldest HIV-positive blood sample") are recorded in *The River: A Journey to the Source of HIV and AIDS* (1999), by journalist Edward Hooper, who theorizes that HIV was introduced into Africans via the polio vaccine programs in the late 1950s. Hooper claims the polio vaccine was prepared using chimp kidney cells contaminated with the ancestor virus of HIV.

When tested for HIV in the mid-1980s, the 1959 blood sample was the only specimen out of 700 stored frozen Congo bloods that tested positive for HIV. Originally collected by Arno Motulsky on a Rockefeller grant, the African sample was one of many sent to the University of Washington in Seattle and used for genetic testing. The sample had been included in a report, "Population Genetic Studies," published in 1966. Around 1970, the remaining 672 frozen blood samples were flown to Emory University in Atlanta for further genetic tests.

In 1985, the specimens again changed hands, this time for HIV testing by Andre Nahmias, a virologist and animal researcher associated with the Yerkes Primate Center at Emory. The Congo specimens were tested along with 500 other blood specimens taken from blacks living in sub-Saharan Africa between 1959 and 1982. Initially, over 90 percent of specimens taken in 1959 tested positive for HIV by the ELISA (enzyme linked immuno sorbent assay) test. However, these HIV-positive tests were later determined to be false-positive. After the examinations at Emory, the specimens were shipped to Harvard University in Cambridge, Massachusetts, for HIV testing in Max Essex's lab.

Three specimens initially tested HIV-positive, but finally only the 1959 specimen from the unidentified Bantu man was confirmed HIV-positive. Around the time of these examinations, Essex's lab was unknowingly contaminated with primate viruses.

In 1986, Essex discovered a new "human" AIDS virus that later proved to be a monkey virus. The source of the primate virus traced back to a captive monkey at a primate center in nearby Southborough, Massachusetts. This primate contamination at his lab resulted in the erroneous green monkey theory, heavily popularized by Gallo and the media.

Also unpublicized is the little-known fact that Gallo's lab at the National Cancer Institute was plagued with contamination by primate viruses. In 1975, Gallo reported a new human "HL-23" virus that eventually proved to be three ape primate viruses (gibbon-ape virus, simian sarcoma virus, and baboon endogenous virus). Gallo claims he has no idea how these viruses contaminated his research.

In 1996, Hooper convinced Nahmias to turn over the remaining 1959 specimen to David Ho of Rockefeller University in Manhattan for PCR (polymerase chain reaction) testing. In 1996, Ho was named *Time* magazine's "Man of the Year," at a time when few people had ever heard of him. Ho is also the director of the Aaron Diamond AIDS Research Center, affiliated with Rockefeller University since 1996. The Diamond Center is also now connected with the New York Blood Center, home of the gay vaccine experiments that gave birth to AIDS.

Ho determined that the tiny amount of the remaining specimen did not contain live virus, nor was the complete virion of the virus present. Instead, some fragments of the virus (about 15 percent of the total genome) were tested and presented to the scientific world as the oldest specimen of HIV in the world. Ho's PCR results cannot be confirmed by independent investigators because the 1959 specimen is now totally used up.

When published in the journal *Nature* on February 5, 1998 ("An African HIV-1 sequence from 1959 and implications for the origin of the epidemic"), Hooper's name appeared on the report, along with Ho, Bette Korber, Nahmias, and others. The report was heavily publicized as proof that HIV existed in the African population in 1959.

Although there are no HIV-positive tissue specimens from Africa from the 1960s and 1970s, and no proven cases of AIDS either, Hooper relies heavily on this 1959 test to support his theory that HIV entered the African population via the polio vaccines programs in the late 1950s. In *The River*, Hooper quickly dismisses the claims of physician Robert

Strecker, the first whistle-blower of man-made AIDS, as well as the research described in Horowitz's *Emerging Viruses* and in my own books *AIDS and the Doctors of Death* and *Queer Blood*.

In condemning AIDS biowarfare research, Hooper declares, "Sadly, supporters of the Streckers have continued to peddle their ill-informed and outdated versions of the myth, blaming variously the Soviets, the CIA, the Germans, and the World Health Organization (WHO) well into the nineties." He dismisses the hepatitis-B vaccine connection to AIDS by noting that only two of the 826 gay vaccinees had developed AIDS by 1983.

Hooper ignores the fact that by 1981 over 20 percent of the men in the trials were HIV-positive and that by 1982, over 30 percent of the men were HIV-positive. He dismisses the World Health Organization's African smallpox vaccine connection by saying, "There is no reason for either HIV or SIV [simian immunodeficiency virus] to be accidentally present in the vaccine." Hooper fails to consider the possibility that the vaccines could have been deliberately contaminated with HIV. Hooper has been a United Nations official, but no details of this are included in his book.

Despite his massive research, Hooper seems naïve about the continuing transfer of viruses between various primate species at primate centers. For example, in 1995 he interviewed Preston Marx at LEMSIP. At that time Marx was a representative of David Ho's organization, the Aaron Diamond Research Center. Hooper writes:

> I was shocked by the cavalier way in which tissues and sera from one species had been introduced into other species, long after the risks of cross-species transfer had been highlighted by the SV40 [polio vaccine] debacle, and I was astonished that survivors from troops that had been stricken by mystery illnesses could have been casually sold to other centers, for use in experiments there. Furthermore, this apparent lack of monitoring and central control seemed to be echoed in other fields, like xenotransplantation (the transplanting of organ or cells from one species to another)—and here, of course, the implications were even more frightening.

By predating his polio vaccine theory back to the late 1950s, Hooper greatly simplified his theory of AIDS origin. He ignored all those animal viruses that were placed into human tissue in the 1960s and 1970s, and all those dangerous viral creations that were genetically altered for cancer research, vaccine research, and secret biological warfare.

THE CHIMP IN THE FREEZER AT FORT DETRICK

On February 1, 1999, Lawrence K. Altman, physician and longtime writer for *The New York Times*, dutifully reported, "The riddle of the origin of the AIDS virus has apparently been solved." A team of researchers, headed by Beatrice Hahn at the University of Alabama, had performed viral studies on three chimps in the African wild and had also studied the frozen remains of a chimp, discovered by accident in a freezer at Fort Detrick. The chimp had tested positive for HIV in 1985. On the basis of all this research, Hahn declared that a common sub-species of chimp (*Pan troglodytes troglodytes*) was the animal source of the virus "most closely " related to HIV.

In a media blitz, U.S. government scientists presented a phylogenetic ancestral "family tree" of primate viruses (which few lay people could understand) to prove that HIV was genetically descended from a chimp virus in the African bush. Molecular analysis of virus genetic data, per-formed by Bette Korber and the supercomputer Nirvana at the Los Alamos National Laboratory in New Mexico, indicated that HIV had jumped species from a chimp to a human in Africa around the year 1930. (Los Alamos is the official home of nuclear bomb-building, alleged Chinese spies, and the laboratory which directed secret human radiation experiments on unsuspecting civilians from the 1940s up to the beginning of the AIDS epidemic.)

Beatrice Hahn theorized that the epidemic started when a hunter cut himself while butchering chimp meat and subsequently became infected. Scientists readily accepted Hahn's notion that the AIDS virus and its closest relatives jumped species from chimps to humans on multiple occa-sions, thereby explaining the origin of the three separate subtypes of HIV-1 (M, N, and O), as well as HIV-2.

Chimps in west Africa are hunted for food, as well as for medical experimentation. Young chimps are especially prized for scientific research and are usually caught by shooting their mothers. Many die from stress and inhumane conditions during capture and transport to laboratories and zoos in western nations. Due to all this killing, chimps are now an endangered species. During the past century the African chimp population has dropped from two million to less than 150,000. Despite the mass killing of chimps, they are still blamed for causing the worldwide epidemic of AIDS.

Beatrice Hahn is no stranger to primate theories, having worked in Gallo's lab when he was heavily promoting the green monkey theory in the mid-1980s and the "close relationship" of the monkey virus to HIV. Hahn's virus was claimed to be a closer relative than the contaminating monkey virus in Essex's lab that formed the basis of the false green monkey theory.

Media journalists paid no attention to these discrepancies. Hahn's new chimp findings, along with the old 1959 blood specimen, fully convinced the AIDS establishment and an adoring media that Africa was indeed the source of HIV and the AIDS epidemic.

THE 2000 ORIGIN OF AIDS CONFERENCE IN LONDON

When Hooper's book appeared in the fall of 1998, molecular scientists quickly used the new chimp virus data to completely discredit Hooper's polio vaccine theory. AIDS in Africa could not be caused by a virus jumping species in the 1950s if it had already jumped species back in the 1930s. Researchers refused to believe scientists could have played any role in the origin of HIV and AIDS.

Hooper bypassed the biowarfare theory by predating HIV back to the 1950s. Now scientists bypassed Hooper by dating HIV back several decades earlier. The fact that there was no African epidemic until the early 1980s did not seem pertinent. To make their view official, a small group of scientists proposed an "invitation only" meeting to settle the origin matter once and for all.

In October 2000, the Royal Society of London held a two-day conference on the origins of HIV. Obviously, the biowarfare theory of AIDS was not discussed. On the contrary, one professor emphatically declared, "All human infectious diseases have an animal origin." Although there was never a disease like AIDS—until scientists started flagrantly passing viruses around to repeatedly break the species barrier—the same professor declared that "natural transfer of these infections is a common event in animal populations."

Using the viral fragments from the 1959 specimen and comparing them with the select viruses contained in the data bank at Los Alamos, Bette Korber refined her computer calculations to establish a likely date of 1940, "with confidence levels extending from 1871 to 1955." The Rega Institute in Antwerp estimated the transfer could have occurred between 1590 and 1760, with 1675 the most likely date.

Hooper spoke, but his views were largely ignored by the molecular biologists. Preston Marx warned about more human diseases caused by viruses emerging from primates. None of the speakers mentioned what happened to the thousands of liters of animal viruses that were passed around the world by the Special Virus Cancer Program in the decade before AIDS.

Instead, the London conferees alerted the public to a new view of medical science, championed by the virologists. The "last word" at the conference was that "all human viral infections were initially zoonotic (animal) in origin. Animals will always provide a reservoir for viruses that could threaten human populations in the future." And the scientists predicted: "There is still a myriad of current unknown viruses in animal populations on land, sea, and air with the potential to cause human disease." Apparently, none of these viruses were present in animal laboratories.

AIDS, CANCER AND GENETIC SCIENCE

Although rejected completely by most scientists, the theory of man-made AIDS is a reasonable explanation for the origin of HIV, based on an awareness of the gene-polluting activities and species-jumping virus experiments of irresponsible scientists during the two decades before the epidemic. In addition, the record clearly shows that scientists and biowarfare scientists experimented secretly on unsuspecting people. Horrific aspects of the Cold War–era human radiation experiments attest to the fact that covert medical experimentation is not an *X-Files* fantasy.

It is easy to understand why researchers might want to obscure the man-made origin for AIDS and blame primates. It is now apparent that most of the major researchers promoting the African primate origin of AIDS were connected with the largely secret Special Virus Cancer Program, or are scientists involved in the transfer of viruses in animal research, particularly primate research.

From the very beginning of the epidemic, researchers disclaimed any connection between AIDS and cancer, as well as any connection between HIV and animal retrovirus cancer research. In 1984, Gallo originally named HIV a cancer-causing "leukemia/lymphoma" virus. To obscure the cancer connection, the name was immediately changed to "lymphotropic" virus.

My own Kaposi's sarcoma research, first published in medical journals in 1981, showed "cancer-associated bacteria" as possible infectious agents in "classic" KS tumors. Before HIV was discovered in 1984, additional papers in 1982 and 1983 showed similar cancer bacteria in the enlarged lymph nodes and KS tumors of gay men with "gay cancer" and AIDS. Since the 1950s, cancer-associated bacteria have been linked to viruses, as well as to mycoplasmas. This aspect of cancer research has been suppressed for decades by the cancer establishment. A history of this research and its relevancy to AIDS is the subject of my books, *AIDS: The Mystery and the Solution* (1984) and *The Cancer Microbe: The Hidden Killer in Cancer, AIDS and Other Immune Diseases* (1990).

Gallo, in his 1991 book, claims falsely that no infectious agent had ever been found in KS. The refusal of AIDS scientists to recognize cancer microbe research, published in peer-reviewed scientific journals, is a further indication that the AIDS establishment seeks to control all aspects of HIV research in such a way that the origin of AIDS will never be connected with early cancer research and covert biological warfare research. This cover-up conceals the possibility that AIDS, in reality, is a new man-made form of infectious and contagious cancer.

Could a small coterie of government scientists concoct a bogus (but scientifically plausible) primate theory of AIDS origin and bamboozle the public to believe it, in order to cover up the truth? It is time for the theory of manmade HIV to be examined fairly. Proponents of this theory should not be dismissed as paranoid conspiracy theorists, and AIDS educators should educate themselves about this hidden history of AIDS and its implications for the origin of HIV.

How many more species-jumping viruses will we have to endure before we question the integrity and the agenda of scientists who still blissfully jump viruses between species in animal laboratories?

The secrecy and scientific disinformation surrounding the human radiation experiments of the Cold War era have taught us how easily government scientists can fool the public on scientific matters. And when it comes to scientific monkey business, researchers know that most people are chumps. ●

References

Cantwell Jr., A. "Bacteriologic investigation and histologic observations of variably acid-fact bacteria in three cases of Kaposi's sarcoma." *Growth* 45: 79–89, 1981; "Necroscopic findings of pleomorphic, variably acid-fast bacteria in a fatal case of Kaposi's sarcoma." *Journal of Dermatologic Surgery and Oncology* 7: 923–30, 1981; "Variably acid-fast bacteria in vivo in a case of reactive lymph node hyperplasia occurring in a young male homosexual." *Growth* 46: 331–36, 1982; "Kaposi's sarcoma and variably acid-fast bacteria in vivo in two homosexual men." *Cutis* 32: 58–74, 1983; "Necroscopic findings of variably acid-fast bacteria in a fatal case of acquired immunodeficiency syndrome and Kaposi's sarcoma." *Growth* 47: 129–134, 1983.

———. *AIDS: The Mystery and the Solution.* Aries Rising, 1984; *AIDS & The Doctors of Death: An Inquiry into the Origin of the AIDS Epidemic.* Aries Rising, 1988; *The Cancer Microbe.* Aries Rising, 1990; *Queer Blood: The Secret AIDS Genocide Plot.* Aries Rising, 1993.

———. "Gay cancer, emerging viruses, and AIDS." *New Dawn* (Melbourne), September 1998.

Faden, R. R. (Chair). "The Human Radiation Experiments: Final Report of the President's Advisory Committee." Oxford University Press, 1996.

Gallo, R. *Virus Hunting: AIDS, Cancer and the Human Retrovirus.* Basic Books, 1991.

Hooper, E. *The River: A Journey to the Source of HIV and AIDS.* Little, Brown, 1999.

Horowitz, L. G. *Emerging Viruses: AIDS and Ebola.* Tetrahedron Publishing Group, 1996.

Lee, R. E. *AIDS: An Explosion of the Biological Time-Bomb?* Biographical Publishing Company, 2000.

Montagnier, L. *Virus.* Norton, 2000.

Special Virus Cancer Program—Progress Report #8. Bethesda, MD: National Institutes of Health, August 1971.

—Fall 2001

Anthrax Bioterrorism and the Insanity of Biological Warfare

by *Alan Cantwell, Jr., M.D.*

Who was responsible for 2001–2002 anthrax bioterrorism? So far, no one knows for sure. Will bioterrorism be the final straw that starts World World III? As Dr. Cantwell notes, unless we want to live constantly in fear, we had better promote peace rather than a war which uses the biowarfare agents our mad scientists have created.

FOR MANY DECADES, physicians, scientists, and military officials have been busy designing infectious agents for the sole purpose of producing mass death. As a result, fear of biological warfare now pervades the planet. There is an old expression that summarizes the extreme dangers of biowarfare: "What goes around, comes around."

Recently, the United States experienced bioterrorism of a sort previously encountered only in Hollywood action movies. The horror was real—deadly anthrax spores were discovered in the Congress of the most powerful nation on Earth. The biowarfare nightmare is just beginning, with no end in sight.

To complicate matters, biowarfare research is always conducted with the greatest secrecy, and the public has little knowledge of the biologic monstrosities the biowarfare experts have concocted to destroy us. However, when deployed, the deadly results of chemical and biological biowarfare are plain to see.

In 1988, Saddam Hussein initiated genocide against the Kurds in Iraq by spraying isolated villages with poison nerve gas. More than 100,000 Kurds are thought to have perished in this genocide program. Despite the killing, the U.S. government continued to loan Iraq billions of dollars.

In 1991, world leaders feared that Iraq would use biowarfare in the Persian Gulf War. A large part of Iraq's chemical and biowarfare arsenal had been supplied by the U.S. government several years before, in friendlier times. To reassure a nervous public, U.S. government officials bragged that America had the capability to gas the entire world population 5,000 times over ("U.S. chemical arsenal dwarfs that of the Iraqis," *Los Angeles Times*, August 17, 1990).

THE JAPANESE BIOWARFARE EXPERIMENTS IN MANCHURIA

Historically, all the major powers have contributed to the biowarfare mess we are now in. Finding a world power "innocent" in biowarfare is as rare as finding a virgin in a whorehouse. In Manchuria in the late 1930s and early 1940s, the Japanese performed the most diabolic biological experiments ever performed on human beings. When the Japanese overran the country, they established Unit 731, a biowarfare research and production facility in Pingfan, near the city of Harbin. In their book *Gene Wars: Military Control over the New Genetic Technologies*, Charles Pillar and Keith Yamamoto write: "At least 3,000 Chinese, Korean, Soviet, American, British, and Australian prisoners of war died horrific deaths at the hands of the Pingfan technicians."

In the biowarfare experiments, the Japanese deliberately infected prisoners with microbes causing cholera, dysentery, typhoid, syphilis, and other infectious diseases. "The work included trials of anthrax and gas gangrene bombs. Prisoners were tied to stakes, their buttocks exposed to the shrapnel flying from a bomb detonated by remote control. The course of the disease was meticulously tracked and recorded as the victims died in agony. Other prisoners were infected with organisms causing cholera and plague, only to be dissected—sometimes while still alive—to monitor the progressive degeneration of their internal organs."

During the post-war Japanese war crime trials, the U.S. Army feared the Russians might benefit from learning the full details of the experiments. To thwart this possibility, the U.S. Army biowarfare department made a deal: Japanese doctors were required to turn their data over to the Army, and in turn the U.S. government would not prosecute the Japanese perpetrators of these war crimes.

The infamous secrets of Unit 731 were kept hidden from the Japanese public until a decade ago. About 200 American veterans, who were held prisoner in Japanese-occupied Manchuria after the fall of the Philippines in 1942, claim to have suffered as guinea pigs in biowarfare experiments conducted by Japanese doctors. The suffering of the aged men remains unacknowledged and uncompensated in the absence of "no known records." David Roach, who has researched the plight of these men, is convinced these POWs were part of a methodical germ-warfare experiment. "But this issue is so sensitive, and our government and the Japanese won't own up. We should tell these guys before they die: Look, you were in a camp where you were experimented upon, and that's why you have been sick for fifty years. It's a moral issue," said Roach ("Truth emerging on ailing POWs, Japan germ unit, *Los Angeles Times*, March 20, 1995).

"ANTHRAX ISLAND" IN SCOTLAND

In a closely guarded secret experiment performed in the summer of 1942, leading British bacteriologists used a small island, 400 yards off the northwest coast of Scotland, to test a twenty-five-pound chemical bomb filled with a thick brown mix of anthrax spores. Thirty sheep were collected from the mainland and as the date of the detonation approached, the animals were ferried over to Gruinard Island. The anthrax bomb was placed on a small mound of earth, and the sheep were tethered nearby. When the bomb exploded, billions of spores formed an invisible cloud over the island and dispersed over the test site and the sea. A day later, the first sheep began to die from anthrax. In further tests, more sheep were brought to Gruinard, and more anthrax bombs were tested. The detailed account of "Anthrax Island" can be found in Robert Harris and Jeremy Paxman's *A Higher Form of Killing: The Secret Story of Chemical and Biological Warfare* (1982).

In the winter of 1943, as part of a biowarfare project that carried the highest security classification, the Allies began to manufacture a biological bomb weighing four pounds and filled with anthrax spores. Under the code name "N," its design was largely British, its manufacture exclusively American. Harris and Paxman consider "N" to be "the greatest Allied secret of the war after the atomic bomb." Proving that the U.S. is no stranger to anthrax manufacture, the authors note that in May 1944 an initial batch of 5,000 anthrax-filled bombs came off the experimental production line at Fort Detrick, the U.S. Army's biowarfare unit located at Frederick, Maryland.

In the ensuing years, various attempts to decontaminate Gruinard were unsuccessful, and the island remained off limits for decades, a testament to the persistent viability of anthrax spores and the military's inability to destroy the spores once they heavily contaminated an area. A BBC report (July 25, 2001) claims an English company was paid a half-million pounds to decontaminate the 520-acre island in 1986 by soaking the ground with 280 tons of formaldehyde diluted in seawater. Finally, on April 24, 1990, the government declared Gruinard safe and removed its red biohazard warning sign. But Dr. Brian Moffat, a leading archaeologist, remained unconvinced the land is safe. Moffat has examined anthrax spores at ancient excavation sites and found them to be still viable after centuries. "I would not go walking on Gruinard. [Anthrax] is a very resilient and deadly bacterium."

PLUM ISLAND AND SECRET U.S. MILITARY EXPERIMENTS

In the 1950s the U.S. military planned to cripple the Soviet economy by killing horses, cattle, and swine with biowarfare weapons developed from exotic animal diseases at Plum Island, located off the coast of Long Island, New York. The two diseases under development were foot-and-mouth disease and African swine fever. According to Norman Covert, base historian and public information officer at Fort Detrick, only a handful of scientists were aware of this project. "In many cases there were only maybe five people who knew what was going on in weapons research. People in one lab didn't know what happened in the next lab, and they didn't ask." One legacy of the Army's role in founding the Plum Island lab is its repository for viruses and viral antibodies of the most dangerous animal diseases in the world. Details of these 1950s experiments remained classified until 1993 ("Plum Island's shadowy past: Once-secret documents reveal lab's mission was germ warfare," *Newsday*, November 21, 1993).

During the 1950s and '60s, secret military biowarfare attacks on unsuspecting civilians took place in many parts of America. The most notorious was a six-day attack on San Francisco in which clouds of potentially harmful bacteria were sprayed over the city. Twelve people developed pneumonia due to the infectious bacteria, and one elderly man died from the attack. This attack was revealed to the public years later when classified documents were finally released ("Army germ fog blanketed S.F. for six days in '50 test," *Los Angeles Times*, September 17, 1979).

In other classified experiments, bacteria were sprayed in New York City subways, in a Washington, D.C. airport, and on highways in Pennsylvania. Biowarfare testing also took place in military bases in Virginia; in Key West, Florida; and off the coasts of Southern California and Hawaii ("Army used live bacteria in tests on U.S. civilians," *Los Angeles Times*, March 9, 1977).

The Army also experimented on its own soldiers. Project Whitecoat, a code name for a series of germ-warfare experiments that took place at Fort Detrick between 1954 and 1973, utilized about 2,300 Seventh-Day Adventist volunteers as subjects. The men were exposed to germs causing tularemia, malaria, anthrax, Queensland fever, Rocky Mountain spotted fever, encephalitis, and a host of exotic diseases. The studies were aimed at preventing, diagnosing, and treating these diseases, as well as the development of vaccines. No one died in the experiments, but critics contend that the men were essentially coerced into participating in research that, despite military assurances to the contrary, could have been used to produce biowarfare weapons ("Adventists' faith put to test; 2,300 soldiers were used in germ-warfare experiments," *The Washington Times*, October 17, 1998).

In preparing America for nuclear attack during the Cold War years following World War II, thousands of U.S. citizens were used as unsuspecting guinea pigs in more than 4,000 secret and classified radiation experiments conducted by the Atomic Energy Commission and other government agencies, such as the Department of Defense; the Department of Health, Education, and Welfare; the Public Health Service (now the CDC); the National Institutes of Health; the Veterans Administration; the CIA; and NASA ("The Human Radiation Experiments," *New Dawn*, September, 2001).

The full extent of these government-sponsored covert biowarfare programs will probably never be known because the entire biowarfare industry is clouded in secrecy. Many incriminating documents remain top-secret or classified. Other documents are often declared as missing, destroyed, or "unavailable," in an attempt to hide the truth from the public. Despite all this, some scholarly accounts of unethical medical abuse by government agencies, not only in the U.S., but also worldwide, are slowly coming to light.

BIOLOGICAL WARFARE AND GENETIC ENGINEERING

As the 1970s began, the U.S. Army's biowarfare program intensified, particularly in the area of DNA and genetic engineering research. It is important to realize that genetic manipulation of cells and infectious agents, as well as the mixing of new and old infectious agents by transferring them between species, all have tremendous potential in the creation of new agents for biowarfare purposes.

In order to placate the fears of critics, President Nixon renounced germ warfare, except for "medical defensive research." But despite the 1972 treaty forbidding nations from developing or acquiring weapons that spread disease, the biowarfare buildup has continued. In order for biowarfare researchers to create a defense against bioweapons, it is necessary to study offensive biowarfare agents.

In 1971, when Nixon transferred a major part of the Army's Biological Warfare Unit at Fort Detrick to the National Cancer Institute (NCI), secret biowarfare experimentation continued under the cover of bona fide cancer research. Utilizing the latest genetic engineering techniques, virologists forced cancer-causing viruses to jump from one species of animal to another. In the hazardous transfer of dangerous infectious agents, new forms of deadly cancer and immunodeficiency diseases were produced in the animals. And, undoubtedly, biowarfare experts took notice of these "supergerms" and their possible use as newly-created biowarfare agents.

In November 1973, a high-level conference entitled "Biohazards in Biological Research" convened at Asilomar, near Pacific Grove in northern California. The cancer virologists freely admitted there was no foolproof way to prevent the escape of these highly dangerous viruses into the community. Robert W. Miller of the NCI reminded people that "the hazards in microbiological research concern diseases that kill a lot faster than cancer." Leaving no doubt that new and dangerous viruses were being created, Miller warned that "laboratory workers have not only heavy exposures to known viruses, but also to the viruses that they invent."

During the 1970s the NCI's Special Virus Cancer Program brought together scientists from the leading medical and scientific institutions in America, as well as from abroad, in a unified attempt to uncover cancer-causing viruses. Some researchers, like myself and others, believe that this Special Virus Cancer Program created HIV, the virus that causes AIDS and that it was seeded into the U.S. homosexual community via experimental vaccine programs undertaken in the late 1970s ("AIDS: Who is to Blame?" *New Dawn*, May 2001).

Not only is the public kept ignorant of biowarfare research, but biowarfare "accidents" are routinely covered up or downplayed by government officials, or blamed on animals. Russian authorities revealed the truth about an epidemic of anthrax that caused at least sixty-eight deaths in 1979 in the city of Sverdlovsk, 850 miles east of Moscow. The outbreak was officially blamed on eating meat from infected animals.

Officials at the nearby top-secret military compound maintained that anthrax spores indigenous to the region's soil were spread among cattle through ingestions of contaminated bone meal, and among humans through the illegal sale of diseased cattle from private farms. In 1992, Russian President Boris Yeltsin finally acknowledged that the cause was not "natural," but due to the accidental escape of spores of weapons-grade anthrax produced by the nearby secret biowarfare installation ("Soviet germ lab caused epidemic in '79," *Los Angeles Times*, June 16, 1992).

DEADLY GERMS FOR SALE

Further complicating the sources of bioterrorism is the sale of deadly microbes to anyone with the cash to buy them. In the mid-1980s, when the U.S. was still on friendly terms with Saddam Hussein, his Education Ministry purchased seventy shipments of anthrax and other disease-causing organisms from the American Type Culture Collection, a non-profit company in Rockville, Maryland. At that time, such shipments were entirely legal and received quick approval by the U.S. Commerce Department ("Germ library's inventory is making detractors queasy," *Los Angeles Times*, March 16, 1998).

In a germ warfare article in *Time* (December 1, 1997), writer Bruce Nelan claims that "Iraq now admits to brewing more than 2,000 gallons of anthrax, but American experts think the true amount was three times that." A fatal dose, says a U.S. Defense official, is smaller than a speck of dust, something you wouldn't even see. One truth about bioweapons is that they can be produced using a recipe found on the Internet, a beer fermenter, a culture, and a gas mask, with a total investment of $10,000. A Pentagon official states, "if you buy commercial equipment and put it in a small room, you can be producing kilogram quantities of anthrax within a month, and each kilo has millions and millions of potential deaths in it." A study by the U.S. Office of Technology Assessment estimated that a hundred kilos of anthrax spread by a crop duster over Washington, DC, could cause 2 million deaths.

Individuals can easily gain access to microbes used for biowarfare. In

1995, U.S. law enforcement officers arrested Larry W. Harris, a former member of Aryan Nations, a notorious neo-Nazi group. Employed in an Ohio laboratory, Harris ordered three vials of bubonic plague bacteria from a scientific supply house. When he was placed on trial, prosecutors discovered it was perfectly legal to possess deadly bacteria. Placed on probation, Harris was again arrested in 1998 for possession of anthrax germs. When it was determined the microbes were harmless, the charges were dropped.

On March 1, 2000, in a bizarre murder-for-hire plot in Irvine, California, the home of biomedical researcher and suspect Dr. Larry C. Ford was searched by police. Ford worked as an advisor to the South African apartheid-era government on biochemical warfare. The next day, Ford shot and killed himself. Police found guns, illegal weapons, and explosives in his house, as well as jars of live germs containing salmonella and cholera bacteria. The *Los Angeles Times* (April 30, 2000) noted that "both bacteria can be obtained from hospital labs," and infectious disease specialist Kenneth Litwack claimed he "knew of no laws preventing researchers from storing the bacteria, though he wasn't familiar with the laws governing its use."

THE POOR MAN'S ATOMIC BOMB

A bioterrorism attack against America has been predicted for years. Joseph Douglas and Neil Livingston, in their prophetic 1987 book *America the Vulnerable: The Threat of Chemical and Biological Warfare*, outline many practical reasons why C/B (chemical/biological) weapons are attractive to terrorist groups. First, C/B weapons are cheap and "the poor man's atomic bomb." Second, C/B weapons can be produced without much difficulty and in a relatively short time. Third, a very small amount of a C/B agent (like a nerve gas agent) can represent a real threat. And fourth, virtually any living target is vulnerable to a C/B attack.

Appearing before a UN panel in 1969, a group of C/B experts estimated that "for a large scale operation against a civilian population, casualties might cost about $2,000 per square kilometer with conventional weapons, $800 with nuclear weapons, $600 with nerve-gas weapons, and $1 with biological weapons. In 1989, Douglas and Livingston concluded that the U.S is completely unprepared to respond either to terrorist attacks on population centers or to covert operations.

As of this writing (December 2001), the anthrax attacks on Americans have been made through mail contaminated with spores. Because the actual number of cases is small, the public has been cautioned repeatedly not to worry or panic. Anthrax-filled envelopes sent to Congress have resulted in the contamination of the Hart Senate Office Building with anthrax spores. Biohazard workers have attempted to decontaminate the building by sterilization with chlorine dioxide gas.

The media stress that antibiotics can easily cure anthrax. However, if anthrax was disbursed by a crop duster, or by a bomb loaded with anthrax spores, the results could be catastrophic. So far, all known strains of anthrax are susceptible to antibiotics. If an antibiotic-resistant, genetically-engineered, and "weaponized" strain were unleashed, the results would be far more serious

On October 18, 2001, the CDC issued an unprecedented alert, asking physicians to watch for cases of smallpox, plague, botulism, tularemia, and even "emerging" African viruses that cause Ebola and Marburg disease. Before the World Trade Center and Pentagon attacks, virologists were expecting these African viruses to originate from animals. Now it is clear (to those who can read between the lines) that the more likely threat comes from crazy scientists and their terrorist colleagues, who will use any deadly infectious agent as a potential biowarfare agent if it suits their national, political, or religious agenda.

Who is responsible for this anthrax bioterrorism? No one knows for sure. There is no firm evidence implicating Islamic terrorists. Could a small group connected with military biowarfare or some militia group be unleashing these attacks to force the vulnerable U.S. government to take bioterrorism more seriously? Certainly with the anger of the American public against Arab terrorists for their role in the World Trade Center and Pentagon attacks, Arabs are likely to be blamed even in the absence of evidence implicating them.

In any war, there are always people who benefit financially. Sales of Cipro, the only antibiotic approved to treat anthrax, have skyrocketed. Produced exclusively by Bayer in Germany, the drug sells for $350 for a month's treatment. A generic version made in India sells for about $10.

The horror of an anthrax attack in the form of bombs is definitely not being emphasized in the media. It is not far-fetched to think that a few anthrax bombs strategically dropped on Manhattan could easily turn New York City into another Gruinard-type "Anthrax Island."

BIOLOGICAL WARFARE IN THE TWENTY-FIRST CENTURY

What can be done to counter more than a half-century of biowarfare buildup? Would a bioattack affecting millions of people lead to World War III?

There are no definite answers to these questions. But people everywhere should ask themselves whether they want to live in a world contaminated and seeded with biowarfare agents, along with all the other "emerging viruses" and plagues to have appeared since the rise of genetic engineering and crazy germ warfare experiments. If we want to live in a better and safer world, it is imperative that we understand clearly the extreme dangers of biowarfare. For decades we have been in denial about biowarfare agents, from which there is clearly no antidote.

Unless we want to live constantly in fear and disinfect our bodies and environment with bleach, formaldehyde, and chlorine dioxide gas, we had better start pushing for peace rather than pushing for war with the kind of biowarfare agents our physicians and scientists have so painstakingly designed to kill us. •

—Winter 2002

The New West Nile Virus Epidemic

Bioterrorism or Mother Nature (Again)?

by *Alan Cantwell, Jr., M.D.*

West Nile Virus is yet another new infectious disease, a form of encephalitis that has mysteriously appeared in the U.S., seemingly out of the blue. Is this another disease that, like AIDS, poses a threat to certain high risk groups? Dr. Cantwell asks: Could the outbreak of West Nile be some sort of biologic "test" (like the anthrax mailings) to wake up people to the dangers of bioterrorism? Are these new "emerging diseases" and "emerging viruses" merely the continuing (and unprecedented) cruel acts of Mother Nature? Or could the hand of man (i.e. biological warfare scientists) be causing these new outbreaks? Is it just a coincidence that these weird bugs and illnesses have erupted in the past two decades? Or is this just "paranoid" thinking?

NEW EMERGING DISEASES: ACCIDENT OF NATURE OR MANMADE ILLNESSES?

DURING THE 1970s it was thought that many infectious diseases had been banished from the industrialized world. But, remarkably, over the last two decades more than thirty "emerging diseases" have appeared in various places. Among the better-known diseases are AIDS, Legionnaire's disease, toxic shock syndrome, Lyme disease, hepatitis-C, "mad cow disease," hanta virus, various new encephalitis and hemorrhagic viruses, Lassa fever, and Ebola virus. (Controversial new diseases such as chronic fatigue syndrome and Persian Gulf War illness, which affects veterans, are not included in the government's list of "emerging diseases.") In addition, older diseases, such as tuberculosis, malaria, and cholera have reemerged in more virulent and drug-resistant forms. After eighty years of steady declines in infectious disease, the mortality rate from infectious disease in the U.S. rose 58 percent between 1980 and 1992.

Health officials place the blame on increased global travel and globalization, population growth and movements, deforestation and reforestation programs, human sexuality (in the case of HIV), and increased human contact with tropical mini-forests and other wilderness habitats that harbor unknown infectious agents. Nowhere in the official list of causes is the fact that for many decades millions of animals and innumerable vials of infectious material have been shipped around the world for commercial and biological warfare purposes. The world trade in deadly agents, coupled with the gene-splicing technology developed in the 1970s, has increased the dangers of new disease outbreaks. In addition, many new viruses have been passed around between various species of animals, and some of these viruses have been adapted to human tissue. This has resulted in the production of new laboratory diseases that have potential biowarfare capabilities. The biowarfare implications of such scientific "advances" have led some conspiracy-minded people to suspect that the hand of man might be responsible for the outbreak of one or more of these newly emerging diseases.

The anthrax mailings that followed the World Trade Center bombings of 9/11 were certainly a "wake-up call" indicating that America was unprepared for a bioterrorist attack. More than a year later, the perpetrators have not been apprehended, and the U.S government's own biowarfare scientists are the number-one prime suspects. On the first anniversary of the anthrax attacks, Barbara Hatch Rosenberg, chair of The Federation of American Scientists Working Group on Biological Weapons, confirms that the strain and properties of the weaponized anthrax bacteria found in the letters originated within the U.S. biodefense program. "Government officials recognized that the anthrax source was domestic less than two weeks after they learned of the letters, and nothing in their investigation has led them to say otherwise," writes Rosenberg.

Rosenberg sounds like a conspiracy theorist when she concludes: "Given the origin of the anthrax and the warnings contained in the letters, the perpetrator's motive was not to kill but rather to raise public fear and thereby spur Congress to increase spending on biodefense. In this sense, the attacks have been phenomenally successful." ("Anthrax attacks pushed open an ominous door," *Los Angeles Times*, September 22, 2002) No doubt a public trial of the perpetrators would open a pandora's box of government biowarfare secrets that would shock the public.

THE NEW EPIDEMIC OF WEST NILE VIRUS ENCEPHALITIS IN AMERICA

West Nile virus infection in humans first broke out in New York City in August 1999. The first sign of the West Nile epidemic occurred in early July when many birds died mysteriously. Half the crows in the New York City area died, as well as some exotic bird species housed at the Bronx zoo. The virus has an affinity for some bird species, and the mosquito acts as a vector for the virus. Thus, the virus spreads from birds to mosquitoes, and is transmitted to humans and other animals via mosquito bites. A few weeks later, the first human cases of encephalitis appeared in local hospitals in northern Queens. By September, nine of twenty-five infected horses with West Nile virus died in Long Island.

Although the virus is contagious among birds, the disease is not contagious among humans. It is estimated that only 20 percent of infected people will develop a mild flu-like form of the illness; but one in 150 people will develop a severe form of the disease, with mental confusion, headache, swollen glands, high fever, severe muscle weakness, and the tell-tale symptoms of encephalitis (inflammation of the brain). Mild cases last a few days; severe cases can last several weeks.

In 1999, the disease was totally confined to the New York City area, with sixty-two cases and seven deaths. As many as ten thousand wild birds died. In the year 2000, there were twenty-one cases and two deaths; in 2001 there were fifty-six cases with seven deaths. By October 8, 2002, the CDC had reported a cumulative total of 2,768 cases of West Nile virus with 146 deaths. It is estimated that as many as two hundred thousand people have been infected nationally.

Until 2002, the virus was confined to the eastern half of the country. By summer 2002, all but six of the lower forty-eight states reported West Nile virus in birds, mosquitoes, animals or humans. In 2002 the CDC confirmed that a transplant patient became infected by West Nile virus after having received organs from a Georgia accident victim infected with the virus. There was also evidence that the virus could be transmitted by an infected mother to her infant during breast feeding. Shockingly, it was announced that West Nile virus was in the nation's blood supply, and there is no blood screening test available to test for the new virus.

At first, infectious disease experts believed that the St. Louis encephalitis (SLE) virus was the cause. Oddly, this endemic virus occasionally causes mild outbreaks of disease in other areas of the U.S., but no cases had ever been seen in New York. At the Bronx Zoo, veterinary pathologist Tracey McNamara suspected a different virus, because the SLE virus was not known to kill birds. Trained at Plum Island, the pathologist suspected a connection between the bird deaths and the human cases, but the Centers for Disease Control rebuffed her concerns. In September, officials reinstituted extensive spraying over New York in attempts to kill the mosquito population and control the encephalitis epidemic.

It was only through McNamara's heroic efforts to enlist the aid of biologists at other national labs, as well as at Fort Detrick, that it was determined, on September 24, 2002, that the virus was indeed West Nile virus—one never before seen in America—and a virus for which there was no testing available in any New York state laboratory.

WEST NILE VIRUS: OUT OF AFRICA OR OUT OF A VIRUS LABORATORY?

West Nile virus was first discovered in 1937 among encephalitis cases in Uganda, in east Africa. African cases tend to be mild, and the virus there does not affect animal and bird populations to any significant degree. In fact, the ability of West Nile virus to infect and kill birds has only been noticed very recently. Could this indicate that the virus has been genetically-altered or "weaponized" for biowarfare purposes during the many decades that it has been available for study in virus laboratories?

Mild outbreaks of West Nile have occurred in Israel in 1951–1954 and 1957, and also in South Africa in 1974. However, since the mid-1990s, outbreaks of West Nile virus have appeared in Morocco, Tunisia, Italy, Israel, and Russia, accompanied by a large number of bird deaths. A Romanian epidemic, reported in 1996, infected 90,000 people and caused seventeen deaths.

Scientists have determined that the closest viral relative of the so-called New York 99 strain of West Nile is a strain that circulated in Israel from 1997–2000. The NY99 strain has remained stable for the past three years. Health authorities suspect the virus entered the U.S. by way of travelers from the Middle East, or via a stray mosquito on an airplane. Other researchers claim the West Nile virus arrived with African animals or birds placed in zoos. But, in fact, the West Nile virus has been housed in U.S. labs for decades, and has been openly sold to researchers around the world. It's hardly a secret that West Nile virus, along with dozens of other infectious agents, was sold to Iraq by the National Type Culture Collection in Maryland during the 1980s, when the U.S. was on friendlier terms with Saddam Hussein.

From the very beginning of the West Nile virus outbreak, there were rumors that the cause was bioterrorism, but these rumors were denied by health officials. CDC spokesperson Barbara Reynolds told CNN that "the possibility of bioterrorism is at the bottom of the list for how some outbreak may have occurred. It appears Mother Nature is at work." (CNN report, October 11, 1999)

Various new theories of origin still appear in the press. For example, a *Los Angeles Times* editorial of September 28, 2002, proclaimed that "scientists think [the virus] may have arrived in the early 1980s when Asian tiger mosquitoes traveled in tire casings from Japan to Houston." One wonders who supplies the press with these bizarre and undocumented stories. None of these theories has deterred Vermont Senator Patrick Leahy from urging federal officials to determine if the introduction of West Nile virus is a terrorist attack. On September 12, 2002, Leahy declared: "I think we have to ask ourselves: Is it a coincidence that we're seeing such an increase in West Nile virus—or is that something that's being tested as a biological weapon against us." Leahy is no stranger to bioterrorism, having received an anthrax-laden letter at his Washington office a year earlier.

The current presence of West Nile virus in the blood supply poses a potentially serious threat. Receiving West Nile virus by a blood transfusion undoubtedly infects the body with a larger dose of virus than a dose received from an infected mosquito. Those at high risk for West Nile virus infection include elderly, debilitated, immunodeficient people (like cancer, AIDS, and transplant patients) and the very young. Currently, all blood is tested for syphilis, as well as for viruses such as HTLV-1 and -2, HIV-1 and -2, and hepatitis-B and -C. A blood screening test for WN virus may be available within a year, and a vaccine might be developed in three years. But, at present, there is no treatment or cure for West Nile virus disease.

SECRET U.S. MILITARY BIOWARFARE EXPERIMENTS ON HUMAN POPULATIONS

A July 24, 2000, report from the Senate Governmental Affairs Committee ("The West Nile Virus Wake Up Call") dismisses the idea of West Nile virus infection as biowarfare, although the CDC was criticized for its "tunnel vision" and its failure "to expect the unexpected." The Committee concluded: "The next outbreak of an infectious disease—whether naturally occurring or deliberately inflicted—may not be so forgiving." The 2001 anthrax attack proved to be the next "deliberately inflicted" biowarfare attack.

It is surprising that the U.S. government quickly eliminated bioterrorism as a cause for the West Nile outbreak, particularly when the government has a long and well-documented history of biowarfare experimentation against unsuspecting citizens. In the 1950s, the U.S. military planned a project to cripple the Soviet economy by killing horses, cattle, and swine with biowarfare weapons developed from exotic animal diseases. The laboratory at Plum Island, off the coast of Long Island, New York, is the Army's repository for viruses derived from the most dangerous animal diseases in the world. For further details read this author's article "Anthrax, Bioterrorism, and the Insanity of Biological Warfare."

AIDS: A DESIGNER DISEASE?

During the 1970s the NCI's Special Virus Cancer Program brought together leading national and international medical scientists in a unified attempt to uncover cancer-causing viruses. During this same decade many human and animal viruses were adapted for commercial and biowarfare purposes. At the end of this decade, new "emerging viruses" began to appear.

Some AIDS researchers believe that this Special Virus Cancer Program (and its covert connection to America's biowarfare program) spawned HIV, an immunosuppressive virus that was subsequently seeded into the U.S. homosexual community via the government-sponsored experimental hepatitis-B vaccine program (1978-1981). These experiments in New York, Los Angeles, and San Francisco utilized only highly promiscuous, healthy, white gay and bisexual men as guinea pigs. Shortly after this experiment began, the first cases of "gay-related immune deficiency disease" (later known as AIDS) erupted in New York City.

The idea of AIDS as a man-made virus deliberately seeded into the American gay and African black population in the late 1970s is considered by most scientists to be a joke. There are many theories pertaining to the origin of HIV, but man-made AIDS is always trashed as paranoid "conspiracy theory." Previous biowarfare experiments against civilians have all been clouded in secrecy; furthermore, the scientific "facts" surrounding these unethical programs were often tainted with government misinformation, propaganda, cover-ups, outright lies, and more than a touch of conspiracy.[1]

KILLER GERMS FOR SALE

Further complicating bioterrorism is the sale of deadly microbes to anyone and to any country with the cash to buy them. From 1985–1988, when the U.S. was still friendly with Saddam Hussein, his Education Ministry purchased seventy shipments of anthrax, West Nile virus, and other disease-causing organisms from the American Type Culture Collection. At that time, such shipments were entirely legal and received quick approval by the U.S. Commerce Department ("Germ library's inventory is making detractors queasy," *Los Angeles Times*, March 16, 1998). Even after Hussein gassed the Kurds in 1988, and even after the Gulf War, U.S. officials continued to supply Iraq with biochemical warfare ingredients ("U.S. was a key supplier to Saddam," *Seattle Post Intelligencer*, September 24, 2002). The CDC also sent WN virus and numerous other biological agents to Iraq during the years 1984 and 1993 (www.newsmax.com/archives/articles/2002/9/23/210336.shtml). The Riegle Report (May 25, 1994) further details biological and biochemical shipments from the U.S. to Iraqi government agencies. It was later learned that these microorganisms exported by the U.S. were identical to those the UN inspectors found and recovered from the Iraqi biowarfare program (www.gulfweb.org/bigdoc/report/riegle1.html).

On October 18, 2001, the CDC issued an unprecedented alert asking physicians to watch out for cases of smallpox, plague, botulism, tularemia, and even "emerging" hemorrhagic African viruses that cause Ebola and Marburg disease. Before the terrorist attacks, virologists were blaming animals in the wild. It is now clear that the more likely threat comes from crazy scientists who will use any deadly infectious agent as a potential biowarfare agent if it suits their national, political, or religious agenda.

WAS WEST NILE VIRUS DELIBERATELY SEEDED INTO THE ENVIRONMENT?

Could the new outbreaks of West Nile virus be a result of decades of animal experimentation and manipulation of the African virus in various laboratories worldwide? Surely over the past sixty years new strains of West Nile virus have been developed and "weaponized" by genetic and/or biowarfare engineers. Once a virus like West Nile is "introduced" into the environment it can spread rapidly on its own. Already the West Nile virus causes sickness in humans and animals unlike that seen in Africa in the 1930s. In late September 2002, media reports claimed that some West Nile patients had developed symptoms of polio, even though polio is caused by a different virus. Could these new manifestations of West Nile virus be an indication that the virus has been altered in a laboratory? Could this more deadly form of West Nile virus reflect manipulation not by Mother Nature but by the hand of man?

The World Trade Center bombing of 1993 did not serve as a wake-up call for the attack of 9/11. Neither did the introduction of West Nile virus into the New York population in 1999 serve as a wake-up call for bioterrorism, because it was followed two years later by successful anthrax letter attacks. How many more wake-up calls with bioterrorism will be required before health officials stop looking in rain forests and African animals for the origin of these new epidemic-causing diseases— and begin to look at the world trade in deadly infectious agents, and the insanities of biowarfare and biowarfare research, as reasons for our current new plagues?

Biowarfare agents are designed solely to kill large numbers of civilians. Any country that is willing to employ and deploy these agents should be fully aware that "what goes around, comes around." •

Note

1. It is possible here to discuss only a small amount of evidence pointing to AIDS as a manmade disease. My two books and articles published in *Paranoia* have covered this research, which has been ignored by the scientific community and the major media.

—Winter 2003

* * *

THE BIG PICTURE

* * *

Declaring War on the Human Spirit

The Media Spectacle vs. the Collective Psyche

by *Frank Berube and Joan d'Arc*

Eight days after the terrorist attacks of September 11, 2001, the Bush Administration unveiled its proposed Anti-Terrorism Act, which broadly expanded current domestic surveillance laws. The resultant anti-terrorism legislation, called the USA Patriot Act, was rushed through Congress on October 26, 2001. This article provides an overview of the potential for this expansion of government power to infringe on the freedom of American citizens. Berube and d'Arc also discuss the role of the media in promulgating government propaganda, and in manufacturing reality during this crisis. Fear of being labeled a "traitor," the authors declare, prevented people from questioning or challenging government-sanctioned viewpoints. The authors conclude, "Most people are too caught up in the frenzy of the moment to notice the totalitarian monster creeping up behind them."

CATASTROPHIC EVENTS on the world stage are being met with overwhelming fear, weakening the foundations of personal integrity and undermining the ability to remain true to oneself. Hoards of people are unconsciously caught up in the whirlwind of technology: cell phone interactions, internet connections, video games and other virtual activities—lost in a world of their own making, scrambling for scraps of security in an ever more dangerous and uncertain world. Yet, how many of us are aware that global media conglomerates have helped to build this egomaniacal madhouse called America?

In 1983, when Ben Bagdikian wrote the first edition of *Media Monopoly*, fifty media corporations dominated the mass media. Now there are six: AOL Time Warner, Viacom, Disney, News Corp (Rupert Murdock), Vivendi Universal (the number-one music company), and Bertelsmann (a private German conglomerate). In the sixth edition of his book, published in 2001, Bagdikian explains the problem this concentration of media ownership raises in a democratic society:

> There was reason enough, even then, for concern that so small a number of dominant firms had such a disproportionate influence on American culture, commerce, and political power. That shrank the status of the individual and more personal groups as voices in society. But today there is an even smaller number of dominant firms–six–(even excluding the AOL–Time Warner deal), and those six have more communications power than all the combined fifty leading firms of sixteen years earlier. It is the overwhelming collective power of these firms, with their corporate interlocks and unified cultural and political values, that raises troubling questions about the individual's role in the American democracy.

As everything is falling apart around us, no one but the most steadfastly oblivious could possibly be unaware of what is happening; yet, far too many people still do not realize what's really going on: We're in a media lockdown. Your mind is being trashed.

Should we censor points of view that we find "unpatriotic"? What if, under all the emotion these points of view conjure, they contain a kernel of "truth"? When it's not possible to establish the truth about anything, that doesn't mean we should surrender our autonomy to media authorities and give up on our own personal intuitions and perceptions. As Bagdikian explains:

> As the dominant corporations' increasing global scale enlarged their importance in the stock market, Wall Street analysts and leading investment houses became a factor in deciding how much and what kind of news and entertainment will reach the public. Wall Street lives and dies by daily stock levels, so pressure on media companies has increased not only to achieve ever-higher profits and stock levels, but also to do it rapidly.

In the frenetic race for attention, media companies adopt any means to freeze viewers' eyes in order to prevent viewers from changing channels. Their pursuit of the huge commercial rewards for this instant fixation has produced significant social and political changes in America's culture and social values.

As most will agree, all eyes were indeed frozen on images of the World Trade Center being struck by airplanes, images shown over and over again until our minds reeled with horror. How indelibly those images are now etched into our minds forever. Dare we open our mouths to ask this question: Should these images be any more appalling than tens of thousands of Iraqi civilians being massacred or hundreds of thousands of fleeing Rawandans being slaughtered? At the very least, the world has caught up to us. But outside of these televised images, how much of the real picture are we being allowed to see?

According to an article in the Manchester *Guardian*, the Pentagon spent millions of dollars to prevent western media from seeing highly detailed civilian satellite pictures of the effects of bombing raids in Afghanistan. According to the *Guardian*, "The extraordinary detail of the images already taken by the satellite includes a line of terrorist trainees marching between training camps at Jalalabad. At the same resolution, it would be possible to see bodies lying on the ground after last week's bombing attacks." But we aren't seeing them. We are seeing carefully orchestrated imagery of what "they" want us to see. And we are hearing only the carefully worded propaganda "they" want us to hear. Through acts of Orwellian censorship, our views and opinions are calculated to fit in with the prevailing media opinions.

After reports of heavy civilian casualties from overnight bombing of training camps northwest of Jalalabad near Darunta, the Pentagon decided to shut down access to satellite images. Interestingly, under American law the Defense Department may legally shut down US civilian satellites in order to prevent enemies from using the images. Instead of invoking its legal powers, the Pentagon simply purchased exclusive rights to all Ikonos satellite pictures of Afghanistan from Space Imaging, the company that runs the satellite. The reason for this? As the *Guardian* explains, if the Pentagon had imposed legal powers, news organizations could have filed a lawsuit arguing "prior restraint censorship." Instead, the Pentagon simply bought the images, end of story.

DEBATE IS NOT DISSENT!

Luckily, Orwell's "thought police" don't run the whole show yet, as much as they would like us to think they do. But we're in danger. Self-censorship must go. Debate does not equal dissent. Dissent does not make you a traitor. "Freedom-loving people" should keep their eyes and mouths open, not shut. Talking about our dissenting opinions brings them out into the open where they can be examined and studied.

The "cryptocreeps" are sabotaging the collective psyche, giving them the psychic power to control individuals from within, without having to force people to conform and behave. But they still have to maintain a complex system of policing and surveillance to see that all goes as expected. It's a good thing we have "civil libertarian" Alan M. Dershowitz.

According to Dershowitz, the proposed friendly national identity card will help stop racial profiling. Neat. As he points out, at many bridges and tunnels across the country, drivers already avoid long delays with "an unobtrusive device" located on the dashboard. In place of the old-fashioned dolt "fumbling for change," the trendy driver is on his or her merry way in seconds and gets the bill in the mail later! Dershowitz calls it a "tradeoff between privacy and convenience." Yes, "the toll-takers know more about you—when you entered and left Manhattan, for instance—but you save time and money."

Dershowitz suggests that an "optional" national ID card could be used in a similar way, "offering a similar kind of tradeoff: a little less anonymity for a lot more security." As he explains, those who have the card could move "more expeditiously" through their day, zipping through airports or building security, and anyone who opts out would be "examined much more closely." We've already got the ad line for this one: "Hey, there goes Bill, on his merry way already, and here I am spreading my cheeks. What gives? The new national identity card. You won't leave the airport without it." Dershowitz claims he is "instinctively skeptical" of such tradeoffs, although he does support a national identity card with a "chip that can match the holder's fingerprint."

So, they're already using the latest atrocity to "up the ante" against dissidents. This means that all of us in the conspiracy business have to rethink our strategies for the future. What's going to happen to us? Have they ratcheted their legal power up a notch and added other forms of pressure to hinder people who go against the grain? There's no telling how far they will take the new police state: they could cart us all the way to the gulag for all the American public could care. It's no longer paranoid to think that another "terrorist attack" like this one would bring the FEMA-tons down on us "turncoats" like there's no tomorrow.

What's worse, this gives media-sedated people another excuse to dig in and hunker down. Forget trying to clue them in; they're scared out of their minds and are ready to submit to whatever it takes to "solve the problem." *Paranoia*'s believability rating just hit rock bottom. We're not just crackpots on the fringe anymore—we're "dupes of the terrorists": spreading their message of overthrowing the government and letting loose the devil on the world. But it's easy for the media to pull off these manipulations when the public mind is so dumbed-down by television. As long as they can keep Americans in "short attention span theater," we're in mental lockdown. The creeps can rewrite history. They can do anything they want. As John MacArthur, publisher of *Harper's*, has noted:

> Americans live in a perpetual present. This is the country with the shortest attention span in the civil world, and it is a cultural problem. We don't know anything that happened six months ago, much less twenty years ago, when we supported the Afghan resistance and bin Laden against the Soviet Union. No one remembers that we were Saddam's ally and supporter during the Iran-Iraq war. Nobody remembers.

Does nobody remember because "somebody" doesn't want us to remember? A notable parallel from George Orwell's novel *1984*:

> For the moment he had shut his ears to the remoter noises and was listening to the stuff that streamed out of the telescreen. It appeared there had been demonstrations to thank Big Brother for raising the chocolate ration to twenty grams a week. And only yesterday it had been announced that the ration was to be reduced to twenty grams a week. Was it possible they could swallow that, after only twenty-four hours? . . . The fabulous statistics continued to pour out of the telescreen.

We would be better able to react to the 9/11 event if we knew how it came about and what aim it was intended to "achieve." But instead, the cover story about bin Laden's orchestration of this event and of the CIA knowing appears to be just that—a cover story—seen from the vantage point of how nicely the outcome of this gruesome act fits in with the precisely prepared steps to deal with "domestic terror." [*Editor's Note:* Here it is 2003, and the hunt for bin Laden somehow turned into a hunt for Saddam Hussein. Who's bin Laden, you ask? That's short-attention-span theater for you.]

Eight days after the terrorist attacks in New York and Washington, the Bush Administration unveiled its proposed Anti-Terrorism Act (ATA), which broadly amended current surveillance laws. In October 2001, overreaching wiretap bills were rushed through Congress by the Bush Administration without hearings. The USA Act (USAA) was passed by the Senate on October 11; the final legislation, called the USA Patriot Act, was passed on October 26.

With the expansion of surveillance authority permitted by these bills, a major concern is that authority is not limited to even a "broad definition" of terrorism. In addition, Congress moved too quickly on these measures in the heat of the moment. The ATA and USAA bills came after the Senate's hasty passage of the Combating Terrorism Act (CTA) (S.A. 1562), which was passed on September 13 after being discussed less than thirty minutes on the Senate floor. A similar bill, the Public Safety and Cyber Security Enhancement Act (PSCSEA), was drafted for introduction in the House, and appears to be a "backup plan" for S.A. 1562. This legislation includes the following:

- Makes it possible to obtain e-mail message header information, Internet user web browsing patterns, and "stored" voicemail without a wiretap order
- Removes controls on Title III roving wiretaps
- Permits law enforcement to disclose information obtained through wiretaps to any employee of the Executive branch
- Reduces restrictions on domestic investigations under the Foreign Intelligence Surveillance Act (FISA)
- Permits grand juries to provide information to the US intelligence community
- Permits the President to designate any "foreign-directed individual, group, or entity," including a US citizen or organization, as a target for FISA surveillance
- Prevents people from providing "expert advice" to terrorists
- Extends the federal DNA database to include every person convicted of a federal terrorism offense that involves low-level computer intrusions

According to the ACLU, law enforcement authorities already had sufficient legal power to investigate suspects in terrorist attacks, including wide authority to monitor both telephone and Internet communications. The scope of the Computer Fraud and Abuse Act (Sec. 1030(a)(5)(A)) has been described as "dangerously broad"; what's worse, the ATA would attempt to redefine violations of the Computer Fraud section as "terrorism."

The ACLU has warned that the surveillance provisions of this legislation would reduce or eliminate the role of judges in ensuring that law enforcement wiretapping is conducted legally and with proper justification, and dangerously erode the distinction between domestic law enforcement and foreign intelligence collection, which protects Americans from being spied upon by their own intelligence agencies. In addition, "the definition of 'terrorism' is too broad, permitting the special surveillance powers granted in this legislation to be applied far beyond what is commonly thought of by the term." The ACLU has warned that under the proposed definition of terrorism, even acts of simple "civil disobedience" could lead organizations to become targets of "terrorist" investigations.

The ACLU has also argued that placing all "computer crime" under the umbrella of "terrorism" is heavy-handed. Under this section, even manufacturers of computer equipment could find themselves in legal hassles since the definition of "transmission" would include the design, manufacture, creation, distribution, sale, and marketing of floppy-disk controllers made faulty by defective microcode. Other such activities could eventually be held illegal under this statute—but it's a crap shoot. As Electronic Frontier Foundation Action Alert writes:

> No one can predict at this early stage what will or will not be considered a violation of this provision. Yet the ATA would redefine all present and future violations as acts of terrorism, with violators subject to terrible penalties, up to and including life in prison without possibility of parole. Additionally, these changes to the law would remove statutes of limitations and become retroactive. This means that any US–based computer security professional who, like many in this field, once upon a time began as a system cracker or other "black hat" hacker, potentially faces criminal prosecution under the ATA.

While it is obviously of vital national importance to respond effectively to terrorism, these bills recall the McCarthy era in the power they would give government to scrutinize the private lives of American citizens.

"CODED MESSAGES" OR OUTRIGHT CENSORSHIP?

Propaganda is a tried-and-true tool of the state during times of national insecurity. You would have caught this one if you had your radar on, when right before our eyes the major television broadcast companies went along with government instructions not to air videotaped messages by men in turbans because they might contain "coded messages."

This is downright silly. As Susan Sontag pointed out, "Does anyone over the age of six really think that the way Osama bin Laden has to communicate with his agents abroad is by . . . pulling on his left earlobe . . . to send secret signals?" No. This was not the true intent of this military-state directive. The government simply didn't want the American public to hear the radical, anti-American views of Islamic culture. It was overt censorship of the media by the military, and they didn't even have to disguise it. All they had to do was put a turban on it.

The true intent of this censorship was made clear in late September (exact date undisclosed) when Pakistani newspaper *UMMAT* featured an interview with Osama bin Laden, which would have been censored by major media no matter who it was about. Views like the following are not "coded messages" but are simply not the views normally aired on major networks in America:

BIN LADEN: There are intelligence agencies in the US which require billions of dollars worth of funds from the Congress and the government every year. This [funding issue] was not a big problem till the existence of the former Soviet Union but after that the budget of these agencies has been in danger. They needed an enemy. So, they first started propaganda against Usama and Taliban and then this incident happened. You see, the Bush Administration approved a budget of 40 billion dollars.

Where will this huge amount go? It will be provided to the same agencies, which need huge funds and want to exert their importance. Now they will spend the money for their expansion and for increasing their importance. I will give you an example. Drug smugglers from all over the world are in contact with the US secret agencies. US secret agencies do not want to eradicate narcotics cultivation and trafficking because their importance will be diminished. The people in the US Drug Enforcement Department are encouraging drug trade so that they could show performance and get millions of dollars worth of budget.

General Noriega was made a drug baron by the CIA and, in need, he was made a scapegoat. In the same way, whether it is President Bush or any other US President, they cannot bring Israel to justice for its human rights abuses or to hold it accountable for such crimes. What is this? Is it not that there exists a government within the government in the United Sates? That secret government must be asked as to who carried out the attacks.

Yikes. Cover the children's ears!

THE HUMANITARIAN COVER

The media overseers are taking it upon themselves to use film and television to present to the public their private view of the way things ought to be. They know that no matter how much this picture may differ from what is really happening, the mind-controlling powers of televisual imagery and film history will supersede other views and change the way these times will be looked on forever after. In *1984*, Orwell illustrated the mutability of the past through the use of Newspeak. The main character, Winston Smith, works at the Ministry of Truth, where his job is to "rectify history."

As in Orwell's novel, all forms of media have been consolidated and standardized, delivering the same views and information to everyone in their homes and communities—setting the specifications for what is considered acceptable behavior and showing people how to play the game. Consider, for example, the stories of severe treatment of Afghan women under the Taliban regime—truly abhorrent and dehumanizing. But if the media can get us to react emotionally, forcing us to participate in a ritual akin to *1984*'s daily "Two Minutes Hate," we won't be capable of reading between the lines. The following is interesting as a media case study in emotional foreplay: During the week of October 15, 2001, an "e-mail petition" directed to the UN stated that the appalling treatment of Afghan women should not be tolerated and "deserves action by the United Nations."

Yet, how would the petition's author propose that the UN address this extremely complicated cultural and religious situation? Any suggestions? Increase the sanctions, perhaps, which would only hurt them worse? Drop some allied "smart" bombs, perhaps, that hit only men, being careful to avoid "innocent women and children" (why is it that men are never innocent?), thus killing the men on whom these women and their children are dependent for food?

But then the allies could drop delicious treats from the skies—manna from the gods! One news report that seemed to be squelched immediately said that the Afghans were burying these food rations out of fear that America was trying to poison them. Whoops. Blew our humanitarian cover. Get rid of that story. Other reports said that these food rations were totally inadequate, consisting of biscuits and jam and peanut butter. There was also the danger of land mine explosions as Afghans ran into the deserts to grab up the rations. According to Sontag, "Afghanistan has more land mines per capita than any country in the world. Humanitarianism is once again being used in this unholy war as a pretext for war."

The humanitarian cover is propaganda at work. We need to see how it subtly manipulates our emotions. The treatment of women under Taliban rule is not a new story. Our government has known about it for several years; only now has it suddenly taken front position. We need to step back and see how complicated this situation is and rise above this one-dimensional image: the one where Uncle Sam takes care of all the needy and desperate in the world, while we ignore how the humanitarian deed was accomplished, if it ever actually was.

As Sontag has argued, the crimes against women in Afghanistan are indeed unthinkable, but the Northern Alliance, the group which would take over the government, is certainly not known for its fair treatment of women either. Intense bombing will only increase Islamic militancy in the Middle East, making it even harder on these women. The bombing campaigns have already sent refugees to the country's various borders where as many as a million may freeze or starve to death. As Sontag notes, "How you're going to dethrone the Taliban without causing further trouble in that part of the world is a very complicated question." And it's not going to be solved with bombs and peanut butter crackers.

Furthermore, since this war is being "brought to you by" the best Orwellian "Victory Gin" money can buy, we won't get to see who we are really dropping the bombs on. As Sontag points out, "There are not very many military targets in Afghanistan. We're talking about one of the poorest countries in the world. What they can do is bomb the soldiers, the camps . . . And you can imagine who they are, it's a lot of kids." A news report on October 16, 2001, stated that only "the poorest of the poor" were present in the city of Kabul during the air raids that week. Islam Online reported that the terrified screams of women and children pierced the air as the bombs fell, killing about 400 civilians and making homeless hundreds more. In one air raid alone, at least 160 were killed, mainly women and children, when a missile fell in an area of traditional Afghan mud houses.

It's unpleasant to have to point out that these are the women that our e-mail petitioner wanted to help. It's not that Americans don't mean well; it's that we are being manipulated by our supposedly open and free democratic media. As Sontag points out, "There's a great disconnect between reality and what people in government and media are saying of the reality. What is being peddled to the public is a fairy tale. The atmosphere of intimidation [behind that] is quite extraordinary."

THE MANUFACTURED REALITY

As long as you don't make waves you won't get into trouble. The glue that holds everything together is the effect of the media on the subconscious minds of the masses. Without the information provided by alternative news sources and "underground" publications, frightened egos have nothing to work with in questioning the party line, and they end up subconsciously going along with the gargantuan media monopoly—a huge blind octopus which only answers to money in its pockets.

The Internet has such enormous potential for inspired corporate capitalists that it must be controlled. In fact, the Internet was the only source of dissenting opinion throughout this macabre experience. Given its remarkable ability to remain a tool of the proles, what will be its future? Long range plan: get rid of the riffraff?

Television is the sacrificial altar upon which the blood ritual is performed daily, until these tragic events lose their power to shock and outrage us. The mental effect of seeing the WTC buildings falling over and over again makes all the horror and suffering seem unreal, simply because it's happening on TV. Whatever the media spectacle of the moment, there is always the element of subliminal subversion embedded beneath the surface of events, ready to trick the distracted mind into making the manufactured view captured on film seem true to life.

To those who have tried to prepare themselves for this day it must seem like a scripted movie, because it's playing out according to the new world order's plans and heading us in the direction of total control. The "event" itself was horrific—the media coverage was stunning—but it was also a very effective way to bring everyone to their knees. When there is no other "authorized" way of getting information about what's happening, all people have to talk about is what they parrot from the news media. Downright fear prevents them from looking any deeper—scared to death of what they might find and be forced to deal with. Strangely, after much of this article was written, *UMMAT* published an interview with Osama bin Laden in which he stated:

> The Western media is unleashing such a baseless propaganda, which surprises us but it reflects on what is in their hearts and gradually they themselves become captive of this propaganda. They become afraid of it and begin to cause harm to themselves. Terror is the most dreaded weapon in the modern age and the western media is mercilessly using it against its own people. It can add fear and helplessness in the psyche of the people of Europe and the United States. It means that what the enemies of the United States cannot do, its media is doing.

The mainstream media is a surreal stage where shocking and terrifying things happen on a daily basis. The apocalyptic scenario is playing itself out for all to see and react in the prescribed way. Knowing how the public reacted to the Gulf War and other atrocities of the 1990s, it's clear that most people are too caught up in the frenzy of the moment to notice the totalitarian monster creeping up behind them.

It's getting harder for ordinary people to withstand these mounting forces of inner chaos—our spirits are weakening from being aware of so much needless suffering and death among animals and humans on this ailing planet. We ought not to believe that we are merely spectators in the grand theater of life, thinking ourselves innocent bystanders to all the death and destruction we see on the nightly news.

The mass media is getting more psycho-technological and, combined with a growing anxiety about other potential terrorist events, fear has an increasingly stronger effect on our lives. We naturally want to close ranks and protect our families. It's hard to ask people to find the courage to search for the truth and try to set things right, when that would mean going up against the new world orderers and risking everything.

How can anything positive gain a firm foothold when the media is run by the cryptocracy, and most people are too scared to lift the curtain to see the great and powerful Oz behind it? Many have referred to these events as a wake-up call, but what have we awakened from and to? As Al Krulick wrote in the *Orlando Weekly*:

> Have we awakened from the notion that we are not alone in this world and that there are a lot of hurt, angry, and desperate people

out there? Have we awakened from the conceit that we may not be entitled to our profligate ways, consuming 25 percent of the world's resources with only 5 percent of its population? Have we awakened from the dream that we can do what we want, live how we wish, regardless of cost—without paying a heavy price? Have we awakened to a world where . . . being conscious of our actions will take precedence over gorging on our pleasures?

Or will the ad men have their way? Will they use their enormous powers of influence and control of the media to lull us back to sleep?

As we know only too well from looking back over the twentieth century, the only way for evil to take root in the world is for good people to do nothing. As long as the human spirit survives in individuals, the forces of good are able to work through our everyday lives, which gives the world-soul the boost it needs to run those inhuman bastards out of morphogenetic city and give the collective psyche back to the people. ●

References

Bagdikian, Ben. *Media Monopoly*, 6th edition, 2001.

Campbell, Duncan. "US buys up all satellite war images," *Guardian*, October 17, 2001.

Dershowitz, Alan. "Why Fear National ID Cards?" *New York Times*, October 13, 2001.

Electronic Frontier Foundation Action Alert, www.eff.org/alerts/20011010_eff_wiretap_alert.html.

Independent Media Institute, www.alternet.org.

Islam Online. "Kabul's Poorest Have No Escape from U.S. Bombs," October 16, 2001.

Krulick, Al. "Gimme a Commercial Break," *Orlando Weekly*, October 15, 2001.

"Surveillance Powers: Changes being considered by Congress," www.alternet.org.

Talbot, David. "Susan Sontag, 'The Traitor,' Fires Back," *Salon*, October 17, 2001.

UMMAT, Pakistan, September 28, 2001. www.khilafah.com.

—Winter 2002

The Police State Is Now a Work of Art

A Retrospective, 1994–2000

by Randy Koppang

Writing prior to 9/11, Randy Koppang argued that the major war being fought by the government is not taking place overseas, but is rather a street war on its own citizenry. In the year 2000, America's penal colony ascended to the two million inmate mark—most having been jailed in the failed War on Drugs—as incarceration became a big business. In fact, crime itself has become a commodity and a national pastime, fed back to us as TV entertainment. Updating this article to the year 2003, the author gives us a glimpse of a frightening future of mega-workhouse prisons and a global police state.

> "The police state is now a work of art"
> —MARSHALL McLUHAN, "TAKE TODAY"

ON MAY 8 AND 9, 2000, there occurred a sequence of events I discerned as vital to the theme that follows. *USA Today* reported on May 8, "Serious crime continued to decline nationwide for the eighth straight year in 1999, dropping an overall seven percent, says the FBI." According to former New York Police Commissioner William Bratton, "We are beginning to see [in this decline,] the long-term benefit of rising incarceration rates and the presence of additional police across the country." And, from the vantage of mainstream media and sensibilities of popular advertising, I would agree.

In contrast, on May 9, 2000, a *USA Today* headline confirmed that human rights group Amnesty International held a news conference on policing, at which grave concern was voiced that nationwide police practices routinely demonstrate the "institutionalization of cruelty"; practices that increasingly resemble torture.

In 1994, I began to perceive a pattern of convergent points leading to a comprehensive analysis of crime which is a bit more technical than Bratton's. The global environment of electronic media surrounding us can be empowering if we use the new perspectives it requires of all of us. Nineteenth-century perceptions of twentieth-century crime are obsolete. Time to move on.

From the hearts and minds of America, citizens express ever louder their concerns for crime and punishment. The *Los Angeles Times* on February 24, 1995 observed that, "Crime [was] the hottest topic on network news . . . In an annual survey of news coverage on ABC, CBS, and NBC, Washington's Center for Media and Public Affairs found that crime ranked number one for the second straight year." As policies are mythologized in media, politics offers yesterday's answers to today's problems.

Consider the following: Are the methods used to police crime a tool used to fine-tune a particular socioeconomic vision? People are hired to assemble in "think-tanks," as consultants with government. These policy "thinkers" have successfully recommended solutions to crime, discussed below.

This article intends to show that popular notions of crime, and policies chosen in reaction to it, are misinforming. However, absent from this discussion is a claim that the policies mentioned are the works of liberals, rightists, extremists, conservatives, etc. This review is not about blame. Such conclusions fall prey to the diversionary tactics of dialectic debate that are so crucial to those of our controlling interests—those who would rather forsake liberty for a tyranny of security. Rather, I intend to emphasize consciousness.

When strung together, basic building blocks of crime and security policy form patterns of insight. To debate differences of opinion on these details is obsolete. This is a composite picture of transformation: a state of policing which we helped to create. This "state" has two interactive orders: the military jurisdiction and the civil jurisdiction.

My first point is inspired by William McNeill's article "A World Transformed," which appeared in the fall 1990 issue of *Foreign Affairs*, the journal of the Council on Foreign Relations.

The simple fact is that the more we tinker with human behavior and seek to manage it in accordance with some deliberate goal, the more we entangle ourselves in processes we do not fully understand. Yet, there really is no choice. Decisions have to be made and policies implemented—somehow. The situation we face in the United States as the Cold War winds down and the arms race peters out—if that does turn out to be the path into the future—is that some new balance among all the special interests and social groupings of American society will have to be contrived. This calls for the sort of political process that went into the redefinition of the role of the federal government after World War II.[1]

It's interesting to note that the above viewpoint suggests that a resolution to the Cold War and the Arms Race will only *perhaps* be our path to the future. Whichever path it is, McNeill feels a "new balance" among the various segments of society will have to be "contrived." Contrived by whom, you may ask? And to what degree has or has not the "arms race" petered out? Cold War–era Department of Defense budgets have been maintained.

The redefinition of the role of the federal government after World War II, which McNeill refers to above, resulted primarily in two creations. The Office of Strategic Services was transformed into the CIA[2]; and the National Security Act of 1947 gave birth to the National Security Council, the National Security Agency (via Executive Order),[3] and our omnipresent National Security State mentality. This war mentality is now archetypal. As a microcosm of the nation, this mentality has so infected the social consciousness that ethnically diverse youth gangs are at war with each other (in and out of prison), and "crime-fighters" are at war with them nationwide, in perpetuity. As Sanyika Shakur writes on page 355 of his Los Angeles youth gang autobiography, *Monster*:

> It's not enough to say that I had transcended the mindset of being a [gang] banger . . . After having spent thirteen years of my young life inside what initially seemed like an extended family, but had turned into a war machine, I was tired and disgusted with its insatiable appetite for destruction . . . I wanted to construct something, which in [gang] banging is tantamount to treason.

The socioeconomic effects we experience today, resulting from a National Security path of governance, were publicly previewed by President Dwight D. Eisenhower when he warned:

In the councils of government, we must guard against the acquisition of unwarranted influence, whether sought or unsought, by the military industrial complex. The potential for the disastrous rise of misplaced power exists and will persist . . . only an alert and knowledgeable citizenry can compel the proper meshing of the huge industrial and military machinery of defense with our peaceful methods and goals so that security and liberty may prosper together.[4]

We did not heed President Eisenhower's warning. The military industrial complex has become the role model for civil police procedures now at federal, state and local levels.[5] This is culturally verifiable daily. View the many crime-fighting dramatizations and news broadcasts called "reality shows," preoccupied with a contrived human interest in paramilitary crime fighting. The media mirrors the social system of crime control paranoia. The clearest demonstration of this role modeling was Waco. BATF forces violated Posse Comitatus (Title 10 U.S.C.) by using military training, tanks, and helicopters in the serving of a warrant on David Koresh.

World War II established a militaristic, media-enhanced consensual reality. Thereafter, the people engaged a political will to continue funding major war preparedness. Yet, Section 8, Par. 12 of the U.S. Constitution states: "Congress shall have the power to raise and support armies, but no appropriation of money to that use shall be for a longer term than two years." (Coincidentally, the National Security Act was passed in 1947, two years after WWII.)

Conscious nurturing of a World War II–era economy still dominates today: no signs of economic conversion have surfaced; budget continues to escalate; there is no post–Cold War budgetary peace dividend. Now, twelve years after the end of the Cold War, the war peacetime budget continues to escalate. In the 2000 presidential campaign, Al Gore pledged to increase Department of Defense budgets, showing no difference between Democrats and Republicans. As militarized themes of conflict/entertainment pervade the daily media fabric (video games, virtual reality), media illusions exaggerate a morphed historical consciousness. Such war economy propaganda is the MK-ULTRA of thought control—a symbiosis of entertainment and the Department of Defense.

In the post–World War II security posture Eisenhower warned against, we've had the Cold War, Korean War, invasion of Cuba, Vietnam, covert war in Central America, Angola, invasion of Panama to arrest Noriega for drugs, the bombing of Libya, the Gulf War, Somalia, Haiti—all global policing "emergencies," but non-constitutionally declared acts of war.[6]

The Cold War may be over, but what now? The "need" for annual military budgets of $250-300 billion should require an impressive security threat. Behold this new image being declared to America and the world: Representing our role in facing the newly invented "threats," the headline on the cover of the October 24, 1994, issue of *U.S. News & World Report* read, "Uncle Sam, Supercop!" The creative thought required for this cover story literally makes the point. Global policing (in collaboration with the UN) is a new American ambition, setting the stage for new domestic wars—wars on drugs, crime, Islamic terrorism, rogue nations, and perhaps "aliens" (not from the third world, but from space).

What ending the Cold War actually defines is the possibility and desirability of peace, per se. Eloquently prescribed in *Report from Iron Mountain*[7] is a social equation: "It is the incorrect assumption that war, as an institution, is subordinate to the social systems it is believed to serve. The fact that a society is organized for any degree of readiness for war [means] war itself is the basic social system."[8] The educational/commercial priorities of war economy are "the balance-wheel" securing our economy. War and peace are social systems. War, as a system, has non-military as well as military functions in society.

A headline in the December 21, 1994 issue of the *Los Angeles Times* reported, "Military's Un-Martial Outlays Scrutinized," nondefense spending in the Pentagon budget was growing. Interestingly, the Pentagon budget included the following expenditures and dozens more: "Breast cancer research, drug interdiction/enforcement, environmental cleanup, financing for public schools, international aid and rifle practice for neighborhood teenagers."

Sooner or later, such nonmilitary functions must substitute for overt war.[9] These are many and the time is now, in peace. Actually, we have peace veiled in Executive Orders claiming continual National Emergency.[10] In May 2000, the Clinton administration proclaimed that now AIDS is a national security threat. In reviewing the *Report from Iron Mountain* we learn:

> Under sociological substitutes for non-military functions of war—war serves to insure social cohesiveness. In post-war (or Cold War), the Job Corps idea can serve to this end for the socially disaffected, economically unprepared, psychologically unconformable [e.g. "Crips," "Bloods," and Mexican Mafia gang members], hard-core

"delinquents," incorrigible "Subversives," and the rest of the unemployable . . . seen as somehow transformed by the disciplines of a service.

As Secretary Robert McNamara has stated, "even in our abundant societies, we have reason enough to worry over tensions that . . . tighten among underprivileged young people, and finally flail out in delinquency and crime . . . where mounting frustrations are likely to fester into eruptions of violence and extremism."[11] This couldn't be more true today. The most volatile social enclave is now that of youth gangs.

THE PRISON SYSTEM: A SOPHISTICATED FORM OF SLAVERY

Social safety concerns many citizens, who feel increasingly unsafe as a result of media portrayals of rampant crime. After all, they voted for the "Three Strikes You're Out" equals twenty-five-years-to-life sentencing. A plan to house greater numbers of prisoners for longer terms could reduce unemployment outside prison, imply greater social stability, and even create a labor force of prisoners. I mention this point in relation to a third reference from the *Report from Iron Mountain* that "it is entirely possible that the development of a sophisticated form of slavery may be an absolute prerequisite for social control in a world at peace."[12]

On 5/6/00, it was reported that national unemployment was 3.9 percent—but how many people are in prison? What follows is evidence that policymakers continue to fine-tune a system whose priorities are outlined above—the control of crime, social cohesion, unemployment outside prison vs. a 'Job Corps' for unemployed prisoners:

ABC News Nightline: November 11, 1994: Inmates in U.S. Federal Prisons, 93,708; State prisons, 919,143. Total U.S. prisoners: 1.01 million (Source: BJS, 1994). In the year 2000, the inmate population was 2 million (*L.A. Times*, February 15, 2000). Do 2 million people equal a sizeable work force?

Los Angeles Times: October 16, 1994: "California's Boom Times for Prison Building." In this article, the picture becomes focused. "During the past decade, Department of Corrections [asserted] get tough on crime policies . . . by building sixteen new prisons and renovating old ones." Anticipating "Three Strikes" sentencing, "terms for many second-time felons will double (as of December 1994, Virginia may abolish parole entirely). As a result, officials estimate [a prison] population . . . of about 100,000 more than today's total—and twenty-five new prisons will be needed . . . [giving] California fifty-eight [state] prisons, plus several minimum security work camps." Construction has begun!

California's constitution mandates education as a budgetary priority over others. But $5 billion has been spent and a bond debt "will double that to $10 billion with interest." "Prison building [is] a multibillion-dollar industry in California, and with the 'Three Strikes' law, an even bigger boom is forecast for coming decades." Clinton's 2001 budget will fund the building of seventeen more prisons. A prison construction boom lasting decades amounts to investment opportunities just like real estate. With "Three Strikes," the nation will imprison in the next five years many more than the increase from 1.01 to 2 million that occurred between 1994 and 2000, at an annual warehousing cost of $25,000 per inmate.[13]

The police state vision takes on added form with the following serious proposal, published in the *Journal of Criminal Justice* in 1993, describing how to make mega-imprisonment cost effective: "By 1990, prison populations in [America] had risen 135 percent since 1980, and most states were facing record deficits." Following more than twelve years of "renewed interest in prison industrialization, and slow, steady, inmate employment growth, most prisons still suffered vast inmate unemployment."

This article proposed a policy for total prisoner employment, and discussed "a number of models" which focused on "the implications of dramatically increasing prisoner employment." The *Journal of Criminal Justice* article showed how prison labor productivity can increase with no "significant threats to the civilian labor force" and that these production centers "can yield economic, institutional and individual benefits."[14]

The pattern of facts presented here shows that the national will to "get tough on crime" exceeds simple bureaucratic success. The "getting tough" amounts to a sort of social surgery, and denies a sincere effort to end crime at its root via economic prevention. In 1994, the Federal Crime Bill gave $20 billion for more police and prisons, which resulted in locking up 900,000 more people to date.[15] On February 15, 2000, America's inmate population (literally, a socioeconomic subculture within) reached the two million mark.[16]

Furthering the econo-political momentum of this burgeoning social enclave, President Clinton's law enforcement portion of his 2001 budget featured yet another "$2 billion in funding for the construction of seventeen prisons."[17]

This article was originally written in 1994. It is perhaps fortunate that it was not published until now, since there have been six years of war on drugs and terrorist crime in the interim. Yet, not much has actually changed: pop-media reports of crime statistics in 1994 said crime was in decline; and pop-media reports in 2000 indicate crime is still down. Given the record increase in our prison populace, what has changed is the higher media profile which crime and punishment have attained via crimertaining news, reality programming, video games, drama, *Court TV* and film. Crime is a big-bucks industry. *Report from Iron Mountain* is on target here: crime becomes a commodity and a national pastime as it's fed back to us via thrilling entertainment, actual or virtual.

Big Imprisonment Is Big Business

As detailed on the front page of the *Los Angeles Times* on March 7, 2000, California went on a prison-building "spree" in the mid-1980s. The Pelican Bay (a modern-day Alcatraz) in Del Norte County "saved their community" in Crescent City. Numerous rural communities "have become dominated by the prison industry."[18] Yet, crime is reported as being down. A case in point: "The number of homicides in New Orleans" declined 47 percent from 1994 to 1998, compared to a 27 percent decline in all of the US. The New Orleans decline continued in 1999—for a drop of 62 percent since 1994."[19] In the state of Louisiana, the average per capita prisoner population rate is 736 per 100,000, "tops in the nation."[20] Is the homicide rate in decline because there are more people in prison?

In answer to this question, we will not pursue an analysis which the question logically suggests. Rather, to make these human warehouses useful, there are now serious proposals to employ all US prisoners as workers in what will then be workhouse prisons. The consensus leadership in America legislates against crime, consciously denying the socio-economics of prevention. In 1994, the Republican Party intended to rewrite Clinton's crime bill by removing all funding for crime prevention. Why? Because policymakers don't act in terms of prevention; they react in terms of problem management, analogous to the absence of illness prevention in the education and practice of medicine.

Ex-cons, stigmatized by their bad reputations, have always been viewed as "negative-economic units." With workhouse prisons they can be more productive. The prison sector of our economy, perhaps? An economic value to be managed?

For many reasons, policy thinkers must have decided crime should be redefined as a resource if it is a given of society, with potential high-yield growth. Noam Chomsky, in a 1998 radio broadcast lecture on the issue of stable profits and the new economic order, established by the General Agreement on Trade and Tarrifs (GATT) said:

A case in point . . . is the early nineteenth century. There was an effort to undermine [the "Right to Live" system] carried over from feudal times; the poor were granted "benefits" (by) the "poor laws" to keep them alive. Because "people" had their "Natural Place" [in the world]. As the "New System" of Industrial Capitalism developed, came an ideology called "Classic Economic Theory," which denied people had a "Right to Live." It stated they had no rights other than by selling their labor power in the market place. Economists like Malthus [argued] it was an attack on liberty and the "Natural Order" to deceive the poor into thinking they had rights.

So, [denying a "Right to Live"] forced people either into the wage system, or into workhouse prisons. [This was early nineteenth century England; working-class riots ensued.] Today, there's to be a market for labor, people have no rights other than [obtainable] on the labor market, capital is protected [by monopoly power and state power]. There will be workhouse prisons, which is what the huge prison systems will become, more and more. The growth of prisons, the increasingly Draconian punishment system is all part of this. Also, part of it is to whip up fears and hatreds; which have an objective basis, e.g., fear of crime and terror. These are the best techniques of social control to suppress . . .

The humane aspects of society are being progressively numbed as youth is vicariously reared with graphic violent reality based TV shows, violent video games, and violent entertainment. From this came the last few generations of children devoid of empathy, increasingly resorting to violent conflict resolution—provoking the "Million Mom March."

The bottom line is, are there sufficient crimes being committed to warrant building so many prisons? Or, who is in prison and why? Popular opinion views violent crime as the main problem. In 1994, *ABC Nightline* quoted 73 percent of their poll as wanting to "build more prisons and give longer sentences."[21] Sympathy for this view is reasonable. However, the August 31, 1994, edition of the *Los Angeles Times* reported, "Although crime has seized the public's attention recently, crime rates are sinking in L.A. County and to a lesser extent nation-wide." The same report stated, "Figures released by [California] State Attorney General's office show . . . a declining homicide rate (excluding murder by gun) for the first time since 1987, [and] echoes federal and local reports." On November 14, 1994, KFWB (Radio L.A.) reported all categories of major crimes in decline. A panic momentum in prison construction ensued and it continues, creating a need which must be filled, while crime statistics reported in 2000 are down, as they were in 1994. As a *Los Angeles Times* headline read on May 17, 1999: "Crime Rates Continue Record 7-Year Plunge."

I agree with skeptics who say statistics can be skewed, favoring biased conclusions. However, I'm not taking a stance for debate. Whether increasing or decreasing, crime is a measure of societal health. On 12/21/94, Sen. Paul Simon released a poll of prison wardens, the majority of whom felt building more prisons won't solve crime. It's a bad policy.

In an age when increasing incidents of violent crime are committed by children (prosecuted as adults in some states), the issue is that the sociology of criminal behavior focuses on crime-management, not prevention. And if crime is generally declining, what is the true reason for the years of advance planning of this prison construction boom, other than to accept the reality that an inequity in our socioeconomics requires the warehousing of millions of prisoners?

The actual use of our megaprison capacity needs to be deciphered. The September 13, 1994, *Los Angeles Times* reported, "stiff drug laws cited for record incarceration rate (i.e., not violent criminals)." "[In 1994] more than 60 percent of federal and 25 percent of state inmates were there on drug charges." Nationwide in 1993, "22 percent [more people were imprisoned] than in 1989." Between 1994 and 2000, 900,000 more people were jailed, and counting. "If California were a nation, it would be the world's leader in incarceration." In 2000, California is home to the largest prison population. "The U.S. Bureau of Prisons estimated that 70 percent of its inmates will be serving time for drugs by 1997."[22]

On March 13, 2000, the *Los Angeles Times* reported "large increases in federal anti-drug budgets." The TRAC researchers at Syracuse University reported (March 13, 2000), "Marijuana was involved in more federal convictions in 1998 than any other single drug." In response to the report, Justice Department spokesman John Russell said, "It's worth noting that the number of drug defendants sentenced has increased 21 percent" from 1992 to 1998. This was the rationale behind the drug war. As of May 17, 2000, the Department of Defense had "about 200 employees in Columbia helping with the anti-narcotics effort" of Columbia's civil war.

CRIMINOLOGICAL SLEIGHT OF HAND

If most offenders filling prisons are drug users/dealers, why is there such a determined effort to outlaw "assault rifles" (Crime Bill H.R. 3355, 1994), and possibly all guns? Are drug abuse offenses synonymous with rape, murder and aggravated assault? Statistics consistently show gun crime is done mostly with handguns—not assault rifles! Perhaps the urban terror of violent crime with guns is a media exaggeration. As of December 15, 2000, the *Los Angeles Times* reported a new local study showing an overall decline in gun deaths of nearly 10 percent from 1998 to 1999.

Clearly, outlawing assault rifles is an erosion of the Second Amendment. A December 5, 1994, *L.A. Times* opinion stated that, "The argument . . . about preserving legitimate sporting and hunting misses the mark: The Second Amendment isn't about hunting ducks. Nor are weapons [that are] only good for killing people exempted from Second Amendment protection; they are at its core."[23]

It seems there is a shrewd sleight of hand in this "debate" on the crime issue, since the debate lacks the recognition that national economic prevention of crime would be wise. Crime is a micromanaged economy unto itself. It begins as a tumor on the host economy of social values. When the health of national values deteriorates—no longer immune to crime—it spreads as cancer. The best approach to crime is conscious prevention; not prison management and "crimertainment."

The political debate on crime gives top priority to illegalizing assault rifles, and perhaps all guns. But guns are a tool in crime, not a cause. There is evidence that the federal government has actually sanctioned the creation of an apparent handgun/assault rifle crime wave. Congress then usurped the Second Amendment and passed laws to control the crime wave.

1. *Handgun Proliferation.* On October 4, 1994, L.A. Radio-KFWB Pentagon correspondent Ivan Scott reported: "A White House spokesman confirmed, President Clinton personally endorsed and

encouraged the importation of seven million 9-millimeter Russian handguns, plus seven billion rounds of ammunition; a trade deal worked out at a recent summit meeting?" "That's all it is . . . a trade deal," a White House official says, "you'd better believe it." The Russian handgun "will sell for about a hundred bucks." I've always heard most gun crime is caused by readily available, inexpensive handguns. So, why would our authorities allow flooding the market with millions more? Political expediency is a prerequisite to consideration of such a deal.

2. *Assault Rifle Proliferation.* On a 1994 *Dateline* TV news magazine, Brian Ross reported the "Deadly Cargo" story. As Ross reported during a national debate to outlaw assault rifles, America imported over one million assault rifles from China since 1987; 965,000 of them in 1993 alone. Under our "most favored nation" trading policy, Norinko Corp., a branch of the Chinese People's Armed Police, was granted a Treasury Department import license, and State Department sanctioning, to import a million of these $129 assault rifles. As L.A. customs agent Joe Charles stated, "We are being inundated by these weapons." A loophole in Clinton's 1994 crime bill allowed importation of the Chinese weapons after becoming law; likewise with sales of 30-round ammunition magazines manufactured prior to the law. William Triflet, former CIA China expert, said such an import decision meant "somebody in the American government is asleep at the switch." When personally questioned on video for this report, Treasury Secretary Lloyd Bentsen and his Assistant Secretary in Charge of Law Enforcement, Ron Noble, said they knew nothing about it and refused discussion.

These two high-level policy decisions should clarify a contradiction in government intent. At the core of a governmental stance that demonized guns for public consumption was an import policy aiding and abetting activities of crime. Such demonization also presumes that our highest incarceration rate in the world is due to gun crime, which is not the case. The public debate to ban guns becomes a "PR ploy" encouraging public support for strengthening the police state, which, in turn, strengthens more as each school killing spree occurs. Rather than focusing on gun controls, perhaps a better question would be: Why are more and more kids being drugged with "stimulants, anti-depressants or anti-psychotic drugs?"[24]

Obviously, the best method for resolving the crime problem would be prevention and systemic revitalization. If military industrial economy prevails among the superpowers, manufacturing of guns is institutionalized. Making civilian guns illegal will not make crime go away; guns would only become lucrative black market commodities. The denial of gun abuse as a function of conditioned behavioral response via media "crimertainment" (including video games) presupposes political "debate" of more gun laws vs. improved enforcement, and the filling of Clinton's seventeen new prisons.

The November 27, 1994, broadcast of *60 Minutes* featured the report, "Arms Supermarket," which reported that since the collapse of the USSR, America has cornered the market as an international arms dealer. In 1993, the U.S. had 72 percent of weapons sales to the Third World; selling to 140 countries. Since then, civil war has ensued in many of these countries, and small arms have ended up on the black market. "Arms Supermarket" reported that, contrary to the policy of previous administrations, Clinton's Department of Commerce teamed with the Department of Defense and major defense contractors to sell arms at international arms expos. In 1993, this amounted to $22 billion in sales. So, what goes around, comes around: America corners the market on material for low intensity warfare, and throughout the land we have exactly that—gangs or individual youth in armed conflict resolution. The populace would deny there is a connection.

In 1992, Clinton pronounced "a long term effort to reduce proliferation of weapons of destruction." Two years later, his government contradicted this pledge, participating directly in profiting upon exactly the opposite. On December 6, 1994, the *Los Angeles Times* reported that President Clinton needed more than the $1.5 trillion he planned for the Pentagon over the following six years. He wanted to add $25 billion more: "This year [alone] the country will spend . . . almost as much as the rest of the world combined" on national security. In 2000, Clinton husbanded a 2001 Department of Defense budget, literally at Cold War levels. Whatever happened to the pacifist-touted peace dividend?

From 1994 to 2000, $1.5 trillion went to battle an unknown force, as 900,000 offenders filled new prisons. As Robert Anton Wilson has said, the only people in America with access to free health care are prisoners and members of Congress. Militarism, policing, and crime have been institutionalized as the "balance wheel" of our social economy. With Echelon global satellite eavesdropping and Clinton's seventeen new prisons, our future will feature mega-imprisoning workhouse prisons and global policing. Crimewar will be analogous to the perpetual warfare in Orwell's *1984*. With TV's pseudo-mythologizing of the police state, a need for ritual arises; we must exorcise our heretics-of-criminality from the body politic.

THE POLICE STATE IS A WORK OF ART

The insight gained by seeing our systems of security as an art form is that it has a life of its own, perpetually perfected. This is important, since crime incidence can actually decline, yet the system becomes ever more invasive and unconstitutional under the color of the law. "The problem (of crime) now is more perceptual than actual," L.A. County Sheriff Sherman Block stated in a news conference reported in the December 29, 1994, edition of the *Los Angeles Daily News*. As also reported, "For the third straight year most serious crimes decreased in L.A. County [by] 12.2 percent.[25] This was incredible, given that California was then, in 1994, in the process of building twenty-five new prisons. I will speculate that crime rates probably fluctuate like inflation; while the economic ills causing poverty and crime are never truly resolved—intentionally.

The twenty-first century is upon us. Soon we may see womb-to-tomb Echelon surveillance, based on mathematical computer probability models used to predict where the future "hot spots" will occur. In scanning our digital telecommunications, the FBI is supposed to get court orders for wiretaps based on probable cause. "In practice, probable cause has come to mean just that the FBI asks for a wiretap."[26] To protect our First Amendment rights, digital phones safeguard privacy with codes. But "the FBI wants us to use codes [they] or the National Security Agency can crack. The NSA has twelve underground acres of computers to crack codes, in Fort Meade, Maryland. It also has little oversight."[27]

The insidious applications of high-tech police work can be summed up with the following technique: a variety of what are called "nonlethal weapons." These weapons are currently being transferred from military research & development to use by local police departments. In collaboration between Psychotechnologies Corp. of Richmond, VA, and Russian military scientists of Moscow Medical Academy, a new control is being introduced. It is called a "psycho-correction technology" designed for security situations "where inaudible commands might be used to alter behavior."

This method of computerized acoustic mind control was to be used on David Koresh[28] but the high-profile publicity of Waco perhaps prevented it. The FBI, CIA, Defense Intelligence Agency, and the Advance Research Projects Agency were all consultants on its use. Legal and political fallout has since vindicated critics of Waco.

The art of security mindedness is creeping into every niche of society. The all-seeing video eye pursues us throughout the land. From shopping mart to roadway intersection, the Orwellian nightmare of sci-fi surveillance has come home to roost.

I conclude with an exchange between two characters in *Atlas Shrugged*, a 1957 novel by Ayn Rand. Government official Dr. Ferris instructs industrialist Mr. Rearden on crime:

> Did you really think that we want those laws to be observed? We want them broken. There's no way to rule innocent men. The only power any government has is the power to crack down on criminals. When there aren't enough criminals, one makes them. One declares so many things to be a crime that it becomes impossible for men to live without breaking laws. Who wants a nation of law-abiding citizens? What's there in that for anyone? But just pass the kind of laws that can neither be observed nor enforced nor objectively interpreted—and you create a nation of law-breakers, and then you cash in on guilt. Now that's the system, Mr. Rearden, that's the game and once you understand it, you'll be much easier to deal with.

This seems cynically excessive. Yet, since this book was published in 1957, we have seen such prolific lawmaking that, in a real sense, there can be few if any fully law-abiding citizens. To which archetypal mythos do we assign this paranoia, with our most common offenses being tax or traffic violations? And whether it's the aforementioned construction boom in prisons, or local government demanding more revenue-bearing traffic-ticketing quotas, we have a real "cashing in on the guilty."

In a police state, virtually all people become law-breakers by definition. Thereby, people become psychologically disaffected via the attitude "how much can we get away with," no matter how seemingly minor the violation. This is especially true in traffic violations or tax evasion. On February 21, 2002, an *L.A. Daily News* article, "Cop Conspiracy," reported the worst case of L.A.P.D. criminal policing. Thus, the system expands to service the growing numbers of violators. On the day you read this, perhaps 2.05–2.1 million may be imprisoned. Baby Boom to Prison Boom.

Due to "Three Strikes" sentencing, the cost effective plea bargain trend in court procedures has lost purpose. Court schedules are clogging up with criminal trials, and civil courtroom uses have no priority standing, being resolved at greater expense elsewhere.[29] Could megaprisons and multimedia computerized "Cyber Cop" methods of justice be viable solutions to crime? No! That approach lacks basic common sense.

This compilation of facts is merely a discomforting reference point. As sensible citizens, a police-state illusion of safety and comfort is not our business. As citizens, healing the root cause of crime is our responsibility. This requires an evolution of our ineffective perceptions of the problem, beyond the reward and punishment system. State of the Art crime management thinking is obsolete, because it is resonant with ancient Hammurabic codes of "An Eye for an Eye" justice. An extreme state of constitutional erosion that forces such justice is not justice at all. The path of social progress means creating true innovations in crime and economic management via prevention and forgiveness.

The prerequisite for a sensible future lies in new perceptions—willing the greater body of citizens into political will congruent with what is now known: our most precious resource is children. So, let's prevent their being enculturated to "accept" crime via role models exhibiting violent conflict resolution: Turn off commercial TV!

ADDENDUM, 2003

Ancient Roman calendars invoked the renewal of symbolic powers during their Ides of March. In the America of 2003, this period resonated with the Roman model of Empire: Imperialism has been cloned onto history in the form of Bushonomics-Part II.

While composing this addendum during these very days, a pall of dark skies loomed as global psychology: the portent of waging a war in Iraq. Diplomatic mantras and technodeath were being orchestrated precisely at a time-immemorial for traditions celebrating spring and the living. The timing symbolizes the ritual that Bush coerces our global village to accept, "You're either with us, or you are against us!" An epithet of neo-fascist order, if ever there was one.

As noted in this article, America reinvented itself when the Cold War ended. With American anti-communism a nightmare of history, the cover of *U.S. News & World Report* for October 24, 1994, prophetically advertised a new-improved America, "Uncle Sam, Supercop!" In propaganda terms, American imperialism moved on from the *Hunt for Red October* to war in the ides of March. This is a bad omen, like the Columbia space shuttle crash. The global reach of corporate opportunism has become the template for theatrically infecting police-statecraft into the world. Disguised as statecraft, the American civilization institutionalizes its artform of policing as a global archetype of power. This is Orwellian newspeak—peace by war.

As a letter-to-the-editor writer, Charles C., of Lake View Terrace, California, said, "What good are Social Security and cheaper medicine and a clean environment if we live in a police state without civil rights, where corporations have usurped our democratic processes and where government is bent on starting unprovoked and self-destructive wars?" (*Los Angeles Times*, September 5, 2002)

Rome, like America, began as a republic, ultimately declining as a sick, decadent empire. This is America now: televisually selling *Fear Factor* protectionism to a post–9/11 world of aid-hooked nations-in-chaos, which it has helped to create. As the *Los Angeles Times* reported, "U.S. Treasury Secretary, Paul H. O'Neill, said he would lobby [industrialized nations] to adopt a new system . . . for nations that are in unsustainable situations, [easing] the chaos the current system creates." (*Los Angeles Times*, September 27, 2002) Meanwhile, this national security contrivance, sold as democracy, is simply a subtle species of neo-fascism, what law-and-order consumerism calls American civilization and what imperial liberals call permissive cornucopia.

Achieving this corporate-interlocked police state of global "wars" on drugs, crime, terrorism, communism, cancer, AIDS, etc., actually requires constitutional erosion. For example:

1. President Bush usurped a Constitutional mandate that war requires explicit declaration by Congress. The Bush Patriot Act of October 2002 supported UN military action. It did not declare war. And "preventive" war violates Nuremburg tribunal codes. Thus, Bush's authority in unilateral action was unlawful. Following this, the Bush Administration asked a federal judge to dismiss a lawsuit filed by five congressmen to prevent war against Iraq without proper Congressional approval.

2. The ACLU challenged the Justice Department's surveillance powers, which monitored people under warrants granted by the super-secret Foreign Intelligence Surveillance Court, or "spycourt." (*Los Angeles Times*, February 19, 2003) This police state authority could also be used in nonterrorist cases.

3. The FBI was shown to usurp constitutional safeguards by two U.S. federal judges, when "false information was recklessly included in the search warrant application." (*Los Angeles Times*, March 7, 2003)

Bush insisted the UN, as an institution symbolic of international law, commit to a resolution to make war. He threatened to disregard the UN as "irrelevant" in global affairs if no resolution was passed. Such a resolution could disguise Bush's doctrine of offensive/preventive war, as he was crossing the line from persuasion to aggression.

Without UN oversight, a de facto American world "government"—or paradigm of management—with a right-wing agenda, could become more likely. Joseph Nye, Dean of the Kennedy School of Government at Harvard, said, "Members of the Bush Administration seem to argue that we're so strong we can do whatever we want. We're stronger than anyone since ancient Rome." (*Los Angeles Times*, March 3, 2003) Remember, the fasces, the Roman symbol of power, is borne over the U.S. Senate dais, as their symbol of authority. Also a symbol of power in fascist Italy, the fasces was removed from the U.S. "Mercury" dime in 1945.

In this era of late-stage capitalistic America, it's valid to use Roman imperialism as a model for defining American unilateralism. Indeed, the *Washington Post* reported that "in recent years, a handful of conservative defense intellectuals have begun [arguing] the United States is indeed acting in an imperialist fashion—and that it should embrace the role." (August 21, 2001) In the hands of globalist reactionaries, the republic has devolved into imperialist "Super Cop." President Reagan's Secretary of State, George P. Shultz, concurred, "It's not too bad to have a good cop–bad cop routine. Rumsfeld is out there reminding people of reality." (*Los Angeles Times*, March 3, 2003)

Our problem is George W.'s primitive dialectic worldview. Bush "reality" is a nostalgic retrieval of the nineteenth century. The UN charter mandates peacekeeping, not conditional force of arms. In the UN Security Council there is no superpower, except the superpower of the human family. As Nelson Mandela described Bush, "One power with a president who has no foresight and cannot think properly is now wanting to plunge the world into a holocaust." Indeed, Bush did just that on March 19, 2003 when he invaded Iraq. The "reality" Bush insists on requires war for insuring the obsolete mechanical-model identity of man. The petrol-identity set is threatened by the free thought/free energy paradigm.

American reality excludes a cosmology beyond—that is, beyond survival-of-the-fittest resource exploitation. Ultimately, Americans can only reconcile their unconscious dependency on this double bind: that their lofty living standards are undemocratically codependent on foreign resources. Thus, Americans are obliged to deny an accurate critique or description of their garrison-state system. They and their institutions are not capable of an open-minded critique, and their system's policies make other members of the global neighborhood fearful. Alas, 9/11!

On October 30, 2002, a *Los Angeles Times* headline read, "In New World Order, Many Fear U.S. Unilateralism." Bush's formal "National Security Strategy" was published in September 2002. It "boldly asserts that the U.S. plans to prevent any combination of other countries from ever challenging its supremacy." This explains the need to make the UN "irrelevant." Edward C. Luck, Director of the Center on International Organization at Columbia University, said, "Other countries think the major security threat to the world is the undisciplined use of American military power," not to mention suspect principles of duplicitous law-making. Located at the heart of American martial globalization policies is empire disguised under color of law. Military readiness is an opportunity, as Bruce Eilerts, a former natural resources specialist for the Navy and Air Force, said: "Military commanders don't want to be told there are other priorities . . . they want to operate without any checks and balances." (*Los Angeles Times*, March 19, 2003)

In the election year of 2004, the question will be not, Where is Osama bin Laden. It will be, How do we know when we are not fascists? ●

Notes

Dedicated to inmates at Coleman in Florida and elsewhere who are avid readers of *Paranoia*.

1. McNeill, William H. "A World Transformed," *Foreign Affairs*, Fall 1990.
2. Marchetti, V. and John D. Marks. *The CIA and the Cult of Intelligence*. New York: Knopf, 1974.
3. Ibid.

4. Eisenhower, Dwight D. "Farewell Radio and Television Address to the American People," Jan. 17, 1961.

5. Marchetti, "Omnibus Crime Control and Safe Streets Act of 1968," 7:2 24–5.

6. For details on Presidential Emergency Powers, see *Perceptions*, Fall 1994.

7. Lewin, Leonard C. *Report from Iron Mountain*. Dial, 1967.

8. Ibid.

9. Ibid.

10. See *Perceptions*, Fall 1994.

11. Lewin.

12. Ibid.

13. *L.A. Times*: "'94 Prison Rolls at Record High,' Study Says," August 28, 1995.

14. Flanagan, T.J. and K. Maguire. "A Full Employment Policy for Prisons in the United States: Some Arguments, Estimates, and Implications," *Journal of Criminal Justice*, Vol. 21, 1993.

15. *L.A. Times*: "Calif.'s Boom Times for Prison Building," October 16, 1994.

16. *L.A. Times*: "A Nation of Too Many Prisoners," February 15, 2000.

17. *USA Today*: "Highlights in President's Proposed Budget for 2001," February 8, 2000.

18. *L.A. Times*: "Prison Is Town's Savior, but at a Price," March 7, 2000.

19. *USA Today*: "New Orleans Homicides Drop," (graph) February 1, 2000.

20. *L.A. Times*: "A Nation of Too Many Prisoners," February 15, 2000.

21. ABC News *Nightline*, November 18, 1994.

22. *L.A. Times*: "Stiff Drug Laws Cited for Record Incarceration Rate," David G. Savage, September 13, 1994.

23. *L.A. Times*: "2nd Amendment: Something for Everyone," Glenn H. Reynolds, December 5, 1994.

24. *USA Today*: "Adult Medication is Used on Young Without Testing," November 30, 1999.

25. *L.A. Daily News*: "Serious Crimes Fall in County," David Bloom, December 29, 1994.

26. *L.A. Times*: "And Constitutional Rights Lag Behind," Bart Kosko, December 19, 1994.

27. Ibid.

28. "D.O.D., Intel Agencies look at Russian Mind Control Technology, Claims," *Defense Electronics Journal*, July 1993.

29. *L.A. Times*: "Courts: '3 Strikes' Crowds Out Civil Trials," November 30, 1994.

For further confirmation of Department of Defense role modeling of crime control, see *Defense Issues*, Vol. 9, #48, April, 1994.

—Spring 2001/2003

* * *

SECRET AND SUPPRESSED SCIENCE

* * *

The Ascendancy of the Scientific Dictatorship: The Origin of Darwinism

by Phillip Darrell Collins

As antiquity gave way to modern times, the religious power structure shifted to an autocracy of the knowable, or a "scientific dictatorship." Subtly and swiftly, the ruling class seized control of science and used it as an "epistemological weapon" against the masses. This article will show that the history and background of this "scientific dictatorship" is a conspiracy, created and micro-managed by the historical tide of Darwinism, which has its foundations in Freemasonry.

IN *The Architecture of Modern Political Power*, Daniel Pouzzner outlines the tactics employed by the elite to maintain their dominance. One of them is "ostensible control over the knowable, by marketing institutionally accredited science as the only path to true understanding" (Pouzzner 75). Thus, the ruling class endeavors to discourage independent reason, while exercising illusory power over human knowledge. This tactic of control through knowledge suppression is reiterated in the anonymously authored document, *Silent Weapons for Quiet Wars* [1]:

> Energy is recognized as the key to all activity on earth. Natural science is the study of the sources and control of natural energy, and social science, theoretically expressed as economics, is the study of the sources and control of social energy. Both are bookkeeping systems. Mathematics is the primary energy science. And the bookkeeper can be king if the public can be kept ignorant of the method-

ology of the bookkeeping. All science is merely a means to an end. The means is knowledge. The end is control. (reprint in Keith, *Secret and Suppressed*, 203)

THE EPISTEMOLOGICAL CARTEL

The word "science" is derived from the Latin word *scientia*, which means "knowing." Epistemology is the study of the nature and origin of knowledge. Therefore, this elite monopoly of the knowable, which is enforced through institutional science, could be characterized as an "epistemological cartel." The ruling class has bribed the "bookkeepers" (i.e., natural and social scientists). Meanwhile, the masses practically deify the "bookkeepers" of the elite, and remain "ignorant of the methodology of the bookkeeping." The unknown author of *Silent Weapons for Quiet Wars* provides an eloquently simple summation: "The means is knowledge. The end is control. Beyond this remains only one issue: Who will be the beneficiary?" (Keith, *Secret and Suppressed*, 203)

In *Brave New World Revisited*, Aldous Huxley succinctly defined this epistemological cartel:

The older dictators fell because they could never supply their subjects with enough bread, enough circuses, enough miracles, and mysteries. Under a scientific dictatorship, education will really work. Most men and women will grow up to love their servitude and will never dream of revolution. There seems to be no good reason why a thoroughly scientific dictatorship should ever be overthrown. (Huxley, 116)

This is the ultimate objective of the elite, an oligarchy legitimized by arbitrarily anointed expositors of "knowledge" or, in Huxley's own words, a "scientific dictatorship." How did the scientific dictatorship of the twentieth century begin? In earlier centuries, the ruling class controlled the masses through mystical belief systems, particularly sun worship. Yet, this would all change. In *Saucers of the Illuminati*, Jim Keith documents the shift from a theocracy of the Sun to a theocracy of science, where priests and rituals were soon supplanted by a new breed of "bookkeepers" and a new "methodology of bookkeeping." Keith elaborates:

As the Sun/Moon cult lost some of its popularity, "scientists" were quick to take up some of the slack. According to their propaganda, the physical laws of the universe were the ultimate causative factors, and naturally, those physical laws were only fathomable by the scientific (Illuminati) elite. (Keith, *Saucers of the Illuminati*, 78–79)

It must be understood that this new institution of knowing is a form of mysticism like its religious precursors. Contemporary science is predicated upon empiricism, the idea that all knowledge is derived exclusively through the senses. Yet, an exclusively empirical approach relegates cause to the realm of metaphysical fantasy. This holds enormous ramifications for science. Do we really know what causes anything? Although temporal succession and spatial proximity are self-evident, causal connection is not. Affirmation of causal relationships is impossible in science. What is perceived as *A* causing *B* could be merely circumstantial juxtaposition. Given the absence of known cause, all of a scientist's findings must be taken upon faith. This is all one can deduce while working under the paradigm of radical empiricism. Thus, the elite merely exchanged one form of mysticism for another.

Returning to Pouzzner's previous statement, "ostensible control over the knowable" is achieved through the promulgation of "institutionally accredited science." (Pouzzner, 75) Now, the elite had to meet two requirements to insure their epistemological dominance: a science specifically designed for their needs and an institution to accredit and disseminate it.

THE BRITISH ROYAL SOCIETY

The new secular church and clergy of the elite originated within the walls of the British Royal Society. The creators of the Royal Society were also members of the Masonic lodge. According to Baigent, Leigh, and Lincoln in *Holy Blood, Holy Grail*:

> Virtually all the Royal Society's founding members were Freemasons. One could reasonably argue that the Royal Society itself, at least in its inception, was a Masonic institution—derived, through Andrea's Christian Unions, from the "invisible Rosicrucian brotherhood." (Baigent, 144)

Jim Keith makes it clear that the Masonic lodge "has been alleged to be a conduit for the intentions of a number of elitist interests." (Keith, *Casebook on Alternative Three*, 20) In service to the elite, the Royal Society Freemasons would resculpt epistemological notions and disseminate propaganda. Keith provides a brief summation of the Royal Society's role in years to come: "The British Royal Society of the late seventeenth century was the forerunner of much of the media manipulation that was to follow." (Keith, *Saucers of the Illuminati*, 79)

Before the advent of the British Royal Society, science (i.e. the study of natural phenomena) and theology (i.e., the study of God) were inseparable. The two were not separate repositories of knowledge, but natural correlatives. In *Confession of Nature*, Gottfried Wilhelm Leibniz established the centrality of God to science. According to Leibniz, the proximate origins of "magnitude, figure, and motion," which constitute the "primary qualities" of corporeal bodies, "cannot be found in the essence of the body." (de Hoyos) Linda de Hoyos reveals the point at which science finds a dilemma:

The problem arises when the scientist asks why the body fills this space and not another; for example, why it should be three feet long rather than two, or square rather than round. This cannot be explained by the nature of the bodies themselves, since the matter is indeterminate as to any definite figure, whether square or round. For the scientist who refuses to resort to an incorporeal cause, there can be only two answers. Either the body has been this way since eternity, or it has been made square by the impact of another body. "Eternity" is no answer, since the body could have been round for eternity also. If the answer is "the impact of another body," there remains the question of why it should have had any determinate figure before such motion acted upon it. This question can then be asked again and again, backwards to infinity. Therefore, it appears that the reason for a certain figure and magnitude in bodies can never be found in the nature of these bodies themselves.

The same can be established for the body's cohesion and firmness, which left Leibniz with the following conclusion:

Since we have demonstrated that bodies cannot have a determinate figure, quantity, or motion, without an incorporeal being [God], it readily becomes apparent that this incorporeal being is one for all, because of the harmony of things among themselves, especially since bodies are moved not individually by this incorporeal being but by each other. But no reason can be given why this incorporeal being chooses one magnitude, figure, and motion rather than another, unless he is intelligent and wise with regard to the beauty of things and powerful with regard to their obedience to their command. Therefore such an incorporeal being be a mind ruling the whole world, that is, God. (de Hoyos)

Of course, this conclusion was antithetical to the doctrine of the scientific dictatorship, which contended that "the physical laws of the universe were the ultimate causative factors." (Keith, *Saucers of the Illuminati*, 78–79) Metaphysical naturalism (i.e., nature is God) had to be enthroned. Meanwhile, God's presence in the corridors of science had to be expunged. To achieve this, the Royal Society created a division between science and theology, thus insuring the primacy of matter in the halls of scientific inquiry (Tarpley).

EVOLUTION: THE OCCULT DOCTRINE OF BECOMING

With the British Royal Society acting as their headquarters of propaganda, the elite had created an institution to provide credibility for their specially designed "science." Now, they needed to introduce the "science." The founding members of the Royal Society were all Freemasons; thus, whatever "science" these men would design would be derivative of Masonic doctrine. In *The Meaning of Masonry*, W. L. Wilmhurst reveals the world view underpinning the new Masonic "science":

> This—the *evolution* [emphasis added] of man into superman—was always the purpose of the ancient Mysteries, and the real purpose of modern Masonry is not the social and charitable purposes to which so much attention is paid, but the expediting of the spiritual evolution of those who aspire to perfect their own nature and transform it into a more god-like quality. And this is a definite science, a royal art, which it is possible for each of us to put into practice; whilst to join the Craft for any other purpose than to study and pursue this science is to misunderstand its meaning. (Wilmhurst, 47)

Later in the book, Wilmhurst reiterates this theme:

> Man who has sprung from earth and developed through the lower kingdoms of nature to his present rational state, has yet to complete his *evolution* [emphasis added] by becoming a god-like being and unifying his consciousness with the Omniscient—to promote that which is and always has been the sole aim and purpose of all Initiation. (Wilmhurst, 94)

With God's exile from science, man's position as *imago viva Dei* (created in the image of the Creator) became obsolete. Freemasonry could now introduce its occult doctrine of "becoming," the belief in man's gradual evolution towards apotheosis. According to *Mackey's Encyclopedia of Freemasonry*, Erasmus Darwin, grandfather of Charles Darwin, was the first to promulgate the concept of evolution:

> Dr. Erasmus Darwin (1731–1802) was the first man in England to suggest those ideas which later were to be embodied in the Darwinian Theory by his grandson, Charles Darwin (1809–1882), who wrote in 1859 *Origin of Species*. (Daniel, *Scarlet and the Beast*, 34)

Erasmus was the founder of the Lunar Society. According to Ian Taylor, the Lunar Society was active from about 1764 to 1800, and its prominent influence "continued long afterwards under the banner of the Royal Society." The group's name owed itself to the fact that members met monthly at the time of the full moon. The membership of this group boasted such luminaries as John Wilkinson (who made cannons), James Watt (who owed his notoriety to the steam engine), Matthew Boulton (a manufacturer), Joseph Priestly (a chemist), Josiah Wedgwood (who founded the famous pottery business), and Benjamin Franklin. It is with the Lunar Society that one begins to identify Erasmus' ties to Freemasonry (Taylor, 55).

Interestingly enough, in an article by Lord Richie-Calder, Lunar Society members were assigned the very esoteric appellation of "merchants of light." This was precisely the same description used for the hypothetical society presented in Sir Francis Bacon's *New Atlantis* (Taylor, 55). Conspiracy researcher Nesta H. Webster, in her examination of J.G. Findel's *History of Freemasonry*, made the following observation: "Findel frankly admits that *New Atlantis* contained unmistakable allusions to Freemasonry and that Bacon contributed to its final transformation." (Webster, 120) Taylor clarifies:

> Webster pointed out that one of the earliest and most eminent precursors of Freemasonry is said to have been Francis Bacon, who is also recognized to have been a Rosicrucian; the Rosicrucian and Freemason orders were closely allied and may have had a common source. (Taylor, 445)

Still, these are tenuous ties at best. Are there any sources that firmly establish a Darwinian/Freemasonic connection? *Mackey's Encyclopedia of Freemasonry* conclusively confirms a link:

Before coming to Derby in 1788, Dr. [Erasmus] Darwin had been made a Mason in the famous Time Immemorial Lodge of Cannongate Kilwinning, No. 2, of Scotland. Sir Francis Darwin, one of the Doctor's sons, was made a Mason in Tyrian Lodge, No. 253, at Derby, in 1807 or 1808. His son Reginald was made a Mason in Tyrian Lodge in 1804. The name of Charles Darwin does not appear on the rolls of the Lodge but it is very possible that he, like Francis, was a Mason. (Daniel, 34)

In 1794, Erasmus Darwin wrote a book entitled *Zoonomia*, which delineated his theory of evolution. Being a Freemason, there is little doubt that Erasmus cribbed liberally from the lodge's occult doctrine of "becoming." Before Freemason Erasmus Darwin penned his precursory notions of progressive biological development, Freemason John Locke had extrapolated the Hindu doctrine of reincarnation into the realm of science, and formulated a theory of evolution. The British East India Company had imported the Hindu belief in reincarnation to England, where it would be adopted by the British Royal Society. A prominent member of the Royal Society, Locke studied reincarnation extensively and, extrapolating on occult doctrine, developed his own evolutionary ideas. In fact, Locke's theory of evolution received the support of the male members of Darwin's family (Daniel 33–34). Two centuries later, his occult concept of "becoming" was transmitted to Charles Darwin, and *On the Origin of Species* was born.

THE DARWIN PROJECT

In the article "Toward a New Science of Life," *Executive Intelligence Review* journalist Jonathan Tennenbaum, writes:

Now, it is easy to show that Darwinism, one of the pillars of modern biology, is nothing but a kind of cult, a cult religion. I am not exaggerating. It has no scientific validity whatsoever. Darwin's so-called theory of evolution is based on absurdly irrational propositions, which did not come from scientific observations, but were artificially introduced from the outside, for political-ideological reasons (Tennenbaum).

Given Darwinism's roots in occult Freemasonry, and Freemasonry's expedient promotion of an emergent species of supermen—the elite—this is a fairly accurate assessment. Charles Darwin acted as the elite's apostle, preaching the new secular gospel of evolution. Darwinism could be considered a Freemasonic project, the culmination of a publicity campaign conducted by the lodge. Evidence for this contention can be found in the controversial *Protocols of the Wise Men of Sion*. Although an examination of the *Protocols* and a critique of their authenticity are not the purposes of this essay, it is important to address the questions surrounding their origin. After all, the *Protocols* have been employed throughout history in numerous genocidal campaigns against the Jews. However, the authors of *Holy Blood, Holy Grail* provide evidence that the document may be Masonic in origin:

> It can thus be proved conclusively that the Protocols did not issue from the Judaic congress at Basle in 1897. That being so, the obvious question is whence they did issue. Modern scholars have dismissed them as a total forgery, a wholly spurious document concocted by anti-Semitic interests intent on discrediting Judaism. And yet the Protocols themselves argue strongly against such a conclusion. They contain, for example, a number of enigmatic references—references that are clearly not Judaic. But these references are so clearly not Judaic that they cannot plausibly have been fabricated by a forger, either. No anti-Semitic forger with even a modicum of intelligence would possibly have concocted such references in order to discredit Judaism. For no one would have believed these references to be of Judaic origin.
>
> The text of the Protocols ends with a single statement: "Signed by the representatives of Sion of the 33rd Degree." Why would an anti-Semitic forger have made up such a statement? Why would he not have attempted to incriminate all Jews, rather than just a few—the few who constitute "the representatives of Sion of the 33rd Degree"? Why would he not declare that the document was signed by, say, the representatives of the international Judaic Congress? In fact, the "representatives of Sion of the 33rd Degree" would hardly seem to refer to Judaism at all, or to any "international Jewish conspiracy." If anything, it would seem to refer to something specifically Masonic. The 33rd Degree in Freemasonry is the Strict Observance—the system of Freemasonry introduced by Hund at the behest of his "unknown superiors," one of whom appears to have been Charles Radclyffe. (Baigent, 192–93)

Baigent, Leigh, and Lincoln conclude:

> There was an original text on which the published version of the
> *Protocols* was based. This original text was not a forgery. On the
> contrary, it was authentic. But it had nothing whatever to do with
> Judaism or an "international Jewish conspiracy." It issued, rather,
> from some Masonic organization or Masonically oriented secret
> society that incorporated the word "Sion." (Baigent, 194)

Given the Masonic language, one can discard the racist contention
that the *Protocols* constitute evidence of an "international Jewish conspiracy." Nevertheless, the document holds some authenticity:

> The published version of the *Protocols* is not, therefore, a totally
> fabricated text. It is, rather, a radically altered text. But despite the
> alterations, certain vestiges of the original version can be discerned.
> (Baigent, 195)

The remnant of the original text strongly suggests Masonic origins.
Having established the Masonic authorship of the *Protocols*, one may
return to the issue at hand: Freemasonic involvement in the promotion
of Darwinism. Consider the following excerpt from the *Protocols*, which
reads distinctly like a mission statement:

> For them [the masses or cattle] let that play the principal part
> which we have persuaded them to accept as the dictates of science
> (theory). It is with this object in view that we are constantly, by
> means of our press, arousing a blind confidence in these theories.
> The intellectuals of the *goyim* [the masses or cattle] will puff them-
> selves up with their knowledge and without any logical verification
> of it will put into effect all the information available from science,
> which our *agentur* specialists have cunningly pieced together for
> the purpose of educating their minds in the direction we want.
> Do not suppose for a moment that these statements are empty
> words: think carefully of the successes we arranged for *Darwinism*
> [emphasis added], Marxism, and Nietzscheism. (reprint in Cooper,
> 274–75)

In addition to establishing the lodge's official sanction of Darwinism,
this excerpt also reveals a direct relationship between Marxism, Nietzscheism and evolutionary theory, which will be discussed shortly.

The grandfather of Aldous Huxley, T. H. Huxley, would act as the "official spokesman for the recluse Darwin." (White, 268) Recall that, many years later, Aldous would propose a "scientific dictatorship" in *Brave New World Revisited*. Whether Aldous made this proposition on a whim, or was penning a concept that had circulated within the Huxley family for years, cannot be determined. Given the family's oligarchical tradition, the latter assertion is a definite possibility. Yet, there may be a deeper Freemasonic connection, suggesting that the concept of a "scientific dictatorship" may have originated within the Lodge.

T. H. Huxley was a Freemason and, with no apparent achievements to claim as his own, was made a Fellow of the Royal Society at the age of twenty-six (Daniel, 34). T. H. Huxley tutored Freemason H. G. Wells, who would later teach Huxley's two grandsons, Julian and Aldous. Both Julian and Aldous were Freemasons (Daniel, 147). Given this continuity of Freemasonic tutelage within the Huxley family, it is a definite possibility that the Huxleyan concept of a "scientific dictatorship" is really Masonic. With the publicity campaigns of the Royal Society, and the avid defense of evolution propagandist, T. H. Huxley, Darwin's theory would be disseminated and popularized. The seed had taken root and, in the years to come, numerous permutations of the elite's "scientific dictatorship" would emerge.

DARWINISM DISMANTLED

Providing a complete and comprehensive delineation of the various concepts constituting Darwinism is a daunting task. The theory itself is a dense amalgam of "isms," thinly veiled occult concepts, philosophical doctrines, and ideologies. Again, Tennenbaum's statement that Darwinism "is based on absurdly irrational propositions, which did not come from scientific observations, but were artificially introduced from the outside, for political-ideological reasons" seems succinct and accurate. But, with what outside sources do these "absurdly irrational propositions" find their proximate origins?

One of the many constituent world views comprising Darwinism is Hegelianism. According to philosopher Georg Hegel, a pantheistic world spirit was directing "an ongoing developmental (evolutionary) process in nature, including humanity," which bodied itself forth as a "dialectical struggle between positive and negative entities." This conflict always resulted in a "harmonious synthesis." (Taylor, 381–82) The same dialectical framework is present in Darwinism.

In *Circle of Intrigue*, occult researcher Texe Marrs, reveals the Hegelian structure intrinsic to Darwinian evolution. The organism (thesis) comes into conflict with nature (antithesis) resulting in a newly enhanced species (synthesis), the culmination of the evolutionary process (Marrs, 127). Of course, in such a world of ongoing conflict, violence and bloodshed are central to progress. Thus, Darwin's theory "gave credence to the Hegelian notion that human culture had ascended from brutal beginnings." (Taylor, 386)

Yet, Darwinism's roots go deeper than Hegelianism, returning to an earlier esoteric source. In turn, Hegel's ideas originated with Fichte, who was "a Freemason, almost certainly Illuminati, and certainly promoted by the Illuminati." (Sutton, *America's Secret Establishment*, 34) In fact, Hegel's dialectical logic reiterates the Masonic dictum, *ordo ab chao* (order out of chaos). It appears that the bedrock upon which Darwinism rests is Freemasonry, a channel for elitist interests.

THE RISE OF THE SCIENTIFIC DICTATORSHIP

Darwinism shares the Hegelian framework with two other belief systems. In *The Secret Cult of the Order*, Antony Sutton states, "Both Marx and Hitler have their philosophical roots in Hegel." (Sutton, 118) It is here that one arrives at the Hegelian nexus where Darwin, Marx, and Hitler intersect. Recall that Nietzscheism, Darwinism and Marxism were mentioned together in the *Protocols of the Wise Men of Sion*. This was no accident. Nazism (a variant of fascism) sprung from Nietzscheism, and communism sprung from Marxism. Both were based upon Hegelian principles. Moreover, both were "scientific dictatorships" legitimized by the "science" of Darwinism. Ian Taylor elaborates:

> However, fascism or Marxism, right wing or left—all these are only ideological roads that lead to Aldous Huxley's brave new world [i.e. a "scientific dictatorship"], while the foundation for each of these roads is Darwin's theory of evolution. Fascism is aligned with biological determinism and tends to emphasize the unequal struggle by which those inherently fittest shall rule. Marxism stresses social progress by stages of revolution, while at the same time it paradoxically emphasizes peace and equality. There should be no illusions; Hitler borrowed from Marx. The result is that both fascism and Marxism finish at the same destiny—totalitarian rule by the elite. (Taylor, 411)

The interest of both Hitler and Marx in Darwinian evolution is a matter of history. While he was living in London, Marx attended lectures on evolutionary theory delivered by T. H. Huxley. Recognizing the odd synchronicity between the communist concept of class war and the Darwinian principle of natural selection, Marx sent Darwin a copy of *Das Kapital* in 1873. Enamored of evolution, Marx asked Darwin for permission to dedicate his next volume to him six years later. Troubled by the fact that it would upset certain members of his family to have the name of Darwin associated with an atheistic polemic, Charles politely declined the offer (Taylor, 381).

Numerous authors have established firm connections between Darwinism and Hitler's Nazism. Darwinian, Sir Arthur Keith, documented the strong links between Hitler's racialist goals and the doctrine of evolution. In his 1947 book *Evolution and Ethics*, Keith wrote: "The German Fuhrer, as I have consistently maintained, is an evolutionist; he has consciously sought to make the practice of Germany conform to the theory of evolution." (Keith, 230) Also, in an analysis of *Mein Kampf*, author Werner Maser, reveals that Darwin was the crucible for Hitler's "notions of biology, worship, force, and struggle, and of his rejection of moral causality in history." (Taylor, 409) Researcher Alfred Kelly, also provides a comprehensive history of Darwinism's popularization in Germany.

CONCLUSION

Returning to the Hegelian nexus that binds Darwinism, Marxism, and Nazism, both the fascist and communist "scientific dictatorships" were a political enactment of evolutionary theory. Marx was greatly influenced by Hegel (Taylor, 381). The concept of class struggle, which paralleled Darwinian natural selection, resulted from Marx's redirection of the Hegelian dialectic into the socioeconomic realm. The proletariat (thesis) comes into conflict with the bourgeoisie (antithesis), resulting in a classless utopia (synthesis). Marx, however, rejected the concept of a world spirit, and relocated the revolution's causal source within the proletariat itself.

The same Hegelian framework was evident in Hitler's genocidal Final Solution. The German people (thesis) came into conflict with the Jew (antithesis) in hopes of creating the Aryan (synthesis). In both communism and Nazism, the results were enormous bloodbaths. This is the natural consequence of Darwinian thinking and the legacy of the "scientific dictatorship." In tangibly enacting the ideas of Darwin, both communists and fascists have murdered millions. Both of these groups find their origins in the elite (the Illuminati), who are still pursuing the same objectives today. According to the Darwinian mantra of "survival of the fittest," victory will demand bloodshed. The Huxleyan new world order shall be eugenically regimented in accordance with Darwinian principles.

In *Brave New World Revisited*, Aldous Huxley warns, "the twenty-first century . . . will be the era of World Controllers." (Huxley, 25) If the scientific dictatorship introduced by these World Controllers is anything like its precursors, humanity may stand to inherit a bloody legacy in the near future. •

Note

1. It has been claimed that the manuscript of *Silent Weapons for Quiet Wars*, dated May 1979, was found in a surplus IBM copy machine in 1986 by a Boeing Aircraft employee.

References

Baigent, Michael, Richard Leigh, and Henry Lincoln. *Holy Blood, Holy Grail*. New York: Delacorte, 1982.

Cooper, William. *Behold a Pale Horse*. Sedona, AZ: Light Technology Publishing, 1991.

Daniel, John. *Scarlet and the Beast: Volume II*. JKI Publishing, 1994.

de Hoyos, Linda. "The Enlightenment's Crusade Against Reason." *The New Federalist*, February 8, 1993.

Huxley, Aldous. *Brave New World Revisited*. New York: Bantam Books, 1958.

Keith, Arthur. *Evolution and Ethics*. New York: G.P. Putnam's Sons, 1947.

Keith, Jim. *Casebook on Alternative Three*. Lilburn, GA: Illuminet Press, 1994.

———. *Saucers of the Illuminati*. Lilburn, GA: Illuminet Press, 1999.

———. *Secret and Suppressed*. Los Angeles: Feral House, 1993.

Marrs, Texe. *Circle of Intrigue*. Austin, TX: Living Truth Publishers, 1995.

Pouzzner, Daniel. *The Architecture of Modern Political Power: The New Feudalism*, www.mega.nu:8080, 2001.

Sutton, Antony. *America's Secret Establishment*, Liberty House Press, 1986.

———. *The Secret Cult of the Order*. Cranbrook, Australia: Veritas, 1983.

Tarpley, Webster. "How the Venetian System Was Transplanted into England," *The New Federalist*, June 3, 1996.

Taylor, Ian T. *In the Minds of Men: Darwin and the New World Order*. Toronto: TFE Publishing, 1999.

Tennenbaum, Jonathan. "Towards a New Science of Life," *Executive Intelligence Review*, 28 (September 7, 2001): 34.

Webster, Nesta H. *Secret Societies and Subversive Movements*. London: Britons Publishing Society, 1924.

White, Carol. *The New Dark Ages Conspiracy: Britain's Plot to Destroy Civilization*. New York: New Benjamin Franklin House, 1980.

Wilmhurst, W.L. *The Meaning of Masonry*. New York: Gramercy, 1980.

—Fall 2003

Marcel Vogel and the Secret of the Fifth Force

by Joan d'Arc

In this article, Joan d'Arc describes the experiments and inventions of the prolific IBM patent holder and inventor Marcel Vogel. As she explains, since ancient times a creative life force or fundamental energy has been postulated to be the vital "fifth force" in all of creation. Vogel referred to this medium as the "information band." Vogel postulated that the information band is a record-keeper of the events which bring an object into being. From his numerous experiments in human-plant telepathy, to his Vogel-cut crystals for information storage and his invention of the "Omega-5," Vogel's work illustrates that magic and science are two sides of the same coin. This article concludes that this powerful occult knowledge remains in the hands of an elite social clique comprising the various intelligence tentacles of the U.S. government.

SINCE ANCIENT TIMES a fundamental energy or "fifth force" has been postulated to be the intrinsic vital force in all of creation. As John White writes in *Psychic Warfare: Fact or Fiction?*, ancient magicians called this force the *astral light*; the Chinese call it *chi*; the Japanese call it *ki*; the yogic traditions of India and Tibet call it *prana*; the Polynesians and Hawaiian Kahunas call it *mana*; the Sufis call it *baraka*; Jewish Cabalists call it *yesod*; the Iroquois call it *orenda*; the Ituri pygmies call it *mgebe*; and the Christians call it *Holy Spirit*. As Eliphas Levi writes in *Transcendental Magic*:

There exists an agent which is natural and divine, material and spiritual, a universal plastic mediator, a common receptacle of the vibrations of motion and the images of form, a fluid and a force, which may be called in some way the Imagination of Nature. The existence of this force is the great Arcanum of practical Magic.

In modern times, Rupert Sheldrake postulated the existence of causative organizing fields he called morphogenetic fields, which he believed accounted for both the evolution (changingness) and stasis (unchangingness) of life forms. Also in modern times, Wilhelm Reich identified through scientific investigations a primordial, massless, and pre-atomic creative life force he called orgone energy. Inventor Marcel Vogel discovered an energy he called the information band as an energetic communication band between all substances, between all life forms. In addition, investigators have noted parallels between this all-pervading medium and the Soviet idea of bioplasma. This energy appears to be the energy recognized in paranormal abilities. White quotes electrical engineer Laurence Beynam:

There is an energy in living organisms that is weak and unpredictable, but it can be refracted, polarized, focused, and combined with other energies. It sometimes has effects similar to magnetism, electricity, heat, and luminous radiation, but it is none of these. Attempts to control and employ the energy have met with little success; investigators have not yet defined the laws governing its operation.

It is likely that as of this writing (2000) the laws governing the operation of this organismic energy have been well defined, and its ability to be focused and combined with other energies has likely been well-researched by the military-industrial complex. Preliminary work in this area was performed by Marcel Joseph Vogel (1917–1991), senior research scientist for IBM in San Jose, whose work focused on "phosphor technology, liquid crystal systems, luminescence, and magnetics." Remy Chevalier writes (www.remyc.com/bigigloo.html) of Marcel Vogel's discovery of the properties of *chi*:

I experienced Marcel's release of stored *chi* from one of his crystals at a US Psychotronics conference back in the late 1980s. When he asked everyone in the audience to stand up, and he aimed the crystal in our direction telling us that three day's worth of *chi* had been stored inside and that he would release it all at once, call it a "psychic wind" blew from his direction to the back of the room, gently freshening our faces. There was no fan on the stage, no sudden burst of the air conditioning system. Just something Marcel was able to do.

We had a long conversation over the phone a few months before he passed away. He explained electromagnetism as a kind of "box" that enabled *chi* to travel, as if *chi* was a passenger on the electromagnetic train, and that *chi* was finer than EM and that EM was just its vessel. Marcel's work has yet to be rediscovered by the "new age" community. Somebody is carrying on his work and surely cashing in on his crystal designs.

Indeed, we can safely surmise that one of these somebodies is the secret government, a covert corporate/military/intelligence apparatus that is above the law. This is likely the same entity that has in its possession the coopted works of Wilhelm Reich, Nikola Tesla, Marcel Vogel, and other modern geniuses "bitten on the ass" by ancient wisdom. Laurence Beynam listed the characteristics of this fifth force or energy as follows:

- It is observed in the operation of heat, light, electricity, magnetism, and chemical reactions, yet is different from all of them.

- It fills all space, penetrating and permeating everything, yet denser materials conduct it better and faster, and metal refracts it while organic material absorbs it.

- It is basically synergistic, moving toward greater wholeness. It has a basic negentropic, formative, and organizing effect, even as heat increases, and is the opposite of entropy, thereby violating the Second Law of Thermodynamics.

- Changes in this energy precede physical, observable changes; therefore, it is a creative force.

- In any structure that is highly organized (crystals, plants, humans), there is a series of geometric points at which the energy is highly concentrated. (This relates also to chakras and acupuncture points.)

- The energy corresponds to certain colors, which can be seen by psychics.

- The energy will flow from one object to another. (According to the Huna tradition, it is "sticky," so an invisible stream of energy will always connect any two objects that have in any way been connected in the past. This is the basis for sympathetic magic.)

- The energy is subject to exponential decay, radiating outward in the course of time. The density of this energy varies in inverse proportion to distance, which sets it apart from electromagnetic and gravitational laws.

- The energy is observable in various ways: as isolated pulsating points, as spirals, as an aura surrounding the body, as a flame, as a tenuous web of lines (mana).

THE EXPERIMENTS OF MARCEL VOGEL

In 1943, Marcel Vogel cowrote, with Dr. Peter Pringsheim, *The Luminescence of Liquids and Solids and their Practical Application*. Shortly thereafter, Vogel founded a company called Vogel Luminescence Corporation. Vogel sold this company and joined IBM in 1957, becoming one of the most prolific patent inventors in IBM history. Incidentally, Vogel did not hold a university degree, but was largely self-taught. Vogel also did pioneering work in man-plant communication experiments, leading to the study of quartz crystals and the creation of the "Vogel-cut crystal," which stores, amplifies, converts, and coheres subtle energies. By spinning water around a tuned crystal, Vogel created a novel information storage system.

When Vogel retired from IBM after twenty-seven years, IBM and Stanford Research Institute donated equipment to his new company, Psychic Research, Inc., which aimed to show the ultimate compatibility of science and metaphysics. Vogel went on to study subtle energies and forces which emanated from the human body, and attempted to identify and quantify these energies. He was also interested in the therapeutic application of crystals and crystal devices, using stored energies to heal the human body.

Vogel invented a radionics machine, the Omega-5, which utilized the psychic power of the human mind and detected fields undetectable by standard scientific devices. The Omega-5 was a subjective type of device that assisted in scientific findings by providing clues on how to proceed, or where to look, to obtain standard scientific measurement. The

Omega-5 worked by use of a pendulum, similar to the telepathic dowsing process. Vogel referred to the unknown fields measured by the Omega-5 as the "information band."

THE BACKSTER EFFECT

Following a 1969 article in *Argosy* magazine entitled "Do Plants Have Emotions?," which explored the research of polygraph expert Cleve Backster, Vogel began to explore the concept of human-plant communication. Interestingly, Cleve Backster was present at the First International Psychotronic Congress in Prague in 1973. His paper, "Evidence of a Primary Perception at Cellular Level in Plant and Animal Life," is listed in the table of contents for Volume I of these proceedings. Backster's work came to the attention of L. Ron Hubbard, founder of Scientology.

Backster is also famous for the development of the lie detector, which was picked up for official use by Hubbard as the "E-meter." Hubbard also performed plant-communication experiments on tomato plants using the E-meter. (Backster's invention is advertised in the scientology magazine *Advance!* as the "Mark Super VII Quantum TM E-Meter" at a regular edition price of $4,650, and a commemorative edition price of $5,530.)

In separate experiments, Vogel was able to duplicate the "Backster effect." He used plants as transducers for bioenergetic fields released by the human mind, demonstrating that plants respond to thought. By connecting the plant to a "Wheatstone Bridge," Vogel was able to compare a known resistance to an unknown resistance. When he held a thought in mind while pulsing his breath through his nostrils, the philodendrons responded dramatically. Vogel's experiments suggested that these human bioenergetic fields were linked to the action of both breath and thought. His findings were that these fields acted outside the known natural laws; they had the same effect on the plant whether the person emitting them was inches away or miles away. This suggested that, "the inverse square law does not apply to thought," and that the effect of thought energy does not diminish with distance.

MAN–PLANT COMMUNICATION EXPERIMENTS

Marcel Vogel was also present at the First International Congress on Psychotronic Research in Prague. In his talk entitled "Man–Plant Communication Experiments," in Volume II of these proceedings (in this author's possession), Vogel presented his findings with respect to the distant influence of thought on ordinary house plants, split-leaf philodendrons specifically. Vogel's basic conclusions after four years of work are most interesting. He concluded, once the experimenter is able to establish a psychic link with the plant, the plant will respond to: "(a) the act of damaging the leaf of another plant; (b) the destruction of another life form, cellular or animal; (c) the release of a thought form of love, healing, mathematics, imagery, emotion."

Vogel explained that each of these thought forms have distinct patterns to them. Vogel also stated that the distant projection of thought forms had been accomplished with a distance of up to 110 miles between plant and person. He also acknowledged that repeatability of experiments had been possible, and that "thought forms of individuals can be repeated."

Vogel discovered that plants respond more to the thought of being cut, burned, or torn than to the actual act. The plants seemed to be mirroring his own mental responses. He concluded that the plants were acting like batteries, storing the energy of his thoughts and intentions. Vogel discovered that when thought is pulsed, the energy connected with it becomes coherent. To Vogel, the only pure force and the greatest cohering agent is "love." Coherent thought, Vogel asserted, can have a "laser-like power." He likened love to gravity, stating that it is an attractive and coherent force, present at every level of existence.

THE VOGEL-CUT CRYSTAL

In his experiments on crystals, Vogel was able to alter the final form of a liquid crystal while focusing on its growth. In one experiment, Vogel, who was a devout Catholic, focused for a full hour on an image of the Blessed Virgin while viewing the growth of the crystal under the microscope. The result was a shape recognizable as the Madonna. Vogel videotaped this anomaly and noted that, "before the melt went into the liquid crystal state, a blue flash of light took place and then immediately after that, the sample transcended into the liquid crystal state." After a year of watching this anomaly, Vogel finally captured a picture at the moment of transition. This anomaly had been discussed in metaphysical literature, but had never before been witnessed and photographed. The flash of blue light witnessed through the microscope was the transfer of information from the level of light-coding to the physical plane. As Vogel wrote (www.vogelcrystals.com):

What appeared on the film was the prefiguring in space of the crystallographic form the system was to assume. The blue flash contained information which formed into a geometric form. This geometric form was the source of the crystallographic form from which the crystal grew and developed.

According to Vogel, once the crystal has ceased growing, its "intelligence matrix" disappears. The form of the quartz is then basically an empty shell until it is enlivened with human bioenergy, accomplished by the transfer of thought-energy via the pulsed breath. Vogel then began seventeen years of research into quartz crystals, discovering that quartz had the capacity to store, amplify, and transfer information. But, because raw quartz crystals could not adequately cohere these energies, Vogel began to cut them into various shapes. Just as light through a faceted ruby can produce coherent energy, Vogel wondered if thought interfaced with a specifically faceted quartz could produce a coherent energy.

One morning in 1974, Vogel awoke with a pattern in his mind similar to the kabbalistic Tree of Life. Over the course of the following year, he was able to grind his quartz into a 3-D representation of the Tree of Life. The resultant four-sided quartz crystal with pyramid-like points came to be known as Vogel-cut crystals. From these experiments came the first instrument for storing, amplifying, transferring, and cohering the energies of the body-mind of an individual. It is reputed that some of the best crystal and diamond cutters in Germany have attempted to reproduce the Vogel-cut crystals without success. Vogel explained that the crystal must be worked with "right attitude, understanding, and consciousness." He maintained that it is not simply a matter of cutting the quartz in the correct shape, but it must be "tuned as a coherent information transfer device." The geometry of the Vogel-cut crystal creates a coherent field of energy that can act as a carrier wave of information.

The ability of crystals to store information is now widely known. According to the September 4, 1994, issue of *Newsweek*, Stanford University physicists have demonstrated the first model of a fully digital device that stores information as a hologram within the subatomic structure of a crystal. The scientists were able to store and retrieve a holographic image of the Mona Lisa. The particular crystal held only 163 kilobytes of memory, but it is expected that these holographic units could store up to one million megabytes. This article explains that crystals store information in three dimensions and could be ten times faster than the fastest systems currently available.

Vogel claimed his crystals could be used for healing the human body and mind, by "removing unwanted vibrations or thought forms from an individual in distress." He discovered that the crystal acted as an "energetic scalpel" in an "etheric surgery," and he developed methods of healing using the Vogel-cut crystals. Vogel also came to believe that the various subtle energy bodies described in metaphysical literature are "gradations of a field that is anchored to the physical body via the water molecule." He discovered that, since the human body is three quarters water, the profound healing effects of the crystal were related to its resonance to water. A web site devoted to Marcel Vogel (www.vogelcrystals.com) explains how these crystals work:

> The crystal is a quantum converter that is able to transmit energy in a form that has discrete biological effects. This is most likely a resonant effect. The human body, on an energetic level, is an array of oscillating points that are layered and have a definite symmetry and structure. This crystallinity is apparent on both a subtle energetic or quantum level as well as the macro level. The bones, tissues, cells, and fluids of the body have a definite crystallinity about them. The structure of the fluids, cells, and tissues of the body tends to become unstructured or incoherent when disease or distress is present. The physical body is comprised of liquid crystal systems in the cell membranes, intercellular fluids, as well as larger structures, such as the fatty tissues, muscular and nervous systems, lymph, blood, and so on. Through the use of an appropriately tuned crystal to which these structures are responsive, balance and coherence can be restored by delivering the necessary "information" or energetic nutrients needed.

THE INFORMATION BAND

Vogel discovered that the information band measured by the Omega 5 exists in and around all matter. He postulated that the information band is a sort of "record keeper" of the specific events which brought an object into being, as well as the responses of this object to these actions, energies, fields or forces. He suggested that these forces and actions combined to build a series of identifying patterns or codes. Since all motion generates a field, the composite of these fields is the ground state of the information band. These perturbations form an energy cloud around the substance. This is the mind of the atom.

Vogel found that there is a rhythmic nature to this field, and a corresponding periodicity to the information band. He discovered that the information band would expand and contract in accordance with its relationship to planetary influences. Vogel even took a clue from Alice Bailey's *The Consciousness of the Atom*:

> We have seen that the atom of chemistry, for instance, demonstrates the quality of intelligence; it shows symptoms of discriminative mind and the rudiments of selective capacity. Thus the tiny life within the atomic form is demonstrating a psychic quality—take the atom that goes to the building of form in the mineral kingdom; it shows not only discriminative selective mind, but elasticity. Let us endeavor to realize that there is no such thing as inorganic matter, but that every atom is a life. Let us realize that all forms are living forms, and that each is but the vehicle of expression for some indwelling entity.

Vogel's contention was that there is communication through the information band. He believed that as long as there is integrity in the system the object holds its geometric form.

KEEPING OCCULT SECRETS

Keeping occult secrets is an unspoken mandate of the national security state. With respect to scientific knowledge of an arcane nature, this information becomes a source of power when it is kept within the control of an elite social clique. The story of Marcel Vogel illustrates that magic and science are two sides of the same coin. Notice that IBM kept their hooks in Marcel Vogel after he left their employ, and Stanford Research Institute donated equipment to Vogel's research lab. What kind of information did this computer industry giant and intelligence think tank receive in return? We can only imagine.

Members of the military and intelligence communities, as Adam Mandelbaum points out in *The Psychic Battlefield*, are highly trained specialists. They are well-drilled in security matters, and always work under threat of extreme penalty for breaches of security. This is also how members of secret societies work. Loyalty to the organization's secrets is taken very seriously. As Mandelbaum concludes, "It is not surprising that occult secret societies have often played a role in the military and political arenas of the world, achieving status as permanent residents in the realm of the military-occult complex." He also notes:

A secret cabal with indigenous contacts, untraceable funding, and a built-in chain of command is just what the revolutionary or the espionage organization ordered. The history of revolution and intelligence provides us with examples of how secret societies have participated in geopolitical struggles, and how occult symbolism and ritual have been found alongside the bayonets and bombs that have changed governments and established—or overthrown—tyranny.

THE SECRET SOCIETY OF THE STATE

An important book written in France in 1960 discussed the implications of this control of scientific knowledge by the secret society of the state. As Pauwels and Bergier wrote in *The Dawn of Magic*, unknown treasures of the past lie slumbering in libraries of Alexandria, Athens, Jerusalem, and Egypt, and many other ancient libraries were torched for political and religious reasons. Much of our ancient history is physically lost, and much of what remains is lost to the tendency of moderns to believe that the progress of knowledge is "discontinuous with hundreds of thousands of years of ignorance." This assumption serves a purpose: to obscure arcane knowledge in order to keep it in the hands of the few.

The idea that an "era of enlightenment" suddenly emerged with no precedent serves to obscure all previous periods of history. Yet, Pauwels and Bergier lament, these periods of time actually contained "truths far too profound to be attributed merely to the intuition of the ancients." For instance, modern methods of rational inquiry were not invented by Descartes, but by Aristotle, and before that, Democritus had his roots in an earlier Phoenician tradition of rational scientific inquiry.

A comparison to modern science shows that the state of affairs is much the same. The rapid growth of technology makes the same secrecy a necessity. As knowledge advances, it is surrounded by secrecy at every level, and the technical language with which this knowledge is conveyed becomes more and more obscure to the lay person. As a result of this secret scientific knowledge, the upper echelons of the cryptocracy have the power to make far-reaching decisions over the heads of a powerless populace. As Pauwels and Bergier warned, we are returning to "the age of the Adepts," and to the era of secret societies. We are on the verge of fully realizing that "magic" is misapprehended science. Yet, the agencies in charge of our so-called national security have known these secrets for a long time. Is this an orchestrated time lag?

Secret societies have always closely guarded their scientific knowledge, their artisan and industrial traditions, and their magical techniques, and have carefully created closed societies and guilds for the propagation and protection of these secrets. The initiates of secret orders were organized to keep their knowledge and techniques underground. In 1960, Pauwels and Bergier imagined that the state would become a secret society in the near future. As is exhibited by the keen interest of the intelligence community in what we might call the "mind sciences," it would appear that this is exactly what is happening. I would add that the state has never been anything but a secret society, and therein lies the root of its ordained power.

Current scientific advances are merely an extension of the safekeeping and continual propagation of secret knowledge in the hands of the few. The safe haven of this hidden knowledge lies in a caste system, which possesses much more planetary clout than governments and political police. It is a secret society above the law of any land. This power elite has its own police force: the intelligence tentacles of the US government, such as the CIA, NSA, Department of Defense, and military intelligence forces. Such secrets are kept secret under the auspices of "national security."

Pauwels and Bergier predicted the secret society would be the future form of government, taking the form of a cryptocracy. They believed that at a certain level intelligence itself is a kind of secret society, and that its powers are unlimited when it is allowed to develop without boundaries. Thus, it is important to reconsider our conception of a secret society. They admitted that this view may seem mad, but explained: "This is because we are saying rapidly and brutally what we have to say, like a man knocking on a sleeper's door when time is running short." ●

References

First International Congress on Psychotronic Research, #JPRS L/5022-2, Vol. 2. Conference held in Prague in 1973; NTIS, (703-605-6000). Previously a government classified document.

"Legacy of Marcel Vogel," www.vogelcrystals.com.

Mandelbaum, W. Adam. *The Psychic Battlefield: A History of the Military-Occult Complex.* New York: St. Martin's Press, 2000.

Pauwels, Louis and Jacques Bergier. *The Dawn of Magic.* London: Panther, 1964.

White, John. "What Is Psychic Energy?" Appendix 1 to *Psychic Warfare: Fact or Fiction?* London: Aquarian Press, 1988.

—Spring 2001

Psychiatry and Psychology

Reexamining a Sacred Cow

by Steven Ferry

According to Steven Ferry, psychiatry is a pseudo-science, a scam parading as science. From German psychologist Wilhelm Wundt, to Swiss psychiatrist Wilhelm Griesinger, to the illustrious Sigmund Freud, Ferry outlines the secret history of the shrink business. According to Ferry, the first error these professors made was that man is an animal without spirit. Freud's psychoanalysis began a largely unchallenged "science" that has subverted religion and has become an insidious industry that has moved into every facet of our world, including our schools. As Ferry concludes, the mental health industry has resulted in multiple real problems in society.

WHAT IS THE COMMON GROUND between genocide by the Nazis in Europe, shooting rampages in our schools, spiraling crime rates, and an increasingly amoral society? The common ground lies with the same group that has managed to kill twice as many Americans under its direct care between 1950 and 1990 alone as have died in all the wars in which America has ever engaged. Although the group is highly visible, it makes itself invisible by engaging in countless activities too incredible to be believed. Anyone pointing out that this "emperor" is wearing no clothes is usually ignored because no group could be so off-base and remain in a position of authority.

Explaining his excesses, Adolf Hitler once boasted that the more outrageous the deed, the less people are inclined to believe it. We are not, today, devastated by economic collapse as the Germans were in 1933, and we do not live in a police state where all media are controlled by the government. We can surely think for ourselves and see when the wool has been pulled over our eyes. However, suppose the information we have been led to believe is reasonable, and which we use to reach our conclusions, is actually flawed? Would we be able to recognize what may be the greatest hoax of the century?

This group of individuals—150,000 of them around the world—has introduced itself into almost every facet of our lives, changing the way we think and view our selves and life as a whole. It has used billions upon billions of taxpayer dollars to finance itself. It uses its own ineffectiveness as evidence that more government allocations are required to combat "the problem," which itself didn't exist until this group materialized two centuries ago and stated there was a problem. Their actions have resulted in multiple real problems in society.

This sacred group, known collectively as "psychs"—psychiatrists and psychologists (and their cousins, mental health workers and counselors)—has achieved nothing since it started. Before anyone rejects this notion, and for the sake of argument, let's suppose that psychs, who have been leading the way in mental health for a century now, had taken a wrong turn right from the get-go? Suppose man isn't just an animal that can be cured of "mental diseases" with chemicals and Pavlovian coercions? This assumption might explain why psychs are hard-put to achieve the improvements in man's condition that one would expect from a science of the mind.

THE EARLY PSYCHS

From the moment Wilhelm Wundt, professor of psychology at Leipzig University, Germany, in 1879 declared the study of the spirit—psycheology—a futile endeavor, the rest of the world has been led by psychs to believe that men and women are no more than animals responding to stimuli from the environment—in other words, victims. Although it shocked the religious majority at the time, who believed that mankind had a spiritual dimension, the idea was far from new. Materialism had been on the rise for two centuries. A pivotal change occurred in 1865, when a Swiss psychiatrist, Wilhelm Griesinger, asserted that because most nerve cells were in the brain, all mental problems must be brain problems. In other words, the mind was the brain, the software was really hardware.

The concept of a field of study that denies the validity of the very field itself is a challenging position to hold. It is certainly an interesting approach to formulating a science. The nebulous nature of things spiritual and mental, however, lends itself to a trusting acceptance of any who would stand and say, "I am an authority." Thus, Wundt's experimental psychology, followed in the late 1890s by Sigmund Freud's psychoanalysis, began a largely unchallenged "science" that has moved into every facet of society today. Freud, whose claims that human behavior was the result of sexual repression, and that neuroses were caused by moral codes, was instrumental in popularizing the new "science," as he called it. He also rejected religion as "obsolete," a collection of superstitions, and the "universal obsession neurosis." Unfortunately, he neither conducted experiments nor published his findings, two critical requirements in any science.

Freud published six case histories during his fifty-six years of psychoanalyzing, falsely claiming each patient had been cured. The cocaine that he sniffed, injected, and smoked could have influenced Freud's science. He claimed cocaine cured his depression and promoted its benefits to others. Freud suffered from psychosomatic illnesses, and was what psychs today call "paranoid" about his competitors harming him. His theories—many of which he lifted from others without credit—were so complex that his followers relied upon him for interpretation. Anyone asking for proof of his theories he dismissed as psychologically impaired for "resisting" his ideas. Incidentally, eight of his associates killed themselves. Freud, hailed as the grandfather of psychology, continues to be a model for psychs today.

PARADING AS SCIENCE

Whatever Freud was doing, it was not science. Today, the "science" of psychiatry and psychology has grown into no less than 250 theories about the mind, each one reportedly better than the other and none able to cure anything, according to the practitioners themselves. Assuming that the good German professors had chanced upon the real nature of man—an animal without spirit in whose brain resided the entire capabilities of the mind—over a century of work should have wrought some significant improvement in man's general condition. Strange, therefore, that psychs are claiming that 48 percent of people today between the ages of fifteen and fifty-four have some mental illness. The figure was 0.1 percent across all ages in the mid-1800s, before psychs started to manufac-ture the myth of mental illness. If a police chief offered crime statistics like this he would be out of office.

The first edition of the *Diagnostic and Statistical Manual* (DSM), the psychs' definitive list of mental illnesses, identified 112 of them in 1952; by the fourth edition in 1994, 370 mental illnesses were listed. One would be justified in wondering how such an exponential rise in insanity could occur within just two generations. Furthermore, each new malady is added to the DSM by a show of hands—who among the psychs at a meeting agreed with the existence of a malady proposed verbally by one of their peers. As Dr. Renee Garfinkel has noted, "The low level of intel-lectual effort was shocking. Diagnoses were developed by majority vote on the level we would choose a restaurant. 'You feel like Italian. I feel like Chinese. So let's go to a cafeteria.' Then it's typed into a computer." Where do the ideas come from? Robert Spitzer, chairman of the DSM-IV committee, thought up "self-defeating personality disorder" on a fishing trip and persuaded his colleagues to include the disorder in DSM-IV.

Bear in mind, therefore, when looking for some explanation for this rise in "mental illnesses," that it is only when the "illness" is listed in the DSM that psychs can bill insurance companies for treating the "diseases," invariably with drugs. Other maladies added recently are "Math Disor-der," "Shopping Disorder," and "Disorder of Written Expression."

Psychs are apparently unable to differentiate between an idea and a reality, because they believe that by coining disease-sounding terms, the diseases then exist. In DSM IV, psychs do not distinguish between mental and physical "disorders." For instance, if a child keeps missing the ball and this upsets the child, or even the parent or teacher, the child is said to have "developmental coordination disorder," and is administered Ritalin or Prozac, instead of being coached.

Not all psychiatrists are so naïve as to fall for the DSM, however. In fact, an international poll of mental health experts in London in 2001 voted the DSM to be one of the ten worst psychiatric papers. Medical doctors are not impressed with the DSM either. Most still believe that a thorough physical exam should be undertaken before any assumption is made that irrational behavior is mental in origin. Dr. Dennis Dorman, member of the Royal College of Physicians of the United Kingdom, described the DSM as "nothing but an extended racket furnishing psy-chiatry a pseudo-scientific aura. The perpetrators are, of course, feeding at the public trough."

FRAUD BY ANY OTHER NAME

If psychiatry started off on the wrong foot by denying the spirituality of humankind as its basic premise, it went seriously awry, beginning in the 1960s, when it encroached on the field of neurology—an actual science that deals with the diagnosis and treatment of physical abnormalities and diseases of the brain. If part of the brain is physically damaged, neurology treats it as a physical problem. Up to that time, psychiatry was meant to psychoanalyze (and render tractable with its other punishment-based restraining and quieting techniques) those patients who had no physical problems, but were behaving irrationally.

Psychiatrists realized in the 1960s that they could create a vast "market," and achieve their goals of social control, by redefining behavioral problems as physical illnesses resulting from chemical imbalances in the brain (the problem), and offering drugs to bring about balance (the solution). By defining more and more peculiarities of human behavior as "diseases," it would be possible to have the entire population of the world buying these drugs. Even those who had nothing wrong with them, other than a disagreement with this strategy, could be labeled as being in denial, having "non-compliance with treatment disorder," and, therefore, chemically imbalanced.

The pharmaceutical industry was quick to support the new theory that emotional and behavioral problems were diseases of the brain brought on by a "chemical imbalance." The problem with this theory is that legitimate medicine requires identification of physical symptoms to diagnose a disease, and no physical basis has been found for any of the 374 diseases listed in DSM-IV, after decades of research with billions of dollars of taxpayer and pharmaceutical company monies. Additionally, no tests exist to determine the chemical status of a person's brain while he is living.

This fact, however, doesn't discourage psychs from fraudulently misdiagnosing tens of millions of people as having these "diseases," or pharmaceutical companies from making psychiatric drugs to treat these made-up diseases. For anyone who imagines that psychiatric drugs actually do any good, consider the 2002 study by psychologists Irving Kirsch and Thomas Moore, published in the online journal of the American Psychological Association. They reviewed forty-seven research test-studies, submitted to the FDA for approval of antidepressants, including Prozac, Paxil, and Zoloft. Their study showed that sugar pills produced better results than these drugs. The manufacturers make over $6 billion a year from the American public for these particular pills—which, unlike real sugar pills, create violent behavior, and psychosis upon withdrawal.

To show how psychiatry and pharmaceutical companies have teamed up to create a cash cow, let's consider a very SAD story: In 1997, Social Anxiety Disorder was invented by psychiatrists to give shyness a "scientific label." Fifty mentions were made in the media of this SAD condition in 1997 and 1998, but in 1999, many, many more media mentions occurred, 96 percent of which also happened to say that Paxil was the only FDA-approved medication that could treat SAD.

The *Washington Post* reported on July 16, 2001, that Glaxo Smith Kline, the manufacturer of Paxil, had hired Cohn & Wolfe, a public relations agency, to coordinate a multimillion-dollar marketing and advertising campaign to "inform thousands of people who previously did not know they were suffering from the disorder," and to encourage many to seek "help." Cohn & Wolfe told the media that it was speaking for doctors and nonprofits—not the pharmaceutical company that was paying its bills. Such altruism is not reflected, however, in Cohn & Wolfe's annual reports, in which they make it clear they are in the business of marketing, not public health. Nor is such altruism reflected in Glaxo Smith Kline's 2000 annual report, which informed shareholders that Paxil had become the number-one prescription in the huge selective serotonin reuptake inhibitor (SSRI) market in the U.S. that year.

The Dutch government has started to tighten the screws on this kind of false public relations, marketing and advertising. The Netherlands Advertisement Code Commission ruled in August 2002 that the country's Brain Foundation could not claim that attention deficit hyperactivity disorder (ADHD) is a neurobiological disease or brain dysfunction, and ordered the Foundation to cease such false claims in their advertising.

When talking about fraud, we must also consider the story of Prozac. In 1978, manufacturer Eli Lilly knew Prozac caused suicidal and homicidal thoughts. The German government refused to approve Prozac in 1984, because trial results showed sixteen suicide attempts (two of which succeeded) in a group of people selected precisely because they were known not to be suicidal. Lilly withheld this information from the FDA when it obtained approval for Prozac in the U.S. Lilly then spent large sums of money defending itself against charges of involvement in murders and suicides committed by people under the influence of Prozac, because "Lilly can go down the tubes if we lose Prozac," stated Leigh Thompson, a chief scientist at Lilly. The FDA's records show 28,623 adverse reactions reported, of which 1,089 were suicides and 1,885 were attempted suicides. However, Prozac suicides may be as high as 108,900, with attempts at a whopping 188,500, since the Government Accounting Office estimates that only 1 to 10 percent of adverse reactions are actually reported to the FDA. Recent studies estimate Prozac deaths in excess of 50,000, with 7 to 10 percent experiencing some adverse reaction.

In its efforts to hide the truth, Lilly pressured its scientists in 1990 to alter records of physician experiences with Prozac, changing "suicide attempt" to "overdose" and "suicidal thoughts" to "depression." The company settled out of court most of the 200 lawsuits over Prozac, with the terms kept confidential. In 2002, in promoting its new version of Prozac, Eli Lilly stated it would not produce "suicidal thoughts and self-mutilation . . . one of its more significant side effects"—an admission made only because it would help with sales of the new product.

Yet, even psychologists can see through the fraud: Jonathan Abramowitz, a psychologist at the Mayo Clinic in Rochester, Minnesota, who worked on DSM-IV, warned "social anxiety is not a chemical problem with the brain. I see it as a problem with normal thinking and behaviors that have gone awry."

These marketing strategies seriously compromise the survival of mankind as a result of physical problems left untreated, and the widespread ingestion of toxic chemicals that result in many physical problems and mental side effects. One study showed that 83 percent of those referred for mental treatment by clinics and social workers were found to have an undiagnosed physical illness. Yet, psychiatrists do not conduct physical examinations. They merely consult a checklist of aberrant mental conduct, and label and prescribe psychotropic drugs for "diseases" they know to have no basis in fact. This violates the informed consent rights of patients and constitutes medical malpractice.

When psychs say that Ritalin, Paxil, Haldol, or any of the many psych drugs, will remedy abnormalities, pathologies, or chemical imbalances within the brain of a child having difficulties in school, they are implying they have detected such an imbalance and know exactly how it is remedied. The problem is that no such studies or findings have ever been made. This level of science is the same as that propounded by the purveyors of quack medicine 150 years ago. Some things never change, and we still find people falling for it. What has changed is that: the government funds it; it is not just being directed at thinking adults, but babies and children, under penalty of law for refusing to cooperate; and the potions are toxic. Psychiatrists and pharmaceutical lobbies also practice unethical behavior by spending billions to create the illusion they are all-knowing scientists working under the mantle of "professional help," while their true motive is personal profit.

THE LOBOTOMY: MIRACLE CURE?

It must be frustrating for professionals to invest so many years of their lives into what turns out to be a scam. Such frustration may have as its cause a reliance on unprovable theories in the place of facts to build a "science." Take the lobotomy, for instance. This practice originated from one event in 1847, in which a crowbar blew through the prefrontal lobes of Pheneas Gage during a rock-blasting operation in the U.S. He survived the accident, it is true, but nowhere in the case history is there mention of any improvement in his condition. On the contrary, he became extremely rude and anti-social.

Based on this one incident, with no case studies, psych Walter Freeman introduced prefrontal lobotomies in the U.S. The procedure, which involves hammering an ice pick through the eye sockets and using it to sever the nerves behind the forehead, has been performed on at least 100,000 people. No record exists of anyone being improved by a lobotomy. Quite the opposite, in fact, since a vegetative state is the inevitable result. The spirited Hollywood beauty, Frances Farmer, was finally broken after a lobotomy. Yet, the lobotomy was touted by psychs as a "miracle cure" in the same way that electro-convulsive therapy (ECT) was promoted in 1938, and psychotropic drugs are promoted today. Prozac is meant to cure everything from weight gain to jealousy and pulling out one's hair—a list that sounds as convincing as the pitch for the potions that quack doctors peddled a century ago.

FRIEND OR FOE?

What if psychs were not as advertised—civilization's last line of defense against global insanity and barbarism? What if they really were the cause of the craziness around us that they insist governments pay them handsomely to prevent? What if psychs were not the rescuing cavalry, but the curse of humanity? The director of the U.S. National Institutes of Mental Health (NIMH), Rex Cowdry, may have unwittingly backed this conclusion, in 1995, when he said, "We do not know the causes (of psychiatric disorders). We don't have methods of 'curing' these illnesses yet." A 1999 Surgeon General report stated, "No single gene has been found to be responsible for any specific mental disorder. There is no definite lesion, laboratory test or abnormality in brain tissue that can identify the [mental] illness."

Consider the words of Norman Sartorius, who, as president of the World Psychiatric Association, announced to fellow psychiatrists in 1994, "The time when psychiatrists considered they could cure the mentally ill is gone. In the future, the mentally ill will have to learn to live with their illness." David Kaiser, one of several psychiatrists with the integrity to blow the whistle on his own kind, stated in 1996 that, "modern psychiatry has yet to convincingly prove the genetic/biologic cause of any single mental illness. Patients have been diagnosed with 'chemical imbalances' despite the fact that no test exists to support such a claim, and . . . there is no real conception of what a correct chemical balance would look like." If these gentlemen are being honest, we have to assume that the other *pronouncements* in the media by psychs of every color are nothing more than high-sounding language with no substance behind them. The millions of victims and billions of dollars and hours spent on research and treatment are all based on a pretend science.

TECHNOLOGY TO QUIET OR KILL

Relying on the theory that man is an animal without any spiritual existence, whose mind is really his brain, it is easy to see how this "science" produced the three key technologies it did: pharmaceutical drugs, the lobotomy, and ECT. Psychs package any observable behavior, reclassify and label it as a mental disorder or disease, and prescribe a drug that turns the person into an addict and/or zombie. Many of the side effects of these drugs are the very symptoms that psychs consider a "mental illness." For instance, the *Physicians' Desk Reference* lists psychotic episodes as a side effect of Ritalin and Dexedrine. This results in more business for the psychs with the increased dosages of ever-stronger drugs. For the patients, there is stupefaction, toxicity, and brain and central nervous system damage. By 1989, more people were dying from prescription drugs than from street drugs. For society, there is increased crime (560 percent increase between 1960 and 1991), a drug epidemic, lowered production, and tragedies like the Columbine High School shooting.

Psychiatrist Loren Mosher resigned from the American Psychiatric Association (APA) in 1998 on the grounds that "psychiatry has been almost completely bought out by the drug companies." He further stated, "The APA could not continue without the pharmaceutical company support of meetings, symposia, workshops, journal advertising, grand rounds luncheons, unrestricted educational grants etc. We condone and promote the widespread overuse and misuse of toxic chemicals that we know have serious long term effects. I want no part of a psychiatry of oppression and social control."

The second technology is the lobotomy, which was essentially replaced in 1954 with the introduction of the drug Thorazine, otherwise known as the chemical lobotomy.

The third technology is ECT—the application of up to 460 volts to the temples of a patient, who is drugged to prevent bones breaking during the attendant convulsions. ECT is applied to create a grand mal epileptic seizure and permanent brain damage from oxygen deprivation. It results in memory loss, learning disability, disorientation, brain shrinkage, coma, and sometimes death due to hemorrhaging or choking. The "reduction in intelligence is an important factor in the curative process," according to one American psychiatrist.

Dr. Ugo Cerletti pioneered ECT in Italy in 1938, after seeing how pigs were administered electric shock just before being slaughtered. He admitted in 1970 that it ought to be abolished. Yet, 110,000 people still receive six to twelve such treatments of ECT each year in the U.S., costing taxpayers and insurance companies (and providing psychs with) $3 billion annually. A study of 340 depressed patients by ECT proponent Dr. Harold A. Sackeim showed that not one person received any lasting benefit from the treatment.

While the latter two procedures have been rejected by most today, they were claimed to be highly effective in their heyday, with no evidence to show any real benefits for those patients who were administered the procedures. Does this sound similar to the latest psychiatric breakthrough—psychotropic drugs to cure mental "diseases"? What are the typical reactions to psychotropic drugs? Minor tranquilizers can cause lethargy, confusion, sexual dysfunction, hallucination, severe depression, insomnia, and muscle tremors. Withdrawing cold turkey can result in seizures and death. Antidepressants can cause drowsiness, lethargy, difficulty in thinking, memory problems, delusions, seizures, fever, liver damage, heart attacks, and strokes. SSRIs result in withdrawal symptoms in 50 percent of takers, sexual dysfunction in 60 percent, and seizures, hearing loss, paranoia, and suicide.

LEGITIMIZING AND INSTITUTIONALIZING A SCAM

German psychologists introduced experimental psychology into a world ignorant of matters of the mind, but which had believed that mankind has a spiritual component. Like all early movements, psychology had some converts among a majority who considered it either absurd or unscientific. Influential American devotees visited Germany and returned to the U.S. to introduce the theories into schools. German professors also came to the U.S. to export their technology and theories. For instance, Ernst Rudin, professor of psychiatry at Munich and director of the Department of Heredity at the Kaiser Wilhelm Institute, visited the U.S. in 1930. He was praised by the leaders of the Carnegie Foundation and supported financially by a large Rockefeller Foundation grant. Rudin was the architect of Nazi Germany's sterilization law. The Kaiser Wilhelm Institute is the place where, until 1990, psychs kept the brains of hundreds of children for psychiatric research—children murdered and dismembered by psychs in the Nazi concentration camps.

By the 1930s, Hollywood was helping to legitimize psychs by including them as positive characters in movies, and by the 1940s, the government was funding psychiatric programs to control the independent and unruly minds of its more boisterous subjects. The infamous, but now forgotten, Alaska Bill fell just a vote or two shy of passing in the mid-1950s. It would have given psychs the power to lock up and electroshock anyone in mental health camps in Alaska, without recourse. The CIA used psychs in an attempt to control minds for their own ends, continuing the research undertaken by psychs in Nazi concentration camps. Today, we have the Department of Homeland Security edging the land of the free closer to such enforced psychiatric-controlled gulags once more.

The facts listed above may paint an alarming picture with a broad brush, but the words, reproduced below, of G. Brock Chisholm and J.R. Rees, founders of the World Federation for Mental Health (WFMH), show plainly that psychs are engaged in breaking down any sense of social and moral responsibility, and creating an ignorant, drug-addicted society that is increasingly in turmoil. Established in 1948, WFMH influences the establishment of psych facilities, agendas, and programs in several countries.

The approach psychs were to take was outlined by Rees in a 1940 speech, in which he said:

Public life, politics and industry should all of them be within our sphere of influence. If we are to infiltrate the professional and social activities of other people I think we must imitate the totalitarians and organize some kind of fifth column activity! If better ideas on mental health are to progress and spread, we, as the salesmen, must lose our identity . . . Let us all, therefore, very secretly be "fifth columnists."

This goal was subsequently executed in the U.S. by four psychiatrists—Robert Felix, William Menninger, Francis Braceland, and Jack Ewalt—who wrote the basis of a legislative bill signed into law in 1946, creating the National Insitutute of Mental Health and a national mental health program funded by taxpayer dollars. The mental health industry was and remains the only branch of medicine to have its training subsidized by taxpayers. NIMH was empowered to carry out psychiatric research, fund psychology training, and assist states with community-based prevention programs.

The three-phase program for world mental health development called for: setting up psych institutions; establishing community outpatient centers, one for every 100,000 people; and introducing parental and pre-marital guidance, child and welfare services, and psych programs in schools. In 1963, Congress authorized $150 million to build the centers and, in 1965, a further $735 million to staff them. The cost for these centers rose dramatically, from $140 million in 1969 to $9.75 billion in 1994—a 6,800 percent increase. By 1980, 55 percent of those attending these centers were being prescribed powerful psychotropic drugs.

The NIMH has funded the training of psychiatrists, psychologists, psychiatric social workers, nurses, and public health officers for years. Today, we find psychiatric theory and influence at every turn: in schools, hospitals and doctor's offices, businesses, media and entertainment, retirement homes, courtrooms, and the list goes on. Let's look at the effects of some key psych programs.

G. Brock Chisholm stated in 1945, "The reinterpretation and eventually eradication of the concept of right and wrong which has been the basis of child training . . . are the belated objectives of practically all effective psychotherapy." The introduction and promotion of the "insanity plea" and other psychiatric "illnesses" or "disorders" in the courtroom have redefined criminals as victims of their past, rather than as responsible for their own actions. They have also made it next to impossible to control crime. Violent crime in the U.S. increased from one in a hundred to eight in a hundred people between 1960 and 1995.

Any courtroom consulting psychs for the prosecution will be fed opinions that counter those of the defense's psych. The American Psychiatric Association itself filed a statement in the U.S. Supreme Court admitting that psychiatric "predictions are fundamentally of very low reliability and . . . irrelevant" in court. Yet psych mumbo-jumbo, and reference to DSM-IV as the authoritative source, still occurs throughout the court and prison systems. Psychs counsel both the police and criminals. The result is three hundred policemen and women commit suicide each year, 30 percent higher than the national average, and 80 percent of criminals end up in prison again. A 1974 study in St. Louis showed that 82 percent of those arrested had received psychiatric treatments prior to committing the crime.

TURNING SCHOOLS INTO MENTAL HEALTH CLINICS

Perhaps more tragic still is the encroachment of psych theories and practices in our schools over the last century, particularly the last thirty-five years. Education was first undermined in the U.S. when psychology courses were introduced in American teaching colleges in 1899. The "Father of American Education," John Dewey, wrote in his *School and Society* that same year: "There is no obvious social motive for the acquiring of learning. It is one of the greatest mistakes of education to make reading and writing constitute the bulk of the schoolwork for the first two years. The ultimate problem of all education is to coordinate the psychological and social factors . . . and schools should take an active part in determining the social order of the future."

Edward Thorndike created "Educational Psychology" in 1903. In his 1929 book, he stated that the three R's were of little value. Psychs also decided to remove the "stress" factors in education, such as academic curricula, disciplinary procedures, and school failure. "Values Clarification" programs were introduced under various names, most recently being called "Outcome Based Education" (OBE). These programs carefully taught children that morals are defunct, and yet tried to teach them how to behave "properly." The psychs, thereby, shifted the emphasis from teaching students to controlling and molding them, making it more difficult for the students to learn, and opening them up to being thought "difficult" and who "needed" drugs to be able to learn properly.

Psych influence in our schools was assured in 1965 with the passage of the Elementary and Secondary Education Act, providing the funding for psych programs, testing and personnel in schools. In 1969, there were 455 psychiatrists in schools, a number that had bloated to 16,146 in 1992. By 1994, psychs and their cohorts in and around schools almost outnumbered teachers. The psychs introduced a plethora of labels to describe typical child behavior (such as fidgeting) as well as redefining difficulty with math or reading as "mental disorders" (DSM Code #315.1 and 315, respectively) rather than a lack of adequate teaching. Could this be because teachers were increasingly being redirected from teaching to controlling? Teachers have been turned into amateur psychologists, pinning labels on their students and turning them over to the psych-pharmaceutical machine now built into our schools.

Pharmaceutical companies have financed "grassroots" groups such as CHADD (Children and Adults with ADHD), which received $1 million from the manufacturer of Ritalin to create an apparent groundswell of public demand for psychiatric drug usage in schools, and to help bring about Title One of the Federal Code, Children With Disabilities Act, and the Supplemental Security Income program, in 1991. These programs provided schools with up to $650 annually for each child diagnosed with a "disorder," giving schools "an incentive to identify more kids with special education needs," according to an Education Department official.

There has been a 1,100 percent increase between 1987 and 2001 in the diagnosis of ADHD in American children, with 20.6 million prescriptions written in 2001. Compare this to the conclusion reached by the world's experts in ADHD at a 1998 conference: "Our knowledge about the cause or causes of ADHD remains largely speculative." In 1996, $15 billion was spent in the U.S. on managing the various psychiatric disorders children were suddenly manifesting. The same is occurring in other wealthy countries: Germany saw the number of stimulants prescribed to children jump from 7 million in 1995 to 31 million in 1999. In 1992, 2,000 such prescriptions were written in the U.K., and by the year 2,000, some 186,000 had been written. This money, of course, goes into psych and drug manufacturers' coffers.

How has this approach to educating U.S. school children affected them? Over 6 million of our primary through high school children are now on mind-altering drugs, compared to 1 million on street drugs. As an observant parent of one child noted, "The drugs rob these kids of their personality. They become quiet little robots." Except, that is, for the reported 4 percent of users (80,000 children), who psychiatrist

Peter Breggin, author of *Toxic Psychiatry*, claims are prompted to violent behavior.

Matthew Cohen, president of Children and Adults with ADHD in Landover, Maryland, has the pat answer to this violence, however: "The medication doesn't produce the violence. The more accurate thing to say is that the medication was insufficient to prevent it." Interesting, as the DEA reports four fifths of amphetamine use in the U.S. is for the "treatment" of ADHD, with production of the stimulant increasing 3,750 percent between 1993 and 2000. In November 2000, 19 million prescriptions were made out to one in five of our school children. Ritalin, which shares many of the pharmacological effects of cocaine but lasts longer, according to a 1995 DEA report, goes for $6 a pill on the black market on school campuses.

The fact that teen suicides have tripled since the 1960s can be laid squarely at the door of psychiatric drug pushers, as well as their twisted sense of education in providing "death education"—stories of death, murder, and suicide, followed by asking children what they want written on their tombstones.

No fewer than 1,336 children age thirteen to seventeen were arrested for murder in 1987. By 1992, the number had risen to 2,829. What of less high-profile crimes? Between 1965 and 1992, teenage drug arrests rose from 10 to 147 per 100,000 juveniles. In 1992, 5,364 rapes were committed by children under eighteen, with 2,049 of these committed by children under fifteen.

Education shows equally alarming statistics. Combined SAT verbal and math scores began dropping in 1963, and have fallen eighty points to 890. In the 1930s, 3 million adults could not read because they had not been to school. In 1990, forty million could not understand what they were reading or perform simple math calculations, even after a decade in school. National Achievement Tests given in 2000 showed that more than two thirds of U.S. fourth graders were unable to read up to grade level. Was this because they were no longer being taught how to read using phonics, or because they really were "mentally disordered, developmental learning types," which is what the psychs claimed?

WEAKENING THE FAMILY

If the psych agenda really is to weaken the individual and make him or her more controllable, the last thing one would want is a strong family to bolster confidence and morale. So it was that G. Brock Chisholm pronounced the following in London in 1948: "The family is now one of the major obstacles to improved mental health and, hence, should be weakened, if possible, so as to free individuals and especially children from the coercion of family life." Today, social service bureaucrats in the U.S. have the power to declare parents guilty of child abuse and to take their children away until the parents can prove their own innocence.

It seems that apart from destroying all concepts of right and wrong, and undermining the family as a unit, psychs have introduced sex education into schools that encourages promiscuity and perversion. One question, about when to engage in sex, offered the answer: "Do what you like and when you want. Your emotions are what count." Parental discipline has been redefined as "child abuse." Parental concern for the upbringing of children has been renamed "overprotectiveness," and enforcing outmoded religious and moral values. "Tolerating" whatever the child does is now a positive parental trait. Hillary Clinton stated as much in her book, *It Takes a Village*.

SUBVERTING RELIGION

In keeping with Freud's dim view of religion, G. Brock Chisholm stated: "To achieve world government, it is necessary to remove from the minds of men their individualism, loyalty to family traditions, national patriotism and religious dogmas." Chisholm and Rees targeted religion for "mental health orientation" through the training of the clergy. Given this hitherto hidden purpose, it is ironic that we find churches looking to psychs for training on the mind and the "true nature of man." The result of this trust has been a severe decline in church membership and activity:

- By 1952, 83 percent of 109 seminaries and graduate theological schools in the U.S. offered one or more psych courses.

- By 1961, 9,000 clergymen had taken psych-based "clinical pastoral" counseling classes. The clergy were referring parishioners to the community mental health centers.

- While, in 1960, 42 percent of parishioners had consulted their clergy for help and only 18 percent had gone to psychs, by 1991, 38 percent were going to psychs.

- Between 1961 and 1991, church membership dropped 25 percent in the U.S.

The recent pedophile scandals in the United States, which have so damaged the Catholic Church, can also be laid in part at the door of psychs who ran completely unworkable rehabilitation programs on pedophile priests, and who, as a body, have made sexual crimes into mental diseases to be "treated."

Captive Audiences

The elderly with health insurance coverage have been prime targets for the psych industry. Fraud has been rampant, as might be expected, and Medicare finally barred eighty community mental health centers from serving the elderly and disabled in 1998. Unfortunately, 73,000 elderly die each year from adverse reactions to the psych drugs they are administered. Psychs have a captive audience in those kept in psych hospitals, usually against their will and often under false pretenses.

Between 1950 and 1990, the number of in-patient deaths in psychiatric hospitals in the country was almost double the total number of deaths in every single war in which the U.S. has engaged, from the Revolutionary War to the Gulf War. Psychs filled a similar role in Nazi Germany: of the 320,000 in-patients alive in psych hospitals in 1939, only 40,000 remained alive in 1946. The last survivor of the Brandenburg Havel institution in Germany, Elvira Manthey, related years later that she and her three-year-old sister, Lisa, were declared feeble-minded and incarcerated by a psychiatrist in 1938. Lisa died in the gas chambers the following year.

There's Money in Them Thar Pills

As Tana Dineen, Canadian psychologist and author of *Manufacturing Victims*, stated recently, psychology is neither a science nor a profession, but an industry that turns healthy people into victims to provide itself with income. From the mouths of Chisholm and Rees, it seems that psychs as a body have set themselves a goal of engineering world government and social control in the guise of helping individuals and society.

How much money are we talking about? Mental health expenditures, paid for by every taxpayer, rose almost 800 percent between 1970 and 1995, to $28.6 billion per annum. Federal funds are provided through the U.S. National Institute of Mental Health to state branches for "research" and to community level programs in schools, courts, welfare agencies, etc. Federal funds are allotted to finance psych programs in our schools, communities, the armed forces, prisons and courtrooms, and the list goes on.

For the psychiatric drug companies, life is also sweet: In 1999, the U.S. market alone for antidepressants and "anti-psychotic" drugs was over $10 billion. As might be expected of a product and service that is based on junk science, psychs do not solve but create many of the problems in society today. When the situation they are paid to remedy continues to deteriorate, they say they need more money to solve the problem with more drugs and reeducation. Most people, from the President to the media, have fallen for this line.

In the wake of the Columbine High shootings, the gun lobby came under attack. With the exception of a few perceptive writers, such as Bev Eakman in the *Washington Times* and Alexander Cockburn in the *Los Angeles Times*, none asked why many school shootings over the last few years had been committed by a child who was on, or trying to come off, psychiatric drugs, with warning labels that include suicide and violence among their side effects. Among those children were the following:

- Eric Harris at Columbine High was on Luvox when he killed twelve classmates and a teacher in Denver, Colorado.

- Kip Kinkel in Springfield, Oregon, was withdrawing from Prozac when he shot twenty-four classmates and family members.

- Shawn Cooper, a fifteen-year-old in Notus, Idaho, was taking Ritalin when he fired a shotgun at school.

- Elizabeth Bush, a fourteen-year-old, was on Prozac when she shot at fellow students in Williamsport, Pennsylvania, wounding one.

- Mitchell Johnson was taking an unspecified psych drug when he shot at fellow students in Jonesboro, Arkansas.

- T. J. Solomon, a fifteen-year-old in Conyers, Georgia, was taking Ritalin when he shot six classmates.

- Jason Hoffman was on Effexor and Celexa when he wounded five students at his California high school.

- Cory Baadsgaard was on Paxil when he took a rifle to his high school and held 23 classmates hostage.

Why has nobody asked why these children were on heavy drugs? Because everyone knows that the problem with so many kids these days is that they are "mentally ill" and we need more drugs to quiet them at a younger age. If we could just clean up the entertainment industry and remove all guns, what would we have? We would have an entire nation on drugs, seething with an inner rage and finding ways of killing others with whatever weapons are still available.

PORTRAIT OF A CON ARTIST

What kind of person is leading us down this sylvan path to the utopia that George Orwell predicted fifty years ago? Let's look at the stats:

The average psychiatrist in the U.S. today is one among 42,000, supported by 12,000 psychiatric hospitals.

40 percent of psychs are sued for malpractice in the U.S.

221 received criminal convictions in 2001—an increase from 100 in 1998—53 percent for health care fraud and 26 percent for sexual crimes against their patients, who are often children.

The largest health care fraud suit in history ($375 million) involved the smallest sector of healthcare—psychiatry. Fraudulent schemes have included billing insurers for therapy given to deceased people, having sex with patients, or letting them watch TV or play bingo. Between $20 and $40 billion in such fraudulent billings by the mental health industry occur in any given year.

Psychotherapists manifest up to three times as many incidents of inappropriate behavior as the people they are meant to be treating.

One in four psychiatrists worldwide admits to sexually abusing his or her patients. In one study, 150,000 patients were found to have been sexually abused by their psychiatrists, and among 21,000 of these patients who subsequently tried to kill themselves, 1,500 succeeded.

The psych scam is so solidly in place that everyone from National Public Radio to the White House pushes the psych lines, championing the "Mental Health Parity" and ignoring the real cause of school shootings. Yet these issues pale in comparison to what happens when psychs are given free reign to operate in totalitarian states, such as Nazi Germany, Stalinist Russia, and even modern China.

A DOCILE WORLD POPULATION CAN'T JUST SAY "NO!"

The genocide we have witnessed this past century has its roots in psychiatry. It was initially touted as racial hygiene. A Nazi psychiatrist summed it up neatly, when he stated, "Only through the Führer did our dream of over thirty years, that of applying racial hygiene to society, become a reality." Then again, if you were wondering about the parallels between the Nazi and the Serb agenda in the 1990s, look no further than two psychiatrists and former Serbian leaders, Radovan Karadzic and Slobodan Milosevic (the former on the lam, and the latter on trial for war crimes). Consider that the real force behind al-Qaeda, chief advisor to Osama bin-Laden, is psychiatrist Dr. Ayman al-Zawahiri, and that psychologist, Ali A. Mohamed, trained bin-Laden's men.

As G. Brock Chisholm stated, psychologists and psychiatrists had to become leaders in the "planned development of a new kind of human being." It seems that George Orwell only had the date wrong. Less than two decades after the date set by Orwell—1984—the legal and psychiatric elements are finally in place. The populace is at the point where it will accept the conditions of a compliant society controlled by psychiatric drugs. A populace that has been dumbed-down cannot think for itself when it is falsely informed that the mind is a physical object susceptible to chemical deficiencies. According to the UN's International Drug Control Board, 330 million daily doses of Ritalin are taken each day in the U.S., compared to 65 million in the rest of the world. The criteria for ADHD diagnosis are so general that virtually anyone would qualify for a prescription.

By forcing or sneaking through federal and state laws, psychiatrists now have the right to examine and determine that babies may be a threat to society, and so add mint-flavored Prozac to their formulas. As the millions of children diagnosed with fake labels and forced onto drugs will testify, they and their parents were cajoled or forced to take them when they ran into trouble at school. This continues despite Article 33 of the 1989 UN Convention on the Rights of the Child, which state that children have the right to protection from the "illicit use of psychotropic substances."

Yet, the use of psychotropic drugs on two- to four-year-old children tripled between 1991 and 1995. A recent study at Michigan State University revealed that both Ritalin and Prozac were being prescribed to toddlers between the ages of one and three. Ritalin's manufacturer, Novartis, states: "Warning: Sufficient data on the safety and efficacy of long term use of Ritalin in children are not yet available." The Oregon legislature passed into law a bill that provides $25 million for a "preventive mental health" screening program to identify and pre-treat newborns who are determined to be at "psycho/social risk." In France, 3,400 one-year-old children have been prescribed psychotropic drugs.

The Mental Health Parity efforts over the last two years are an effort to provide unlimited funding for psychotropic drug usage throughout the country. It is pushed heavily by the National Alliance for the Mentally Ill (NAMI), a psych front group with strong ties to the pharmaceutical industry. This parity legislation encourages doctors to assign a code from DSM-IV to their patients, so they can be paid for psychiatric drug prescriptions. With the passage of the euphemistically named "patient confidentiality" law in 2002, neither an individual nor his heir has the right to see his or her own medical records, even though a label of some "mental problem" will stigmatize him or her forever. Worse, he or she will become an easy candidate for "civil commitment," as may occur under Florida's Baker Act or California's Code 5150.

Civil commitment is carried out by a police officer, an Emergency Medical Services worker, a pastor, the principal of a school, or by any medical doctor, psychologist, social worker, or probation officer, to forcibly take an individual into custody. The person would be brought to a mental hospital for treatment and/or observation of a "mental, emotional, or behavioral disorder," as found in the latest version of the DSM.

Nearly twenty years ago, President Reagan called the Soviet Union the Evil Empire. It was a political entity in which citizens who disagreed with the government were labeled mentally aberrant and imprisoned in mental institutions until their thinking had been adjusted by psych drugs and conditioning. It is still being done in China, where members of the peaceful Falungong spiritual group are imprisoned in mental hospitals.

Obviously you weren't consulted, but is this vision of a new human being something you really want? Is your concept of the ideal human being an amoral, promiscuous, criminally-inclined drug addict, who is just one animal among many, with some animals less equal than others? Maybe this is what G. Brock Chisholm and his ilk see when they look in the mirror, but are the majority of us really like that? ●

References

Baughman, Fred A. "History of the Fraud of Biological Psychiatry," www.adhd fraud.org, July 19, 2000.

Breggin, Peter. *Toxic Psychiatry: Why Therapy, Empathy, and Love Must Replace the Drugs, Electroshock, and Biochemical Theories of the New Psychiatry.* New York: Prometheus Nemesis, 1994.

Citizens Commission on Human Rights (CCHR). "Psychiatry, Harming in the Name of Health Care," 2002, www.cchr.org/doctors/eng/cchr-harming.htm.

———. "Psychiatry, A Human Rights Abuse and Global Failure," 2000, www.cchr.org/failure/eng/cchr-failure.htm.

———. "Children and Adults with Attention-Deficit/Hyperactivity Disorder (CHADD)—What They Aren't Telling You," 2002.

Lapon, Lenny. *Mass Murderers in White Coats.* Springfield, MA: Psychiatric Genocide Research Institute, 1986.

Szasz, Thomas. *Pharmacracy, Medicine and Politics in America.* New York: Praeger, 2001.

Weber, Mary and Douglas and Sandi Payne. *Open Letter to the Office of the Surgeon General,* www.PetitionOnline.com.

Whitaker, Robert. *Mad in America.* Boston: Perseus, 2001.

Wiseman, Bruce. *Psychiatry: The Ultimate Betrayal.* N.p.: Freedom Publications, 1995.

For more information on the human rights abuses of psychiatry, see Citizens Commission on Human Rights, www.cchr.org.

—Winter 2003

* * *

MIND CONTROL/ THOUGHT CONTROL

* * *

Concentration Campus
Thought Control in American Education

by Robert Guffey

In this article, award-winning science-fiction writer Robert Guffey traces the parallel lineage of compulsory schooling and military entrainment, concluding that thought control in America began when Wilhelm Wundt, the true father of experimental psychology, suggested the abolition of voluntary schooling. The concepts of "licensing" and academic "degrees" in an authoritarian structure were part of Wundt's social engineering, which he believed must start with children. As Guffey explains, fragmentation was part and parcel of this: splitting subjects into disparate specialties as a way to divide and fragment the mind of a child. Without the provision of connections between disparate subjects, Guffey writes, each one became "an island of isolated facts with no ties to the future or the past." And what better way to create islands of time but by the ringing of bells: the logic of schooltime. Guffey asks, "How is it possible to develop a logical train of thought with a bell clattering in your head every forty-five minutes or, for that matter, every seven minutes if you're a hardcore television addict?" Welcome to modern mind control. As Guffey points out, "a commercial interruption carries with it as much of a fragmentary effect as any church bell in the Middle Ages."

HOLES ARE FORMING in the brains of your children. Big Bird is hawking Prozac from inside a colorful box sitting in the center of your living room. Ronald McDonald has become a doctor.

It all began on the battlefield.

In 1995 Lt. Col. Dave Grossman published a revelatory book entitled *On Killing: The Psychological Cost of Learning to Kill in War and Society.* The main point of the book is simple: Left to their natural instincts, soldiers in combat are unlikely to kill. During World War II, for example, only 15 to 25 percent of combat infantry were willing to fire their rifles. By the Persian Gulf War, however, the shooting rate had increased to 95 percent. How did the military manage to raise the firing rate so dramatically within only forty-five years?

In his 1978 book *War on the Mind: The Military Uses and Abuses of Psychology,* Peter Watson revealed the Mengele-like conditioning techniques used by the U.S. Navy to train assassins. A Naval psychiatrist, Commander Dr. Thomas Narut, explained his method as follows: He first exposed his subjects to "symbolic modeling" involving

> films specially designed to show people being killed or injured in violent ways. By being acclimated through these films, the men were supposed to eventually become able to disassociate their emotions from such a situation. The men were taught to shoot but also given a special type of *Clockwork Orange* training to quell any qualms they may have about killing. Men are shown a series of gruesome films, which get progressively more horrific. The trainee is forced to watch by having his head bolted in a clamp so he cannot turn away, and a special device keeps his eyelids open. (Grossman)

As you can see, Stanley Kubrick's cinematic version of these techniques is ass-backwards. In *A Clockwork Orange* the onslaught of violent images sensitized Malcolm McDowell to violence, whereas in the real world these images actually served to *desensitize* Narut's military subjects. Grossman expands on this point:

> In [A] *Clockwork Orange* such conditioning was used to develop an aversion to violence by administering a drug that caused revulsion while the violent films were shown, until the revulsion became associated with acts of violence. In Commander Narut's real-world training the nausea-creating drugs were left out, and those who were able to overcome their natural revulsion were rewarded, thereby obtaining the opposite effect of that depicted in Stanley Kubrick's movie. The U.S. government denies Commander Narut's claims, but Watson claims that he was able to obtain some outside corroboration from an individual who stated that Commander

Narut had ordered violent films from him, and Narut's tale was subsequently published in the London *Times*. (Grossman)

So what does all this have to do with Ronald McDonald and Big Bird and the holes in your kid's brain? Very simple. . . .

Compulsory schooling, as with military entrainment, was born on the battlefield. In 1806, Prussia's army was defeated by Napoleon at the battle of Jena. Prussia believed that its defeat was caused by soldiers *thinking for themselves* in the midst of combat. Far too many soldiers were refusing to fire their weapons. The Prussian government wanted to know how to prevent such pesky inconveniences like "free will" in future generations, so they approached the brilliant psychologist Wilhelm Wundt of the University of Leipzig and asked him for advice. Wundt, the father of experimental psychology, suggested that voluntary schooling be abolished. Wundt recognized that to control a population it was best to begin with children.

Fragmentation was the order of the day. Wundt began by dividing traditional school subjects up into subsets. He shattered them into divisions—not unlike military divisions—precise regiments of lifeless facts marching through the children's porous little minds six hours a day, five days a week: History, English, Mathematics, Biology, Physical Education, etc. It was very important that no connection be made between these disparate subjects. Each was to stand alone, islands of isolated facts with no ties to the future or the past. The best way to ensure this fragmentation was to create *specialties*. Each instructor would be licensed to teach a specific subject, nothing more. If they tried to overstep their bounds they would be severely punished, ostracized from the academic world.[1]

The origins of "licensing" and academic "degrees" grew out of this authoritarian structure. The Ph.D. itself, based on the ideas of Francis Bacon in *The New Atlantis*, was introduced in Prussia in the early 1800s. The concept of "licensing" was later expanded upon by Andrew Carnegie in the steel industry in the United States. The purpose, according to John Taylor Gatto, author of *Dumbing Us Down*, was to "tie the entire economy to schooling and hence to place the minds of all the children [in the hands] of a few social engineers." (Gatto interview)

These social engineers, led by Wundt, knew that fragmentation was the key. Once they had divided the subjects, they then set about dividing the children by segregating them according to age groups. As Gatto has pointed out, this kind of segregation exists nowhere else, certainly not in the adult world. In what office setting do you find all the fifty-five-year-olds working in one room? Before compulsory schooling, in the era of the one-room schoolhouse, the older children were encouraged to teach the younger children. This system is known to work much better than by ordering children to sit back passively and accept like a drone what their "superior" tells them.

Or like a soldier on the battlefield.

Just as a drill sergeant enjoys rattling a broomstick inside a garbage can at four in the morning in order to torture his recruits, the school system has a similar, though far more systematic, instrument of control.

THE BELLS, THE BELLS

How the danger sinks and swells,
By the sinking or the swelling in the anger of the bells
—EDGAR ALLAN POE, "THE BELLS"

Bells are the most basic tool of Pavlovian conditioning. As any freshman psychology student is well aware, Ivan Pavlov was a Russian physiologist known for his breakthrough work with the conditioned reflex. This work consisted of ringing a bell prior to feeding his dogs; he did this regularly over an extended period of time. Eventually the dogs would salivate upon hearing the bell, even when there was no food around.

In the vast laboratory known as public education, however, the experimental subjects—children in this case rather than dogs—are not conditioned to do something as trivial as salivate. No, the goal is far more sinister.

Let John Gatto, "New York State Teacher of the Year" for 1991, tell you in his own words:

I teach children not to care too much about anything, even though they want to make it appear that they do. How I do this is very subtle. I do it by demanding that they become totally involved in my lessons, jumping up and down in their seats with anticipation, competing vigorously with each other for my favor. It's heartwarming when they do that; it impresses everyone, even me. When I'm at my best I plan lessons very carefully in order to produce this show of enthusiasm. But when the bell rings I insist they drop whatever it is we have been doing and proceed quickly to the next work station. They must turn on and off like a light switch. Nothing important is ever finished in my class nor in any class I know of. Students never have a complete experience except on the installment plan.

Indeed, the lesson of bells is that no work is worth finishing, so why care too deeply about anything? Years of bells will condition all but the strongest to a world that can no longer offer important work to do. Bells are the secret logic of schooltime; their logic is inexorable. Bells destroy the past and the future, rendering every interval the same as any other, as the abstraction of a map renders every living mountain and river the same, even though they are not. Bells inoculate each undertaking with indifference. (Gatto, *Dumbing Us Down*)

There is an historical precedent for the use of bells as a Pavlovian conditioner. Bear with me as we launch into another extended quote, this one from none other than Dr. Timothy Leary, whose research into psychedelics as a behavior modification tool was supported and funded by Dr. Henry Murray, chairman of the Department of Social Relations at Harvard and head of the CIA's Psychology Department. Murray was also the man who oversaw the mind-control experiments performed from the years 1958 to 1962 on a young student volunteer at Harvard named Theodore Kaczynski, whom the FBI would later dub the Unabomber (Cockburn). To be fair, it's quite possible Leary's intentions were honorable, but at this late date I'm afraid it's clear that the motives of his financial backers were far from benevolent. Either way, Leary's knowledge of the history of behavioral control is extensive, which makes the following insight that much more impressive:

Over a thousand years ago [there existed] an organization of light-wizards that controlled and programmed minds from Istanbul, Constantinople, and Greece, through southern Europe and northern Europe, all the way up to the British Isles. We're talking, of course, about the hyperdelic, cyberdelic, shamanic brain-fuckers centered in the Vatican. Those guys knew how to program minds.

How'd they do it? Well, first of all, they developed the notion of a bell. If you were a peasant in Constantinople or Romania or France or wherever, the loudest sound you ever heard in your life was that bell five times a day. And where was that bell? On top of the church steeple. And the only sound you ever heard louder and stronger than that was lightning, and you know who's in charge of the lightning bolts. (Leary lecture)

What Leary neglects to mention is the fact that the center for behavior modification shifted in the early 1800s from the Vatican to the arena of public education, which is why Murray was a chairman of Harvard and not the Vatican. If a researcher like Leary had existed a thousand years ago he would have been forced to solicit funds from the Pope rather than the CIA.

In an argument with a friend. I maintained that I had learned absolutely nothing worthwhile in high school. My friend countered with a non sequitur, insisting that kids *need* to graduate from high school in order to get a good job. Despite being a patently false comment (employers tend not to care about your grades in high school or college), it did inspire me to ask the following question: Since when did education devolve into a glorified trade school? It wasn't that way in Plato's day, nor was it that way before Wilhelm Wundt and the implementation of compulsory schooling.

Only while researching this article did I come across the answer. During a 1994 interview conducted by Jim Martin in *Flatland* magazine, John Taylor Gatto brilliantly laid out the following information: Between the years 1807 and 1819, a stream of American dignitaries travelled to Prussia to consult with Dr. Wundt. They were so impressed by his work that they immediately began advocating his system of behavioral control for American education. The sons of the American elite were shipped overseas to study at Wundt's feet, and by 1900 all the Ph.D.s in the U.S. were being trained in Prussia.

Between 1880 and 1910, the American successors to Wundt became the heads of the departments of psychology at all the major universities. Henry Murray was no doubt among them. Wundt's main protégé, James McKeen Cattel, trained 322 Ph.D.s who in turn set up the new discipline of educational psychology; this discipline quickly grew in influence with the help of the Rockefeller and Carnegie foundations. Ultimately, Wundtian experimental psychology gave rise to infamous behavioral scientists, such as James B. Watson and B.F. Skinner, whose work was used for the specific purpose of raising the firing rate in the U.S. military and training assassins to kill more effectively. As Gatto explains:

The next step came when Andrew Carnegie [realized] that capitalism—free enterprise—was stone cold dead in the United States.

Men like himself, Mr. Morgan, and Mr. Rockefeller now owned everything. They owned the government. Competition was impossible unless they allowed it. Carnegie said that this was a very dangerous situation, because eventually young people [would] become aware of this and form clandestine organizations to work against it. . . . Carnegie proposed that men of wealth reestablish a synthetic free enterprise system (since the real one was no longer possible) based on cradle-to-grave schooling. The people who advanced most successfully in the schooling that was available to everyone would be given licenses to lead profitable lives. . . .

[Y]ou need to look at what occurred in the two decades following Carnegie's original proposal (1890–1910). You're talking about the realization of Carnegie's design. These licenses, which now extend to bus drivers and all sorts of people who never had to be licensed, are then tied to forms of schooling. So they've reserved that part of the work market. Through the cooperation of the government, many of the government positions have very precise schooling requirements. You can in fact control all of the economy by tying jobs to schooling, and therefore you have a motivation for people to learn what you want them to learn. (Gatto interview)

CONTROL

Today, at the start of the twenty-first century, a single bell atop a church steeple would no longer be effective as an instrument of control. The population is too large, too spread out. The instrument of fragmentation has become more sophisticated. The controlling toll of the church bell has been replaced by the controlling mainstream entertainment of Hollywood. Why waste valuable time and money surreptitiously planting electrodes in people's brains when you can sell them television sets instead? The CIA's MK-ULTRA program has long been obsolete, which explains the recent explosion of books and movies and magazine articles, and even comic books concerning the subject. As Marshall McLuhan liked to say, quoting James Joyce, "pastimes are past times." Anything that's popular is twenty to thirty years out of date.

Thought control has morphed into mind control, mind control into soul control. No implants required. Just sit back and relax. Take a toke, dude, and trip out on those pixels on your TV screen. Go with the flow. Accept the fragmentation.

How is it possible to develop a logical train of thought with a bell clattering in your head every forty-five minutes, as it does in Kurt Vonnegut's classic science-fiction story "Harrison Bergeron"? Or, for that matter, every *seven* minutes if you're a hardcore television addict? In fact, a commercial interruption carries with it as much of a fragmenting effect as any church bell in the Middle Ages.

All is not lost, however. Wundt was right; the best way to control a population is to begin with the children. But the opposite is true, as well. What was once fragmented can be made whole again. The primary reason kids hate school is obvious: they know, at least subconsciously, that they're being lied to. If you begin to respect them and teach them history undoctored by propaganda, they'll *want* to learn. But that would require a radical alteration, a veritable paradigm shift, in the present system. It would first require the decertification of the teaching process and the destabilization of institutional schools.

"Oh, no!" cries the voice from the audience, "but how will little Johnny learn to read and write?!"

I'm glad you asked me that, ma'am.

You're living under a false assumption if you think the school system teaches reading and writing. As Gatto has pointed out:

> The truth is that reading, writing, and arithmetic only take about one hundred hours to transmit as long as the audience is eager and willing to learn. The trick is to wait until someone asks and then move fast while the mood is on. Millions of people teach themselves these things, it really isn't very hard. Pick up a fifth-grade math or rhetoric textbook from 1850 and you'll see that the texts were pitched then on what would today be considered college level. The continuing cry for "basic skills" practice is a smoke screen behind which schools preempt the time of children for twelve years. (Gatto, *Dumbing Us Down*)

This same point—the relative ease with which children can learn given the right set and setting—was proven over seventy years ago by A.S. Neill, creator of an experimental live-in school called Summerhill. Influenced by the psychoanalytic work of Wilhelm Reich, Neill created a school geared toward helping the "rejects" of the British school system. In the words of investigative journalist Jon Rappoport:

> Neill operated on the idea that if you allowed students and faculty to participate, by vote, in the running of their own school, they would be more real, more alive. And then if you gave students,

with no tricks, the license never to come to classes until they were ready to learn, they would live out their childhood fantasies to the hilt. A child might play in the fields and the mud with his companions until he was fifteen—every day—and then finally school would begin to interest him. At that point he would come to class to stay. At that juncture, twelve years of education might be telescoped into two or three years, without stinting. The classrooms at Summerhill were not remarkable. There was no effort made to "interest" the child in a subject through special aids. Neill forbade this. He saw that when a child wanted to learn, the teaching became easy, and when he didn't the introduction of seduction was a cruel thing. (Rappoport)

A. S. Neill proved beyond a shadow of a doubt that kids learn much more efficiently when you leave them alone. Forget the "concept mapping" (otherwise known as "brainstorming" or "webbing") nonsense so prevalent in education today. That's the big thing in high schools now: forcing complete strangers to bounce ideas off each other until the "gestalt" inevitably reduces the very worst of these ideas into a form acceptable to the status quo. Teachers claim it encourages cooperation, but in reality it just instills conformity. Its sole purpose is to merge our children into a single hive mind consisting of brainless organic robotoids who eat alike, drink alike, sleep alike, and think alike. A regiment of tiny toy soldiers marching into oblivion to the same dissonant tune.

THE SCAN-TRON

The purpose of school is *not* to teach. If you don't believe me, study an average Scan-Tron sheet—or as I like to refer to them, "Scam-Trons." A Scan-Tron is a rectangular blue-and-white slip of paper that is used to grade a student's answers to a series of multiple choice questions, each question having four possible answers. For each answer the student is expected to mark one of four available circles with a No. 2 lead pencil. When the student is finished, the teacher feeds these little slips into a machine that reads the answers. (The machine reads by electrical current, hence the need for a pencil with "lead"—really graphite, which conducts electricity.) With such back-breaking work, one wonders why teachers aren't paid more.[2]

The Scam-Tron is one of the most basic examples of behavioral programming one can find in the school system. Its intent is to instill in the student the idea that there exists only a limited number of answers for any given question—a closed universe of possibilities. I have a close friend who works as a teacher in Seattle. She tells me, and I know this is true from my own experiences at Torrance High about ten years ago, that all the kids prefer taking the multiple choice Scan-Trons. This is, statistically speaking, crazy. It should be obvious that an open-ended, subjective, nonlinear written test in which you have to actually formulate an essay provides you with a much better chance of receiving a good grade. But this doesn't matter to the majority of high school students because they've simply forgotten how to think, if they ever knew in the first place.

My teacher friend in Seattle recently included a question on a test for her students in which she asked them to do nothing more than give an *opinion*. Anything at all, even written semicoherently, would have earned them at least a passing grade. Many of the students chose to leave the question blank. When she asked them why they had done this, they replied matter-of-factly that they couldn't come up with their own opinion.

FRAGMENTATION

This is where NLP comes into the picture. Neuro-linguistics programming was created by Jim Grinder and Richard Bandler in the 1970s, though the basic techniques are related to the work performed from the 1940s to the 1980s by the psychiatrist Dr. Milton W. Erickson, under the close supervision of the CIA (Bowart). Essentially, NLP is the art of mastering the "language of the unconscious" to influence not only yourself but others as well. A baseball player might want to use it to improve his batting average—"creative visualization" could be used for this purpose—while a CIA agent might want to use it to coax vital information from a reluctant source. In the latter case, our hypothetical agent would try to "mirror and match" the source's physiology—sit the way he sits, gesture the way he gestures, breathe the way he breathes. In this way he could win the source's confidence within a surprisingly short period of time. But NLP doesn't rely on only gestures and body language, it also relies a great deal on words—words written or spoken with such precise tonality and timing that they slip into the subconscious as embedded commands.

If you think this is just a bunch of hocus-pocus, keep in mind that in 1983 Major General Albert Stubblebine formed an interagency team called the Jedi Project to disseminate NLP skills throughout the U.S. Army. According to John B. Alexander, a U.S. Army Psy-ops Colonel, even soldiers with no prior experience firing a .45 pistol learned better and more quickly when neuro-linguistics programming was used on them (Mandelbaum). If NLP could enable complete amateurs to fire a standard service sidearm with even middling accuracy, what other effects could it have on human potential—or inhuman potential for that matter?

Walter Bowart, author of *Operation Mind Control* and a NLP practitioner himself, calls neuro-linguistics programming the twentieth century's most important technology of empowerment or enslavement. It can be used to help people—to "influence with integrity"—as with curing a serious phobia within minutes, for example; or it can be used to harm people, to persuade them to purchase an oh-so-unique brand of cigarettes or alcohol or coffee or ketchup or thirty-six-inch television set.

My associate in Seattle has sent me numerous examples of high school exams that were purposely embedded with neuro-linguistics programming techniques. Once you're familiar with these techniques, you can detect them right off the bat. To site one example, a test might consist of a series of sentences and paragraphs that have been spelled incorrectly or have incorrect grammar, the ostensible purpose of which is for the student to correct the mistakes. Anyone familiar with NLP will tell you that this is exactly the wrong way to teach anybody anything. Visualization, suggestion, and *positive* reinforcement are the main tools of learning. Humans don't react well to negative programming—unless, of course, your goal is to teach them negative behavior.

No matter how much money is thrown at local schools, they will not improve, because they're failing on purpose, just like that other ignoble experiment we call the war on drugs. As Bowart notes:

Most students of NLP know that negative phrases can be used as effective embedded commands to produce the opposite effect. Most parents know, when dealing with a young child, to try a little reverse psychology. The "Just Say No" slogan, and the billboards with a photo of a man with a gun up his nose and the slogan "Say No to Cocaine" under it, were just part of the successful psy-ops campaign which got Americans to take more drugs. It's well-known by now that the war on drugs is a complete failure. The extent to which the cryptocracy's black funds depends upon the drug trade is also widely noted. George Bush gave the game away, many believe, during one of his televised debates with Clinton when he wiped his nose in an involuntary response after he said the word "cocaine."

I would add that George W. Bush demonstrated the same involuntary "sniffing" reactions all throughout his debates with Al Gore. Under the new, improved Bush administration I predict that an unprecedented amount of money will be spent on the war on drugs and the results will be just as effective as the war on cancer and the war on domestic violence and the war on guns and the war on illiteracy and the war on terrorism. There hasn't been a more strategically fought conflict since *The Mouse That Roared*.

THE STRATEGY OF TENSION

Yes, the strategy of tension is about to get a lot more tense.

Of course, such tension serves the cryptocracy well. Mae Brussell, the late political researcher and talk show host, recognized this fact in the 1960s while investigating the Kennedy assassinations, realizing that most of the crazed "lone nuts" of that tumultuous decade arose from the same intelligence milieu: Lee Harvey Oswald, Jack Ruby, Albert DiSalvo, Sirhan Sirhan, the SLA, Charles Manson, the Zodiac, Jim Jones, Ted Kaczinski. Authoritarian regimes thrive amidst chaos like this. The populace just rolls over and allows any dingbat with a wealthy father, a charming smile, and a balled-up fist to waltz into a position of power and protect them from the creeping chaos. "Only a return to the values of the past can save us!" Unfortunately, the values of the past are the values of now. The modern day equivalent of the MK-ULTRA chaos investigated by Brussell is the rash of school shootings sweeping the country in the past few years, Columbine being the most destructive of all.

Which leads me to a revealing comment made by Dr. John Hagelin, a university professor and quantum physicist who ran for president on an independent ticket in 2000. At the State of the World Forum held in San Francisco in October 1999, Hagelin delivered a speech in which he discussed the school shootings. He identified a disturbing common denominator that tied the shootings together. According to Hagelin, many of the "lone nut" teenagers responsible for these shootings were suffering from a brain dysfunction that tends to resemble a "hole" in the brain when seen in CAT scans. These children don't have literal "holes" in their heads, of course, merely dark spots where the neurons have ceased firing. The brain centers most affected are those in charge of emotional control and decision-making; they've literally atrophied due to lack of use. Doctors who have studied this phenomenon refer to it as "cortical fragmentation." Hagelin believes that this dysfunction is directly caused by the process of *education* itself.

Do you begin to see the connections now? Has it become clear to you yet?

FRAGMENTATION IS THE KEY

Pause a moment and wrap your mind around this: The process we are currently engaged in is known as in-depth pattern recognition. Skeptics would call it "conspiracy theory." But what is conspiracy theory if not the ability to pick out patterns, like Edgar Allan Poe's resourceful fisherman who is able to free himself from a whirlpool by noticing which pieces of wreckage are ejected from the maelstrom and attaching himself to one of them? The point of Poe's classic story "A Descent into the Maelstrom" is clear. You *must* study the debris. Don't turn your eyes away from it just because it isn't pretty, or because it doesn't seem relevant to you at the moment.

What doesn't seem relevant now may save your life in the future. But most people have no ability even to begin comprehending the complicated process of in-depth pattern recognition. You can't blame them. They've been systematically conditioned to *not* see the patterns affecting their lives due to twelve years of constant fragmentation. They're caught in a maelstrom they don't even know exists, a maelstrom imposed upon them by a vast array of authority figures, beginning with their parents and continuing on up to their elected officials and clergymen and bosses and doctors and drill sergeants and teachers. And advertisers. Lately, however, it's been very difficult to tell the difference between those last two.

IN-SCHOOL MARKETING

Instruments of operant conditioning are being introduced day by day into the school environment on an ever-increasing basis. These instruments include surreptitious advertisements, pharmaceuticals, and toxic junk food smuggled onto the campuses by corporate underwriters. In September 2000 the U.S. General Accounting Office released a significant report entitled "Commercial Activities in Schools," which states:

> In-school marketing has become a growing industry. Some marketing professionals are increasingly targeting children in school, companies are becoming known for their success in negotiating

contracts between school districts and beverage companies, and both educators and corporate managers are attending conferences on how to increase revenue from in-school marketing for their schools and companies.

In the past few years high schools have become nothing more than laboratories for corporate-backed market researchers. Pfizer hands out highly-addictive stimulants like candy, causing six million normal children to become speed freaks for the express purpose of reinforcing our belief in a nonexistent disease some social engineer decided to call Attention Deficit Disorder. Microsoft and Toshiba "graciously" donate computers outfitted with the appropriately named "Zap Me" Internet portal that bombards students with a constant stream of advertisements for its own products, while also collecting data on the web-browsing habits of children. Recently, market researchers went so far as to pass out disposable cameras and twenty-page booklets to elementary school students and requested they document their lives in both photographs and words so the researchers could better understand "what sparks kids these days." The booklets were titled *My All About Me Journal.* An "educational cable TV channel" named Noggin paid one school in New Jersey $7,500 for the privilege of butting into the students' lives.

According to Amy Goodman of Pacifica Radio's *Democracy Now*, even *Sesame Street* has gotten into the act. The show that brought us Big Bird and Kermit the Frog now hawks pharmaceuticals to kids. Traditionally, *Sesame Street* would end with an announcement that the episode had been sponsored by, for example, the letter P and the number 2. These days, however, you might hear instead, Eli Lily brings parents the letter P for Prozac, over the images of a parrot and children playing with a big toy letter block, essentially a fifteen-second commercial for an antidepressant manufactured by Eli Lily. PBS chooses to call these segments "enhanced underwrited account announcements" rather than "commercials." (*Democracy Now*)

PBS, like the Democratic Party, is nothing more than controlled opposition—a pseudo-alternative for what the Stanford Research Institute likes to call "Societally Conscious Achievers," conformist consumers who need to believe they're actually nonconformists before they can, "in good conscience," part with their money (Meyer).

Advertisers and politicians know this and purposely cloak their true intent behind a façade of being societally conscious. McDonalds, for example, established Ronald McDonald House to help children with cancer, a disease perhaps contracted from their own McToad burgers. Vice-President Al Gore—who, by the way, studied neuro-linguistics programming under none other than Col. John Alexander back in 1983 (Bowart)—professes to be an environmentalist, but he does not mention the fact that he's as much of an oil man as George W. Bush.

In the September 25, 2000, edition of the *Los Angeles Times*, Michael O'Hanlon reported that:

> Most tellingly, the budget proposals of [George W. Bush and Al Gore] differ by less than 2 percent. Remarkably, for perhaps the first time since the 1960s, it is the Democratic candidate who proposes spending more on the country's defense. Gore proposes allocating $100 billion of the ten-year surplus, or about $10 billion per year, to the armed forces. Bush's budget plan would provide the Pentagon about half as large a real dollar increase. Either way, defense spending would remain about $300 billion a year. That is as much as the world's next ten military powers spend in aggregate.

Bush's and Gore's budgets differed by less than 2 percent. What, then, were those two idiots debating about on television? Answer: nothing. They don't need to debate anything, just so long as they keep their lips moving. The content of the media doesn't matter. Marshall McLuhan was the first to point this out in *Understanding Media*, and it's a good bet that the powers that be are well aware of this. There's a reason why the NSA regularly consults McLuhan's book *The Laws of Media*, and uses his theory of the "Tetrad" to manage world affairs (Dobbs). The future of humanity can be predicted by studying the future of its technology. Control technology and you control humanity.

When Tipper Gore and Senator Joseph Lieberman complain about the Hollywood film industry—the very same industry that provided a significant chunk of the financial backing for the Gore/Lieberman presidential campaign—you never hear them mention the fact that the very same ultraviolent virtual reality video games that so offend their delicate sensibilities were specifically created by DARPA (the Defense Advanced Research Projects Agency) to entrain American soldiers to kill on the battlefield without hesitation (Steinberg).

The reason you won't hear Lieberman bring up that particular tasty tidbit is simple: He's as much of a hawk as Dick Cheney or George W. Bush. As he's so proudly stated on more than one occasion during the 2000 campaign, Lieberman was the first Democrat to express his support for the Persian Gulf War on the floor of the Senate. Progressives should be happy that Bush stole the election from Gore. It's better to know the killers are coming rather than open the gates for a Trojan Horse. Remember, in a dictatorship you have only one choice, in a democracy you have two choices, and in a cryptocracy you have one choice disguised as two.

The ultimate point is this: The techniques of modern day public education were specifically created, via behaviorist entrainment and Ericksonian negative neuro-linguistics programming, to discourage nonlinear thinking among our nation's school children and encourage fragmentation.

The fragmentation is all around us. Our most brilliant theoretical physicists have been submerged in unprovable claims for a hundred years, wading through a sea of elementary particles in search of the ultimate irreducible integer of matter. Our major political institutions, bickering amongst themselves, are incapable of even stealing an election properly anymore (things certainly have decayed since Kennedy's day). That nice old lady over there, your kid's second-grade schoolteacher, whose body cells are now dividing uncontrollably from years of cigarettes sold to her forty years earlier, thanks to a bombardment of television, radio, and magazine ads in that long-lost golden era when the *Journal of the American Medical Association* claimed smoking was actually good for women. And that kid standing in front of you right now, the cute one with the hole in his brain and the gun in his hand—he's pointing it directly at your face. His finger is tightening on the trigger. Do you recognize that emotionless look in his eyes? You should. After all, he's your son.

Think fast, daddy. ●

Notes

1. This process continues in modern times. Witness the harassment suffered by Wilhelm Reich, a psychologist, when he dared to enter the field of biology; or the similar treatment showered upon Immanuel Velikovsky, a physician, when he dared to propose a new theory of planetary evolution.

2. In high school I knew a guy named Bill who would coat the edge of the sheet with Vaseline. The Vaseline had some kind of mirror-like effect and would screw up the laser, causing the machine to interpret all of his answers as correct. Eventually he grew more clever and dabbed the Vaseline on only *some* of the answers, so the results would be more believable. Word to the unwise.

Special thanks to Randy Koppang for his invaluable research assistance.

References

Bowart, Walter. *Operation Mind Control*. Ft. Bragg, NC: Flatland Editions, 1994.

Cockburn, Alexander. "We're Reaping Tragic Legacy From Drugs." www.latimes. com [July 6, 1999].

Democracy Now, Pacifica Radio KPFK, Los Angeles, September 18, 2000.

Dobbs, Robert. Dave Porter interview. *Genesis of a Music*, Pacifica Radio KPFK, Los Angeles, September 24, 1994.

Gatto, John Taylor. *Dumbing Us Down*. Gabriola Island, BC, Canada: New Society Publishers, 1992.

———. Jim Martin Interview. *Flatland* 11 (1994).

Grossman, Lt. Col. Dave. *On Killing: The Psychological Cost of Learning to Kill in War and Society*. Boston: Little, Brown, 1995.

Hagelin, John. Lecture delivered at State of the World Forum, San Francisco, October 1999.

Leary, Timothy. Lecture delivered at Millenium Madness Conference, Los Angeles, May 29, 1993.

Mandelbaum, W. Adam. *The Psychic Battlefield: A History of the Military-Occult Complex*. New York: St. Martin's Press, 2000.

McLuhan, Marshall, and Wilfred Wilson. *From Cliché to Archetype*. Viking Press, 1970.

Meyers, William. *The Image Makers*. New York: Times Books, 1984.

Rappoport, Jon. *The Secret Behind Secret Societies*. San Diego: Truth Seeker Books, 1998. www.truthseeker.com.

Steinberg, Jeffrey. "The Creation of the 'Littleton' Culture." *The New Federalist*, August 30, 1999.

—Winter 2001

The Third Reich of Dreams

Charlotte Beradt's Diaries of the Night

by Frank Berube

In her book The Third Reich of Dreams, *Charlotte Beradt collected dreams that centered on the everyday political realities of prewar Germany. Published in 1966, it provides a glimpse of the subconscious messages and warning signs of the emerging totalitarian state. In this poignant article, Frank Berube describes in chilling detail some of the dreams of a dehumanized and terrified populace as the German subconscious mind was invaded by totalitarian fear. These dreams are described as parables of the subconscious mind. As Berube explains, "Something within us is registering these disturbing vibrations and sending out signals of danger to the frightened conscious mind." Beradt described how people, dreaming these diaries of the night, were able "to recognize the aims and principles of totalitarianism and foresee their consequences, so that their dreams ring prophetic in retrospect."*

"Lose your dreams and you will lose your mind."
—"RUBY TUESDAY," THE ROLLING STONES

DURING THE 1930S, Nazi Germany's rise to totalitarian power was well under way. Warning signs of the terror to come were being felt by increasing numbers of people. Among them was a young woman of great courage and insight, Charlotte Beradt. In her book, *The Third Reich of Dreams*, she recorded people's dreams about the Nazi government's domination of their lives—dreams which tell of the painful political realities of the emerging Nazi state. In an essay at the conclusion of the volume, which was published in 1966, Bruno Bettelheim described what a shocking experience it was to read this book of dreams and see how effectively the Nazis murdered sleep, "forcing [their] enemies to dream dreams that showed that resistance was impossible and that safety lay only in compliance."

The following was dreamed by a man who lived in Berlin during the early years of Nazi rule. It demonstrates the potential of our dream worlds to produce stories that reflect the psycho-political conditions under which we live. Something within us registers these disturbing vibrations and sends out signals of danger to the frightened conscious mind. The dreamer in this story is describing not only how one comes to accept conditions as they are, but also the state of mind in which such acceptance grows. This consists of a readiness to be deceived and a tendency to construct alibis for oneself. Once conditioned long enough by the right combination of pressure and propaganda, one becomes so receptive and malleable that all will to resist disappears.

In the dream, the man was told by Nazi authorities to report to the Berlin railway station on a Sunday morning to collect money for the Party. Before leaving he said to himself, "What the heck, I won't be bothered." So he brought along a pillow and blanket—no collection box—and took it easy. After about an hour Hitler appeared, wearing high patent-leather boots, dressed as a comical cross between a circus clown and a lion tamer. The dreamer watched Hitler use exaggerated, artificial gestures to win the hearts of schoolchildren. Then he adopted a stern attitude as he lectured a group of older boys and girls. At last, he turned coquettish to impress a group of old maids. Suddenly, the dreamer began to feel uncomfortable under his blanket. He grew afraid that Hitler would notice that he had no collection box—he might be recognized as one of "the group of those who pretend to sleep." If caught, he imagined confronting Hitler and telling him that he doesn't approve of concentration camps.

As the dream went on, Hitler continued his appearances around the station, interacting with different groups of people, and the dreamer was amazed to see that no one seemed to be afraid of him. He noticed that someone even kept a cigarette in his mouth while talking with him, and many more were smiling! After completing his stint at the station, the dreamer picked up his pillow and blanket and went down the main stairway in the station.

Then the dreamer saw Hitler standing at the top of the stairs, concluding his appearance with a song from an imaginary opera called "Magica," mesmerizing the crowd with extremely theatrical gestures. Everybody applauded. He bowed and then went tearing down the stairs, looking foolish in his purple trousers and holding his trainer's whip. Hitler passed by with no bodyguards and stood in line at the cloakroom like everyone else, waiting patiently to get his coat. At this point, the dreamer thought, "Maybe he's not so bad after all. Maybe I needn't take the trouble to oppose him." All at once, the dreamer realized that instead of carrying a pillow and blanket, he was carrying a collection box.

This dreamer sees Hitler as a manipulator par excellence—an animal trainer—and yet the big act that Hitler puts on works in the end: The dreamer begins to feel that things are not half bad and maybe he doesn't have to worry about Hitler after all. Likewise, in the novel *1984*, Winston Smith, sipping his Victory Gin with tears of gratitude in his eyes, reached a similar conclusion about Big Brother, although he got there by a different route.

The average person struggling with his or her conscience in the face of dehumanizing conditions, is, like Orwell's hero, "neither good nor bad, up against the effects of a political system which in the end leaves open but one direction in which he can move—the one toward the movement." Individuals are embedded in a repressive psycho-political system, unable to act independently or resist the forces that are propelling the motion of society in the direction of Nazi domination.

The Third Reich of Dreams tells a compelling and revealing story about the hidden side of World War II. It portrays how the German subconscious mind was invaded by totalitarian fear as the Nazi's plans reached fever pitch during the 1930s. Hitler and his evil cadre, the rise to power of the Nazi Party and the mobilization of the country for total war were all carried out with cold-blooded determination and ruthless precision by human beings whose very souls had been violated and whose minds were controlled.

Beradt collected hundreds of dreams from 1933 through 1939, referring to them as "diaries of the night." The dreams, drawn from the lives of ordinary people who found themselves confronting the terror of the Third Reich, provided a view into the inner world of fear and confusion people were feeling as their personal integrity disintegrated and their lives fell apart. They show that this was a war on the human spirit. It was secretly about capturing inner ground and blowing apart the national psyche: destroying the progress gained over centuries of psycho-spiritual development, doing away with a whole generation of artists, writers, and scientists, and burying the work of these creative people beneath the rubble and ruin of total war.

As American citizens, we should have learned from Nazi Germany that psychologically terrified people can be pressured into giving up their democratic rights and living in a police state, once political power has been stolen from them and their lives have been turned upside down. We now know that Nazi propaganda was bolstered with psychotronic technology that fostered an atmosphere of psycho-political terror, desensitized feelings, and thought control. We have to remember that for more than a decade the frightened minds of average German citizens were unable or unwilling to resist the insane domination of Nazism, and so could not, or would not, question authority. Horrifying things were happening and were beyond anyone's control, so the public was swept along by overpowering Nazi propaganda and terror, too fearful to object to the abuse of power, or to do anything about the atrocities carried out against Jews and Communists, or others who threatened to undermine the Third Reich.

The Nazis imprisoned and executed people whom they considered subhuman, and those considered enemies of the state. How they got the public to accept this, however tenuous their consent, is something not entirely explainable or understandable by simply saying that Hitler "hypnotized" the masses. How can human beings stand by and allow their government to enslave and kill people in such a brutal manner, or find an acceptable justification for it?

Such inhuman behavior cannot be explained merely in terms of people being numbed into apathy for the fate of their fellow humans, or allowing themselves to be herded into the mass hysteria of a faceless mob. We must look beyond the explanation of nationalistic frenzy for the causes of this herd mentality. Racism and ideology go only so far in explaining the soul-boggling horror involved in their participation in mass slaughter. Concepts of patriotism and blood were the "front men" for the Nazi state and provided a vessel into which poured the forces of the collective unconscious.

THE MENTAL STATUS QUO (MSQ)

It's because of the work of renegade researchers and writers like Charlotte Beradt that we are able to see beyond the conventional historical perspective and open our minds to reviewing controversial material. This allows us to understand, however vaguely, the underground forces and occult underpinnings of the Third Reich. Propaganda and state terror carried the population along on a wave of hysteria, with millions obeying the rules and regulations of the Nazi mental status quo (MSQ). Yet, Beradt writes, "from the very beginning people from all walks of life and in all their fear and anxiety were able, while dreaming, to recognize the aims and principles of totalitarianism and foresee their consequences, so that their dreams ring prophetic in retrospect."

Now, sixty years later in the United States, the technology of mass mind control is vastly improved and is deadly in its effectiveness. Consequently, the population of the United States is in a worse situation in terms of being forced into mental slavery than were the inhabitants of Germany, Italy, or Russia earlier in the century. American citizens are facing the 1990s form of totalitarian fear, and just as the German people thought sixty years ago, believe that it could never happen here. But it's clear by now that the vast majority of Americans still do not possess an adequate understanding of how their minds work, nor are many citizens any closer to comprehending how the national psyche is being manipulated. In short, we're unable to come to terms with the fact that our subconscious minds are being controlled.

Only century-spanning, transgenerational, psychic genocide can account for the subjugation of the mind that made possible the appalling events of the twentieth century. Mass mind control technology has made leaps and bounds of progress over the past half-century, and has succeeded in keeping millions of people bound to lower levels of consciousness and a self-absorbed existence. Our minds are sinking into the paralyzing stupor of the MSQ, while our freedom slips away from us and we come closer to facing the apocalyptic abyss that the German people faced a half-century ago.

There are many inexplicable things about our volatile century that beg understanding, and that are, more often than not, without answers, or end up producing more questions. Nothing can be fully understood without knowing oneself within. Our inner world is much bigger than we imagine, as our dreams allow us to see. There is a hyper-dimensional world of vast inner space within your mind that is beyond the reach of the senses, accessible only by transcendent means. This hidden inner world exists beyond the perceptual horizon of the MSQ—it is the undiscovered realm of the deep psyche where our dreams originate.

Unknown to the programmed mind, your awakened perception has access to other dimensions beyond the brain and the senses, and hidden somewhere in that vast uncharted territory is your inner self, your true self. But ego-bound people are afraid that if they sail too far beyond the perceptual horizon of the MSQ, they'll fall off into an inner abyss, like the ships of the "flat earth" that sailed beyond the horizon plunged over the edge into bottomless space.

During earlier centuries, people from Europe knew nothing of the existence of the continent that would become known as America. These days we're prevented from exploring higher states of consciousness and discovering our true selves by an ocean of unconsciousness that isolates us on an inner island, limiting our perceptual horizons within a short ego range. There are still too many people in this world who are unaware these other dimensions of consciousness are part of our inner geography.

As citizens of America we can already see ourselves losing our right to privacy, and we have to retreat further and further away from society in order to escape from the ubiquitous intrusions of the media and other silent invasions of our psyche. Soon there will be nowhere to hide and no privacy for anyone, and we will be facing the horrible political conditions faced by the citizens of Germany during the 1930s and 40s, as their world fell apart around them, a scary situation illustrated by the following dream.

In 1934, a forty-five-year old doctor dreamed that he was relaxing on the couch reading a book after his consultations, when suddenly the walls of his apartment disappeared. He looked around and saw, to his horror, that all the other apartments in his building didn't have walls either. Then he heard a loudspeaker boom, "According to the decree of the 17th of this month on the Abolition of Walls . . ."

Some time later, the doctor realized what had provoked the dream. His block warden had come around to ask him why he had not hung a flag at his window. Putting him off, he thought, "Not in my four walls." In another dream, the doctor found that the only real escape from "life without walls" was to withdraw from the public realm, because those who give in and go along become part of the Nazi scene. They must surrender their autonomy and conform to whatever mental and social conditions are required of them. In his dream, he wrote, "Now that no home is private anymore, I'm living at the bottom of the sea."

THE NAZI MSQ

Conforming to the Nazi MSQ means going along with a set of rules for inner behavior (which is thought control)—and conforming to political conditions means doing what the authorities say—(which is social control). As a result of having to deal with the rules and regulations of the Nazi regime, people were coerced into maintaining the MSQ: a state-approved way of thinking and behaving that came to be known and practiced by everyone. To say or do otherwise meant putting your life in danger.

The Nazi mentality provided the mind with the linguistic rules and regulations of the German MSQ, which enabled its citizens to think and speak in standard terms. This manufactured mindset channeled thought and conversation in the direction of conformity, and accounted for the underlying set of beliefs that made up the dogma of the Third Reich, a state-sanctioned view of reality.

In 1933, a 30-year old woman, liberal-minded, pampered, and with no profession, had the following dream. Street signs had been abolished and posters were set up in their place on every corner, proclaiming the twenty words people were not allowed to say. The words on the posters were listed in English; the first was "Lord," the last was "I," and the rest were unclear. This dream anticipates the radical restrictions on freedom of expression about matters relating to one's identity and beliefs that totalitarian regimes have exploited during the twentieth century. In the dream, the posters had been substituted for the prohibited street signs, conveying the idea that people had lost their direction, were looking for signposts in their lives, and were finding that they couldn't speak about God or reflect on who they were. The dream is a parable that illustrates "the dialectical relationship that exists between the individual and the dictatorship."

THE UNTOLD STORY OF THE UNCONSCIOUS MIND

"What if something should go wrong with the psyche?" asked psychologist Carl Jung more than thirty years ago. Jung was a cartographer of inner space, and provided humanity with maps and charts of the lost realms of the deep psyche. Without the knowledge and inspiration of Jung and other pioneering psychologists, we would still be crawling around in the dark of the mind, classifying altered states of consciousness in religious terms, and dumping any kind of transcendent experience into the psychotic and delusional category.

Telling the story of the unconscious mind is difficult because it's not so easy to put into words. All the words that could be useful have been taken over by the authorities and corrupted to the core. The reason we find it so difficult to think clearly or speak coherently about the hanky-panky going on in the unconscious mind is because most of the terms used to describe renegade states of consciousness have been stripped of their original meaning and painted over with a glossy sheen. Dictionaries and encyclopedias give descriptions of altered states of consciousness and nonsensory dimensions of the mind like they were psychotic episodes to be neuro-chemically controlled or rendered inactive by psycho-surgery.

It's useless to depend on words when they have so little power over the shackled thoughts of the mentally enslaved, who wouldn't dream of leaving the prison even if they had the keys to unlock their cells. We've been so dumbed-down that these alien ideas are full of verbal booby traps, and the terms used to describe our inner world as natural and sacred have lost their ability to inspire and guide us. Now we have no structure of thought upon which to build an understanding of our inner selves.

Controlling thought in this way reduces the threat that the mind might be led astray by renegade thinking. Perhaps people will discover the inner curtain and pull it aside, expose the shady dealings of the subconscious mind, and put an end to the long-running ego drama. Inner explorers who want to throw light on the darker side are forced to use matches to illuminate the way, because orthodox religion, behavioral psychology, and materialistic science are drawing most of the illumination from these concepts through their domination of consensus reality and control of language. You can't talk about mind control, you can't talk about a secret government, you can't talk about hyper-dimensional realities, you can't talk about hidden history, you can't talk about the age-long story of the fight for the human Spirit. You can't so much as whisper the naked truth that there exists a portion of our mind that we can't understand. Whatever is enforcing rampant unconsciousness in modern humans must be very powerful, because it will not allow any self-reflection or renegade knowledge to threaten its subliminal authority and challenge its hold on the conscious mind.

THE GUILT OF THE GUILTLESS

The woman who dreamed about the twenty words that couldn't be spoken considered herself to be quite self-centered, yet her dreams reflect a deep understanding of what was at stake if one surrendered one's mind to the Nazis. Her series of dreams occurred between April and September 1933. Not long after her dream about God and self, she dreamed that she was all dressed up, sitting in a box at an opera house with several tiers, being admired by many people as she watched her favorite opera, *The Magic Flute*. When the line, "This is the devil certainly" was sung, some policemen came stomping in and told her that a machine had registered that she thought about Hitler when she heard the word "devil." She looked imploringly to the crowd for some sign of help, but they all ignored her. She glanced over to the old gentleman in the adjoining box trying to catch his eye, but he turned and spit at her.

This dream manages to capture the way so-called respectable people behave when they're called upon to respond to unfairness and injustice in their midst. The opera house with its levels of curved tiers is filled with people who do nothing but stare straight ahead when someone who they could help is in trouble. Later, the woman described the thought-control machine in her dream as being electric with a maze of wires, envisioning remote-control devices and other electronic methods of monitoring and control that were coming into use during the 1930s and '40s.

One night, after being deeply disturbed by radio reports about book burnings, in which the words "truckloads" and "bonfires" were used repeatedly, the same woman dreamed that all books were being collected and burned. Not wanting to part with the copy of Schiller's *Don Carlos* that she had since her schooldays, she hid it under the maid's bed. When stormtroopers arrived to take away the books, they marched straight to the maid's room, pulled the book out from under the bed, and threw it on the truck. At this point she discovered that she had hidden an atlas and not her copy of *Don Carlos*.

When we dream, psychological mechanisms censor our unconscious motives by distorting them, preventing us from fully realizing that which we do not wish to know. If people are subjected to extraordinary conditions of control caused by political repression, their dream content will be distorted. One explanation is that the mind is attempting to alter the circumstances that lead to surrendering control of our lives. Because of this self-censorship, many dream scenarios that deal with themes of submission and complicity have bizarre overtones, perhaps in an attempt to change the character of threatening thoughts before they manifest themselves in dreams.

In the same woman's next dream, the milkman, gas man, news vendor, baker, and plumber are standing around her in a circle, holding out their bills. This did not upset her until she noticed a chimney sweep among them. The two *S*'s in the German word for chimney sweep, *schornstein-*

feger, along with his black outfit, made him appear like a threatening member of the Gestapo. The situation reminded her of the German children's game, *Schwarze Kochin*, in which people hold out their bills with arms uplifted in the same gesture, chanting, "Your guilt cannot be doubted." What had provoked the dream? The day before, her tailor's son showed up, wearing the uniform of a storm trooper, to collect the bill she owed his father. She was outraged because, before Hitler, it had been customary to send the bill through the mail, and she demanded an explanation for a government official collecting the money. The embarrassed young man replied that it had no special significance, he just happened to be in the neighborhood and wearing his uniform when he stopped by. "That's ridiculous," she said, but paid the bill anyway.

The woman was aware of how the newly established block warden system functioned and how intrusions were sanctioned by the Party uniform. Her dream indicates that she felt guilty about yielding to slight pressure and settling the account. It was a minor sin of omission, but a significant one, if it had led to more grievous abdications and lapses, "barely recognizable injustices" which might build up, producing a repressed state of mind that is hard to describe. "The guilt of the guiltless" comes from the accumulation of these tiny abdications, which are hidden away in the subconscious until they show up disguised in dreams.

THE LANGUAGE OF CONSCIOUSNESS

It's simply not possible to think about and discuss matters of importance, such as the survival of the life of the mind and the preservation of our democratic rights, if the terms and concepts used to describe psychospiritual freedom have had their original meaning squeezed out of them. Today, we cannot speak of threats to our inner freedom, because terms like mind control, secret government, conspiracy theory, the unconscious, paranoia, hidden history have negative connotations attached to them and deflect the mind away from investigation and study.

It's an academic given that all these subjects are not to be taken seriously. The inner world beyond the borders of the MSQ appears incomprehensible to people who have never experienced other dimensions of their psyche. But there is no question that an unconscious realm of the human psyche exists. Its psychological conquest and subliminal colonization has been the deepest darkest secret of the twentieth century.

Controlling our thoughts by controlling language keeps them safely within the bounds of the MSQ. Unable to seriously address things like psychotronic warfare and a global cryptocracy is a good example of language controlling thought, because if you speak of these things you'll be classified as a "conspiracy theorist," or you'll be thought of as downright crazy by members in good standing of the MSQ club.

The same dreamer had several dreams that repeatedly dealt with the new environmental conditions of total control. Her dreams pictured her neighbors sitting in a large circle around her, silent and expressionless, leaving her feeling progressively more alone in each one. Finally, one dream says it all by containing no images, only words: "Am going to bury myself in lead. Tongue is already leaden, locked in lead. Will lie immobile, shot full of lead. When they come, I'll say, 'The leaden cannot rise up.' Oh! They want to throw me in the water because I'm so leaden."

The woman had this dream on New Year's Eve, 1933, after the custom of pouring molten lead. Like the doctor's dream of seeking refuge at the bottom of the sea, she wished to become buried in lead, wanting to completely withdraw from the public realm and hide from herself in the process. These dream fables are a warning of the insidious mental intrusions that were gradually taking over the consciousness of the people, interfering with their relationships with their inner selves.

The profusion of prohibitive regulations, along with the steady control of the population, placed increasing pressure on people's lives. It wore down their will and tore away their defenses, leaving many people compliant slaves at the feet of their mental masters in only a few short years. Yet, while this may have been taking place imperceptibly, so that people became gradually accustomed to the takeover of their minds, their dreams were showing this process taking place quite clearly. All the small steps it took to get to a groveling position can be seen in their dreams. If one reflected on such dreams and discerned their wisdom, perhaps people wouldn't allow themselves to become disconnected from their inner selves, which is why even dreamland is invaded by "the gestapo."

THE MSQ RENEGADES

The Nazis' intrusive regulation of people's lives drove some people to death and others into denial. If they had no way to deal with these forces of coercion and repression, the only thing they could do is surrender to the authorities and submit their lives to the will of the Nazis. But some people felt they must attempt to resist these insidious intrusions by performing simple acts of defiance. Such everyday refusals to take part in the ritual destruction of human dignity show the human spirit surviving in the midst of dehumanization. These were the freethinkers whom the Nazis feared the most, because they had discovered their inner power. They were more threatening to the stability of the Nazi state than all their other enemies combined.

The following was dreamed by a student whose brother had been arrested. The arrest had caused considerable strain on him. In the dream, there was a party going on in a large building. In a small attic room, a group of people had gathered, all of whom could be arrested for political crimes against the Nazi regime, among them degenerate artists and performers, one-time socialists, and relatives of concentration camp inmates. They were joking and making fun of the well-dressed guests arriving downstairs.

The dreamer crept downstairs and overheard someone remark that the whole house was filled with tension, and that the stairs to the attic had caught fire as a result. "The suspects have to be saved," the dreamer yelled into the bedlam. The well-dressed guests only shrugged, saying, "Why shouldn't the suspects go up in flames?" In short, everyone is a potential enemy of the state, lumping together internee and relative, artist and friend, activist and employer, into the single category of "suspect."

The following dream, which occurred in the autumn of 1933, was dreamed by an elderly woman who was a mathematics teacher. In her dream, it was forbidden under penalty of death to write anything having to do with mathematics. This woman took refuge in a night club, which in waking life she would never have set foot in. The place was filled with drunkards and prostitutes and the music was blaring. She took a piece of tissue paper from her pocketbook and wrote down a couple of equations in invisible ink, all the time frightened to death.

Her dream reflects how absurd it is to attempt to ban something that people do naturally every day. When asked to comment on her dream, she replied simply, "It is impossible to forbid what they are forbidding here!" In the dream, she chose a night club to perform her act of defiance, a place no one would expect to find her, and where other forbidden things are going on.

Sitting at a table in the dimly lit club, she worked with the tools of spies to copy the equations that would ensure that her profession survived the destructive forces set against it. As the environment was being transformed by the machinations of the Nazis, people were becoming alienated from one another and disconnected from the activities that made up their daily lives. Individuals were being taken away from their communities and being turned into obedient servants of the Reich. Yet, there are always the defiant ones who resist becoming dehumanized, who keep alive within themselves the flame of the individual human spirit.

THE AMERICAN MSQ

As George Orwell warned in *1984*, once you take over the language, there is thought control, and then it becomes impossible to think for oneself or question authority. We need a viable language that relates to secret dimensions of consciousness and hidden aspects of history. In a mathematical way, physics was confronted by the same problem earlier in the century, when its formulas and equations ran up against hyper-dimensional phenomena it couldn't explain with current theories. There had to be a bigger picture to what was happening, and relativity and quantum theories provided that greater perspective.

Our media-saturated minds are being anesthetized with overdoses of "doublethink" and overflowing mouthfuls of "newspeak." Our beleaguered brains are being subliminally and vibrationally assaulted every day, to the point of dangerous psychic depletion and extreme spiritual vulnerability. New dimensions of language are needed to orient our minds to hyper-dimensional realities and to provide a linguistic structure for renegade ideas. The transcendent dimensions of language that address the inner life of the mind continue to remain inaccessible to most of us. There are powerful occult forces keeping people unconscious, so it may be expecting too much to think that we could overcome our intense fear of waking up to transcendent dimensions.

With the New World Order closing in fast, our language needs to undergo a corresponding revolution, as the written word attempts to define and conceptualize other dimensions of reality beyond the range of the MSQ—the prevailing consensus reality. There is no other way to approach this perceptual transformation of our minds—the power of words—freely thought, spoken and written. Our psycho-spiritual freedom depends upon it.

THE UPRAISED ARM

During the 1980s and '90s, American citizens lost, and have continued to lose, more individual political power and rights through the encroachment of frightening federal laws. Many are waking up to what's going on behind our backs, or beyond our comprehension. People today are con-fronting the same fear of unknown forces that the German people were facing during the 1930s, and the subconscious minds of individuals are registering the steady erosion of freedom and its debilitating effects. As the New World Order closes in fast, perhaps people in the United States are dreaming similar dreams.

Three days after Hitler seized power in Germany, Herr S., a sixty-year-old factory owner, dreamed that he was under so much pressure trying to reconcile his worldly ambitions with his conscience that he "cracked" from the stress, "breaking his backbone." It left him a moral invalid. In the dream, Goebbels was visiting his factory and had all the workers line up in two rows facing each other. Herr S. had to stand in the middle and raise his arm in the Nazi salute. It took him half an hour to get his arm up, inch by inch. Goebbels showed neither approval nor disapproval, as he watched him struggle. When he finally got his arm up, Goebbels said, "I don't want your salute," and turned to the door. There, the dreamer stood, arm raised, in the midst of his workers, able to keep himself from collapsing only by staring at Goebbels's clubfoot as he limped out of the factory.

Herr S. was a man with lifelong political convictions, who had a strong paternalistic attitude toward his employees. Through several demeaning dream episodes, he was forced to humiliate and debase him-self in front of his employees by having to submit to conditions that made him lose self-respect; by being coerced into conforming to laws that are unfair and immoral. In one recurring version of this dream the dreamer stated, "The effort of lifting my arm was so great that sweat poured down my face like tears, as if I were crying in front of Goebbels." In another, "I looked to my workers for a sign of comfort but their faces showed absolute emptiness, not even scorn or contempt." Finally, while struggling to lift his arm, his back—his "backbone"—broke. Herr S. stated he was once a proud man who commanded respect, but now felt "alienated not only from all that is real in his life but also from his own character, which has lost its authenticity."

Dreams like the ones Beradt collected were dreamed by ordinary people confronting repressive conditions, who were looking for psycho-logical ways of dealing with the silent impact of explosive social changes. Beradt had difficulty gathering material because people were afraid to confide in her, and she often heard them say, "I dreamed it was forbid-den to dream, but I did anyway." She states that the dreams of German citizens during the 1930s, unlike the dreams of the victims of wars and revolution of previous centuries, were distinctive in character and content, because "their origin in time and place is explicit: they could only have sprung from man's paradoxical existence under a twentieth-century totalitarian regime, and most of them nowhere but under the Hitler dictatorship in Germany."

At some point during her investigation, Beradt realized that these dreams were important seismic readings registering the debilitating effects of totalitarian stress on the minds and lives of ordinary German citizens. Looking at how each dream reflected a personal journey toward dehumanization, with the dreamers backing away step-by-step from their former way of life, demonstrated to her that "the minor incident, the personally relevant factor, shows how Nazi totalitarianism functioned." She wrote:

> It occurred to me from time to time that a record should be kept of such dreams, a thought that now became a plan. They might one day serve as evidence when the time came to pass judgment on National Socialism as a historical phenomenon, for they seemed to reveal a great deal about people's deepest feelings and reactions as they become part of the mechanisms of totalitarianism. When a person sits down to keep a diary, this is a deliberate act, and he remolds, clarifies, or obscures his reactions. But while seeming to record seismographically the slightest effects of political events on the psyche, these dreams—diaries of the night—were conceived independently of their author's conscious will. They were, so to speak, dictated to them by the dictatorship. Dream imagery might thus help to describe the structure of a reality that was just on the verge of becoming a nightmare.

At the end of her book, Beradt says that these dreams contain "the warning that totalitarian tendencies must be recognized before they become overt—before the guise is dropped . . . before people no longer may speak the word 'I' and must guard their tongue so that not even they understand what they say, and before we begin to actually live the 'Life Without Walls.'" ●

—Fall 1999

Troll Cams: The "All-Seeing" Eyes of GOG (Global Occult Government)

by John Paul Jones

The New World Order has arrived on time, with facial recognition systems, Internet webcams, and nationalization of the telecommunications industry. As John Paul Jones tells us, once the video cameras seen most everywhere have metamorphosed into webcams, the intelligence agencies just need to download it to a central computer facility. By the time you drive up to the customs agent at the U.S. border, the optical scanning system that reads your license plate will have already accessed the records of the Immigration, Customs, and State Department to retrieve your vehicle registration, driver's license and police records. As Jones concludes, an "instant infernal nightmare of Orwellian proportions will no longer be fiction but brute fact," and we, the taxpayers, will have funded our own enslavement.

AS THE VIDEOCAMS we see in homes, airports, grocery stores, banks, convenience stores, gas stations, parking lots, and highways are connected to the Internet as webcams, they will become, in effect, a vast matrix of government eyeballs—always awake and alert, twenty-four hours a day, seven days a week, and placed almost everywhere we need to go.

By intercepting internet traffic, either surgically at ISPs (as with "Carnivore") or directly from the Internet backbones (e.g., Menwith Hill), U.S. intelligence agencies will be able to scan for any individual's digital face print, using a system that will:

T   *Tag:* Tell the software who to look for

R   *Recognize:* Scan for target based on a digital face print

O   *Observe:* Collect images containing targeted person

L   *Locate:* Infer location and time of target's appearance

L   *Log:* Record results for possible software analysis or human perusal

Not only is the above technologically, politically and legally feasible, but the necessary components of this incredible surveillance system have already been developed, tested, and partially implemented. Thanks in large part to the Clinton Administration, but thanks also to the rampant denial, deceit, and apathy which always grease the cogs of impending tyranny, the electronic and legal infrastructure is now established that could one day be used to implement a police state the likes of which would make Nazi Germany look like Camp Snoopy.

But why, it might be asked, should we assume that these cameras we see most everywhere will be linked to the Internet? Well, suppose you owned a Las Vegas resort and you wanted to show off your wares? You might think of converting your surveillance cameras to World Wide Web cams so potential customers could take a look at your accommodations. Or suppose you owned several department stores. By linking all your surveillance cams to the Internet, you could centralize your surveillance facilities at one location to reduce overhead. Or suppose you owned a radio station and wanted your listeners to feel like the DJ is their drinking buddy? You might put a web cam in the studio so your fans can see what antics the DJ is up to.

It's already started, but we ain't seen nothing yet. Already, according to the March 23, 2001, issue of the *Denver Post*, the Colorado Department of Transportation, in conjunction with Adesta Communications, launched a joint $180 million public–private venture to place web cams along fiber-optic backbones extending along major highways through Colorado to New Mexico, and across Kansas through Colorado to Utah.

This dubious public–private funding was made possible by the Telecommunications Act of 1996, which blurred the line between private corporations and government entities, allowing corporations and federal "bloatocracies" to join into amorphous megacorporations like In-Q-Tel, a CIA taxpayer-financed communications company. The project, which began in the fall of 1999 and is expected to be completed in 2002, is likely to provide the model for future endeavors to create "smart roads" across the country. Similar projects in Iowa and Minnesota are currently delayed due to lawsuits claiming highway departments will compete unfairly with private companies by using taxpayer money. These web cams will join the host of other surveillance cameras already posted on the nation's borders by the INS.

As detailed in *The Surveillance Society*, by Grant Jeffries, whenever you drive your car up to the Mexican or Canadian border, a sophisticated long-distance camera automatically scans your license plate, whereupon the computer system compares your plate number against a national registry of motor vehicle files, the customs search-and-seize list, and the national police and security files of the U.S., Canada, and Mexico.

By the time you drive up to the customs agent, the optical scanning system that reads your plate has already accessed the records of the Immigration, Customs, and State departments to retrieve your vehicle's registration, driver's license, and police records. Each time you cross the border in your car, that fact is recorded on the Customs and Immigration computers of the United States and Canada. Although the INS video cameras are not yet connected to the Internet as far as I know, it's not unreasonable to suppose that, as the nation's intelligent highway system develops, they will be.

DIGITAL FACE SCANNING

In addition to scanning for license plate numbers, these systems are capable of automatically zooming in and focusing on a driver to identify him by his facial characteristics. Much of this information pertaining to the government's use of digital face scanning software can be verified by visiting www.viisage.com and www.visionics.com, the web sites of two companies involved in development and testing of facial recognition systems for the government.

As detailed on the Visionics Corporation's web site and elsewhere, the digital face scanning systems are surprisingly sophisticated and not as easily fooled as might be expected. According to Joseph Atick, Visionics president and professor at the Computational Neuroscience Laboratory at Rockefeller University in New York, the "FaceIt" software uses a mathematical construction called local feature analysis (LFA) "to automatically derive a local topographic representation of any class of objects, such as human faces, from an ensemble of examples." FaceIt won the competition of face recognition systems conducted as part of the U.S. Advanced Research Project's FERET program in 1996.

Superior to a previous technique called eigenfaces, which used global face representations, LFA entails local, feature-by-feature analysis not easily fooled by deformations in the face or changes of pose or lighting, according to Atick. LFA analyzes individual features, such as mouth, nose, cheek or jawline, as if they were "Lego" blocks, which means that each feature can be analyzed independently of the face, thus avoiding a pixel-by-pixel analysis of an entire image.

The FaceIt technology combines LFA with "eigenheads," an older technique also developed by Visionics. Eigenheads is a low-dimensional representation of the three-dimensional human head, which is obtained from shading information in a two-dimensional image. The eigenhead is not dependent upon pose or lighting. FaceIt software uses eigenheads to compensate for variations in lighting and pose, then feeds the information to the LFA code, which builds a unique "faceprint." This faceprint can then be matched to a database of digital images in real time, and can obtain images from either live video feeds or from static images.

It is no wonder, then, that a host of federal agencies, including the NSA, DARPA, INS, Department of Defense, and the U.S. Army Research Laboratory, plus almost a dozen state governments, invested large sums of taxpayer money to test, acquire, and implement this control-and-tracking technology in the last half of the 1990s. Research projects, such as FERET, Newham, and the SENTRI trial run, have demonstrated the effectiveness, reliability, and unparalleled possibilities of facial recognition systems beyond any doubt, beyond belief, and beyond George Orwell's worst visions of dystopia unbound.

Given that the technology exists to implement TROLL cam surveillance on a national basis, and given the likelihood that most or many surveillance cams will soon be replaced with webcams, we are still left with a crucial component of the hypothetical TROLL cam surveillance system missing. Or are we?

DRIVER'S "PRIVACY PROTECTION" ACT

In order to scan for and locate targeted individuals via these webcams, the government would need to possess a vast database of digital face prints. That is, before you can tell the software to look for somebody, the software needs some idea of what to look for. In the same vein, the Carnivore system presumably needs to be given an individual's e-mail address before it can tag transmissions containing the target's e-mail address. Likewise, TROLL cam surveillance would require a digitized photo of the people targeted for tracking before it could identify somebody via the world's webcams.

Not surprisingly, given the past history of the intelligence cults, the feds went to great lengths to acquire just such a database of digital face prints, not only for known or suspected criminals, but for almost every citizen of the United States. This was done under the guise of a grossly misnamed and insidious federal law enacted in 1994: the Driver's Privacy Protection Act (DPPA), which requires states to release private DMV records to a multitude of federal agencies under various federal programs. It also permits departments of motor vehicles to sell drivers' information, including names, social security numbers, addresses, and digital photographs, to private third-party organizations (see *Media Bypass*, March 2000).

Although the DPPA was attacked in court as unconstitutional because arguably it violated the Tenth Amendment, the Supreme Court later reversed three lower court rulings from South Carolina, Colorado, and Alabama, which held that the law was indeed unconstitutional. Thus, the DPPA joins a slew of other legislative monstrosities pushed through by the Clinton Administration with the backing of a few constitutionally-challenged alphabet soup agencies.

According to *Media Bypass*, "Under the DPPA, the federal government will take full control over all state-held driver and motor vehicle records. The sole purpose of this act was, in fact, to wrench away authority over these records from the states." Since motor vehicle records contain digital photos of most adult citizens in the United States, these provide the missing link in the evolution of police state America and a vital component of the TROLL cam surveillance system.

Soon after the falsely named DPPA was adopted, a company called Image Data, of Nashua, New Hampshire, was formed specifically to develop a huge database of driver records for use by retail outlets in verifying customer identity and reducing fraud. Image Data began purchasing records from several states based solely upon the newly granted authority under the DPPA.

The company intended to install small "image monitors" at retail outlets using their service, which would display the customer's driver's license photo during transactions where identity needed to be authenticated. The equipment would have allowed stores to run credit cards through a reader, which would then retrieve the "verifying" photos and other data through phone wire connections to Image Data's database. Children's photos taken from state-issued identity cards were also included in the database.

In a series of articles in late 1999, the *Washington Post* reported that the Secret Service provided the funding for the Image Data operation. Consequently, due to public outcry, the Image Data project was postponed, and three states, which had signed contracts to sell 22 million photographs to Image Data at about a penny per photo, cancelled their contracts. Florida Governor Jeb Bush cancelled a contract to sell 14 million images, and Colorado Governor Bill Owens halted the sale of 5 million photos. But as a consequence of the Supreme Court ruling in 2000 upholding the DPPA, government and businesses could again begin building databases like the one undertaken by Image Data.

That said, consider the components required to implement a TROLL cam surveillance system of U.S. citizens on a global basis:

- Super-fast digital face scanning software.

- Federally-accessible database of digital photos of U.S. citizens.

- Downlink of Internet traffic to federal computer sites.

- Webcams posted at key places throughout the U.S. and overseas.

DIGITAL TELEPHONY ACT OF 1994

There is good reason to believe that all components, except perhaps the last one, are either operational at this time or soon will be. As detailed above, it was no mere coincidence that these requirements fell into place just before the last prerequisite—webcams everywhere—seems about to happen. Nor was it a mere coincidence that the legal groundwork was laid down via the Digital Telephony Act of 1994, the DPPA, and the Telecommunications Act of 1996, not to mention the taxpayer-financed spread of webcams onto highways, public schools, Indian reservations, and elsewhere.

Keep in mind that Carnivore, which some had already considered inevitable long before news of its existence hit mainstream media, came to us compliments of the Digital Telephony Act of 1994—a virtual nationalization of the telecommunications industry, according to Simson Garfinkel, author of *PGP: Pretty Good Privacy*, a book on PGP encryption. This gives the feds the legal authority to place surveillance equipment or software in the communications infrastructure, e.g., on ISP servers, Internet backbones and NAPs (Network Access Points), etc., and corporations must comply or be severely penalized.

Thus, once the video cameras we see most everywhere metamorphose into webcams and proliferate, spawning a vast matrix of interconnected electronic eyeballs, the intelligence agencies need only intercept the traffic and download it to a central computer facility, such as the NSA headquarters at Fort Meade or the Menwith Hill site in the U.K. (located over the Internet backbone carrying traffic to and from Europe). The webcam images can then be scanned with sophisticated digital face scanning software to identify and track targeted people using digi-photos, now available to the feds, thanks to the DPPA.

Voila! As if from some hoary midnight sci-fi flick, an instant infernal nightmare of Orwellian proportions will no longer be fiction but brute fact. Who will ultimately be financing this *Brave New World* wide web of evil? Why, you, of course—the taxpayer—will have funded your own enslavement. So work hard. Big Brother depends on you, my virtual fellow cyberslaves of the new world order. ●

References

"Approval of Facial Mapping Reviewed." *Denver Post* (July 15, 2001).

"Big Brother on the Way." *Media Bypass* (March 2000).

"Clinton Unveils Plan to Close Digital Divide on Reservations." *New York Times.*

"Colorado To Map Faces." *Denver Post* (July 4, 2001).

Garfinkel, Simson. *PGP: Pretty Good Privacy.* 1995.

"Information Highway Hits the Road." *Denver Post* (March 29, 2001).

Jeffries, Grant. *The Surveillance Society.* 2000.

"News & Views." *Dr. Dobbs Journal* (December 1998).

"Sale of License Photos Sparks Uproar." *Washington Post* (January 30, 1999).

"Smile: You're On Scan Camera." *Wired* (March 14, 2001).

"U.S. Helped Fund Photo Database of Driver IDs." *Washington Post* (February 18, 1999).

www.visionics.com.

www.viisage.com.

www.innoventry.com.

www.EarthCam.com.

www.webcam.com.

"Your Face Scan Dollars At Work." *Wired* (August 15, 2001).

CONTRIBUTORS

Frank Berube may be reached at fberube57@yahoo.com. Please feel free to drop him a lifeline.

William Patrick Bourne is an independent researcher who has published scientific papers in *Chronology*, and *Catastrophism Review*, *Leading Edge*, and *The Theoscientist*. He may be reached at wpb4@mindspring.com.

Alexandra Bruce is the author of *The Philadelphia Experiment Murder*, the latest in an underground series of books related to The Montauk Project, published by Sky Books. She has articles and RealTV/Audio interviews currently posted on www. incunabula.org and www.disinfo.com. She can be reached at intuit7@yahoo.com.

Dr. Alan Cantwell, Jr., is a physician and author of two books on the manmade origin of AIDS: *AIDS and the Doctors of Death: An Inquiry into the Origin of the AIDS Epidemic* (1988) and *Queer Blood: The Secret AIDS Genocide Plot* (1993). His books are available in the U.S. from Book Clearing House, 1-800-431-1579, or through Aries Rising Press, PO Box 29532, Los Angeles, CA 90029. He may be reached at AlanRCan@aol.com.

Phillip Darrell Collins is a mass communications student at Wright State University. He gives all the glory to his Lord and Savior Jesus Christ. He may be reached at thefaceunveiled@excite.com.

Scott Corrales is a writer and translator of UFO and paranormal subjects in Latin America and Spain. His work has appeared in magazines in the U.S., U.K., Japan, Spain, and Italy. Corrales is also the author of *Chupacabras and Other Mysteries* (Greenleaf, 1997), *Flashpoint: High Strangeness in Puerto Rico* (Amarna, 1998), and *Forbidden Mexico* (1999). He lives in Pennsylvania, where he edits *Inexplicata: The Journal of Hispanic UFOlogy*. He may be reached at lornis1@juno.com.

Joan d'Arc is co-founder and co-publisher of *Paranoia: The Conspiracy Reader* (www.paranoiamagazine.com). She is the author of *Space Travelers and the Genesis of the Human Form* and *Phenomenal World*, published by The Book Tree, 1-800-700-TREE[8733] (www.thebooktree.com). She may be reached at joandarc@compuserve.com.

Steven Ferry is a Brit who was working as a butler on the West Coast when he noticed an incident of repression and investigated the issue. When his article was published by a national journal, he switched careers and, in 1994, began a commercial writing and photography business called Words & Images, based in Florida. He has written numerous articles and has published thirteen books, which are available at his web site, www.words-images.com. His e-mail address is steven@words-images.

Robert Guffey is a graduate of the 1996 Clarion West Science Fiction Workshop, which was begun in the late 1960s by Robin Scott Wilson (a former employee of the Central Intelligence Agency). His first short story, "The Infant Kiss," appeared in Jeremy Lassen's 2000 anthology, *After Shocks*, and received an honorable mention in the 2001 edition of the *Year's Best Fantasy & Horror*. Guffey's second story "Esthra, Shadows, Glass, Silence" is scheduled to appear in the twenty-seventh issue of the British science fiction magazine *The Third Alternative*. His articles have appeared in *Paranoia*, *Steamshovel Press*, *Flatland*, and the 1999 anthology *The Conspiracy Reader*. He may be contacted at rguffey@hotmail.com.

Al Hidell is the co-founder and co-publisher of *Paranoia: The Conspiracy Reader* (www.paranoiamagazine.com). An award-winning videographer, he is currently pursuing a certificate in graphic design. He has studied international relations under former National Security Advisor Tony Lake, and has completed courses in journalism, copywriting and playwriting. Hidell, who is single, lives at an undisclosed location with his two cats.

John Paul Jones is a writer and computer programmer, whose numerous programs and several articles have been published in nationally distributed computer magazines and on CD-ROMs. Currently, he is working on fully automated web development software for the Nicholas Owen Society. He can be contacted at 1550 Larimer Street, #527, Denver, CO 80202.

Kathy Kasten is a researcher and targeted individual living in Los Angeles, and is on the staff at the University of California, Los Angeles. Four years as staff liaison to the Human Subject Protection Committee/Institution Review Board developed her awareness of the worldwide need for human subject protection policies.. The other day when she looked in the mirror, she noted she was looking more and more like Ms. Marple (she wanted to grow up to be either Sherlock Holmes or Ms. Marple), and she considered it a better disguise than looking like Holmes: As she learned from the Spy-Cruise, little old ladies are less sinister looking than tall, skinny, skeletal males.

Katie Klemenchich may be reached at kxk24@scientist.com.

Randy Koppang is a researcher and media ecologist, who has authored several articles on a comprehensive set of topics for *Paranoia*, *Perceptions*, *Flipside*, *Atlantis Rising*, and on the web site www.xenochrony.net. He can be contacted via email at the.occupant@horizon.net.

Andy Lloyd lives in Gloucester, England, and may be reached at andy3751@hotmail.com. His web site, The Dark Star Theory, is located at www.darkstar1.co.uk. Andy is also part of the team behind the Cosmic Conspiracies web site at www.ufos-aliens.co.uk.

Jorge Martin may be e-mailed at jmartin@prcinternet.net.

Acharya S is an archaeologist, classicist, historian, mythologist, linguist, and member of the American School of Classical Studies at Athens, Greece. She has served as a trench master on archaeological excavations in Corinth, Greece, and Connecticut. Acharya has traveled extensively around Europe, and she speaks, reads, and/or writes in Greek, French, Spanish, Italian, German, and Portuguese. She has also cross-referenced the Bible in the original Hebrew and ancient Greek. Acharya is the author of the best-selling and controversial book, *The Christ Conspiracy: The Greatest Story Ever Sold* and *Suns of God: Krishna, Buddha and Christ Unveiled*. Acharya S has appeared on a variety of radio programs. Her website appears at truthbeknown.com, and she may be contacted at acharya_s@yahoo.com.

Dan Smith's Eschaton web site can be found at www.clark.net/pub/dansmith, and "Pecking Away at Heaven's Gate" can be found at www.clark.net/pub/dansmith/Bopeep.htm.

Brian Tuohy is an award-winning screenwriter and occasional conspiracy author. The majority of his work can be found online at various web sites. If you have any comments about his article or information to add/share, please e-mail Tuohy at mofo2E@wi.rr.com.

Tracy Twyman is a prolific writer, publisher, and film producer, as well as a recognized expert on ancient and medieval history, secret societies, and the occult. For the last six years, she has been the publisher of *Dagobert's*

Revenge magazine and has written extensively on the subjects of Freemasonry, the Knights Templar, the Priory of Sion, Rosicrucianism, Hermeticism, conspiracies, and esoterica. She has appeared on numerous television and radio programs, including *Coast to Coast A.M.*, and her writing has been published in a variety of magazines, newspapers, and books. She has a bachelor of arts degree in Film and Video, and has produced a handful of short films related to her chosen areas of research. More information can be found by visiting www.dagobertsrevenge.com. For a sample issue, send $7 to Tracy R. Twyman, PO Box 18331, Denver, CO 80218.

INDEX